Hugh Allan

Fresh Views of old Truths: Church sermons.

Hugh Allan

Fresh Views of old Truths: Church sermons.

ISBN/EAN: 9783743349056

Manufactured in Europe, USA, Canada, Australia, Japa

Cover: Foto ©Lupo / pixelio.de

Manufactured and distributed by brebook publishing software (www.brebook.com)

Hugh Allan

Fresh Views of old Truths: Church sermons.

Fresh Views of Old Truths:

CHURCH SERMONS

BY

THE REV. HUGH ALLAN, M.A.

VICAR OF RAVENSTONE AND VICAR OF
WESTON UNDERWOOD.

Church of S. Laurence, Weston Underwood.

"Every scribe which is instructed unto the kingdom of Heaven bringeth forth out of
his treasures things new and old."—*S. Matthew* xiii., 52.

OLNEY: H. JACKSON, MARKET PLACE.
LONDON: H. WILLIAMS, 17, WARWICK LANE.
1875.

TO HIS PARISHIONERS AT RAVENSTONE AND
WESTON UNDERWOOD,

WHERE THESE SERMONS WERE RECENTLY PREACHED,

AND TO

MEMBERS OF FORMER CONGREGATIONS;

AND OF THESE LATTER

MORE ESPECIALLY TO THOSE AMONG WHOM

HE HAS MINISTERED

IN THAME AND ITS ADJACENT VILLAGES,

AND IN

HIGH WYCOMBE AND HAZELMERE—

THIS VOLUME

IS AFFECTIONATELY INSCRIBED

BY

THEIR MOST SINCERELY ATTACHED FRIEND,

THE REV. HUGH ALLAN, M.A.,

VICAR OF ALL SAINTS, RAVENSTONE, AND VICAR

OF S. LAURENCE, WESTON UNDERWOOD.

ERRATA.

Page 42, line 30, " an" should be " and."
Page 46, line 8, " too" should be " took."
Page 46, line 42, " shamed" should be " ashamed."
Page 49, line 32, " if it is" should be " of it it is."
Page 92, line 16, " agreement" should be " argument."
Page 96, line 24, " count" should be " court" and " court"
  " count."
Page 103, line 44, " when" should be " where."
Page 107, last line, " Drummond" should be " Heber."
Page 180, last line, " Dr. Alexander" should be " Mrs. Alexander"
Page 209, line 47, " privilege" should be " heritage."

PREFACE.

IT is undeniable that there is often a wearisome sameness about
Sermons which has afforded sad occasion for the contempt only
too readily expressed for them by an irreligious world. The Author
hopes and believes that he has at the least avoided this fault. The
repelling element of constantly recurring religious common-places, and
the stock phrases which are meant to cover, but never really conceal
from the intelligent, poverty or confusion of thought, will not be found
in these Sermons. Very early in the days of the world they became a
just cause of complaint. Even by the godly Job they were found
intolerable: and he signified his impatience of them in the plainest
language. "How forcible (says he) are right words. But what doth
your arguing reprove?" "I have heard many such things: miserable
comforters are ye all! Shall vain words have an end? I also could
speak as ye do: if your soul were in my soul's stead, I could heap up
words against you, and shake mine head at you. But I would strengthen
you with my mouth."

The conventional terms too, so appropriate to systematic theology,
are but very sparingly introduced; the Author considering them out
of place in Parochial Sermons, as inconsistent with the simplicity of
the Gospel, and irrelevant to the plain teachings that the Preacher
should be setting himself to gather in a practical form from the passage
before him.

One aim which, among higher ones, the Author has kept steadily
before himself in the preparation of these discourses, is the infusing a
freshness of thought and achieving an originality of treatment in a
subject so worthy of the most thoughtful and reverent handling, as the
relationship of man to his Creator, Redeemer, and Sanctifier, and to the
future life and world.

If he has in any measure succeeded in this aim he will have so far realised his Lord's will that "every scribe which is instructed unto the kingdom of heaven is to bring forth out of his treasure things new as well as old." (S. Matthew xiii., 52.) That will he has set himself to study here. And to God, whose he is and whom he serves, he commends the work he here dedicates to Him in deep humility and consciousness of imperfection. He earnestly prays Him to accept his unworthy offering; and to bless it to the edification in grace and " the knowledge of Him," of all those readers to whom it has been his happiness to minister in the Gospel of Salvation. "Unto Him be glory in the Church by Christ Jesus throughout all ages !"

And if the volume shall reach a wider circle of readers than his own present and former flocks—and its publication shall tend in any degree to the magnifying in their eyes the glory and the grace of his All-Worthy Master—and if in days to come when he shall have "served his own generation by the will of God," he being dead should yet speak here to some that come after, and be permitted to cast a ray of light from God's glorious Gospel on any that walk in the darkness of this otherwise strange uncertain life—the dearest and longest cherished wish of his heart will be fulfilled.

> And gratefully to Thee, O Lord,
> Shall all the praise be given,
> For every gracious thought and word
> That leads them nearer Heaven.

" Glory be to the Father, and to the Son, and to the Holy Ghost !"

CONTENTS.

SPRING TIDE IN NATURE AND IN GRACE.

Rise up, my love, my fair one, and come away, for lo, the winter is past, the rain
is over and gone; the flowers appear on the earth; the time ·the singing of birds
is come, and the voice of the turtle is heard in our land."   *Canticles ii 10-12.*

This is a text that can hardly fail to suggest itself at the beautiful
season it describes. It is not my purpose however, in choosing it to
expatiate on the charms of Spring-tide ; nor to take up the sublime
invocation of that heart-stirring song we have taken from the Apocrypha
into our Church Service, and invoke the works of nature to combine to
the setting forth the glory of their High Creator. " O, all ye green things
upon the earth, bless ye the Lord : praise Him and magnify Him for
ever " It would be superfluous for me to introduce the subject of this
discourse, by enlarging on a theme, exhaustless as are the topics it
affords, which has been handled so often and so admirably as this by the
best of our poets and writers. Who does not love the glorious Spring-
tide ? Every eye brightens, every face gladdens, every step becomes
more elastic and buoyant, every heart becomes involuntarily more hopeful as the gracious and encouraging words of my text are borne from
heaven itself by the soft vernal gales, the messengers of God, and whispered into the listening ears of us all, even the unthankful and evil.
" Rise up " those favored and blessed of the Lord "and come away for
lo, the winter is past, the rain is over and gone ; the flowers appear on
the earth ; the time of the singing of birds is come, and the voice of the
turtle is heard in our land."

In obedience to the powerful summons constraining us, in spite of
all things adverse, to quickened life, and fresh hope, and new energy, we
all feel ourselves roused, and going forth in spirit from the comparative inaction enforced more or less upon us by the dreary and lifeless
winter, to greet God's fair and happy spring.

Now the human mind has a natural delight in allegory, in figurative representation of the unseen and unknown, and an interest in
parables taken from common objects to set forth higher and hidden
truth. The Bible ministers to this sentiment of imagination on its
almost every page. The things that are seen, the objects, the relations
of this world, are all a pattern of things in the heavens. a figure of
things that are not seen This world itself is a shadow of the world
beyond. And the Bible teaches that all its material things have their
counterpart in the future life.

I accept literally the description of Revelation of the world to
come. Very painful to me would it be to hear explained away the living
and abiding no less than attractive words in which the Spirit tells of

golden streets, and pearly gates, and jewelled glory, and glassy sea, and emerald rainbow, and living creatures, and trees bearing all manner of fruits, and white robes of the redeemed, and harps and crowns of gold. There are those indeed who cannot be so persuaded, as I am, that these things are realities, that—

> " There everlasting spring abides,
>   And never withering flowers."

Very beautifully is their feeling of doubtfulness expressed in a recently published hymn—

> O, shining city of our God
>   And shall we see thee here?
> Thy pearly gates and golden streets'
>   It doth not yet appear.
>
> O, healing tree of twelvefold fruit!
>   O, river pure and clear!
> And shall we touch, and shall we taste?
>   It doth not yet appear.
>
> O, crowned and white robed choir on high,
>   Our elder brethren dear!
> And shall we blend our songs with yours?
>   It doth not yet appear.
>
> O, Rainbow Throne!   O, court of Heaven?
>   And are ye truly so?
> Or signs of things we cannot yet
>   In faintest semblance know?

But whatever may be the view that different minds will take of the relation of earthly things and objects to *heavenly*, it cannot be questioned that they represent in a figure things *spiritual* and relating to the soul. And so the Spirit of God has in the text aptly seized on the emotions of which the most unimpassioned of us cannot be altogether unconscious at the spring-tide, and applied them with wondrous and attractive power to things spiritual.

With the engaging and powerful symbols—as they have been found by the devout soul in all ages of the Church—with which this book abounds and principally deals, the Spirit has set forth to us in the imagery of the text, three phases at least of the religious life and experience, three facts in the teaching of the gospel about the life of the soul. I shall dwell on one and only merely allude to the other two.

And first in the words of the text, Christ who is the speaker addressing the to Him so precious soul, which He has redeemed at the cost of His own Sacrifice, invites the new convert to arise from the inaction of his former unquickened life, and the despondency which always accompanies first convictions of sinfulness, "Arise" says He "Awake thou that sleepest, and arise from the dead," from your former unregenerate unprofitable state. "My love, my fair one!" he deigns to say. For says he by His Prophet "Since thou wast precious in my sight, thou hast been honorable and I have loved thee."

Indeed we are very dear to Him, any and all of us, despite the offensiveness of our natural state of evil. There is none of us who may not turn from ourselves with all the self-humiliation that a knowledge

of our true state before Him must bring, and say as we look with unbounded confidence to our Redeemer, " Jesu, lover of my soul." Do
you know, by the way, where that oft quoted and assuring expression
in the well-known hymn beginning with these soothing words comes
from. The expression might seem to us too bold and familiar were it
not so commended to us by the Spirit of God in Solomon's " Song of
Songs." The expression was borrowed from the Apocrypha, and occurs
in the Book of the wisdom of Solomon ; and the passage will bear
quoting : " Thou lovest all the things that are, and abhorrest nothing
that thou hast made :" (you will observe in passing we are indebted
to this passage likewise for a well-known phrase in the Collect for Ash
Wednesday, " For never wouldst thou have made anything, if thou
hadst hated it. And how could anything have endured if it had not
been Thy will ? Or been preserved if not called by Thee ? But thou
sparest all, for they are Thine, O Lord, thou lover of souls."

" Come away " our gracious Lord goes on to say in the text to the
soul that he is awakening, and leading from the world to Himself.
This is always the call of the Gospel, " Come unto me ! " and " Come
out and be separate." " Away " that is ' laying aside every weight.
and the sin that doth most easily beset." " Away " from thoughts
and cares of this world only, that hitherto have engaged your heart, to
higher considerations, and better hopes, and more exalted affections.

It is the voice with which He raises the spiritually " dead in trespasses and sins," as of old he did in the flesh, " Damsel arise," Young
man, I say unto thee arise," " Lazarus come forth," from the tomb,
the narrow bounds which have hitherto kept your now freed and living
spirit, " Come forth " to follow me to new enterprise and conflict and
life.

" For lo the winter is past " the years, that is, spent in ignorance
and sin, unfruitful and uncomfortable as that dead season of the year.
Struggle against it as we may, an atmosphere of discontent enwraps us
in the winter time, as we look forth or walk in the cheerless world un-
enlivened by the Sun, which is the light of life. Vitality must be strong
in him or her, who does not know its chilling influence on the spirit as
well as the body. Which thing is an allegory. For hide it from us as we
will, a subtle atmosphere of discontent and gloom, that blights and
checks the spirit's life, involves each unregenerate man. And for the
most part you may detect it in his very features, and hear it in his very
tones, " who will show us any good ? "

But " Lord lift Thou up the light of Thy countenance upon us,"
and it vanishes like the gloom of nature before the Spring-tide sun.
When the new convert arises from the despondency which I said for
the most part attends the awakening of conscience, and the conviction
of sin, " The rain is presently over and gone." The gloomy season
attended with storms of excited feeling, perhaps uncontrollable emotion,
which follows the penitent's conviction of his guilt and danger, and
precede the peace he afterwards enjoys in believing, passes over the
horizon of the soul. The tears of godly sorrow are dried when Christ's

words, " Son be of good cheer, thy sins are forgiven thee," come home
with reassurance to the soul. The Sun of Righteousness breaks forth
with healing in His beams, and diffuses a rapture of gladness. As the
winter of nature flees before the power of the spring tide sun, so

> All the winter of our sins,
> Long and dark is flying
> From His Light to Whom we give
> Laud and praise undying.

So it was with David and Peter, whose bitter tears of penitence He
presently wiped away. So it was with Saul the persecutor at Damascus,
and the cruel jailor at Philippi, and the very murderers of Jesus who
obtained mercy on the day of Pentecost. So has it been in our past
experience, if happily we are of their number who can recall

> When first on that most blest of days
> We felt His quickening breath,
> And dead souls woke to love and praise
> The Vanquisher of death.

" And the flowers appear in the earth." The opening blossoms of holy
affections and desires show themselves. Words too of gentleness, and
works of kindness and charity spring up in the path of the godly. And
they give forth to his neighbours the odour of a fair reputation, and
cast in the way of the weary world the charm that the spring flowers
do before our eye and beneath our feet.

" And the time of the singing of birds is come." The converted
soul is clothed with the garment of " praise for the spirit of heaviness."
When the Lord turns again the captivity of the rescued soul, then as
with Zion, is " the mouth filled with laughter, and the tongue with
song."

The believing soul

> " delights to raise
> Psalms, and hymns and songs of praise."

" A new Song is in its mouth, even of thanksgiving unto God."
Its feelings of grateful love to the God of its salvation are those of the
Psalmist " I will sing unto the Lord as long as I live, I will praise my
God while I have my being." " Bless the Lord, O my soul, who for-
giveth all thy sin; and healeth all thine infirmities."

" And the voice of the turtle is heard in the land." We are at no
loss to interpret this of the blessed Spirit, who chose to reveal Himself
under the form of a Dove. The Dove is the well-known natural emblem
of gentleness and grace, and faithfulness and purity. And the emblem
commends itself to us all. The very name of the fair creature is soft,
and its form is graceful, and its eye is eloquent of chastened and winning beauty.

And the voice of that Spirit is heard then as it never was before.
Indeed it may be heard even in the winter of the soul. It comes soft
and low, and plaintively, like the wood dove's from the deep and far-off
glade, when all around is hushed and still. And when the tumult of
passion, or the roar of the restless world is silenced for a little space in

devotional hours, or in Providential visitations o sickness, or bereavement and affliction, or in thoughtful serious moments, that still small
voice is heard,

> For His that gentle voice we hear,
> Soft as the breath of even,
> That checks each fault, that calms each fear,
> And speaks of heaven.

But when the spring-tide of grace has come, the voice of the turtle
is heard with redoubled power. The voice of the Dove in those lands,
as that of the Cuckoo in ours, is heard all the day long in the spring-
tide season. So is His voice then. The time is come for the admonitions and persuasive teaching of the Spirit of God taking of the things
of Christ and showing them to the seeking soul: opening the eyes of
the understanding to behold wondrous things out of God's Word:
teaching, as our Saviour says it is His office to do, and bringing to
remembrance whatever He has said. And this voice of the Turtle fills
the believer's heart with melody.

In the same way may this passage be also accommodated to signify
the believer's renewed comforts, after the often recurring wintry season
of temptation and discouragement. As when for example " the Lord
turned the captivity of Job." As when " the Angels ministered to "
our Lord, after his seasons of conflict with the evil one. As when the
churches had rest after the great persecution that arose about the death
of Stephen. As when God comforted the troubled and downcast
Apostle by the coming of Titus.

The unwatchful and careless Christian in particular, knows well
this too often recurring winter of the soul, when he has forfeited the
light of God's countenance through allowed or too faintly resisted sin.
Often is he in a like case with the hapless mariners, the fellow voyagers
of the Apostle in the wild Adriatic, who loosing from Crete instead of
hearkening to him, had " neither the light of sun nor stars for many
days, and no small tempest lay on them, so that all hope they should be
saved was then taken away."

The tempest, to speak figuratively, that comes rushing down upon
the backslider, as it did literally upon Jonah, fleeing from the presence
of the Lord, how much do the records of the Bible, and the history of
almost every Saint unfold of its dark experiences! When he eats for
a while of the fruit of his own way, and is filled with his own devices,
when he proves how evil and bitter a thing it is to depart from the
living God—he knows what it is to find himself like the disciples in the
thick of the storm, and the midst of the sea, while the Master is out
of sight on the shore. But ever is it with him as with them that in
the fourth watch of the night, when it is at its dreariest and darkest,
Jesus comes. And presently the well-known voice " It is I be not
afraid! " adds—as it did to Peter then, and as here it is in the text
" Come." " And immediately there is a great calm " in the soul. " And
lo, the winter is past, the rain is over and gone, the flowers " of hope

spring up around the soul to which the message of reconciliation comes, and is welcomed by faith. And the voice of the Turtle is heard in response to the repentant cry

> Return O, Holy Dove! return
> Sweet Messenger of rest,
> I hate the sins that made Thee mourn,
> And drove Thee from my breast.

Where verily is the believer, who has not frequent occasion to testify of the fulfillment to himself of the words before us, and to say in the words of Addison's Hymn,

> When worn with sickness, oft hast Thou
> With health renewed my face;
> And when in sin and sorrows sunk,
> Revived my soul with grace.

And very soon that glorious hour shall strike of which every successive spring-tide here is intended to remind us. And the blessed teaching of my text shall force itself in all the reality of its hitherto untold significance on the Sons and Daughters of the Lord Almighty. I pray God you and I may hear it to our eternal joy! The voice shall yet come from the clouds of heaven that shall wake to the great resurrection the slumbering bodies of the just. "Rise up my Beloved!" "Come ye blessed of my Father to inherit the kingdom prepared for you."

For lo, the winter of the grave is past, the reign of grief and tears is ended. The flowery land of heaven is outspread before you. And the voice of the Turtle is heard in the land; the land and home of my Father, and His Holy Angels.

And the words of the Spirit of God answer to those of the Son of God, for thus saith He in His Revelation of the future "God shall wipe away all tears; and there shall be no more death, neither sorrow nor crying, neither shall there be any more pain; for the former things are passed away." And the voice of the Turtle is that of invitation too. For "the Spirit saith come!" And let him that heareth, COME!

THE RELATION OF LESS AND GREATER IN THE DESIGN OF PROVIDENCE.

" Without all contradiction the less is blessed of the better."   *Hebrews* vii, 7.

This saying is a Paradox, that is an assertion of which the very opposite seems at first sight to be the truth, but like all Paradoxes it expresses in a sententious form a fact which when brought out is admitted to be unquestionable.   In this instance being an utterance of the Spirit of God, we may expect the truth to be as it is a profound one.   At first as I say we are startled at the sentiment.   It seems to bely facts of our own common observation.   "The less is blessed of the better." " Blessed," that is benefited or served by.   "The better," that is the greater, the higher in position, capacity or resources.   Let us test the statement by the experience of daily life, let us for example take an illustration from our Lord's teaching, " which of you having a servant plowing or feeding cattle, will say unto him by and by when he is come in from the field, go and sit down to meat," and allow the less to be served by the better : " and will not rather say unto him make ready wherewith I may sup, and gird thyself, and serve me," and so make this word of no effect ?

Does the assertion hold good here—is the barbarian in the bondage of his superstition, the uncared for victim of poverty or ignorance in his destitute state—is the unbefriended sufferer from calamity, the slandered who have none to make their righteousness clear as the light, or their just dealing as the noonday —are the down trodden, when on the side of their oppressor there is power and there is none to plead their cause and spoil the soul of those that spoiled them—are the neglected, by inconsiderate neighbours and selfish relati es, who never know the attention or the affection that nature or humanity prompt ?   Are these, or can they in any sense be said to be, benefited by the greater ?

Not manifestly if by the greater are to be considered those wno stand in this immediate relationship of superiority.   And here is the key to the Paradox.   The " great in the sight of the Lord," the higher natures that bless and benefit the lesser may not be, and often times are not, those in man's judgment relatively greater.   *Moral* and *social* greatness are two utterly distinct things.

Undoubtedly the less may not be blessed of and served by their betters in the scale of human greatness.   But without all contradiction, as saith the Spirit of God here, the less are always being ministered to by the greater   They are indebted in an infinity of ways to the services of the greater, than themselves in capacity, in intelligence, in real excellence of any and every kind   Accompany me to the first adjacent town, and let us walk its streets a while together, and see if the case be not as the text declares.

As we pass along the thoroughfare, the skilled doctor comes out hastily from his house, into which he has perhaps but just entered after nours of incessant and trying labour. Perhaps the summons that has called him out found him already in the study or writing of some valuable professional work to which his genius is contributing results which will presently affect many a human life. Or perhaps it roused him from the meal he has hardly leisure to eat to prolong his own. His carriage passes us at a rapid rate, and it pauses presently at some humble dwelling it may be miles away. And the worn and weaned practitioner is bending over some sufferer's couch, and entering with assiduous care into the particulars of the case.

Possibly the patient is a worthless character. By his restoration to health the neighbourhood may be all the worse instead of better. He may have received the injury which the other devotes himself so carefully to redress in the way of sin or mischief. Or the object of the visit may be one at least by whose recovery from the sickness or accident the other is called in to relieve, society will be no gainer: while by the exhaustion of that doctor's life in labours more abundant than it is equal to it will one day be sadly the loser.

Let imagination supply you with some such case as this, and you will say "without all contradiction the less is blessed of the better," here. Now step with me into the court of Justice, that rears its imposing front hard by. Note that pleader at the bar, who is defending the accused or criminal, note the other personages of the court bringing the almost infinite resources of their marvellous learning and wondrous patience to the unravelling of some tangled web of deceit or sophistry. Or perhaps it is a law suit between two obstinate persons whose pride prevents them from settling the matter amicably, as it might be done in a few moments. You listen admiringly to the eloquence. You follow the sagacity of the Counsel. You observe the astonishing industry he has displayed in acquainting himself with every point of law that can bear upon the trumpery case, you begin to realise the lavish expenditure of time, thought, and talent, you cannot but feel might have been directed to more profitable ends to society at large. And we say as we leave the court together, passing our reflections on the unworthy party who is the object of so much interest and labour on the part of his advocate, "Without all contradiction the less is blessed of the better!"

We are again in the street, and we notice the honest builder at work on the humble cottage, or the artistic decorator on some pretentious building. We see them in the burden and heat of the day, labouring in the sweat of their brow, with infinite pains and prolonged toil, and we ask perhaps who is to be the future inmate of the houses in preparation. On enquiring we ascertain that the cottage is to be tenanted by a lawless, reckless, or idle vagabond who has been the curse of his home, the pest of the neighbourhood, and a warning pointed out to his own family by every respectable householder. And the mansion adjoining is designed for some wealthy but self-indulgent man, whom when the ear heard of it never blessed, when the eye saw it never gave witness to, who never went forth to the deliverance of the poor that had cried, nor him that had none to help him; on whom the blessing of him that was ready to perish never fell, and whose open hand or feeling heart never like Job's set the widow's heart a singing. As we pass musingly on we observe to each other, there again " Without all contradiction the less is blessed of the better." A little longer yet we linger in the streets, and as the hour when the midday meal is over arrives, we see fathers returning to their factory work or other labour, early rising up and late taking rest to provide for a number of children, perhaps troublesome and mischievous, but at all events useless as yet to the world, and we see the sentiment verified again.

And now let us turn aside from the street, and enter the home. There in the cottage sits the woman of low degree, and in the house the lady of superior rank. The one is known if not spoken of—for merit too often invites to depreciation rather than admiration—as a model of humble but untiring diligence; and the other of cultivated but equally unwearied energy. They are both mothers, and they are devoting all the thought and activity of their whole being—thought and activity and service of worth inestimable—they are lavishing too all the wealth of that wondrous affection with which God has endowed their nature, on some perhaps unconscious infant whose existence is a matter of perfect indifference to the whole world beside. We reflect how utterly valueless is that infant life to the world, perhaps a sickly life which it is clear must soon be extinguished. We consider what might be the worth of the humble mother's powers of service if devoted to others. We think how fitted the lady evidently is to shine in society, and to be a centre of admiration, or the adornment of that social life from which she almost excludes herself for the sake of her offspring. We are almost ready to exclaim, but for our knowledge that thus God would have it be, " Wherefore this waste." ? But we once more admit to each other. " Without all contradiction the less is blessed of the better."

And as we cast our hurried glance at the honest artizan it may be steadily labouring for a worthless employer; the pale dressmaker with aching eyes and trembling fingers, the mainstay of a widowed mother or younger sisters, but a very bondslave to the exacting haste and heartless tyranny of fashion; the sleepless provider of literature preparing for the idle and dissipated that will presently yawn over the produce of his over worked brain:—As we see every real worker of of whatsoever craft he be, the result of whose toil goes only to the aggrandizement or amusement, or good of the inferior in mind, though it may be the superior in worldly circumstance, we are no more inclined to doubt the wisdom of this profound truth. " Without all contradiction the less is blessed of the better."

And if we turn from nature to revelation, from things temporal to things spiritual, we find it to be the same. As we read the long prophetic roll of those commissioned in olden times to live and labour and minister for that disobedient and gainsaying, stiff necked and perverse people, who too often would none of their counsel, but despised all their reproof. As we read in the very words that concluded the Chronicles of their nation. " The Lord God of their father's sent to them by His messengers, rising up betimes and sending ; because He had compassion on His people, and on His dwelling place . but they mocked the messengers of God and despised His words, and misused his prophets." As we open our New Testament and find how last of all the provoked but long suffering Father sent unto them His Son saying. " They will reverence My Son." As we read how He went about doing good to that unthankful and evil generation. As we linger on the records of " The Holy Apostles," and Martyrs of whom the world was not worthy : and ponder the tale of a self sacrifice and devotion that make us for the while utterly despondent about our lesser puny trifling lives. And as we think in the very words of one of the greatest of them, how not unto themselves but unto us they minister, like the Queen of Sheba there is no more spirit in us. And we can only faintly and with infinite self humiliation assent once more to the decisive position the text. " W tho it all contradiction the less is b'essed of the better. "And lastly as we think how Angels "that excel in strength," that are " greater in power and might," are " all sent forth to minister unto the heirs of salvation." As we exclaim with the surprise of Elizabeth at the condescending visit to her of the great mother of her Lord. Whence is this that the Angels of my Lord should come to me! Lord what is man that Thou so regardest him. Thou hast made him lower than the Angels and yet crowned him with such honour that Thou hast given Them charge to minister to him !—Verily we admit as we finally decline to challenge the strong and evidently undeniable affirmation. " Without all contradiction the less is blessed of the better."

And yet this despondency and self humiliation in the sense of our inferiority to the greater that thus minister to us—Angels, Martyrs, Apostles, Prophets, -need not be cherished. For it is the very law of Heaven, which Jesus Christ embodied in all His life, that the less *should* thus be blessed of the greater. The greater are only so in order that they may may bless and benefit and serve the less. They are only great in God's estimation as long as they do so bless and serve them. There must needs be the less and the greater, but each are what God made or has allowed them to be.

And the practical bearing of the subject before us is in the application which may be made of it to each class, to the less and to the greater. And there comes here first the lesson to the less. The less need not despond or vex themselves that they are such, any more than should the greater triumph for that they are what *they* are. .

The world condemns pride in the great. But there may be. as. much pride in the less, in the less who refuse to receive, as in the great. who boast to give If the Spirit of God has thus truly said that the. less is actually blessed of the greater, it is equally beyond contradiction that thus God would have it to be.

So says Adelaide Procter

> "I hold him great who for love's sake
> Can give with generous earnest will,
> Yet he who takes for loves sweet sake,
> I think I hold more generous still.
>
> Glorious it is to wear the crown
> Of a deserved and pure success,
> He who knows how to fail, has won
> A crown whose lustre is not less."

Indeed believe me it may be the easier to be the greater than the less. The same Poetess says

> Many if God should make them kings
> Might not disgrace the throne He gave,
> How few who could as will fulfill,
> The humble office of a slave.
>
> Great may he be who can command
> And rule with just and tender sway,
> Yet is diviner wisdom taught
> Better by him who can obey.

I know nothing that so surely marks a noble and generous mind as the contented acquiescing in an inferiority which is manifestly the will and dispensation of the Lord of all our lives.

Thus the last becomes the first. And the less according to the outward appearance, is transformed into the greater in the estimation of Him that judges righteous judgement. "To take the lowest room," or to be content to remain there if rudely pushed into it by the self seeking fellow creature or adverse fate—to be content to remain there till Providence says "Friend come up higher,"—is the highest attribute of greatness.

Yea it is Divine Greatness. It is the very principle of faith. It is the very spirit of Christ. "He endured the cross, despising the shame." "He became obedient unto death," even the death of the slave. "He humbled and made Himself of no reputation," He could say "I seek not mine own glory." "I receive not honour from men." "I am among you as He that serveth." And His own Divine teaching is—And whoever but He or before Him, taught such a lesson?—Who in the schools of philosophy? who in the lands of heathenism?—"Ye know that they that are great exercise authority: but it shall not be so among you: but whosoever will be great among you, let him be your minister, and whosoever will be chief among you let him be your servant even as the Son of man came not to be ministered unto, but to minister."

And so we are brought to the application of this subject to the greater. Some of us must needs be such. The gifts of rank, of wisdom, of powers of attraction, of opportunity for improving those around us are apportioned by God as He will. And for this purpose are they given to those who are thus rendered great that with them they may benefit and serve the less. If the one dependent upon you, or who crosses your path in life is without what you can impart, what you have an aptitude for, what you have it in your power to do to raise him higher in any respect, to smooth his harder lot, or gladden his wearier way, you are called upon to serve him. As the Apostle says "having then gifts differing according to the grace that is given to us."—whether some capacity for ministering no matter how lowly or even mean the sphere— "let us wait on our ministering;" or he that teacheth on teaching, he that giveth let him do it with simplicity; he that ruleth with diligence, he that sheweth mercy with cheerfulness."

> How truly blessed from the snare
> Of earthly pride set free,
> In singleness of heart and aim,
> Thy servant Lord to be.
>
> The hardest toil to undertake,
> Is joy at thy command,
> The meanest office to receive,
> Is pleasure at Thy hand.

Think of this you whose tasks seem irksome and thankless, you who imagine none know the painful struggle it is to you, to bear up through the sameness of monotonous days and an unchanging round of labour. "Do it as to the Lord, and not unto men." Do it in consciousness that His approval follows you, as He watches you pursue your ungracious, perhaps only half requited task, with His own ever unwearied interest. And you shall know

> How happily the working days
> In His dear service fly!
> How rapidly the closing hour,
> The time of rest draws nigh!
>
> When all the faithful gather home,
> A joyful company,
> And ever where the Master is
> Shall His blest Servant be.

"For He cometh," and "His reward is with Him." Yea, and He has Himself foretold one further and delightful verification of the text. "Blessed" says He "are those servants whom their Lord when he cometh shall find so doing. Verily I say unto you that He shall gird Himself, and make them sit down to meat, and come forth and serve them."

> O, happy servant he
> In such a posture found!
> He shall his Lord with rapture see,
> And be with honour crowned.
>
> Christ shall the banquet spread
> With His own Royal hand;
> And raise that faithful Servant's head
> Amid the Angel band.

Then verily shall the less be blessed of the better. For He ou the Throne shall feed and lead beside the living waters, and introduce them to the converse and companionship of one another, and guide them ever further into the knowledge and acquaintance of the mysteries and joys reserved for the blessed.

And as He causes them to know and see more of the love wherewith He has loved them; aud goes on, and ever yet further on, to satisfy them from the inexhaustible stores of its provision, the experience of eternity, like that of time, shall be one prolonged expression of the assurauce of the text "the less are blessed of the better." For the Redeemed shall never cease to be ministered to by their Redeemer.

THE WHEAT AND THE GARNER.

" He will gather His wheat into the garner." *Matthew*, iii, 12.

St. John Baptist who spoke these words was a child of the country.
From early years when he was left an orphan by his parents, who at
the time of his birth were already old and well stricken in years, he
was in the desert we read till the day of his showing unto "Israel," i.e.
till his public career of Ministry begun. And he was very familiar
therefore with country scenes. We have striking indications of this
acquaintance with country life in his preaching; he draws his illustrations
from the sights and objects among which he had all his days been conversant. He enforces his teaching in the very passage from which my
text is taken, and the corresponding one in St. Luke, by reference to
the vipers of the desert, and the scattered stones and rough places of
its almost untrodden ground; and the precipitous steep and the
pathless mountain, the tangled thicket, and the woodman with his
axe, and husbandman with his fan or winnow. From the lonely
heights of the rocky fastnesses, in which the Spirit of God had fixed the
bounds of his recluse habitation he had gazed too, as we see here, on the
distant meadow and corn fields, and watched "the mower fill his hand,
and he that bound up the sheaves his bosom." And like all the prophets
he looked ever on, and especially as we are led to do by the sights of
harvest tide, to the end of all things. For "the harvest," says the Great
Interpreter of nature is the end of the world and the reapers are the
Angels. In the verse from which the text is taken he compresses
much of that parable of his Master where He showed how the field was
the world and the good seed the children of the kingdom, and how the
Son of man should gather out at the length all that offend, and cast as
the refuse of the field, "into the furnace of fire " But I choose rather
now to dwell on the more pleasing aspect of the eventful and coming
day this present season prefigures, and to speak to you—who I pray
God to include in the number and ingather with his saints to glory
everlasting—of his wheat, and its destined homestead. " He shall
gather His wheat into the garner."—His wheat and the garner, lift we
our hearts to God as we dwell upon the words, and pray Him for the
love of his Son and by the grace of His Spirit,

<blockquote>
May we the Angel reaping o'er,
Stand at the last accepted,
Christ's golden sheaves for evermore,
To garners bright elected.
</blockquote>

" He shall gather His wheat !" The wheat stands out for many a month exposed to every wind and storm, and blighting, chilling influence of the outer world. And the Master it may be passes it by but seldom. And it abideth alone. Is not this the picture of our present state. God hideth himself and seems far away ; and we are left, like the frail stalk to bow before the blast of affliction and to brave the rough, cold outer world as best we may, though aided ever like the corn of wheat by the hidden resisting force, and the secret springs of strength that God has implanted in, and will communicate to our regenerate life.

But all the while " God knoweth them that are His " ; and the refining, perfecting process of sanctification is being brought about by the apparently adverse surroundings.

All is tending, to us who are called according to His purpose, to the maturing of the wheat. And " the joy of Harvest " to " the husbandmen " who St. James says " waiteth for the precious fruit of the earth, and hath long patience for it," to us who rejoice in His goodness today, is nothing to the joy over His people, and the eagerness with which as His own Son has said, " When the fruit is brought forth immediately He putteth in the sickle because the harvest is come."

You will observe that of all the different kinds of grain with which the harvest season is associated, *wheat* is chosen as the symbol for the people of God. *Wheat* because it is the produce which of all others is the most valuable to ourselves. We might dispense with any product of the ground sooner. And while other productions have their inferior value as of secondary importance to us, or as food for the animals that minister to us, wheat is of the first consequence, and regulates the value of all other grain. Beautiful indication have we thus in the words "He will gather His wheat" of the price our gracious Lord sets upon us, of the estimation in which he holds our unworthy selves.

His wheat—How do the words show us our true nobility as the redeemed of the Lord ! How do they arouse us to cherish carefully in sanctification and honour the bodies and souls which are sustained in life for such in-gathering. *His wheat* are we! And shall we debase the bodies on which he sets such store, which he has so fearfully and wonderfully framed, and which he upholds in being with such unceasing care, by intemperance, or excess of any sort. *His wheat* are we? And shall we neglect the pursuit of and attention to ought which a Christian should know and believe to his soul's health ? *His wheat* ! And can we suffer the powers of the body to be impaired by sin, or those of the spirit by the neglect of the means and Sacraments ordained by Christ and His Church, for its strengthening and refreshing ? *His wheat* are we ? And shall we (not merely in our Service of gratitude today, but hereafter and always) labour to show forth our sense of his favour " not only with our lips but in our lives, by giving up ourselves to his service, and by walking before him in holiness and righteousness all our days ?" Shall we not take up therefore the Psalmist's words " I will sing unto the Lord as long as I live." "I will praise my God while I have my being?" Shall we not out of the fulness of our grateful souls take up the words of the hymn I have before quoted.

To Thee O Lord our hearts we raise,
In hymns of adoration
To Thee bring sacrifice of praise,
With hymns of exultation.

Bright robes of gold the fields adorn'd,
The hills with joy were ringing,
The valleys stood so thick with corn,
They laughing seemed and singing.

And now on this our festal day,
Thy bounteous hand confessing,
Upon Thine altar Lord we lay
Tne first fruits of Thy blessing!

By Thee the souls of men are fed
With gifts of grace supernal,
Give soul and body daily bread,
Keep us to life eternal.

Keep us we say here to that life. And so we come to observe the blessed destiny of God's precious and preserved wheat, "He will gather it says the text into the garner," O cheering thought, that shelter of security which awaits the blessed when the Great Husbandman brings home His sheaves rejoicing! when the time of exposure to the sorrow and temptation we are subject to here draws to a close, and we are transplanted to the everlasting habitations! comfort yourselves Christian servants of the Lord with this prospect; rouse yourselves ye unprofitable ones—servants only in name—to the sense of what you are missing.

"The garner," the word indicates in the original the reserved spot. And how much does it suggest! We know what a reserved seat is at an entertainment, reserved ground when a park is set open for the entrance of visitors. What must be the beauty and the adornment, and the provisions for enjoyment such as no imagination can picture of the mansions and the better country where God has prepared for His own a habitation! "No eye hath seen O God beside Thee," says the Prophet "What He hath prepared for him that waiteth for Him." "The garner" It doth not yet appear what it shall be.

But blest must be that land of God,
Where saints abide for ever
Where golden fields spread far and broad,
Where flows the crystal river.

The strains of all its holy throng,
With ours to day are blending
Thrice blessed is that harvest song,
Which never hath an ending.

It is a beautifully apt arrangement of our Church that calls us at the very time of the ingathering of the harvest festival, to celebrate and keep in memory the day of St. Michael and All the Angels. We could believe the arrangement was suggested by our Lord's very words, as it is in accordance with His own interpretation already alluded to of the harvest field. "The reapers are the Angels." This much is clear that our Lord would have the sight and thought of the reapers call up before our soul the vision and the contemplation of those spiritual beings—"The Angels that excel in strength," and fill the field of this our world with their mighty energies—We think in our fond self-importance that we are the great agents in the world which is given into the hands of man. But there stand those among us whom we know not, the prompters and helpers and the real great workers in the world. Ever are they swiftly flying to and fro. Unseen they operate through what we call the powers of nature, " doing God's commandments and hearkening to the voice of his word." " The visible intervention of the Angels, (says a late Archdeacon—Evans—of our Church, in a passage I consider so well weighed and conclusive as to be worth quoting,) has become indeed a fact of past history. But the existence of these Angels, and their actual though invisible intervention, in our affairs is a present external reality which we cannot safely overlook. However we may be unable to see what they have to do with us or we with them, as to any directly practical purpose, yet sufficient has been revealed for us to regard them with a lively interest and real sympathy. And our Church has not been wanting in her usual wisdom of provision in placing their ministry before us, among the rest of the dispositions of the kingdom of the Redeemer, and assigning a day for its especial consideration. And if the naturalist be allowed so freely to indulge in the boast that his survey of the creatures *below* us adds much to his sense of the goodness and glory of God, shall the Christian's contemplation of the creatures *above* us be deemed less edifying ? And if Scripture natural history be a favourite study with many, though they may never have seen, and have little chance of ever seeing, and have nothing to do with any of those animals in which they take most interest, why are they to be blamed who feel an interest in those superior beings who are announced in Scripture as having a lively interest in us, being ministering spirits who attended our Lord in His earthly ministration, and are still sent to minister on account of the heirs of salvation ? Is not their study more excellent in the proportion of heavenly to earthly ? And is it not a much nobler employment of the imagination, to picture to us Michael rather than a lion, and Gabriel rather than a cedar of Libanus."

And this shall be the last lesson and thought I would leave with you to-day. As you have been looking so often, during the last few weeks, on the fields in which the busy reapers have now effected so sweeping a change, hear the word of the Lord, and the moral of the harvest scene that has now passed before your eyes, "The reapers are the Angels." They are hovering and waiting ever around the field of your inner life. Have They found in your soul any wheat to in-gather into the garner of the Lord? Do grateful and loving hearts beat here to-day, yielding fruits of righteousness to God's honor and praise which observant Angels may upbear from these courts of the Lord, an offering well pleasing to God? Does Their penetrating gaze detect here what the most quick-sighted and far seeing human eye might overlook—for we have no such insight as they into the hidden things of the spirit, fruits of the Holy Ghost, " Love, joy, peace, long suffering gentleness, " goodness, faith, meekuess, temperance? " As the Vine dresser, in our Lord's parable of the barren fig tree, comes seeking fruit so verily do they. And the Revelation of God tells us that they bear aloft our prayer and praises from the midst of the Congregation here to the great one above. What think you have those reapers to carry up to heaven's treasury to-day. Can They shew—

> " Holy offerings rich and rare,
> Offerings of praise and prayer,
> Purer life, and purpose high,
> Clasped hands uplifted eye ;
> Lowly acts of adoration
> To the God of our salvation ?
> Fervent wishes, earnest thought
> Into worthy action wrought,
> Air and words and garb of pride
> Put for conscience sake aside,
> Lawful luxury foregone
> To relieve some needy one ?

Can They tell of the renunciation on your part of

> " Sinful thoughts and wilful ways,
> Love of self and human praise,
> Pride of life and lust of eye
> Worldly pomp and vanity,
> Loveless life and joyless mood
> Chill of cold ingratitude ?"

Can They announce about you to the listening and glad ear of God,

> " Brighter joys and tenderer tears,
> Fonder faith more faithful fears,
> Lowlier penitence for sin,
> More of Christ your souls within ? "

At least let Them bear back your loving aspirations, and holy resolutions for the future, " I will love Thee O Lord my God," " Thou art my God and I will praise Thee," " Thou art my God I will exalt Thee I will yet praise Thee more aud more, my lips shall greatly rejoice when I sing unto Thee, and so will my soul which Thou hast redeemed."

THE WALK TO EMMAUS.

Luke xxiv, 13-35.

This is one of the most life-like descriptions in the Bible. It has affected the imaginations of multitudes most powerfully. I know no Scripture incident which has been the theme of so many and such touching verses. There was a noted unbeliever once, who has left upon record that he never could read this passage without being moved to tears. I have often pondered it, and I doubt not you too have done so, with enchained interest. And as a Minister I have witnessed the marked attention with which its recital is generally received. I venture here in dependence on the Great Spirit that suggested the record, to handle the subject myself.

Now we like to know all that is to be known about the parties to any transaction, for the story of their doings is otherwise of lesser interest. " He appeared unto two of them," says S. Mark "as they walked and went into the country." Who were the two ? The name of one of them, says the text was Cleophas. But how about the name of the other ? It may be answered it is not revealed, and as the Angel of the Lord said to Manoah, " Why askest thou after the name seeing it is secret ? " If your neighbour tells you some part of a matter that concerns him, but keeps silence about some other part, you have the grace to respect his reserve. Refined or delicate feeling restrains you from expressing or indulging even any curiosity about what is the other's private concern.

Still in the Bible I think there are a good many things not mentioned not because God wishes them concealed, but to stir us up to more diligent search, and to awaken our interest and enquiry. And we may observe that the two travellers here speak as though they were a part of the Apostolic company (see verses 21, 22, 24). They could hardly have identified themselves if one of them at least were not of the Twelve, and the other, if not one also, at all events very nearly connected. So, knowing that Cleophas was not one the Twelve, we should be led to suppose his companion was. We observe further that they both constrained the Lord to enter the house, which seemed to belong equally to them, with an apparently equal right to invite Him. And so we should be inclined to think the two companions very possibly related. Now the one of them was Cleophas, and he was the husband of Mary, the mother of James the less. And S. James was one of the Twelve. What more likely then that he was the other, the companion of Cleophas on his journey to Emmaus ? If so Cleophas being his father would naturally speak as we have seen he did, identifying himself with James and the other Apostles.

The joint invitation they gave to enter the house would thus be explained. For if thus related they would have equal right of access to it. If they were not so related, it would seem the invitation could only have come naturally from the one who had the right of entrance, not from the companion who would only have entered himself in the right of his friend. I conclude therefore the other was very probably S. James.

But leaving one's own conjecture we learn for certain that one was Cleophas. And though we do not read of his presence at the last dread scene in our Saviour's life, we read of his wife as one of our Lord's most faithful and devoted followers,—" Now there stood by the cross of Jesus Mary, the wife of Cleophas." And Cleophas might well say, as we saw in verse 22 " Certain women of our company made us astonished." for in this same chapter we are told that Mary, his own wife, was one of the blessed women, who having gone to visit the tomb, and seen the Angels Who declared Him risen, came back to tell these things unto the Apostles. His wife was the more prominent figure in the story. His discipleship was perhaps equally true, his love equally real. But her understanding was more keen, for she we are told " remembered His words," and after the vision of the Angels, seemed to grasp the whole matter, while he later in the day was, as the text shows us, still hesitating and uncertain. Her faith was more clear, and her zeal more forward. She was already satisfied, for early that morning she had seen the Lord. But he at the day's close was still talking of all these things that had happened, and of doubtful mind.

But though he had not the faith to stand by the Cross of Jesus like her, and despise the shame;—though the grey dawn of that third day had not seen him hastening in the eagerness of the blessed Mary's love to the tomb of the crucified.—Though hope perhaps had already died within his more desponding heart. And he had abandoned all expectation of seeing again the beloved Master, whom his wife and his son had followed so long and so far, and he himself through her had consecrated his substance to so willingly.—Though all to him seemed over now, and the courage of his wife in vain, and her confidence, enthusiasm, and further delay in Jerusalem useless.— Though the things which had come to pass there appeared a mystery, a troubled vision, which he would fain forget, and as he was doing at the time of which the text tells turn his back upon.—Though all this were true the bruised reed the patient Saviour would not break, and the smoking flax he would not quench.

That day should not pass till the light of His countenance should rest on the sad and troubled face of Cleophas. And to him as well as to Mary should be given " the light of the knowledge of the glory of God in the face of Jesus Christ." That very day should salvation come unto him, for that he himself was a child of Abraham. And the gentle rebuke " be not faithless but believing." And the Revelation of Himself to him should gladden the desponding heart of Cleophas, and send him

" on his way rejoicing " not in hope, but in the full assurance " of the glory of God."

So the Lord even Jesus appeared to him and his companion in the way. He accosted them with kindly interest as a stranger sympathizing in the grief which their troubled faces and earnest tones betokened, " What manner of communications are these that ye have one to another as ye walk, and are sad." And Cleophas replied for them both. If the other was S. James he would naturally so answer as the Father. And, with an expression of surprise that the stranger could wonder at his sadness or ask what subject filled his mind at such a crisis of the nation's history, and such a time of desolation for every feeling soul, he spoke as did the prophet in his book of Lamentations: " Is it nothing to you that pass by ! Behold and see if there be any sorrow like unto this ! "

Little did then Cleophas imagine how applicable his reproachful expostulation would become in after times and countries to unthinking multitudes who call themselves after the name of Christ, but whose hearts never thrilled as did those of Cleophas and his companion with the story of His Sacrifice and His love, His Cross and passion, His precious death and burial !

" Art thou only a stranger," he being dead yet speaketh to the absent or retreating ones who desert the banqueting table spread to recall " the exceeding great love of our Master and only Saviour thus dying for us, and the innumerable benefits which by His precious blood shedding He hath obtained for us ! " Art thou only a stranger and carest not to celebrate the continual remembrance of His death ! " A stranger only," and the minister of Christ has perchance overlooked you. and left you unbidden to receive the pledges of His love to your great and endless comfort !

" Art thou only a stranger," and carest for none of these things ! The words of the holy man come echoing to us from beyond the veil of the world that though unseen is so near to us all. I fancy I hear them echoing down the aisles of many a Church in Sabbath Service hours where listless eyes and wandering glances betoken apathetic souls that hear unmoved the tidings of salvation. I seem to see the earnest Cleophas gazing with wondering eyes into prayerless pews, on closed lips that utter no response, or rigid forms that know no bended knee, or careless worshippers that come and go from " the great Congregation," without interest stirred, or feeling roused, or conviction awakened, or resolution strengthened, or a hope confirmed, or zeal enkindled, or love shed abroad in the glowing soul. Art thou only a stranger ! And is this Divine Service nothing to you ? Are you only looking on at a ceremony, assisting at a form which concerns it may be some few present but not yourselves ? Are you only an outsider with no part nor lot in the matter " a stranger to the covenant of promise, an alien to the commonwealth of Israel having no hope and without God in the world," Have you

No sins to mourn, no good to crave,
No fears to quell, no soul to save ?

Nay says the Apostle " ye are no more strangers and foreigners, but follow citizens with the saints, and of the household of God." Claim your privilege, take your part you have a Saviour who died for you, as well as for your devouter neighbour, yea is risen again for your justification.

The stranger in the dim twilight joined Himself to Cleophas and his companion. " And beginning at Moses, and all the Prophets He expounded unto them in all the Scriptures the things concerning Himself." And did, ever such gracious words proceed from the lips of even the Lord Jesus before! He was even (if Divinity could be so), better qualified now for a Teacher and Revealer of the hidden things of God than He had been before. For He had now penetrated the to us strange mystery of death, and solved the solemn secrets of the tomb.

The seven and a half miles (for such was the distance between Jerusalem and Emmaus) was traversed, though after an exciting and weary day, as no such journey had ever been passed before even in the most entertaining and endeared companionship. Well might they say to one another "Did not our hearts burn within us, while He talked with us by the way, and while He opened to us the Scriptures." For who ever heard such an exposition of Scripture before or since? We may have known what it is to have felt our hearts burn within as we listened to some gifted preacher revealing to us our own thoughts and feelings and declaring to us the counsel and grace of God.

> We know how dear the winged hour,
> Spent in Thy hallowed courts O Lord !
> To feel devotions soothing power,
> And catch the manna of Thy word.

We have felt our souls uplifted in sympathy with the fervent worshippers in the earthly sanctuary, and borne aloft, as on Angels wings, with the incense of their united prayers. We have followed the minister of the most High as he has led us in imagination into the midst of the heavenly host till we have seemed for the moment to be kneeling side by side with Cherubim and Seraphim before the throne of God. We have almost been able to persuade ourselves

> That with yonder sacred throng,
> At His very feet we fall ;
> Have joined the everlasting song,
> And seen the Lord of all.

We know some of us,—many I hope, would that we all did—the enthusiasm of Divine worship. But till we come, as of God's infinite mercy I pray we may, to where Cleophas and his former companion on the road to Emmaus are now conversing with their Lord again we can never know how their hearts on that first Sunday evening burned within them while He talked with them by the way and while He opened to them the Scriptures.

" He made as though He would have gone further, but they constrained Him saying, Abide with us, for it is toward evening, and the day is far spent. And He went in to tarry with them." Where he would have gone, and what blessed ministrations further on in the lone country would at that late hour have engaged his service, we cannot tell.

Suffice it only to learn that the genuine invitation and loving constraint "Abide with us." was enough to stay the onward steps of the risen and triumphing Redeemer, and draw Him a willing guest within their humble roof. Thank God it is always so ! And the longing for solace and sympathy and companionship which the sorrowful, or careworn, or sin-burdened soul expresses in that simple appealing cry. " Abide with me," shall never be left unsatisfied. " And He went in to tarry with them." "And if any man love Me" says the Saviour—and only love it is that can prompt this genuine cry, Abide with me. " I will love him, and come unto him, and make my abode with him." And again in the last Revelation of Himself that the Bible contains, lest we should think that since His Ascension, He is beyond the reach of our earnest and inviting call, " Behold I stand at the door and knock : if any man hear my voice and open the door, I will come in to him, and will sup with him, and he with Me."

The story before us is not one of the bygone "days of the Son of Man," which He tells us we may not expect to see, however we may desire to have it repeated. But it is one which, having been a continued experience through all the ages since, may become the history of ourselves to day. Only make the petition of Cleophas and his companion yours, and see if it be not answered.

Yea if it be with you toward evening and the day far spent—if the sun of hope, and vigor, and energy, and perhaps life itself be going down—if bereaved and disappointed and perplexed life seem in your darkened moments a mystery and the world a blank—if like them what you trusted in has failed and what you loved disappeared—he will enter at your call the desolate soul and set before it, as before them the bread of Life that satisfies, and the Wine of the Gospel that revives. He will spread a table before you and bless you with the light of His countenance, and the joy of His fellowship. And he will make himself known to you, as He did to Cleophas and the other, but as He does not to the world.

But He will not vanish out of your sight, as He did from theirs. But come more and more into it, " until the day dawn, and the shadows flee away ;" "and the Lord Jesus be revealed from heaven to be admired in His saints " and to bless and satisfy them with His presence for evermore.

> Abide with us, the evening shades
>   Begin already to prevail ;
> And as the lingering twilight fades,
>   Dark clouds along the horizon sail.
>
> Abide with us, the night is chill,
>   And damp and cheerless is the air,
> Be our companion, stranger still,
>   And thy repose shall be our care.
>
> Abide with us, Thy converse sweet,
>   Has well beguiled the tedious way,
> With such a friend we joy to meet,
>   We supplicate Thy longer stay.

Abide with us—for well we know
  Thy skill to cheer the gloomy hour;
Like balm Thy honied accents flow,
  Our wounded spirits feel their power.

Abide with us—and still unfold,
  Thy sacred, Thy prophetic lore:
What wondrous things of Jesus told!
  Stranger we thirst, we pant for more!

Abide with us,—and still converse
  Of Him who late on Calvary died:
Of Him the prophecies rehearse,
  He was our Friend they crucified.

Abide with us.—our hearts are cold,
  We thought that Israel he'd restore,
But sweet the truths Thy lips have told,
  And stranger we complain no more.

Abide with us,—we feel the charm
  That binds us to our unknown Friend;
Here pass the night secure from harm,
  Here stranger let Thy wanderings end.

Abide with us—to their request
  The stranger bows with smile Divine;
Then round the board the unknown Guest,
  And weary travellers recline.

Abide with us,—amazed they cry,
  As suddenly whilst breaking bread,
Their own lost Jesus meets their eye
  With radiant glory on His head!

Abide with us,—Thou Heavenly Friend,
  Leave not thy followers thus alone!
The sweet communion here must end,
  The Heavenly visitant is gone!
                              RAFFLES.

SIMON THE PHARISEE AND THE WOMAN THAT WAS A SINNER.

Luke vii 36-50.

It is not often that our Saviour draws attention to His wants. His hard lot, or His unworthy treatment on earth as the Son of Man In the intensity of that ever present thought of His soul, consideration for the woes of earth, and unwearied labour to relieve them, He for the most part overlooks His own and suffers the slights and neglect of which He was the object to pass unobserved. For none ever so magnanimously fulfilled the rule of his own, inspiration, and set it forth in example "look not every man on his own things, but every man also on the things of others." But when he does glance for a moment at the neglect and scorn which he had to suffer at the hands of those He held so dear, the glimpse afforded us into the feelings of that human heart of our Divine Lord is very affecting. "He came unto His own," says S. John, and His own received Him not."

When we hear Him sadly contrast His own persecuted, homeless, and outcast life with the security and shelter enjoyed by the wild animals and birds, whose lives men hold for the most part of little value—"The foxes have holes, and the birds of the air have nests, but the Son of Man hath not where to lay His Head"—we gaze upon the noble speaker, the despised and rejected of men, till our eyes almost run down with tears, and our hearts, aye our very frames, are conscious as we realise His suffering, of a thrill of sympathy and shame For we know that we could not bear to turn the meanest cur, or miserable stray cat from our roof, hospitable however humble, that came whining to our door in the hour of its famished or exhausted need, or in that of approaching darkness, or of storm, to crave the shelter or the food which its Maker seemed to have forgotten to provide for it.

And the same feeling of startled pity and indignation commingled comes over us as we read our good Lord's description in the text of the contempt of this proud Pharisee. Simon thought quite sufficient honour bestowed on our blessed Lord by his invitation. And he treated Him with indifference on His arrival Travellers in that country for all except very short distances went barefoot. It was customary and needful therefore for entertainers to provide their guests with water for the feet, as here spoken of. And those high in position and dignity were always greeted as Samuel did Saul, with the salutation of respect and the scented oil, which our Lord here mentions as also withheld from Him

What condescension on the part of the blessed Jesus to submit so calmly and expostulate so gently in this treatment of His own contemptuous creatures ! We should verily have expected that Simon would have come out himself to Him, as Naaman expected Elisha would to him, to offer every service, and the whole household should have vied with one another who should pay Him the most attention. We would almost fancy therefore the expectant Jesus lingering a moment on the threshold to receive the token of homage which was ever accorded at such a meeting to the King or the noble, and be conducted to the post of honour but

> Man had no love to give Thee here,
> No words of peace, no look of cheer,
> No tenderness his heart could move,
> He gave Thee hatred for Thy love,

King of Kings and Lord of Lords was He, accustomed to the ministration of Angels, and the bosom of the Father. But no, He knew what was in man. And though His own words show how grieved He was, He was not surprised. Truly as saith the prophet, "He was despised, and we esteemed Him not." I am not going to ask you to cast the stone of your reproach and condemnation at Simon, nor do I wish to stir one feeling of indignation within you at the heartlessness of the Pharisee. It is a very easy thing to censure others. And when they are manifestly deserving of it, and of the gravest and severest, as this man was, it is vastly flattering to our own self-righteous and self-complacent souls, to exclaim loudly at their misconduct. But unless we are called by any public office or duty let us beware. We are at all times and in all persons boldly to rebuke vice, but the same Spirit of God who had made it His charge, that we should not in any wise "suffer sin in our neighbour," has sternly said, "Therefore thou art inexcusable, O man, whosoever thou art that judgest." And if the prayers of any of us be cold, and the praises feeble, and the devotion slight that we show to the Lord of our faith and lives. If the tokens of earnestness and fervour in His worship or the study of His word be lacking, which of us will be bold to say that we either have given the to Him grateful water and precious oil of our honour and regard. And which among us but must feel that, while we may have bent to Him in formal worship, as even Simon may have done as He came in at his door, ours like his has been the cold glance, the slight recognition of acquaintance, rather than the hearty grasp of faith, and the warm embrace of love! But we may trace the indifference of Simon even further. It would appear that until Jesus said, " Simon, I have somewhat to say unto thee," Simon had not even listened to Him. No doubt Jesus had been all the time conversing with those around the table. Bnt though he was in His very presence Simon was holding no communications with Jesus, but taken up wholly with his other guests. And Christ is in our presence and speaks still. " Now then says S. Paul we are ambassadors for Christ, and as though God did beseech you by us, we pray you in Christ's stead." It is true we do not speak like Him. All words are and must be faint and feeble in comparison with the weighty burning sayings of truth, and words of love of Him into whose lips grace was poured without measure.

The blush of confusion may well rise to the preacher's brow as he reflects how inadequately he is exhibiting even when the flow of utterance is most enlarged to him, the interest of his Master's word, the wonders of His love, the richness of His Gospel. Yet the Word preached in spite of the imperfections attending its delivery is the power of God, and the wisdom of God. And if this be so, and Christ has spoken here often, though as S. Paul says it be in the foolishness of preaching, and the Word preached has not profited you, and you have given so little heed to the things that are spoken, that you are still as much tied and bound with the chain of evil habits or tempers or deeds as ever, as earthly or worldly minded, Ah! then it is not for such a one to say a word as to the coldness or inattention of Simon to the words of Jesus.

Follow out this thought a moment more. Could you name the sins or point to the unholy affections or worldly tastes which in consequence of the preaching of the Word, you have been induced to renounce, or at all events resist ? Could you enumerate the fruits of the Spirit, which by His blessing upon the Word preached have begun to live and grow in you ? Can you tell of a meetness for heaven, a desire after holiness, a study to please God in your daily life, an increasing conformity to the life of Christ ? In your baptism the injunction was laid upon your parents and sponsors, and the Congregation of the Church that witnessed your reception into the kingdom of the Redeemer that they should call upon you to hear sermons. And such you have heard and been taught to consider that you should hear at least every week. Have they awakened in you an interest in Divine truth, a pleasure in God's ways, a longing for His favor, and set you on seeking to become prepared for His kingdom ? In one word has your heart like Lydia's as you listened to the Word, been opened to attend to the things that have been spoken. We feel justly surprised at Simon that he could sit even for a few minutes, and give no heed to the words of Jesus. And yet some of us may for years have come here before God, as His people come, and sat before Him, to quote the prophet Ezekiel's words, as His people sit and heard, unmoved to earnest seeking, of the joys of heaven ; and, to anxious avoidance, of the pains of hell, and gone our way as careless as ever.

But what was Simon doing all this while ? Thinking perhaps how well his table was spread, or how the guests must be admiring his costly furniture, and the admirable appointments of his well ordered household. Or he was talking. The guests were many, and the conversation was not likely to flag. I dare say he was conversing with one or other of them about their respective business or the members of their families, about their future plans, or their neighbours' doings, and very likely misdoings, where they had been, what they had seen, or what they intended to see. This is the very explanation of the too general inattention to God and the things concerning salvation. You have enough in one way or another to occupy your thoughts, and many coming and going ! So you have you imagine no leisure. One day follows hard upon the last with its fresh and inevitable engagements and your dealings with one another. And all the while there is one as near to you as Jesus to Simon, waiting and longing to purify your worldly hearts and rectify your views, and guide you to all truth and happiness. And patiently does He continue to whisper as He waits, as you watch to catch your neighbours eye in the busy throng, " I have somewhat to say unto thee." " Let me counsel you, as Eli so well did the young Samuel, what answer to give my waiting Master." " Speak Lord for Thy servant heareth." But another personage comes now before us than this respectable and honourable Pharisee, a woman in the city that was a sinner. God who has highly exalted His Son and given Him a name which is above every name that all men should honour the Son even as they do the Father, will not suffer Him, and never has done from the first, to go without the honour due to His name. When He brought in we read His first Begotten into the world knowing that being in the form of an Infant He would and must for a while be unnoticed and unhonoured of the world, He said, " Let all the Angels of God worship Him:" And if Herod and all Jerusalem refused as they did to own or worship the Holy Babe, the untaught Shepherds should do so and from the far East should come heathens wiser than the Jews to bring Him their gold, and incense, and myrrh. When the rulers and chief of the Jews rejected and despised Him He yet gave Him favour in the sight of multitudes, and " the common people heard Him gladly," " Though the heathen rage " says God in Psalm ii, " and the people make much ado yet will I set My King upon My Holy Hill of Sion." And so here. Though Jesus was not careful to urge His own claims on the worship and regard of Simon and his guests, His Father would see to it that those claims should not be overlooked, but that attention should be forcibly drawn to them. Reverence should be shown to Him. And the just Pharisee who withheld it should be put to shame by the woman that was a sinner who yielded it. And thus as He has so often done " He chose the foolish things of the world, to confound the wise! and base things of the world and things which are despised to bring to nought things that are, that no flesh should glory in His presence."

And so we come to consider her.—Her name is unmentioned. And perhaps there is something of judgement in the fact. " Their sorrows shall be multiplied," says the Spirit of God, speaking of sinners in Psalm xvi. " nor will I take up their names into my lips." And says Solomon, " Though the righteous shall be held in everlasting remembrance, the name of the wicked shall rot." Very likely her name was a byword and a reproach in the city that was ashamed to own her as one of its inhabitants. And perhaps the omission is intended to warn us of what will be the dread omission when they are assembled before God's bar of judgement and the books are opened, and no names are read out but those which are written in the Lamb's Book of Life, those who have penitently and earnestly sought pardon, and been justified by faith, and walked religiously in good works.

With the same eagerness which in that awful day you will listen to or it announced, from the catalogue which the Great Judge will read th, of the blessed of His Father, when He is commanding them to possession of His glorious Kingdom—seek to make sure of its out now.

But if her name is not given her character is. She was a woman that was a sinner. And what do we learn from this, but that God looks rather at what we are in heart and life, than what we are in outward circumstances. Whether indeed she were a sinner or not the mention of her name was of little import. It matters little or no whether you have a name in the world, whether you are widely known as one of high family. or great genius, or extensive learning or much wealth or importance. This you may or may not be. But God (and the wise I may add) think neither more nor less of you on that account. It has been well said poverty and riches, obscurity and fame are but the drapery of existence, are but clouds which throw their shadows over us.

The incidents of our mortal story, the objects which line our pathway, the associations of our earthly lot, the position we maintain in the world will soon disappear and be forgotten. But what we are within and in relation to Christ, whether love or indifference to Him be supreme within; whether benevolence or selfishness guide our ways in reference to our fellow creatures is recorded in an imperishable record and will be remembered in the day when all shall come up for judgment."

Your soul is as precious in His eyes, however humble be your lot or unnoticed your life, as that of the squire in his mansion, the lord in his castle, or the Queen in her Palace. And the loving Redeemer desires its salvation as much, and the blessed Spirit of grace waits as anxiously to guard it from sin, and sanctify and save it to life eternal.

Your name like this woman's may not be known beyond the village in which you dwell or the neighbouring town. You may be like her a perfect stranger to the world around you. But your works whether for good or evil, and the state of your heart is open to Him to whom all desires are known, and from whom no secrets are hid. By your humble efforts to please God, and to act as He would wish you to do : or your forgetfulness of Him, evil words or dispositions; or it may be even bold disregard of His laws—on this principle alone He judges, and will hereafter judge you. His estimate of you is formed not on the observation whether you are well or badly off, clever or ignorant, but whether you are yielding to and pursuing on the one hand, or resisting and avoiding on the other that which is evil.

The woman before us was unhappily in the former case. She was we are told a sinner. We are not told in what way. Perhaps she was a bad wife, and neglected her duties and mismanaged her house, and wasted her husband's goods, and neither loved nor assisted him as she vowed before God's altar she would do. Or perhaps she was a bad mother, and did not train her children to worship and fear their Great Lord and Friend, but allowed them in their own way in everything, and suffered them to form companionship with other irreligious children, and to mingle among them, and learn their ways of contention, dishonesty, deceit, profanity, Sabbath-breaking and wilfulness.

Or perhaps she was one of those contentious and angry women, with one of whom the wise man wisely says that rather than live in the most spacious and goodly residence, he would prefer solitude in the corner of a house top. Or perhaps she was a bad neighbour a mischief making or quarrelsome woman, one of those whom S. Paul describes as wandering about from house to house, idle, tattlers, busy bodies, speaking things which they ought not, and striving too often as effectually as earnestly to upset the peace of their betters.

Or perhaps she was a bad servant, paying as little attention as possible to the commands, much less the wishes, of her employers; and thinking more of idle company, or pleasure taking than of serving them heartily and faithfully, and ensuring thereby as servants are promised the favour of the great Master of us all. But more surely than all she had been a bad daughter, and had heeded not the advice of her father and had forsaken the law of her mother. Frowardly she had resolved to walk in the ways of her heart and the sight of her eyes. And she had entered, in the headstrong folly of youth, into the counsel of the ungodly, and stood in the way of sinners, and sat in the seat of the scornful. And thinking to be a law to herself, and, hating the instruction, and despising the reproof of the more experienced, she had fallen into evil, and misery, and shame, and into the foolish and hurtful lusts, to quote the words of inspiration which presently drown such giddy and self willed victims of their own infatuation in destruction and perdition.

And now she had eaten of the fruit of her own way and been filled with her own devices. She had sown to the flesh and reaped corruption. And at this time she had perhaps become bad in all or most of the above mentioned particulars together. For our Lord, who only knows, says Himself her sins had been many. And her feet were in Solomon's expressive words going down to death; her health wasted, her property consumed; her friends alienated. And they of her acquaintance more virtuous than she kept away from her, or thanked God in their hearts as they passed her by that they were not so lost and fallen.

This woman heard that the prophet of Nazareth was in her city and in the house of her fellow townsman Simon. And the Divine impulse that stirred the prodigal son prompted her too, in that her day of grace the acceptable time for her salvation, to seek for mercy as he; and to go and cry before Him who never suffers the penitent to cry so in vain. Father I have sinned against heaven and before Thee, and am no more worthy of thy regard. Yet I beseech Thee to hear me good Lord, be merciful to me a sinner! To quote the words of that beautiful mission Hymn that calls the outcast so engagingly to repentance. The Spirit of God made his invitation heard within that hardened bosom.

> Have you sinned as none else in the world have before you?
> Are you blacker than all other creatures in guilt?
> Yet if penitent fear not! the mother that bore you
> Loves you less than the Saviour, whose blood you have spilt.

> Then come to his feet and lay open your story,
> Of suffering and sorrow, of guilt and of shame,
> For the pardon of sin is the crown of His glory,
> And the joy of our Lord to be true to His name.

It would appear from the way in which she acted that she must have heard of Jesus before. And she believed Him to be the very Son of God with power on earth to forgive sins, and to cleanse from all unrighteousness. She appeared to know that that same God whom she had been provoking every day, had so loved not only the world generally but that very city, just like this very village and congregation, in particular, that He had sent the Redeemer not then to punish the world for its evil, and the wicked for their iniquities, but as His Apostle says " to bless by turning away every one of you from his iniquities." She need not then flee from the city as the devils fled before Him saying. " I know Thee who thou art, the Holy One of God! Art thou come to torment me before the time ? " No rather would she go and tell Him all in the confidence she had Divinely learnt, as we are Divinely taught, whether or no we have learnt to believe it like her. " If any man sin we have an advocate with the Father. Jesus Christ the Righteous : and He is the propitiation for our sins." Now that we have seen the woman hastening to the house of Simon, we can afford to suspend our interest as to her reception for thank God we have no doubts on that account. It had ever been said of Him and it ever shall " The broken and contrite heart Thou O God wilt not despise." We need not follow her tremblings teps to know the end. For we have heard and seen in all such instances, as the Apostle says, " the end of the Lord ; that the Lord is very pitiful and of tender mercy."

Let any repentant soul turn back to God through Christ, and the end shall always (praise to our long suffering God), be the same. " Let it be footsore with long wandering or soiled by contact with the world's pollution, or crushed by the burden of life's labours, or palsied by disappointed hopes ;—let it come back sick and weary, feeble and sorrowful, yet penitent and believing, looking to the strong for strength, to the wise for wisdom, to the healer for remedy, to the Saviour for the common salvation." And there shall be joy in the presence of the Angels of God over one such sinner that repenteth. And within the bonds of the covenant of unfailing mercy. And under the shadow of the cross. And on the steps of God's everlasting mercy seat it shall find repose and comfort, and pardon, and peace.

PART 2.

We come now to see how the woman sped upon the errand that was matter of life and death to her. We can however stop a moment to watch her as she passes knowing that she cannot fail to be welcomed to the embrace of eternal love. For this is the confidence that we have in Him, that if we ask anything according to His will, he heareth us and that " this man receiveth sinners," receiveth them to "restore to the path of righteousness and to save them for His name's sake "

We will therefore pause I say to look at her : for could we but see the sympathizing and guardian spirits that throng around the sons and daughters of the Lord Almighty, we should see fixed on her their eager gaze as they rejoiced over her return to God and His Christ. She is, as we learn from the story, gracefully adorned by the Author of beauty with thickly clustering hair : for God gives His gifts to the unthankful and the evil. And in long rich tresses it falls around her shoulders. Such was and is the graceful fashion of the East, the arrangement of nature, and that which the great Apostle thought it not beneath the dignity of inspiration to notice and commend, saying " If a woman have long hair it is a glory to her."

And she carries something evidently very valuable which she presses to her bosom as she hastens along the streets. She has some costly and very precious ointment of a sort which was used in wealthy households for the very purpose of anointing distinguished guests before they sat down to meat. Oil was more commonly provided as our Lord intimates in v. 49. of the text. She may possible have been rich and have been in the habit in the past of giving great entertainments herself such as Simon was now doing. Or it may have been given to her when a guest at some feast, or as a present from some friend. And at once it occurred to her that she would devote it to the honor of Jesus, in the spirit of the direction given in the Scriptures of her nation to those who would enter the presence of the most High. " Bring a present and come into His courts." Perhaps she had heard how the blessed women from Galilee ministered to Him of their substance, and how He—though the earth was His and the fulness thereof, had been pleased to receive these offerings. And she would not come before Him empty. Or, as I think is very probable, she knew her fellow citizen the proud Pharisee well enough to be assured or to suspect at the least, that he would not bestow this customary mark of honor, upon his lowly guest. And so she would supply his lack of service. And so too truly did she find it to be the case on reaching Simon's house. There in His wondrous self abasement sat the Great Lord of all unsaluted and unhonored. There had been none to minister to Him in His hour of human need. From our Lord's description, I am inclined to gather that in her exceeding haste the woman arrived almost directly after Jesus, and was a pained witness of His contemptuous reception. In the 37th verse it is said " when she knew that Jesus sat at meat in the Pharisee's house," she came and acted in the manner we are to describe. But Jesus says " From the time I came in she hath not ceased" so to do.

So quickly had she hurried to His presence! And as the throng of guests assembled she came in and mingled unobserved among the rest. And she watches eagerly her Lord as he enters. But no obeisance is paid Him. The greeting which was usually bestowed upon a superior as the mark of respect and honor, is unoffered. The water that it was usual to bring to cleanse, and the ointment to mollify the bare and way-worn feet is scornfully withheld. And while to quote S. James' words to one and another the invitation is courteously given, " Sit thou here in a good place," Simon's demeanour seemed to say to Jesus, to quote them further, " Stand thou there or sit anywhere under my footstool," No marvel verily that the woman wept. But is He not often treated still with something of a like disregard! No! you say indignantly. And you think you can appeal, as many will do we read at the last day when charged with neglect, to Him who knows all things and say, " Lord when saw we Thee in need and did not minister?" And perhaps your appeal may be allowed and the attachment of many of you be declared to have been sincere and true. I pray God only the number be multiplied! But it may be and it is otherwise with some of us. Like Simon we look one upon another. We care for our acquaintances and take affectionate thought about our friends. And we neglect not it may be to entertain or act kindly towards strangers. We are courteous enough and considerate to friends and neighbours, and delight to do and show them good. But where is the water and the oil we offer to our Lord? Where the attention and the honour He calls for? Where the assiduous waiting upon Him He, rightfully claims and patiently expects? Where is that, of which the kiss is the token and the seal, the devotion and love of which He is so supremely worthy? Yes! I ask those of you who think you love the Lord most where?

Oh if that blessed woman, blessed in this her deed of true devotion to the all worthy One, were on earth now and were to watch us for one single day. If she could look into our hearts as she looked into Simon's house, and observe our feelings towards her honoured Master, as she observed that Pharisee's demeanour, would she find us more forward in our devotion more fervent in our love than He? What signs would she notice of a desire on our part to be attentive to His wishes? What intimations would she gather from our actions of a watchfulness to do honour to Him, whom we confess deserving of all our obedience?

And be ye well assured that the Redeemer who though unseen stands ever by your side, looks as really for the tokens of your heart's regard and worship, as he did for the water and oil, and the embrace of Simon. And what marks of homage you ask will He have you render, and how shall your respect be shown? Very simple is the reply and I press it upon you in your Lord's own words, " If ye love me keep my commandments." You shall show it by doing your daily work in the spirit of ready alacrity, and the single aim to God's will that He did His, by bearing your hourly troubles and little cares in the patience and cheerful fortitude hat He bore His ; by conducting your transactions with those with whom you have to do on the pure and righteous principles of the gospel. Crush down the rising irritability, ignore the petty mortification that would set your spirit in a ferment if you dwell upon it, " Be not overcome of evil."

And more acceptable I tell you shall be such offering and sacrifice of the heart, more nobly shall you have honoured the Lord of Heaven, by whom all the strange discipline of life is ordered than had you received Him in the days of His flesh at your table as Simon did ; prostrated yourself before the lowly One, on the threshold in the presence of the great and the proud in the neighbourhood as He did not, brought forth water and oil to minister to His needs, and placed Him on the right hand as the Man you delighted to honour with the warmest welcome of affection and reverence.

But we return to the thought of the woman whom we left weeping. I said no marvel that she wept if the Lord of love were thus lightly esteemed. And yet I think not that this was the cause of her tears. It was not so much the haughty Pharisee's contempt of Jesus, as her own, that pierced her now tender and contrite heart and drew from her those tears of sorrow and of shame. Ah ! it is for those who are not convinced of the evil within themselves to reflect upon their neighbour's misdeeds. But in the penitent the mouth of accusation is quickly stopped. And sensible as he is of the wrongs of sinners against his Lord, the feeling of his heart is ever " of whom I am chief."

Simon's was a base and heartless sin. But it reminded her only of her own. Against that Blessed One she had likewise sinned times without number. Like Simon she too had slighted Him, His religion and His law, and even as he had put Him to an open shame. And thus it was and therefore that she wept. Indeed I doubt not not she had good cause beside to weep. She was a sinner we read. And the way of transgressors is ever hard. Though rough and thorny be the road, the narrow road that leads to God, is not the broad and flowery path of sin rough and thorny too ? And no doubt as other sinners she had as Solomon so forcibly pictures the end of the way of death. She had to " mourn at the length and say : How have I hated instruction and my heart despised reproof," to mourn over blighted hopes, and utter disappointment saying. " What fruit had I then in those things whereof I am now ashamed for the end of those things is death." " Vanity and and vexation of spirit," must ever be the sinner's portion." There is no peace " saith my God to the wicked.'

And here we leave the woman again in that godly sorrow which will work repentance unto salvation, and look to the next scene in this painfully interesting picture. Our eyes revert to the master of the feast. There he sits at the head of the board. And self complacency is stamped on his whole features and demeanour. He is on the best of terms with himself, and with the whole company. With himself: for is he not a man of unsullied reputation and blameless life? He observes all things that are written in the law and the prophets. And he gives tithes of all he possesses, the tenth part of his income to the purposes of religion. In prayers and attendance on the ordinances of Divine Service in the synagogue, he is an example to the city. He is true and just in all his dealings, and his liberality is notorious. Aye, and his righteousness or merit exceeds he is now thinking that of many. For has he not received the prophet of Nazareth to his house, while many of his own rank and sect are abusing Him with all manner of blasphemy and conspiring to take His life. Has not he thrown this day the shield of his patronage around the much reviled Jesus, and is not his loving protection likely, if not to make Him great or greater, to do Him a valuable service in the eyes of those who will think the better of Him for the court that Simon has paid Him now?

And so as Simon thus thinks of Jesus, and is reminded of His almost forgotten presence, his eye wanders down the table to see where this guest of his is sitting. And as it does so he looks at and speaks to one and another, and they all flatter him. And as they look admiringly on him he looks complacently on them. Well but where is Jesus? And now he begins to look more attentively. Ah! there He is. But see! Oh horror and shame! What! Can he believe his own eyes! There standing behind the prophet of Nazareth there is no mistaking. the person is in very deed.—what can she be doing there—the woman that was a sinner? Amazement depicts itself on Simon's face. He starts in his seat, and his knife drops heavily from his hand, and he pushes aside his plate, and sets down his just filled but as yet untasted glass. But ere Simon has time to express his surprise in a single word he sees she is doing what he had not only contemptuously but inhospitably neglected to do, and his mouth is instantly shut. For he is self convicted. She is only doing, though in a strange manner, what is customary towards honoured guests, and what he had left undone. Then her views about Jesus of Nazareth are different from his, and he feels instinctively that she is right. He cannot then object to her conduct or he might draw a reproof upon himself; or at least suggest by his very words his own neglect. But he can object to herself; for "she is a woman that is a sinner." Captiousness will ever have something to object to. Foolish man! As if a sinner may not turn to honour and cherish the Lord he has hitherto despised. Did Simon believe the prophets? and had he ever read " let the wicked forsake his way, and the unrighteous his thoughts: and let him return unto the Lord, and He will have mercy upon him ; and to our God for He will abundantly pardon?" It is not the touch of a sinner that can defile a man but the participating of his evil deeds or the countenance of his sin. But the thought had hardly occurred to his heart. The guests had scarce time to catch from the expression of Simo 's countenance that there was something amiss with him or in the room, when a voice as of one that had authority interrupted the conversation and the merriment of the assembled company. From the lower end, or from some recess or obscure corner of the room towards which point they saw Simon's gaze directed, was heard the voice of One who spoke as never man beside Him spoke. And every tongue was still and every sound was hushed. And the Master himself the great and proud Simon was visibly overawed. And what were the words that demanded audience of the Pharisee? Were they such as he would love to hear. Of the Pharisees Jesus had said they loved greetings and to be called of men Rabbi, Rabbi. Did the speaker then introduce his remarks with flattering titles and pompous courtesy? O Simon, the first of all the Pharisees here! thou worthy to be the leader and head of all this company, thou man of unblemished integrity and spotless life. Thy prayers and thine alms are come up for a memorial before God. Nothing of all this. But in tones of the mightiest majesty though in words of the simplest kind, and each word of the short sentence suggestive, thus He spoke.

Simon! as though he had said I know thee by name, and have an intimacy of knowledge and perfect understanding of all your thoughts. I, whom thou has not noticed and regarded, but who have the highest claim upon thy attention have something to say to thee. Thy other guests have been talking and thou hast listened to them with pleasure and with interest. But I too whose conversation thou hast not desired nor sought have likewise remarks to offer and a tale to tell. And my communication is to thee. Thou dost act as though thou neededst no instruction or admonition, as though the prophets' exhortations were all for others rather than for thee, as though thou wert above His teaching and needed not His help. But nevertheless I have a message from God, and am waiting to deliver it unto thee. And the words of this brief sentence contain a lesson for you. Have not some of you allowed the words of God to pass as it were over your heads as though they were applicable to other than yourselves? Is there no secret thought in your heart, as there was in Simon's, that you need not the reproofs, the instruction in righteousness that others do?

All well you think it is to preach to the heathen, to teach the utterly ignorant, to rebuke and denounce the judgments of God, upon the lawless, and disobedient, the unholy and profane. But what can the preacher have to say to you? You are not such, you need no repentance or change in your life of the kind they do! It may be so. And what our Lord had to say to Simon was different of course from what He had to say to the woman. Her He had to convict of all her ungodly deeds which she had ungodly committed. But Simon of a coldness of love towards his Saviour and a neglect to take thought of or to do Him honour.

We may not say what effect the address that followed produced on that cold proud hearted man. But Charity hopeth all things. And as there is nothing told to the contrary, we may trust that those clear and striking though gentle words of reproof were not uttered in vain. He received them with evident meekness, the spirit, as we are taught, in which the word when received is able to save the soul. When the Lord condescends to remonstrate in person and to plead His own cause as He does here and in the case of Jonah; and when we find as in both these cases, the remonstrance received in respectful silence, and not in the self-justifying spirit of Cain,—we are fain to hope the best. We think we can recognise in this case, and in that of the brother of the prodigal son in the parable with whom his father expostulated in a like manner the spirit of Job when God entered into judgment with Him "Behold I am vile, what shall I answer Thee, I will lay mine hand upon my mouth."

We would believe that the story our Lord proceeded to tell about the two debtors; who both owed though one more largely than the other and which ended with the significant words, "He frankly forgave them both" was predictive of the result that followed its telling. We wil not think that the words "He forgave both" are put in merely to complete the story, but that the penitence and forgiveness of Simon followed hard upon that of the woman that was a sinner. At least his Lord beautifully and graciously suggested that He would forgive and bless him too.

And Jesus turned and dismissed the woman with His blessing of peace. And reassured by His open acknowledgment of her humble earnest faith, with her forgiveness ratified and sealed before the chief of her fellow citizens, she went her way "steadfast in faith, joyful through hope, and rooted in charity" to abide in His love unto her life's end. But what new thoughts arise in the hearts of the guests that remained, and self questioning! "Who is this they begin to say within themselves that forgiveth sins also?" Some believed no doubt the word that was spoken, and some believed it not. So it was at Athens with the Word preached, and so it always is, Some no doubt said it in scorn, and took it up as a new handle against Him. "Who is this that speaketh blasphemies? Who can forgive sins but God alone?" But others I am inclined to think uttered the words half believingly, half doubtingly, as though the news that there was power on earth as well as in heaven to forgive sins was too good to be true. Thank God it is not so, and the Son of Man who had power on earth to pronounce sins forgiven, has left that power with His Church still. And, as the Ministers of reconciliation we claim the right to pronounce the penitent absolved, and to bid the oppressed go free. And some of the guests then present as they saw in the penitent's deep contrition her conviction of sin, and heard the assurance given her of its pardon, had a sense of sin and a longing for deliverance awakened within them which had never existed before. And they spoke the words enquiringly. Was there anyone so near who could indeed give release from such an evil? They wished to be satisfied as to the reality of such a fact. And what strong consolation to them would there be in the fact that this fellow citizen of theirs whose sins the Lord declared to be so many was justified freely, and dissmised in peace!

Perhaps as in the case of S. Paul "for this cause" she then and there "obtained mercy that Jesus Christ might show forth all long suffering for a pattern to them which should hereafter believe," and that we too might be emboldened to seek pardon, renewal and peace, and led like her to "find grace to help in time of need."

THE YOUNG MAN THAT WENT AWAY SORROWFUL.

When the young man heard that saying he went away sorrowful." *Matthew* ix 22,

"Very sorrowful" says S. Luke in his account of the incident. Did you ever see a person going away sorrowful from the house or presence of another, and not feel touched with the feeling of his grief? Did you ever see one turn unsuccessful or disappointed from the face of his neighbour, his errand fruitless, his application rejected, his purpose defeated, his hopes put completely and finally to confusion? Were you ever in such a case yourself? Perhaps none beside you knew the bitterness of the grief, the anguish of the blow, the dismay and hopelessness that attended that repulse. Perhaps you never spoke of it afterwards, and now it is a thing of the past. And you try to hide from yourself the painful recollection of the hour in the days long ago, when you too "went away sorrowful" from your fellow creature's door. Recall it for a little moment that, in living it over once again you may be able to enter into this painful but touching story. "When the young man heard that story he went away sorrowful." *Whose* saying was it, and what that sent the young man away so sad? And *who* and *what* was the young man that went away so very sorrowful?

And first *whose* was the saying that left so pained an impression on the young man's mind? It was the saying of none other than the gentle and gracious Jesus: from whose lips never fell a harsh sentence on any enquiring or seeking soul. It was He whose words fell evermore so sweetly and soothingly on the heavy laden and sin-conscious, whose office it was as the great Physician to "bind up the broken in heart and to give medicine to heal their sickness" And more than this it was in the most accepted time, when all the human sympathies of Jesus were engaged in his behalf, and all His loving tenderness was going forth for the salvation of that young man's soul. "Jesus beholding him loved him," says S. Mark, "and said unto him" those words that sent him away sorrowful. It was when that Divine look of unutterably attractive power that won the love and chained the hearts of His Disciples to Himself, was actually resting on the young man's face, that he turned from Jesus and went away so sorrowful. And what were the words that caused this strange effect? They were not as we might almost have supposed by any experience, as I said, of our own in the past, they were not the repulse DEPART, but the invitation COME. Come with me, Words that in things pertaining to this life are wont to give encouragement to the backward, and confidence to the doubting. "Come follow me," were the last words that were falling from the good

Master's lips, as the cloud gathered thickly on the young man's open brow, and the tear of disappointment started to his trembling eyelids. "Come follow me," they were the very same words that have roused the impulse, and awakened the slumbering love of every religious soul from that day forward. "Come follow me" the words that we only long to hear more clearly, and watch to recognise more steadily. "Come follow me" the words that are ever the stimulus of our Christian zeal, and the mainspring of all our faith and hope in God. "Come follow me—" the words the newly converted would give his all if he could only believe addressed to himself individually. The words which every hour of our spiritual life we wait and long to hear from the good Master's lips. The words which are our confidence and our joy as our faith increases, and we know they are meant for us, and are being spoken to us each, and that continually. It was even these that occasioned this strange agitation in the young man's soul, and startled him from his dream of self deluded piety, and sent him exceeding sorrowful to his Christless home. And yet it had not seemed likely that he should have been deterred by that word "Come."

For says S. Mark when the Lord was gone forth into the way There *came* this very one running and and kneeling to Him. And so who was he, we proceed to ask and *what*? He was no lukewarm or apathetic being, this that came running to the Lord. And no cold or unimpassioned one that in the presence of the mixed crowd, scoffers, and unbelievers included, cast himself on his knees before the lowly and by too many despised Jesus. There was earnestness in the young man's manner, and devotion in his gestures. The fire of holy fervour that was kindled in his soul was mounting to his glowing face, and glancing from his ardent eye. Young man! I would learn a lesson myself and I would we may all do so from thee! I see thee running! Thou didst rightly judge that the seeking of the good Master would brook no delay. I see thee kneeling humbly and prostrate before His holy feet! And I would learn thy reverence and copy thy very attitude.

Let us pause to look at that young man hasting in the impetuosity of his fresh emotions of awakened earnestness, in his heaven-inspired conviction of the value of life eternal. "What shall I do that I may inherit eternal life?" He is kneeling! Oh how I long to see this a more general posture in the congregation! How I rejoice when I see a man or woman "kneeling" as the Psalm bids us before the Lord our Maker! How it helps to persuade me of their earnestness! And without earnestness what is religion worth, and how can it exist! Without earnestness our preaching is vain, and your faith is also vain. *Kneeling*, —it is the attitude that prepares for victory. The soldier kneels as he fires his rifle. And the Christian soldier does the same. And the evil one knows the coming advantage over him that the posture betokens,

For Satan trembles when he sees
The weakest saint upon his knees.

Let us observe the instinctive consciousness that his running betokened, that the kingdom of heaven could only be secured, as

Jesus. taught, by violence, and that the violent might and should take it by force. And which of us has not much to learn from this young man? As we see him regardless of any but the Master's presence kneeling humbly and suppliantly before the Blessed One, awaiting the teaching and the guidance that could alone make him wise unto salvation, we are convicted—I should think all of us in our own conscience—of our far greater unconcern about things spiritual. And we are sensible of our far greater lack of reverence towards the Holy One, and His Spirit, and His Church, and His Word through which He reveals himself now.

And S. Luke tells us he was a Ruler moreover. He was no untaught or uninfluential personage with no fame on his brow, and no weight to his character, and no handle to his name. He was invested with the greatness of magisterial authority. And he was high in the estimation of his neighbours and the power of his influence. He was a Ruler. But he had the faith to recognise his superior in the humble Nazarene before whom he knelt, and whom he owned as Master and thought himself prepared to accept as Guide. And he was moreover what the world would have thought a good man and a just. He had borne a stainless character ever since he had been known as a religious youth. No blot of dishonour had ever fastened itself on his virtuous fame. And there was something so engaging and attractive in that external goodness that had won the admiration and honour of his neighbours that "Jesus Himself beholding him loved Lim" and was at the very first moment of acquaintance drawn as we say towards him. Let us too, as we behold so far, admire like Jesus and imitate all here that is beyond our own present attainments and worthy of our taking example by.

And now the secret of his unlooked for sorrow is very simple. "He went away sorrowful for he had great possesions." And from those possessions he was not ready at the Saviour's bidding to sever his heart or himself. The love of what was of earth was too strong to sutler him to seek the love and favour of God and heaven. I doubt not the literal sacrifice which he was called to make for it is one that is not demanded of us. To leave all literally to follow Him is not now needful. We can retain our substance, the wealthiest of us, and minister to Him of it. But to make the things of this world, the wishes, the hopes, the aims, the labours that have reference to it secondary, subservient to those that relate to things spiritual, is what we must as surely do as he was bidden if we would inherit eternal life. The young man was required as matter of course in the circumstances of those times if he would be one of the companions of His life on earth which our Lord was willing then to make him, to relinquish as the rich S. Matthew, and the well to do S. James and S. John had done, his position and his calling ; to lay aside his Office as a ruler of the Jews ; and abandon what in his youth he was rejoicing in, of the advantages of the world around him and the honour that cometh of men. But when the young man heard the same call he went away sorrowful. So the one of the two in the same circumstances was taken and the other left. No wonder. that he went away sorrowful. He had true cause for sorrow. He had deliberately made his choice. And as sometimes we do, at the very moment that we *have* deliberately made a choice, he *knew* that his choice was wrong and undeniably foolishness. He knew the Scriptures and how " by faith Moses " esteemed the reproach of Christ greater " riches than all the treasures " of his home. And he had knowing the Scriptures and the power of God, " who is a rewarder of them that diligently seek Him " — chosen the contrary part; not the good part which could not be taken away from him, but that even the portion of this life, which presently must.

The treasure in heaven promised distinctly by one who was able also to perform he had foregone. And that which could endure but for a little while, and then must vanish away, he had the infatuation to prefer.

And as he went away sorrowful he must have known that this was but the " beginning of sorrows. " For they that will be rich, said the Apostle, " have erred from the faith, and pierced themselves through with many sorrows." And though these words were not then written the Person that indited them afterwards, and who was at that hour working within his soul, would suggest them, and convince him of their truth. And as he went away, and Jesus looked after him with that look of lingering affection which he cast on Zion, when the things belonging to her peace were hid from her eyes because she had rejected the day of her visitation, there was a greater sorrow than that of the young man in the heart of his forsaken Guide and Master. We know no more of the misguided and worldly soul, his form vanishes from the page of Scripture and the presence of the Redeemer as far as we know for ever. And a solemn awe steals over our own anxious and self-distrustful souls as we see the many as the Evangelist S. John records who in every age " turn back and walk no more with Jesus." And a voice from the too often deserted Master falls appealingly on our ears." " Will ye also go away ? "

> When any turn from Zion's way,
>   Alas ! what numbers do !
> I think I hear my Saviour say
>   Wilt thou forsake me too ?
>
> Ah Lord ! with such a heart as mine,
>   Unless Thou hold me fast,
> I feel I must I shall decline,
>   And prove like them at last.

" Hold Thou me up," let each of us say with the Psalmist " and I shall be safe yea my delight shall be in Thy Statutes." " Keep me by Thy power through faith unto salvation." And suffer me not now or at any future hour to fall from Thee!

THE CONQUEST OF EVIL.

Be not overcome of evil.   *Romans* xii, 21.

The battle is not to the strong says the Bible.   And the experience of all of us has ofttimes illustrated the truth.

In worldly matters it is the part of the wise to be ready to give in when fairly beaten. You must admit sometimes that you are defeated, that you have failed to secure your end, that you have not been a match for the forces that ranged themselves against you, that the advantage and the success you contended for lies with your neighbour No matter however you think you have the right on your side, however fair was your aim, however worthy your object, it is the mark of humility, as well as of wisdom to be not unwilling if needs be to give in.   However natural it be to take pride in p rsisting the obstinate will not be respected, and does not deserve to be

But in Spiritual things the very reverse of this is commendable. In regard to moral evil it becomes you nd r e as sworn soldiers of the Cross never to yield.   Whatever be the forces arr.yed against us, whatever the weight of concurrent opinion, whatever the inducement on the one hand to persuade you to evil, or on the other to crush and disable you in your pursuit of that which is good and right, the command of inspiration is laid upon you. " Be not overcome of evil."   Now we are daily and almost hourly liable to be so overcome.   In worldly matters our natural pride and independence prompt us to persevere even to excess.   But in Spiritual things we have not this ally to fall back upon and urge us to resolution.

And therefore we have great need indeed to ponder the counsel of the text.   " Be not overcome of evil."   The occasions when this counsel is applicable are as various as they are constant.   When you have laboured, perhaps fervently and long, to do some good to another or to others, and find yourself as far from securing it as ever.   When ingratitude or misapprehension is the only return you seem likely ever to meet with from the dense an unappreciating mind of your neighbour. When you have set some object before you as worth aiming at or striving for, but its fair image is only to others visionary, and they mock at your enthusi sm, or mistake your aim.   When moral efforts produce no result and you seem like the discouraged Apostle as " one that beateth the air," how hard to comply with, yet in how perfectly intelligible a light does this direction present itself " Be not overcome of evil."   One must needs in handling an abstract direction of this kind deal to a certain extent in general terms.   But a little attention and thoughtful application of it to your own individual and special circumstances will invest this g neral direction with a significance to each of you. "B3 not overcom3 of evil." Evil! it is a most general term. W cannot give one portra t of the many-sided and parti-coloured monster. But we all know when we meet with it in our daily life. You are contradicted in your sentiments. You are thwarted in your purpose. Other wills range themselves unexpectedly in opposition to your own. You arrange thoughtfully. And lo, disorder and confusion is the result. You strive perhaps to be conciliatory and say with the Psalmist, "I labour for peace. But when I speak unto them thereof they make them ready to battle." You know what some of these experiences are. And as as you live on, they will be repeated till the heart will sometimes become faint, and the hands of enterprise hang down, and the knees firm set for progress wax feeble. "Be strong and of a good courage saith the Spirit have not I commanded thee.' "Be not overcome of evil." Let not the personation of evil see the advantage he has gained in discouraging you by his formidable presenc e.

I know in the records of inspiration no finer instance of the spirit, which this direction enjoins than one from the life of Jehoshaphat The children of Moab and Ammon, each as formidable in themselves as could be, and others, we are not told whom, came against him to Eagedi. And Jehoshaphat feared, we read, and set himself to seek the Lord and proclaimed a feast throughout all Judah. And stood with those of Judah that gathered themselves together to ask help of the Lord, an l said in the house of the Lord, "If when evil cometh upon us we stand in Thy presence, and cry unto Thee in our affliction, then Thou wilt hear and help. Now O our God we have no might against this great company that cometh against us; neither know we what to do: but our eyes are upon Thee."

It is true there are brave and gifted spirits who rarely experience the power of this inducement to give up the struggle for right, who are absolutely braced anew for theencounter by theappeauance of opposition "Did I fear a great multitude," said Job, "or did the contempt of families terrify me, that I kept silence, and went not out of the door?" "In Thy name we go against this multitude," said Asa as he went against Zerah the Ethiopian with a million of men. And there are moral heroes too in this our day. And we come across them even in obscure towns and villages, and wonder at their fortitude. And yet we need not wonder, For "this" says S. John, "is the victory that overcometh the world even our faith." And faith is the gift of God: His gift to His children to day just as much and as really as it was to kings, and mighty men, and prophets, and Apostles, and martyrs of old.

And many a David goes daily forth with no sword in his hand, save that of faith; and prevails over Philistine giants of evil, and silences the doubter, by his wondrous confidence, and puts the mocker to confusion, and presently carries back the head of his foe, while the disdain at first so freely uttered is silenced And like Saul to Abner the wonder of the spectator is whispered "Who is this that travelleth in the greatness of his strength." Aye the victories tha the page of history records are daily eclipsed by the triumphs gained in many a home around us by Christain men and women, in the moral battle fields of life. And recording Angels are perhaps the only witnesses of the mighty deeds thus wrought and wonders worthy of the name they bear.

And why think you does the Bible record so fully, with such manifest admiration, and so much detail the achievements of the warrihrs of God, judges and kings, but because these things are an allegory, and because they so aptly illustrate the lesson, shall I say the *great* lesson of the Bible "Be not overcome of evil." Be ye followers of them who through faith and patience have gained such distinction! And soon the last difficulty shall be overcome, and the last enemy destroyed. And the great cloud of witnesses, that have watched all through from the unseen world your struggle of faith, shall press toward heaven's open doors to welcome you, a conqueror through Him that loved you. May it be your joy and mine in life's last hour to catch the congratulating voices of that heavenly host. May it be ours to welcome, or be welcomed by each other in those matchless words.

> The strife is o'er, the battle done,
> The victory of life is won,
> The sona of triumph is begun.

Yea what shall be infinitely more blessed still to catch the greeting of the Master whom we love so far beyond the dearest fellow servant in our Lord's household the Church, that greeting which speaks to us even now, from this most blessed Book, that greeting which in weary hours and doubtful moments, we seem to hear and take fresh heart again.

"To him that overcometh will I grant to sit with me on my throne even as I also overcame and am set down with my Father on His throne."

THE MINISTRATION OF ONESIPHORUS TO THE IMPRISONED APOSTLE.

2 *Timothy* ii 16-18.

Of what romantic interest we feel, as we read the allusions to it in this Epistle, would be the story, if wo only knew it, of S. Paul's last imprisonment at Rome! About these, the last words of his closing days there is an inimitably tender and touching tone, a tone that the coldest and most unimpassioned soul cannot but be struck and moved with. A strange and deep interest gathers around the personages mentioned iu this letter as prominent figures in his last captivity. "Alexander the coppersmith who did him much evil, and greatly withstood his words." And Demas, who for love of this vain world faithlessly forsook him in that sad hour when the dying Apostle craved his sympathising presence and kind ministrations so earnestly.

Tychicus, Crescens and Titus, whom the call of duty summoned to Christian work in other parts, when he would fain have retained them to stand by him in his approaching hour of martyrdom.—Erastus, his old fellow labourer, whom his duties as Chamberlain of the city detained at Corinth as he was journeying with him to Rome.—And Trophimus, whose sickness prevented him from accompanying S. Paul as he had purposed further than Miletum.—Eubulus, Pudens, Linus afterwards Bishop of Rome ; and—more interesting to us than all—Claudia, whom history informs us was a Princess of our own land, the first recorded convert to the religion of Christ from the British isles.

How we long to hear of these companions of the Great Apostle, of their words and deeds and life, at this eventful period! But except so far as the imagination may paint the tale we long in vain, and shall till the page of the Church's history is enrolled in the world to come, till the books which this world could not have contained, but the records of which are all in the archives of heaven, are unfolded for our delighted perusal throughout the ages of eternity. And here is another of the great characters recorded in this letter to Timothy, Onesiphorus, whose works of faith and labours of love in that critical hour of the history of the Church, " are unknown in the dark, and whose right-eousness is in the land of forgetfulness."

Onesiphorus, the bringer of assistance, or conferer of benefits, as is the meaning of his name. What was the refreshment bodily or spiritual that he bore to the aged and tried prisoner of Jesus Christ? What were those frequent occasions, and how did they arise, on which it was his privileged lot to minister to the exalted, yet after all the so thoroughly human Apostle of the faith ? What was the shame attending the bonds of S Paul, of which Onesiphorus was so nobly and gloriously unmindful? What was the reproach that for the Apostle's sake fell upon him from which Demas shrank, which Onesiphorus stepped forth so generously to overcome ? What was the contempt that was poured upon him for his open and avowed allegiance to the persecuted one, which he not merely despised, but thought it his high glory and honour to bear ? What were the pains he too as the text indicates to seek S. Paul out of the lowest and the vilest of all the unnumbered captives of Rome ?

How did he proceed in that long and repulsive task, at which the text glances, when in Rome he sought him out very "diligently like the good Shepherd until he found him. And what, as I said in the end the relief that this high and wealthy citizen of Ephesus was permitted to bring, as in days gone by it was notorious, as the text shows, he had done at Ephesus " in many things. ? " We cannot say. We do not know, but the day shall declare it when you and I before the bar of God shall stand side by side with Onesiphorus and S. Paul. Then we shall hear our common Master proclaim it in its detail as He says to the one while He points to the other. " I was hungry, Onesiphorus, and you gave Me meat. I was thirsty and you gave Me drink. I was a stranger and you took me in. I was destitute and you clothed Me. I was sick and you visited me. I was in prison and you came unto Me ! " Let me apply with slight alteration two stanzas from James Montgomery's beautiful parable of our Saviour's teaching that whatever is done for a sick, distressed, reviled, or suffering disciple of His, He takes as done for Him—Inasmuch as ye did it to one of the least of Mine ye did it unto Me —

> I saw one wrongfully condemned,
> In prison, insulted, and forlorn :
> The tide of lying tongues I stemmed,
> And honoured him mid shame and scorn.
>
> My friendship's utmost zeal to try,
> He asked if I for him would die
> The flesh was weak, my blood ran chill,
> But the free spirit cried I will.
>
> Then in a moment to my view
> The stranger started from disguise,
> The tokens in His hands I knew,
> My Saviour stood before my eyes!
>
> He spake : and my poor name he named,
> Of Me thou hast not been shamed,
> These deeds shall thy memorial be.
> Fear not thou didst them unto Me!

You cannot but observe the unusual and exceeding earnestness that S. Paul expresses for the final salvation of Onesiphorus. And it is my opinion from the observation of th s, that the Apostle had strong doubts as to whether Onesiphorus was yet in a state of grace, and in the way of salvation. There is an air of pained anxiety about S. Paul's words which this supposition only will fully account for. Onesiphorus nobly sided with Christ and His cause, and that too when tribulation and persecution had arisen, and so many were therefore drawing off from Him. But there seems an apprehension on the part of S. Paul, that he was yet not quite decided, not far indeed from the kingdom of God, but not yet a partaker of it. And this fear or knowledge must have been agony indeed to his grateful and affectionate soul. And yet there are such instances. We see them in the present, as we have read of them in the past, amiable, kindly, generous natures in whom the impulse of humanity is by nature strong, but who are for all that strangers to the promptings of genuine piety.

It was such a one that our dear Lord followed with infinite regret as the young man whom we read Jesus loved, and who had kept all the commandments, in a blameless youth, went away exceeding sorrowful. And over some such gentle unsaved women, that he cried as he went to Calvary to die. "Daughters of Jerusalem weep not for Me. But weep for yourselves." O to the Christian it may and it must be painful truly to see hard and impenitent souls open and lawless sinners treasuring up to themselves wrath against the day of wrath! But bitterer far than than the contemplation of the lot of such graceless souls, is it to stand in doubt of the real sincerity and the genuine godliness of the pure, and amiable, the high principled, and the generous whom you cannot but love and be drawn to. In such cases the only consolation, encouragement, and confidence, (but thank God there is here room for the strongest), is in the imitation of the Apostle's resource here. This care is one which may indeed be cast with the fullest confidence upon the God who careth for, and is drawn to such dispositions as much as we ourselves can be.

The effectual fervent prayer of the righteous—for such especially. I am of opinion—availeth much. I can entertain no manner of doubt that S. Paul's for Onesiphorus prevailed. How it is that the prayers of the righteous should be not only instrumental to, but the direct occasions of the salvation of those for whom they intercede, is like the effect and operation of all prayers, one of the mysteries of the kingdom of God. We are sure of the fact. But we cannot explain the mode of its being brought about. Regardless of the impossibility of accounting for it, ours be it to act in simple faith upon the knowledge. And we have our reward. We know not what blessings in consequence of the ardent aspiration of the text descended upon the household of Onesiphorus. But with what measure he meted we are very sure it was measured to him again. And when the father had been it may be for years in the overshadowing presence of that God of mercy to whom the dying Apostle commended him " good measure pressed down heaped together and running over," did a mindful Providence pour into the lap of his household. "The just man," saith the Spirit of God " walketh in his integrity, his children are blessed after him." " Blessed is he that considereth the poor," or as the word indicates the afflicted and the down-trodden. The Lord shall deliver him in the time of trouble."

And when possibly in long days afterwards persecution arose, "because of the word" in the great city of Ephesus, and the household of that benevolent and generous father had to share the common lot of Christians in those evil days, there is we are sure a yet untold story which in the ages of eternity may interest our wondering attention of a strange interposition and unexpected relief and unexampled deliverance that befell the household of Onesiphorus.

Their father has heard it long ago (if from the unseen world he did not witness it at the time) as one after another of his family entered the heavenly habitations There are they gathered into the common presence of the God of mercy, with himself who obtained it first, and the Apostolic friend through whose intercess on the whole family of Onesiphorus were safely brought by God their Saviour into His kingdom of blessedness.

THE FAITHLESSNESS OF DEMAS TO THE IMPRISONED APOSTLE.

Demas hath forsaken me, having loved this present world and is departed to Thessalonica. 2 *Timothy*, iv, 10.

This touching passage in the last recorded words that were ever penned by the inspired Apostle is one that we cannot dwell upon without deep emotion and interest. As we peruse with Timothy the letter from which it is taken our hearts are filled with admiration for the veteran Saint. And we are conscious of a kindling of zeal within and a prompting to follow after it, we may perhaps attain something of the eminent devotion and ardent piety of the writer. And as we linger on this its latest page we feel that if ever in his life Timothy had aroused himself to an unwonted earnestness and haste, it would be in compliance with the twice repeated and almost pathetic summons. "Do thy diligence to come shortly unto Me!" " Do thy diligence to come before winter!" How eagerly we delight to think would that true hearted Son in the faith say to himself as he read the letter. "I will go and see him before he die!" And how almost impetuously would the young man start for Rome, if haply it might be his privileged lot to minister to the loneliness of the noble prisoner, and to cheer S. Paul's last hours on earth with the consolations of that Gospel he had so faithfully proclaimed, and wherewith Timothy himself had by his testimony been so abundantly comforted as he must have been by this letter.

Two points do these painfully sad words bring before us. First the conduct of Demas who forsook his Apostolic friend. Next, the cause of his so doing. "He loved this present world," And first we have presented to our notice a broken friendship! Friendship is an aspiration of our nature, that as implanted by Him, is throughout Scripture recognised by the Father of our spirits. The love that we may feel and bear toward our fellow creature is treated by Him as a sentiment not only of a strong, but of a sacred kind. Indeed it is incidentally mentioned as if it were the highest of all human attachments and coupled by God, with the closest of relationships. "If thy brother, the child of thy mother, the wife of thy bosom, or *the friend that is as thine own soul*." And if it is no less true as the prophet Malachi says of the other that " the Lord saith that He hateth putting away." " Thine own friend and thy father's friend, forsake not," it is written again.

It is under this amiable character that the blessed Jesus Himself would gain our hearts and win our confidence. For He was called and revealed Himself as " the Friend of sinners." " With Him is no variableness neither shadow of turning." He is Himself the Faithful

and the True. He makes it His very office to bind up the broken in
heart from whatever cause, and heal wounded Spirits. And so He must
in any case abhor and will resent—for the Lord is the Avenger of all
such—the treachery and insincerity that makes causeless sadness in the
heart of man, and desolation in the world of God.

He revealed Himself to Israel under the particular title of a
covenant keeping God, and covenant breakers He classes in the Epistle
to the Romans, among those who in His judgment are worthy of death.

"See that ye fall not out by the way," is the injunction of the
of our Father in Heaven, just as is it was Jacob's to *his* children. Be
very sure He does not look on indifferently at the description of any
of those bonds He has ordered or sanctioned or knitted in his Providence
whereby to restrain the unruly wills or affections of sinful men. And
that they cannot be lightly or with impunity sundered in the case of
individuals any more than in families or nations.

"Woe to him" saith the Prince of Peace, "by whom any offence
cometh!" And in some of the most startling and awful words He ever
uttered He goes on to say, that it were better for a man than that he
should offend one of the least of His, that a millstone were hanged
about his neck, and that he were drowned first in the depth of the sea.
Had Demas I wonder ever pondered these words? Have you?

Worn with years, and labour, and the care of all the Churches, but
ripe for glory and for heaven, S. Paul the valiant soldier of the cross
had well nigh finished his course, and his work was almost done. From
incidental mention of them elsewhere we know that his eye was dim,
his natural force abated, and his trembling hand could hardly pen to
Timothy his farewell charge.

> For now the winter of his age
> Spread o'er his locks its snows:
> And he could feel his pilgrimage
> Fast drawing to a close.

He had recently stood and answered for the Christian faith
before the nobles and Emperors of Rome. In a few weeks during
which he had been remanded he was to do so yet again.

And that coming day he knew well was to hear his latest testimony
to Christ, and sentence him to the immediate possession of the martyr's
crown. Meanwhile he tarried a patient prisoner of the Lord, in the cold
and cheerless dungeon. Many a one hitherto had as he tells us often refreshed him then by pious converse, by welcome tidings of the Churches
he had planted and visited, and the progress of the faith, and not been
ashamed of his chain. And now it was his hour of utmost human need
"In prisons frequent and deaths oft," the hardships of this last captivity had told, perhaps rapidly upon his enfeebled frame. And though
his faith was never more vigorous, and his hope never more steadfast,
the strong man of nature began, as Solomon puts it in his
description of the infirmities that precede the dissolution of this earthly
tabernacle, to bow himself. And he would fain have leaned upon some
human arm, as Christ His Cross upon the back of Simon, as with
faltering steps he halted onward to his long looked for, and indeed to

him most desirable and welcome grave. And then it was that as he entered the valley of the shadow of death the staff of human sympathy on which he had hoped to lean gave way, and pierce in so doing, his hand, and his heart. And in the text we have the momentary exclamation of pain wrung rom the lips that had only just uttered the triumphant words of faith. "I have fought a good fight, I have finished my course, I have kept the faith, henceforth there is laid up for me a crown of righteousness, which the Lord the righteous Judge shall give me at that day."

Then smitten with the sudden pain of his faithless friend's desertion he broke out as it were into the words of the Psalm, "My soul is full of trouble, and my life draweth nigh to the grave. I am shut up and cannot come forth. Thou hast put away mine acquaintance far from me." Demas hath forsaken me!

And yet doubtless even in that sad hour it was not so much for himself as for the unhappy Demas, that the generous Apostle grieved. It was not in the mere indulgence of what has been termed the luxury of a selfish grief that the noble minded man seems for a time so sore amazed and very heavy. He could take comfort for himself when the moment of bitterness was past. "Notwithstanding the Lord stood with me, and strengthened me." And again he says in this same Epistle. "He abideth faithful." He could say as the Psalmist with perfect confidence. "The Lord forsaketh not His saints."

There is an arm that still prevails,
When human props give way ;
There is a love that never fails,
When eathly loves decay.

Well we know that the disciple was not above his Master. His Lord had stood unbefriended before the Governor, the deputy of Rome. And His heart had felt the pang of a greater desolation still. For not only had He seen His own familiar friends whom he trusted forsake Him and flee, but the Father of Heaven for a while—because that on Him was laid the iniquity of us all—hid His face from Him in the Garden and on the Cross.

For himself then S. Paul could say "yet I am not alone for the Father is with me." But what comfort could he take for the faithless Demas ? It was for him far more than himself, that heaviness filled the the Apostle's soul, and that as he wrote to Timothy even weeping tears of regretful compassion blotted the hand writing of the heroic prisoner.

As is sometimes the case with warm and generous natures the less Demas loved him, the more abundantly as he declared to the Corinthians it was in their case, was he loved. Went not his heart with the apostate Demas as he departed to Thessalonica ? And mourned he not for him—seeing that the backslider in heart is to be filled with his own devices—as one that had little hope ? Of what befell Demas in the future we have no certain knowledge. Tribulation and persecution had arisen because of the Word and he was offended ; and went back to walk no more on earth with his sainted friend. "Fear and evil" humanly speaking were the remaining days of the Apostle in Rome.

And Demas had set a thorn n the crown of martyrdom, that was to cruelly pierce to the last, his hoary head. Then snared by the love of a world he could not forgo he went away. And as he goes darkness closes around his path, and the horror of an unknown future almost repels our further enquiry. We watch with anxiousness his figure vanishing from the page of Scripture. And as we know how few that go back to the world return again to take hold of the paths of life, we share what seems to be in this sad sentence, the Apostle's fearful looking for of judgment. Wisely we feel is the veil of uncertainty drawn over his after career, for our warning and admonition. And we read with trembling, and resolution I trust to apply our hearts more earnestly to our Lord s advice, the moral of his story. " Watch and pray lest ye also enter into temptation."

We limit not the power of the Almighty. We are persuaded the good Shepherd will leave in no case any course untried, consistent with that solemn responsibility of free will he has imparted to his higher creatures, to restore his wandering sheep. He even says " I will heal their backslidings." And He is infinitely willing. And may a one has He brought back again over the mountain barriers of aggravated sin, after years of unwearied pursuit, and placed in the fold to the joy of sympathizing Angels and the delight of " the spirits of the just made perfect," who best can tell the value of a recovered soul. Can none of us bear Him witness

> Perverse and foolish oft I strayed,
> But yet in love He sought me,
> And on his shoulder gently laid,
> And home rejoicing brought me.

Mark who likewise had forsaken S. Paul at one time, was by God's Grace thus reinstated. So the Apostle tells us in this very Epistle. But it was his last. And he never wrote another in which in the same way we might have learnt what became of Demas. He departed to Thessalonica. In that great and busy city of the heathen world, the second of Macedonia he disappears. And we shall know no more of him who made such a shipwreck of his faith, perhaps of his soul altogether, till the record of its inhabitants is read in our ears in the judgment day.

One faint ray of possible hope, it may be but a gleam of fancy, seems to me to cast itself on the after history of Demas. Well is it for ungrateful man that there is no place where the workers of iniquity can hide themselves from the Divine presence : no place they can flee to, where the hand of the Lord may not reach to arrest them in their backsliding, and convince them of their sin, and turn them from the error of their way! Well it is for him to use the figure of the Naamathite that when he flees from the iron weapon, it often happens that in a gracious Providence a bow of steel strikes him through! Thus perhaps it was with Demas! The Lord whose religion and servant he had deserted had already if I may use the figure, a detective in Thessalonica well skilled and commissioned to arrest such fugitives as he.

He had a Church there, a witness and a keeper of two inspired letters, written by this very Apostle. Highly would those letters be prized by the faithful in the city. Dear would they be to many a loving disciple there, that had seen the Apostle when he first visited the place as recorded in the seventeenth of the Acts! Dearer still would they be now that report, perhaps Demas himself, announced that they would never see him again. And well known there would those letters be, and read of all Demas had most likely not seen them before. In Thessalonica from curiosity or accident he might peruse or hear them read.

Did I say that God's Word was like a detective commissioned to arrest and confound the transgressor? Yea! "For the word of God is quick and powerful and sharper than a two edged sword, piercing even to the dividing asunder of soul and spirit, and a discerner of the thoughts and intents of the heart." Look those Epistles to the Thessalonians through with a view to the case of Demas. And you will say that if anything could touch his heart, and bring him again to repentance, there are passages there that unless he were utterly reckless and hardened, certainly might. Observe the expressions of affectionate solicitude for the steadfastness of the Thessalonians in the first Epistle and the last few verses of the chapters ii and iii.

Notice the exhortation in c. v. verses 10 and 11, to respect and love those their pastors that had loved them so earnestly, and watched for them as having to render an account. And think what Demas might have felt had they come to his notice. As he read moreover that God would make it a point of justice to recompense those that had troubled the Christians 2 Thess. i. vi. And again how he asks them to pray that he may be delivered from unreasonable and wicked men, " for all men have not faith," adding so affectingly. " But the Lord is faithful and we have confidence in *you*."

We might fondly hope that such words of God would not be in vain to Demas were it not that we see how vain they often are when received by worldlings like him amongst ourselves. Words like to them are repeated weekly by the preacher in every form and persuasion. And yet souls continue unawakened, hearers indifferent, their hearts unconverted, their lives unchanged, the world unrenounced, God's favor unsought, sins persisted in, and duties neglected, despite all the Minister's efforts, and the Gospel's provision, and the Saviour's entreaty, and the Spirit's inner whisper to the soul.

Often in the retirement of his study does the anxious Pastor think upon his flock, calling over to himself many a one by name, and setting individual cases before his mind. And often does he think within himself as he prepares for the Pulpit. " Surely there shall be for this a reward and mine expectation shall not be cut off." And often I can assure you does he betake himself there again, when the address is delivered, and his word has, as far as he can see and know, returned to him void, and sigh with the Prophet Jeremiah, " We would have healed Babylon, but she is not healed." And thus are we too well prepared to contemplate in the future of this miserable man the other alternative. And who shall say it is not the most probable one in the view of such passages as this same Apostle was inspired to put on record? " It is impossible for those who were once enlightened, and have tasted of the heavenly gift, and were made partakers of the Holy Ghost, and have tasted the good word of God, and the powers of the world to come. If they shall fall away to renew them agian unto repentance." And again " Let us not be of them that draw back unto perdition, for if any man draw back, my soul shall have no pleasure in him." We read in the Prophet Jeremiah "Thou hast forsaken me and art gone backward. Therefore will I stretch out my hand against thee and destroy thee." This was the fate that S. Paul apprehended for the faithless Demas, when the cry of the text escaped his lips, and his clear vision followed him on to the close of his worldly life, and his entrance on that dark valley of death which he was passing through himself when thus treacherously abandoned. Unhappy Demas! " The friendship of the world is enmity with God" it is written. Thou didst choose the one and consent to incur the other.

Thou didst forsake the saint of God of whose friendship thou wast so unworthy, whom the Holy Church throughout all the world hath never ceased to venerate as next to Christ, the chief corner stone, its most exalted mainstay, and whom even the world thou didst prefer instead might well deem a far grander hero than its mightiest and its best! Thou didst forsake him Demas! and left the venerable man to go forth alone to die! There was none—as far at least as we know, and as far as thou wast concerned—when the time of his departure came to take him by the hand, as it was said of Zion, of all the sons he had brought up. None to whisper the consolations of religion into the old man's ear, to reflect the light of Christian love before his closing eye, to lend an arm to uphold the feeble steps of the wasted prisoner, as he went forth to suffer without the gates of Rome, or to bear from his dying lips the last messages of his holy affection to the orphans of a fatherless Church.

Thou didst forsake him Demas! And when he bared his neck to the executioner's sword, his eye wandered enquiringly over the assembled crowd. But there was not from thee the responsive look of recognition and support in the smile of which he had hoped to die. And stranger hands took up his headless body, and carried it to those " Catacombs where alone the persecuted Church could there find refuge for her living and sepulchres for her dead." Gladly would we hope that Demas retraced his steps, that he was restored to the communion of the Church he had abandoned. Gladly would we say to the Apostle as he did to Philemon of another " Perhaps he therefore departed for a season that thou mightest receive him " again for ever." Gladly would we hope that when Demas' time of departue came, he had friends above to receive their once sinning but by the grace of God forgiven brother, into everlasting habitations. Fain would we fancy that S. Paul himself the happiest of their number, was at the gates of heaven, to welcome the ransomed soul. But after all we must face as only too probable the other and the dark alternative.

To Demas there certainly came an hour when that unsubstantial world, for which he had betrayed his Master and his soul, began to fade from his earnest gaze, and shrink from his tenacious grasp. What then think you was the pleasure, or riches, or honour, that lured his soul to Thessalonica, from God and heaven, and tempted him to turn from his good Master's side ? What to him who had worshipped and served the creature more than the Creator, and bowed his spirit to the slavery of an imperious world in preference to the ennobling rule of his former Lord, was then the profit of his bargain? Every once prominent object of the hopes and affections of his worldly life, for which he had been content to barter the favour of the Most High and the Kingdom of His Son, had vanished. And of all men was he not one of the most miserable ? though hardly more so than anyone of us shall be, who live and die like worldly Demas! S. Paul, his former friend, had testified, " The fashion of this world passeth away." And now the world left him alone with the crowding thoughts and realites of a dying hour, aye far more alone than ever had been the forsaken prisoner of Rome.

For O Demas! we exceedingly fear that when flesh and heart were failing thee, thou didst not find, as thy steadfast Master did, that God was the strength of thy heart, and thy portion for ever. We may " not be deceived, God is not mocked : for whatsoever a man soweth, that shall he also reap." It shall always be so sooner or later. Thou didst sin against the clearest light and the most perfect knowledge. And we are sure that sin must have found thee out. Faithless Demas! when the terrors of death compassed thee round, the death of the careless and impenitent, and Christless, the death that brings with it no Saviour to take away its sting, no light from above to chase its gloom, no arm of Godhead to lean upon its untired depths, no guide to ford its swellings with us, or upbear those steps of sinking nature that feel no ground to rest upon, but seem sinking away we know not where thy remorse and despair we can too probably imagine.

But amid the crowding ghosts of former iniquities that would press upon thy wretched soul with the heel of despair, when in that hour God brought them to remembrance, thy conscious memory would raise once more the figure of thy sorrowful and deserted friend, as he looked for thee at the Prison door, the morning thou didst abandon him to follow thy downward course. And the tear of disappointment that stood upon his aged cheek, and the pang of bitterness that wrung the good man's failing heart, when the unlooked for news had reached him that thou also hadst gone away, and renounced thy fellow-labourer, thy Lord and faith—we forbear to point the agony with which it must have tortured thy remorseful soul. We leave thee Demas and thy fate ! But suffer us not O Lord now or up to our last hour to fall from thee. Hold Thou up our goings in Thy paths, that our footsteps slip not. And keep us through faith unto salvation.

> When any turn from Zion's way,
>   Alas what numbers do !
> I think I hear my Saviour say
>   Wilt thou forsake me too ?
>
> Ah ! Lord ! with such a heart as mine,
>   Unless Thou hold me fast,
> I feel I must I shall decline,
>   And prove like them at last.

Our Lord Jesus Christ says this same Apostle to the Galatians gave Himself for our sins, that he might deliver us from this present evil world. And says he, of that world—its objects and its aims, which so many like Demas seeking wholly after have erred from the faith and pierced themselves through with many sorrows—" O man of God flee these things and follow after righteousness, godliness, faith, love, patience, meekness." You denounce the conduct of Demas. You think you never could have acted so base a part as he, you are sure you would not have consented to his counsel or deed! Ah! it is so natural to us all to shrink with a pious horror from another's guilt, while all the time we allow our own. Our Lord detected it in the men of his age, and exposed this imagination of our self deceiving hearts with masterly power. We almost resent the words when first we read them. They are so bold and startling in the revelation of the thoughts and intents of the " desperately wicked" heart.

But ponder we awhile and we shudder to find them so true. " Woe unto you! because ye build the tombs of the prophets and garnish the sepulchres of the righteous and say, if we had been in the days of our fathers, we would not have been partakers in the blood of the prophets. Ye are the children of them which killed the prophets." And he goes on to tell how they would certainly fill up the measure of their fathers crimes. When he said " ye are their children," he implied that there was a like spiritual resemblance in their disposition toward God and His servants to what there was in their fathers, as there is a likeness of natural feature between a man and his child. They did not believe it then. " God forbid!" they said as He told them, as it described themselves, the parable of the householder, and how the wicked husbandmen shamefully treated his servants and his beloved Son. And undoubtedly they meant it, and in their calmer moments repelled the thought of such iniquity, And yet within a while they crucified the Lord of Glory who was generally regarded as at all events a great prophet. Therefore says this Apostle, "Thou art inexcusable O man, whosoever thou art, that judgest."

There is no temptation that has befallen those who are set on the page of Scripture for our imitation or warning that we are not prone to, and which may not be to some of us an occasion of actual falling. And the sin of Demas assuredly comes very near to us all. The world appeals as powerfully, as it did in the case of Demas successfully, to every passion and aspiration of our nature. He loved this present world, says the Apostle as he gives the cause of Demas' fall. He loved it more than the faith of Christ, the worship and service of Him, the communion of His servants, the friendship of His Apostle, the work of His religion. By the world that lured Demas into the ways of ungodliness S. Paul does not here specify its amusements, wealth, or cares; nor do I mean any of these in particular. " The world" is a comprehensive term. We may enlarge upon it, for manifold are the applications it is susceptible of. But we shall lose it if we attempt to limit it. It is all that you see and hear, and your hands handle, and your hearts dwell upon, and things pertaining to this life. It is that which encompases your path, and is about all your ways. It is all that, until higher influences are admitted to give objects to your pursuit and direction to your aims, engages your hopes, and prompts your life. We do not know the particular worldly advantage that drew away this unhappy Demas from his venerable friend. We do not know the particulars of the occasion that might have extorted from the Apostle's lips the complaint of God, " What iniquity have you found in me that you have gone far from me and walked after vanity ?" We do not know the object at Thessalonica that appealed so strongly to the earthly preferences of the natural mind, and made him start aside like a broken bow. But we are not ignorant of the world's devices ourselves to draw our hopes and aims from heaven, and our souls from the fellowship of the spiritual life of the Saints of God.

It has been well said, " There are two worlds that are rivals for our supreme regard. The one crowds upon our notice in unnumbered ways, and tempts us to forego for it all thought and care about the other. Sooner or later we come all to choose between the two masters that claim our allegiance, and to feel more and more our choice must be complete." Thus it is that gradually men come to hold to the one, the present, and despise, or at least disregard the other. And ever more from amongst ourselves, while the change is more or less perceptible, the world is gathering fresh recruits. and they go in heart and life, perhaps in outward character, the way of the apostate Demas. And Paul and his teaching is abandoned afresh, and Christ and His great salvation neglected ; and the history of Demas and his faithlessness is perpetuated through all the ages of the Church.

The love of this present world, mighty is its fascination over the hearts of men, and myriad are the victims of its spell! For it, the child carefully trained in the nurture and admonition of the Lord, as he comes to the years of discretion breaks off from the commandment of his father, and forsakes the law of his mother! For it, the Sunday scholar, religiously and virtuously brought up under the hallowed influences of his Church's faith and doctrine, ceases to obey the voice of his teachers and to incline his ear to those that have instructed him! For it, the young men and maidens of our villages are found preferring to walk in the counsel of the ungodly to the companionship they were taught so earnestly to keep ; and beginning to stand deliberately in the way of known sinners in the idle corners of the streets, until they sit down soon in the seat of the scornful, and walk as others walk, defiling their earliest youth in the ways of reckless sin ; and—as Jeremiah complains of those whom he saw, breaking the yoke and bursting the bonds of law and religion—rebelling against the salutary restraints of home, and from almost childhood eager to rush into a froward self pleasing and lawless liberty! For it, from the very midst of the congregation of God's professed Saints they who ought to be in all holy and blameless life and godliness patterns to the flock live in habitual inconsistencies, to the grief of the Minister and the lasting scandal of that unworldly religion by which they are called! For it, the baptized person forswears the vow he made before God and the

Church to renounce the world with all its pomps and vanities! And those newly Confirmed go forth from the imposition of hands to slight and disobey alike their Pastor's counsel and their Bishop's charge!

And even so—drifting heedlessly along the current of common opinions and ge eral practices, with no conscious effort to rise superior to the average knowledge of spiritual things, and the prevailing tone of religion—contented go the multitude of our hearers, following, like Demas, the well frequented road to Thessalonica! And Paul is left, his life uncopied, his precepts unobeyed, his crown of life unsought, as though heaven were nothing to strive for, and the world nothing to conquer, and sin nothing to struggle with.

"This is the victory that overcometh the world, even our faith," says S. John. In that faith which walks through life with its eye and aim for things eternal, may we as S. Paul become daily " more crucified to the world" and the world to us.

Lord Jesus! King of Paradise!
O keep us in Thy love,
And guide us to the better world
Of perfect rest and love,
Where loyal hearts and true

Are " numbered with Thy Saints" in glory everlasting.

THE SEA OF GLASS.

And before the Throne there was a sea of glass like unto crystal.—*Revelation* iv. 6.

Such is the constitution of our nature that we all of us place as on the throne of our mind some central object before our thoughts, on which, before all else, we fix our attention, and around which we gather our chief hopes and affections. Be it a creature or the Creator, a real or imaginary, a worthy or unworthy object, there is always something in each man's mind that rises above the level of all things beside. Whether it be a person, a possession, an occupation, or a study, there is one, though it may be often exchanged for another at different periods of life, that to each towers above all else as on a throne high and lifted up. In the world to come that throne that is the ever foremost and highest object to the soul of the citizens of heaven is filled by God and by the Lamb. " Whom have I in heaven but Thee ?" says each. On Him that sits thereon is concentred the admiration and the love of a multitude that no man can number. To the contemplation of His glory, the study of His ways, and the service of His kingdom are devoted all the powers and faculties of those exalted and glorious beings that gather around His throne. Differing vastly in gifts, in character, and even in nature, " as one star differs from another in glory" as one man is unlike his fellow here, yet in that Great and Infinite God who " filleth all in all" all in heaven find the highest source of attraction, the most perfect fountain of that particular excellence to which their souls aspire. No matter how diverse from another's its endowments, the Lord of all Light is the Sun to each. Every knee bows to Him ; every heart is occupied with Him ; every one presses forward to serve Him. Before that Throne, therefore, from which He manifests Himself, and from which He fills all with His own grace and joy, there is represented here to be stretching a mighty expanse whereon the hosts of heaven may gather. The words of the text are concise, but suggest a variety of ideas.

And first the mention of the sea before the throne leads us to consider how visible and accessible to all is that throne that fills their view. The sea is a level surface. In the Latin tongue, with which S. John as a prisoner of Rome was familiar at the time he wrote this book, one of its common names is given to it from this circumstance.

Look forth on land to a distant object, and your view is partial and uncertain. There a hill rises, and there a clump of trees or row of houses, and intercepts your vision. But on the great and wide sea, when calm, as here, there is no such alien obstacle either to your vision or approach. On the highway of its open waters you can make straight on to the haven where you would be. No hills to climb, no rivers to ford, no tangled thicket to perplex your steps, no barrier of art or man's device to stay your free course with a restrictive " Hitherto shalt thou come, but no further." You gaze unhindered, you pass unchecked toward the point desired. And thus is it to be with the redeemed hereafter. Now " Clouds and darkness are round about His throne." The mists of earth and barrier-sins uptowering intercept from the believer's view the vision of the Almighty. If, in the still moments of calm meditation, when conflicting passions are chastened into still-ness by the Spirit of Peace, the believer can catch a glimpse on the eternal hills of that high throne and the surpassing glory of Him that sits thereon, he is thankful and encouraged, his soul is filled with wonder and his mouth with song. But he shall see greater things than these. " Blessed are the pure in heart, for they shall see God."   " They shall see Him as He is" says this same Apostle John in plain words that correspond to these figurative ones. Before the throne we are there-fore told there is outspread a level sea. The mountain becomes a plain, the hills are brought low, the rough places smoothed, and the crooked ones straightened, that all may see unhindered, as John the Baptist ex-presses the same idea, the salvation of God.

Encouraging is the prospect to those who can say with Jacob, " I am waiting for Thy salvation, O Lord." The rising doubts that obstruct now the freedom of your approach to God, the fear that hath torment that conflicts with and destroys your confidence of love, the wandering thoughts in holy exercises that you disallow and strive against, the mists of earthliness that come between God and your longing gaze, the obliquities of the soul's vision that since the fall has never been clear and single—all these withholding influences you here may learn are to pass away.

Now you are to a greater or less extent blind, and cannot see afar off. The very beauty of holiness dazzles you, and you sympathze with the abashed seraphs as they hide their faces in the august presence of God in their pure white wings.

At your very best estate as regards all the objects of heaven you see not more perfectly than the man in the Gospel to whom men seemed as trees walking. But on that unruffled sea you shall one day gaze with open face on the glory of God. With no disturbing thoughts to still, no fears to quell, no difficulties to struggle over, no spiritual foe to stand maliciously before you, and cloud with his dark presence the open firmament of God—you shall stand before Him continually, and lift up your undismayed head in the light of the Lord Most Holy.

But in the second place the sea before the throne, the pavement on which the redeemed shall be assembled with all the host of heaven, was like the sea in its immensity as well as the level of its surface. The ancients could hardly conceive a limit to the expanse of ocean that rolled before them. " That great and wide sea," says the Psalmist. When Zophar the Naamathite would speak to Job of the unsearchable judgments and perfections of God he said, " The measure thereof is longer than the earth and broader than the sea." God himself challenged the knowledge of Job on the subject—" Hast thou walked in the search of the depth ?" And when the prophets would signify the widest prevalence of righteousness in the future they predicted that it should cover the earth as the waters the sea. Here, then, we have the idea suggested of how boundless is the heavenly world. So many are the mansions in our Father's house, so vast the family of the angelic and the redeemed children of God that they are gathered before Him as it were upon a sea.

And well can the believer value this delightul topic of revelation. What joy will it, for example, give to Noah to stand there with the multitude, whom no man can nubmer, after standing alone in the faith and fear of God in the world before the flood! What will be the joy of Lot when, after vexing his righteous soul, as the only just man in Sodom, he comes to stand on that sea of glass, alongside the general assembly and Church of the firstborn! How will Elijah feel as he converses there with the seven thousand in Israel he never knew, that had not bowed the knee, nor kissed the hand to Baal, all the time he thought himself the only remaining worshipper of God in the land! How the few in Sardis that walked in white, while the multitude of the great rich city defiled themselves with sin! And Isaiah, Jeremiah, and the other prophets that stood and witnessed alone for God in an evil age, when on that far reaching sea, they come to stand before the throne of God with an innumerable company of Angels and just ones made perfect that perhaps none but Divine arithmetic can compute!

Do any of you seem to stand alone in your religious life, as on a deserted plain ? Do you look upon the thoughtless members of your household, upon the godless company of your workfellows or neighbours, and sigh within with the painful reflections of David and S. Paul. "How are the faithful minished from among the children of men." " I have no man like minded." Are you an Abraham journeying to the land of which the Lord hath spoken to you, but forced to see Terah your father preferring to live and die in the godless Haran ? Are you an Isaac an obedient God fearing one, and your brother Ishmael a mocker? Are you a Moses who having gotten you out thence by the grace of God, have left your kindred in the land of Midian amongst His enemies ? Are you a Mary sitting at the feet of Jesus, and the sister of your heart so careful and troubled about many things that she has not yet chosen your good part ? Are you treading a solitary path to heaven.

No hand but yours to take part in the strife,
No heart to beat high but your own.

Yet a little while and you shall see a different sight: From the little flock of earth, the one of a family the two of a city, you shall turn away for ever your grieved and desponding eyes. For before you shall stretch a sea of which no man has conceived the margin. And from the four quarters of heaven shall gather thereon a goodly company to dwell, to converse, and worship with you, before the glorious throne. The sea moreover is to a great extent unpolluted. No work of man has marred its beauty, as it has so many a fair spot of nature. And no stain of earth has destroyed the comparative purity its Maker in a gracious provision well worthy of remark, has ensured its waters. Not all that the river floods have borne to its bosom from the beginning have to any appreciable extent defiled its waters or permanently changed its fast rich colour. The salt wherewith it is salted has never lost its savour. It has this element of purification within itself. And yesterday to day and for ever it abides in its glory and beauty; fresh and fair as when its Maker prouounced it good, unblemished as when the morning Stars shouted for joy to see it break forth at His Word from the depths of the earth, and gather within those unseen doors that set its tidal bounds

> Time writes no wrinkles on its azure brow,
> Such as Creation's dawn beheld it, it rolls now.

And such are the holy heavens above! If once there was war even there, and its fair threshold was stained with the iniquity of that proud fiend that dared fight with the Lord of heaven, and drew after him the third part of all heaven's host Satan was soon cast out, and its former purity restored. And never again has or shall we are told sin intrude its accursed presence into that "habitation of holiness." "Nothing that defileth shall enter there," No lapse of ages shall bring any alloy to its ever fresh and sparkling tide of happiness. "The nations of them that are saved shall bring their glory and honour into it" we read. But none of them all shall contribute an element of individual infirmity, or an atom of defect, to mar the peace, to interrupt the harmony, or cast the shadow of a moment's uneasiness or discomfort over the happy and united family. No root of bitterness shall spring up to trouble one of the redeemed. " Ephraim shall not envy Judah, and Judah shall not vex Ephraim." Abraham shall have no occasion to expostulate with Lot; Barnabas to disagree with Paul; or Paul to reprimand Peter. Earth will pour its rivers into that great sea; but every sediment of earthly sort will have settled into the great abyss : and no particle shall be traced in that expanse of perfect purity where these waters commingle. The sea before the throne, where the life of heaven goes on, is thus like the sea of earth. No human power can interrupt its divinely ordered course. No agency of man can ever change its nature. " The heavens wherein dwell righteousness " abide for ever.

"Like unto crystal " says the text. And the interpretation is almost as clear as the glorious symbol. Bright as the light in which they walk shall be the ground on which the redeemed shall tread. They shall no more be led by a way they know not, and feel their path doubtful and their steps uncertain. In the darkness of error and remaining sin they stumble often now and their footsteps slip. Painfully and hesitatingly they go like a man on dangerous ground. Snares encompass their path. And here and there are pitfalls varied and multiplied in which despite their greatest watchfulness they fall not seldom. But there they shall be in no doubt as to their position or standing before God, as they were so often here. Many a point is there now which they long to know, and which often causes them anxious thought. But on

all and each shall they be perfectly clear then. They walk by sight on
that crystal sea. They are in no more doubt as to the works, or ways,
or words of God. The difficulties therein that so sorely staggered them‘
the mysteries that they pondered with so great searching of heart, shall
be difficulties and mysteries no more.

Do any of you know what it is to be uncertain of your ground, to
be often not at all sure about the exact path of duty? You would
gladly act for the best; but which is the better of two or more courses
you wot not. You are most anxious it may be to know accurately on
some point what " is the will of the Lord concerning you." But no
answering voice it may be has replied with the precision you desire,
" This is the way walk ye in it." I know this is sometimes your case.
For though you have a Divine Counsellor, yet as a part of your probation you are frequently more or less uncertain. You are studying
sincerely how to walk and to please God; and on the whole you are
graciously guided by the Spirit and kept by the power of God through
faith. His word is a light to your feet; yet for your discipline, you
know you walk sometimes in darkness. Comfort yourselves if such be
your case with these words of the text, and anticipate the here promised
happiness of standing with your fellow saints with unfaltering steps, on
heaven's transparent pavement.

The clearness of the crystal conveys however not only the idea of
a clearly revealed and safe standing ground, but of an exceeding brightness for the eye to rest upon or rejoice in. And so it seems to me, that
when we read that the very pavement on which the redeemed shall tread
is of such exceeding glory, that the very ground there is so bright an
object for the eye to contemplate—it is intended that we should gather
that the every thought, and feeling. and observation of those in heaven,
is of an ecstatic and glorious kind, as though heaven's commonest things,
if I may say so, were clothed in light. Not alone when they fall before
the throne in the moment of heaven's most exalted worship to give
adoration to Him that sitteth thereon, and to contemplate the glory of
the Lamb—

> And songs of all the sinless
> Sweep across the crystal sea.

Not alone when as the voice of many waters, every creature which is in
heaven, from time to time breaks forth into the ascription of blessing
and honour, and glory and power,—not then alone when everyone is
wrapt in a fervent enthusiasm of love and worship—will the whole
being be thrilled with a joy unspeakable and full of glory. But in the,
if we may so say, more ordinary contemplations of all the varied
wonders that heaven presents, of all the objects that shall engage the
thoughts and study when the treasures of the world to come are
laid open and its possessions entered on, in all these shall visions of
glory fill the soul, and subjects of exceeding brightness and attractiveness
crowd upon its notice.

Heaven indeed is bright above, but dull is the ground beneath.
You lift your eye to heaven, and it sparkles with hope. You turn it to

earth, and it is dim with tears. For the curse of Eden is on the ground. Thorns and thistles does it bring forth figuratively as well as literally. For the shadow of sin lies athwart it; and on the heart, full of heaviness through manifold and anxious considerations occasioned by the things below, it casts its reflection of "lamentations, and mourning, and woe." But in yonder world, look which way you will, there is unsullied brightness. Upwards there is lustre round the throne, for "there is a rainbow about it in sight like unto an emerald." Downwards: a lustre plays upon the very pavement, for it is "like unto glass clear as crystal." Here on earth, between gladness and sorrow, your spirit wavers with conflicting feelings. Partly joyous and partly grievous is your daily life-long experience. Let me speak to you on one subject, and your faces shall be lit up with a smile. Let me touch the chord of some hidden grief, the smile has vanished, and instead therof has come in a moment a responsive sigh. In the balance of Providence your mind is trembling. Anon it rises, and anon it is depressed again. Yet a little while, and into the scale your God shall cast an exceeding and eternal weight of glory, and it shall vibrate between the two no more again. Yet a little while, and in Zion, with everlasting joy upon your heart, and sorrow fled away, you shall exclaim, "My heart, O God, is *fixed.* I will sing and give praise." Look where you will there shall be no element of pain, no shadow of faintest gloom, no subject for a momentary care.

There shall be *no* mote in Heaven's clear light, *no* speck in its pure rivers of pleasure, *no* alien thought to mingle with its perfect gladness, *no* disturbing ripple on the bosom of that unruffled sea that lies spread before the throne "like unto glass as clear as crystal."

And such is a glimpse of Heaven! Are you won by its beauty? Are you dazzled by its brightness? Would you long for its glory? Would you seek to enter there? "The Lord will preserve me unto His Heavenly kingdom" said the Apostle, in the confidence of faith. And the grace on which he thus relied, is it not equally offered and pledged to you if you will avail yourself of it? offered already in the Gospel, pledged already in Baptism. "Members of Christ! children of God! inheritors of the kingdom of heaven! take heed lest a promise being left you of entering therein any of you should come short through unbelief, or fall through the deceitfulness of sin.

> Oh! by Thy love and anguish Lord!
> Oh! by thy life laid down!
> Grant that we fall not from such grace,
> Nor cast away our crown.

Would you seek to be preserved unto that life eternal. In the midst of you stands my Master. He has the keys to admit you, the blood of atonement to purify you, the sevenfold gifts of the Spirit to sanctify and make you meet for that glorious home. And now by me He repeats to you those words of His to His Church in Philadelphia. "Behold I set before you an open door," words that are to hold good till the end of all things when "they that be ready go in with Him, and the door is shut." "For when Thou hadst overcome the sharpness of death, Thou didst open the kingdom of Heaven to all believers."

God, who hath called you unto His kingdom and glory, arouse you to give diligence to make that calling sure; " for so an entrance shall be ministered unto you abundantly into the everlasting kingdom of our Lord and Saviour."

PERSEVERANCE.

He that endureth to the end shall be saved.   *Matthew* x, 22.

This text is repeated in the 24th chapter and 17th verse. Twice as recorded in this gospel our Lord exhorts His disciples to perseverance in these words. First when sending them out as described in this passage, on the highway of a world at enmity with Him; and then again when communicating to them His last instructions before he suffered. In both these passages there is evidently a primary reference to their exposure to special circumstances of trial in the early days of His Church.

Indeed we cannot but see, as we trace through His whole teaching the constant repetition of the thought here presented to us under every variety of argument and illustration, that there must have been something then in the relative position of the world and His Church, to account for its so prominent enforcement.

And this explanation is not far to seek. Of Christ it was foretold that He was to sit as a refiner and purifier of silver, that His fan or winnow was to be in His hand, thoroughly to purge His floor. And though the prophecy is to receive its highest fulfillment at the second coming it was most remarkably verified at His first. Through the whole period of the Incarnate life this process of separation between the wheat and the chaff, the genuine and reprobate metal, went on outwardly and visibly as it never has since. In the light of His all-searching eye, and the power of His all penetrating word, when sojourning among men and conversing with them personally, the thoughts of many hearts were quickly revealed, and the sincerity of His followers' professions speedily tested. It was with the Church then as with the Jews all through their Theocracy. Neither sins nor good works could long be hid, while Deity sat as a Prince on the Throne of His Kingdom. Hypocrisy on the one hand was readily detected, and faithlessness and want of earnestness exposed in His professed adherents; while on the other hand they which were approved were as soon made manifest.

In those days "the offence of the cross" was set unmistakably before the eyes of all. And when those who set out to follow Christ at the first sound of His Gospel came up to it, it was easy enough to see whether when tribulation and persecution arose they would be offended and turn back to walk no more with Him or no. And so, as Jesus of Nazareth took resolutely His way directly in the face of the world's sentiments, and maxims, and pursuits, and practices, and therefore as directly in the face of its opposition; and as He cried to those He beckoned after Him, " Whosoever will be My disciple let him follow Me," we cannot wonder that the exhortation to endure was so constantly in His mouth. The character of those to whom the word of Christ and His Gospel came was sooner cleared up, I think I might say more rapidly matured, than has since or can again be the case now that He is absent, and His judgment on us and things relating to and affecting us suspended, and our probation prolonged. We see thus clearly enough why the need of Perseverance was so urgently pressed! on His disciples' consideration, the blessedness of it so often the subject of His discourse. And so, bearing in mind what special occasion there was to call forth this line of teaching, it may seem to us that such solemn and rousing appeals to hold fast our confidence cannot be now so imperatively called for.

If we are holding fast the form of sound words, and contending earnestly for the faith as it was once delivered to the Saints—if, having been baptized into Christ's Church, we have from childhood been religiously and virtuously brought up in it, and come to own it to be our constant duty to follow after holiness, and to " add to our faith, virtue, knowledge, temperance, godliness, patience, brotherly kindness, and charity—we may start perhaps with surprise from such a subject as that which is before us, and repel the imputation that we can be in any peril of apostacy.

In these days, when a lively interest in the advance of the faith of Christ is absolutely fashionable, when a profession of it, more or less earnest, is conventionally demanded of us all as a passport to decent respectability in the eyes of the world, we have not certainly the same strong temptation to deny our faith or renounce our profession. We have no cruel mockings and scourgings, bonds and, imprisonment, spoiling of our goods or terror of death threatening us that those had to whom these words were first addressed. So the character of steadfastness on the one hand or backsliding on the other is not so soon observed in us by others, the tendency to it is not, I think, so easily recognized in us by ourselves.

Yet our age of proud self-assertion, of refined worldliness, of luxurious self-indulgence, is found to foster a forgetfulness of habits of self-renunciation and Christian endurance that I suppose, from the very nature of things, no preceding one can have done. And so not the less because the trials of our faith have in these days taken other forms less outwardly severe, yet not less searching, are exhortations to the maintenance of that faith requisite. Not the less, because temptations to let it go are for the most part specious and subtle now instead of gross and shameless as in the days of heathenism, are warnings against those temptations to be heeded by us all. " Endure afflictions," " endure hardness as a good soldier of Jesus Christ," the injunctions of S. Paul to Timothy, is the direction that was sounded in our ears in unconscious infancy as we were brought for the first time to the House of God. And this burden of our Baptismal charge we have had laid upon us every time we have entered that House since, so that " yourselves know perfectly we are appointed thereto."

In the matter of worldly crosses it is almost superfluous to do more than just allude to the endurance of them to which we are exhorted when we are bidden to " fight manfully under the banner" of Him who endured the like.

Is your heart faint in the day of some adversity? Have you a vexatious Hagar within your household as Abraham had? an obstructive Shimei that plants himself ever in your pathway as it was with David? Has the voice of the slanderers, disturbed your peace, or the tongue of the envious carped at your reputation, or the malicious threatened you to your disquietude and alarm? Has the friend that you trusted betrayed your confidence, and he that did eat of your bread, risen up to take your contrary part, as was the case with David and Job? Have the children of Belial, as they did Saul, despised you and brought you not your due? Has a gloom of Providence overspread your sky, and you walk in darkness and see no light? Have you sowed much, figuratively, and brought in little? Has a light of heaven seemed to mar your very enterprise, loss seized on your merchandise, the blessing of him that alone maketh rich been withheld from your basket or your store, and your handiwork not prospered as others has, or as your own did in days gone by when the candle of the Lord shone more favouringly upon you? If it be a mere worldly loss or sorrow of this sort that you are called to endure, the text no doubt includes it, and the promise applies to it. And the condition to which the promise is attached is Perseverance, " He that endureth to the end." Though days of weariness, months of vanity, and years, it may be even, of failing hope, may precede, at length there cometh the end. By him that is not overcome of evil the end will surely be reached when the garb of sackcloth shall be laid aside for the festal robe; when sorrow and sighing shall have fled away; when patience is approved and submission receives its exceeding great reward—

> Then heaven's rest will be the dearer
> For treading these rough ways,
> And its light will seem the clearer
> For the gloom of such dark days.

But far richer still is this promise of the text in its application not to that cross which is the common lot of all men, but to that which is, which must be, inevitably ours in our character of Christian soldiers striving against sin, if happily we are so striving. As the great poet of our Church has said—

> When worn and tired we sigh,
> With that more fearful war within,
> When passion's storm is loud and high,
> And brooding o'er remembered sin,
> The heart dies down

How needful to awake our slumbering love again, to quicken our almost overmastered zeal, such a word as this of the text admonishing us with our Master's kind voice of sympathy, that we be " steadfast unmoveable always abounding in the work of the Lord," that we " be not slothful but followers of them who through faith and patience inherit the promises." "He that endureth to the end shall be saved!" Of what endurance shall we interpret this so much as of the whole life long struggle with evil, to which the Christian soldier is sworn. "Blessed" says S. James, "is the man that endureth temptation for he shall receive the crown of life." And if, as I said, the temptation the faithful Christian is called to undergo, in regard to the faith to the maintenance of which he is pledged is not what it was in those early days, it is yet real sharp and strong. To some it comes in the form of oppositions of science falsely so called, that would invite them to set up once again the already subverted imaginations of unassisted reason in antagonism to the Revelation of God. So the Philistines set up their subverted Dagon before the ark of the Lord, only to have their idol laid prostrate in a more ignoble fall! To some it comes in a vain philosophy that in the face of the warning, with which the sacred volume concludes, would add to or detract from the words of God with theories of its own: political theories, social theories, ecclesiastical theories, "new gods that have come newly up," hazardous deviations from old paths, good, and tried, and safe. To many it comes in that which is a great and dangerous tendency of the present day, to join the world in a dishonest liberality, a liberality that would treat the distinctive doctrines of Christianity for which Christ testified, and many of His martyrs died as comparatively unimportant, as to be relegated to the domain of curious speculation, and as having no practical bearing on the ordinary duties which society looks to see performed. To some it comes very powerfully in an inclination to follow the multitude in their unworthy unsatisfying life of mere self seeking or pleasure seeking. And to "all that will live godly in Christ Jesus," it comes, if not in the open contradiction of sinners and the gainsaying of the irreligious, at least in their contempt, their neglect, hardest of all perhaps their misrepresentation of the Christian motives and principles by which the godly are actuated "Lest ye be wearied and faint in your minds consider Him that endured the same " says S. Paul.

And indeed the consideration of Him, the Great Author and Finisher of our faith, who endured as we are called to do ; and love for Him, for "Charity endureth all things," says the same Apostle, are the believer's great sustaining principles in his life-long resistance to the world without and sin within. And conjointly with these there is yet one other sustaining principle, that to the power of which as a motive our Lord appeals in the text. There is the object of our faith, salvation, as well as the exemplar of it, the Saviour. "He that endureth to the end shall be saved." This is the prospect which one of the Twelve here addressed holds out to us to move us to patient continuance in welldoing and submission in suffering even as here it had been held out to him. S. Peter exhorts the believers that the trial of their faith might be found unto praise, and honour, and glory. And he encourages them to this perseverance by the added promise of their then receiving the " end of their faith, even the salvation of their souls."

And how enviable shall be that "praise and honour" which the Apostle here says shall surely be the gracious reward of the persevering

" at the revelation of Jesus Christ." Even the world yields its glowing admiration to constancy. They are only the words of a song, but they will bear quoting even in this sacred connection, and illustrate what " He will render to them who by patient continuance" in well-doing ensure that nobler "glory and honour" which He has promised in so many words—

> I have stood by the pilot at dark midnight,
>   When the storm came sweeping by,
> And I've marked by the pale dim compass light
>   How calm was that pilot's eye.
> And I've watched from far on the battle field,
>   When the foe were as ten to one,
> And I've seen how the one has scorned to yield,
>   Though the ten came rushing on.
>
> And I've gazed on the lonely mourner's cheek,
>   When all save heaven was lost,
> And that sad one seemed like some frail wreck
>   On the world's wild surges tossed ;
> And oh ! when I've seen how these held on
>   The truth it has forced from me
> That the noblest sight beneath the sun
>   Is the true heart's constancy.

Thus to the Christian presently cometh the end, when the last enemy is subdued, death being swallowed up in victory, and the last step is gained, and the last cloud breaks away. And he who sometimes in the hour of despondency, like S. Paul "in Asia pressed out of measure above strength, despaired even of life" is greeted with the gracious welcome to eternal life by " the Author of eternal salvation," " Well done, thou good and faithful servant," " Thou hast borne and had patience, and for my Name sake hast laboured and hast not fainted," enter into the joy of Thy Lord, who, having endured the cross, is set down at the right hand of God. " And I heard," says the inspired Divine, anticipating in his book of visions the glad response with which this summons shall be met by the faithful unto death, " I heard a great voice saying Now is come salvation."

THE IMPORTUNATE WIDOW.

Luke xviii., 2—6.

The subject of this parable is importunity. The Bible gives several instances of it, mostly as employed by women. Importunity is an instrument with which those who set themselves to wield it can exert a wondrous influence over their fellow-creatures. As it has been ably remarked by the late Dr. Guthrie, some passages from whose writings on this parable I shall quote, "Nature herself prompts to importunity, and by it in a sense the weak things of the world confound the mighty, and foolish things the wise." It is the first resource of nature to secure the needed sustenance which as yet there is no ability otherwise to obtain, " for the infant cries till the roused mother takes it to her breast." It needs a firm parent indeed to be proof against the winning importunity of the earnest and beseeching child craving for some indulgence it is in the parent's power to grant. It was, we imagine, to this that Adam yielded when, won by the persuasion of the woman, he took of the forbidden fruit, and thus cast his crown to the ground and laid his honour in the dust. "For Adam," saith the Scripture, "was not *deceived*, but the woman being deceived, was in the transgression." And therewith she "stoops to conquer" ever since. For if pride will only suffer her to avail herself of this the great engine of the weaker over the stronger nature, what purpose may not be achieved, what end not obtained, what petition not granted through importunity! There are few indeed who can keep on persistently refusing what is uninterruptedly and untiringly solicited. We do not wonder at the result described in the text, for it is so manifestly true to nature. Who, if she be ready so to humble herself to persistent and earnest entreaty, could, any more than this judge, refuse such a suppliant? "The soft tongue breaketh the bone." It was thus, we remember, that the treacherous Delilah befooled her infatuated lover till she had extorted from his reluctant tongue the secret of his superhuman strength, and then cast the fond and credulous victim of her heartlessness from her caressing arms into the fierce grasp of the Philistine foes. Like her, or like the Syrophœnician woman — another Scripture instance—the woman in the text had the instinctive knowledge that it was by this means only her triumph could be won. And the object being to her unspeakably important she would not disdain to adopt this, perhaps humiliating, yet certain mode of procedure.

Travellers tell us this art of importunity is carried to its highest perfection in the East, and to a degree which would not be supposed possible, as it could not be employed in our country. Our law forbids the annoyance of accosting and following another with importunity, which is common in other countries, and even to some extent in Ireland. This woman was therefore free to exercise this means of inducing the other to compliance; and she did.

"So soon as ever this unjust judge took his seat at the gate of the city. Where in the East courts are held, and all cases heard, his eye as it roamed over the crowd fell on her. There she was, and always was, sorrow in her dress, but determination in the flash of her eye; her form bent down with grief, but her spirit unbroken, resolved to give that judge no rest till he had avenged her of her adversary. Now breaking in on the business of the court she is on her feet passionately demanding justice; and now stretched on the ground at his feet she piteously implores it." The Judge could not fail to notice her. There is a power about a resolute eye, which enforces observation. I know no feature of character that you can sooner recognise in another than that of decision. It needs no profound study of human nature, no great sagacity, to recognise persistency in the face of a fellow creature. You may if you judge by the outward appearance be often strangely mistaken in the estimate you form of your neighbour; but you shall hardly mistake the resolute. There is a nameless something that you cannot confound with vacillation or indecision. And you may be very sure the judge who was accustomed to read the human countenance so often, and compare it with the nature of life as it came under his notice, was at no loss to perceive very quickly the force of character, that underlay this humbled suppliant. There was a hidden resolve, and a determination to do and suffer anything so that she might secure her end, which all her overpowering grief could not dissemble. The darkness of a desolate widowhood had gathered over her life, but the light of earnest will was in that flashing eye. And it seemed in her speaking countenance to say in the great Apostle's words "troubled on every side, yet not distressed; perplexed, but not in despair; persecuted, but not forsaken; cast down but not destroyed." I can well believe that from the moment the unjust judge first heard her case, and we read "he would not for a while," his heart misgave him as to the final result. If he had any experience in human nature, I say it must have done so. And so it proved, the stern judge could not shake the widow off. And if he had any hope of doing so he soon gave up all expectation. The battle was in her hands from the beginning. *He* had the power to all *appearance* but *she* in *reality*. *He* had the position. *But she* was the master of it. *He* had the authority but *she* the influence that was to overrule it. *He* the directing but *she* the disposal of matters. And she soon, with the keen instinct of a woman's nature, saw that it was so; and applied herself accordingly. As I said before she stooped to conquer. We must often be willing so to do. "Denied her suit, she follows him to his house to interrupt his leisure and imbitter his pleasures. Her voice, ringing loud on the threshold, demanding entry, she bursts into his presence. She is quickly enough dragged away by the servants and thrust out, but only to return by some other door or at some very speedily recurring opportunity: as the ball struck rebounds, as the billow shattered on the rock falls back into the deep to gather volume and strength for a new attack. And as by constant dashing the waves in time cut into the cliff, which yielding to the incessant action of the weaker element some day bows its proud head and falls into the triumphant waves—so the persistence of the widow overcomes the resistance of the judge." "The waters wear the stones" says Job. A day came when he could bear it all no longer. His chafing spirit could no more tolerate these interruptions. And like we read of Samson in the case we referred to, "It came to pass when she pressed him daily with her words, and urged him so that his soul was vexed unto death," that the unjust judge, provoked as we say beyond endurance, exclaimed "Though I fear not God nor regard man, yet because this widow troubleth me I will avenge her, lest by her continual coming she weary me." And he gave sentence that it should be as she required.

And " He spake the parable," says the inspired historian, " to the end that men ought always to pray and not to faint." And says the Divine speaker Himself, " hear what the unjust judge saith! And shall not God avenge His own elect, which cry day and night unto Him?" There is however a strange and a great dissimilarity between the point of the story and its application, apart altogether from the contrast between the unjust and the Just Judge. The importunity in the one case was deprecated as intolerably wearisome, in the other it is enjoined as positively pleasing and acceptable to God. I know no assurance that we have about prayer more grateful and encouraging than this. To come again and again, as you and I have to come to the throne of grace ever with the same dreary tale of failure and of sin—to come to tell so repeatedly how we have been baffled in the conflict of duty and shamefully and ingloriously cast our shield of faith to the ground, and laid our honour as Christians in the dust—to go over in word or thought the tale of the same shortcomings—to feel over and over again our self-respect forfeited, and our sins and misdoings inexcusable—to dwell upon them in the first place till " the remembrance is grievous and the burden intolerable," and then to go on and tell them over and over and yet over again, though it be to a pitying Father, and a long suffering Redeemer, and a patient Spirit of grace, whose tenderness is inexhaustible.—Oh this is the great trial of the religious life, to which no other can compare! It makes us come to think that the conflict is an utterly hopeless one, yea perchance that we are " nothing better but rather grown worse." You know this feeling, you that are spiritual, know it well! But to you He spake this parable that men ought always to pray and not to faint ; because to Him there is no disgust at the monotony of the tale, and no weariness at the unbroken importunity. You and I cannot hear a person tell the same story, repeat the same circumstance, or describe his experience or emotion on any subject *more than once*, without feeling tired of it all. And if it comes to be very often repeated we are very sick of it. But His thoughts on this subject happily are not our thoughts. You shall kneel before your Father in secret to-night and tell Him the failure of the day or week past ; and though it be almost or quite the same as it was a week ago, He will not spurn you even in thought from His presence. He will listen to you as graciously as He did the first time that with a truly penitent heart you out-poured to Him all your soul. We shrink from importunity when it attacks ourselves. Though we may admire persistency in the abstract or the distance, we hate to be made the victims of it. But *He* delights in it and welcomes our most constant applications. There are no servants of His as of this unjust judge to thrust us away saying, " Trouble not the Master." There are no unfeeling disciples to drive us from the door, as they did the Syro-phœnician woman. " send her away for she crieth after us ;"or as they did the women that brought their little children to share the caress and blessing of their Redeemer. For His heart has by this time come to be better known. And the Spirit and the Church say Come !

We sometimes, do we not? (if I may interpret your experience by my own, and the study of his own heart tells a minister much about his people's,) we sometimes think as we kneel before the Lord our Maker, I have told God this so often, I have asked this blessing for myself or another so repeatedly, that I must give over now ; I can hardly dare to mention this person for whom I intercede, this want for which I supplicate relief over again. Persevere if it be the desire of your heart, and dread not a vain repetition. Let your request be made known unto God though you have made it a thousand times before. You have no fresh mercy it may be to seek, no new good to crave, but only the old longing of your soul to outpour again, be it for pardon, or for help for yourself, or for the welfare of the friend you love. But ever acceptably shall come up before the Great Judge of all the oft told petition. The offering it up again is the sign that you are still looking to and waiting upon Him. So the old prayer comes before Him like incense, and the lifting up of your hands is grateful to Him as the evening sacrifice. Aye, and if you have nothing at all you feel prompted to ask still persevere like the widow in the attitude of the suppliant. I can well suppose there were times when she cast herself before the unjust judge and had no words to speak. What could she say more than she had said already? But the very attitude of earnest waiting and mute entreaty spoke eloquently to the unjust judge, he interpreted it as plainly and it was to him as forcible as the most impassioned appeal. And if you only assumed her attitude of mind as you knelt before High Heaven, I should care nothing at all though no word escaped your lips. For oftentimes the Spirit makes intercession with groanings which cannot be uttered. What are words to Him that can read the thoughts ?

Prayer is the soul's sincere desire
Uttered or unexpressed,
The motion of a hidden fire
That trembles in the breast.

Prayer is the burden of a sigh
The falling of a tear,
The upward glancing of an eye,
When none but God is near.

And so it is that in that matchless service the Communion Office' the Church knowing that then if ever, the hearts of her devout children may be overcharged with feelings too deep for utterance, breaks off for a moment from continuing to put words into lips tremulous with perhaps uncontrollable emotion. And with exquisite and touching significance—like a mother that can read her children's spirits—she exclaims in a perfect understanding of the high wrought emotion with which they draw near the table of their Redeemer " Lift up your hearts." And the beautiful response comes from those who know well what it is to be unable at times to say a single word, or offer a single petition " we lift them up unto the Lord. "

And last of all when it occurs to you—as again presuming to interpret heart by heart, I doubt not it often will—that in the matter of praise like that of prayer your heart is too full to find expression ; when in the words of the hymn with which I conclude you say

> O God we feel the praise of thee
> A task beyond our powers!

—bear in mind that the attitude to Him of the adoringly grateful uplifted soul is everything. Though the words of thanksgiving die upon your faltering tongue, and the sense of His great love chokes your overmastered spirit, be the worshipping attitude of the prostrate widow before her judge, the posture of your grateful soul before your God. And he will read and be moved by it even as the other was. And the unspoken prayer shall be as effectual and the unuttered praise of the heart as acceptable as the loud voices of the worshipping multitude before the throne of heaven.

Lord we offer Thee that tribute from our full souls now !

> Yea now the wants are told that brought
> Thy children to Thy knee,
> Here lingering still, we ask for nought,
> But simply *worship Thee*!

THE DISAPPOINTED EXPECTATION.

The harvest is past, the summer is ended, and we are not saved! *Jeremiah,* viii. 20.

Here is a consideration very suitable for Harvest-tide. These words were spoken by the besieged inhabitants of Jerusalem, when, after vainly waiting for many months for help from Egypt against their Chaldean invaders, they finally gave up all hope. The season when alone it was possible *that* assistance could be rendered then was over, and they here admit to one another with a pathos of disappointment that is very touching, the hopelessness of their condition.

In the Prophets Isaiah and Jeremiah, we have frequent instances of this dependence which Israel placed upon Egypt. The Egyptian and Assyrian powers, were rivals, and each looked jealously on the interruption by the other of what politicians call the balance of power. They were not unready therefore to take part with Israel—whose rich and prosperous land, aroused the envy of each from time to time—one against the other. But their readiness to interfere when Israel was attacked being prompted by a purely selfish motive, it was natural that when it did not appear to their interest, or convenience, to interfere they should hold back. And much distress and disappointment to their confiding ally was the result. It is true the distress was self inflicted; for Israel had been expressly forbidden to seek help in such cases from their heathen neighbours, instead of from God, the temporal Sovereign of the nation, who had covenanted always to render it. So He says " Woe to the rebellious children that take counsel but not of me, and that cover with a covering but not of my Spirit, that walk to go down into Egypt, and have not asked at my mouth, to strengthen themselves in the strength of Pharoah, and trust in the shadow of Egypt ! Therefore shall the strength of Pharoah be your shame, and the trust in the shadow of Egypt your confusion." But the disappointment, because it was foretold, was none less bitter. We remember how, the city of Jerusalem was taunted with thus misplacing its confidence by Rabshakeh " Thou trustest in the staff of this broken reed on Egypt, whereon if a man lean it will go into his hand and pierce it : so is Pharoah king of Egypt to all that trust in him. "And we learn too how the insincerity of Egypt, for that the Lord is the avenger of all, such called down upon that land His judgments. For though he had, in a gracious care to avert the inevitable dissappointment, forbidden Israel to trust the Egyptians, He was no unmoved spectator of the poignant suffering their misplaced confidence in their faithless neighbours occasioned them. " All the inhabitants of Egypt shall know that I am the Lord because they have been a staff of reed to the house of Israel. When they took hold of thee by the hand thou didst break and rend all their shoulder : and when they leaned upon thee thou breakest. Therefore thus saith the Lord, behold I will bring a sword upon thee. And the land of Egypt shall be desolate and waste." The words of the text then are the affecting exclamation of the besieged and hopeless people, when in the words of a former verse " They looked for peace but no good came," when the season for military operations and the anticipated relief was now over, and they found themselves betrayed.

It is often so in the history of a nation. Another prophet has told us that " the inhabitant of Maroth " in the like circumstances " waited carefully for good, and gave presents to Gath, but the houses of Achzib were a lie to the kings of Israel." And in recent times we remember, and the tale was very painful, how France invaded by a relentless foe and distracted by faction, set her eyes on our own country and on others hoping they might stem the tide that was too strong for her. But she hoped as vainly as earnestly.

It is and it has been so oftentimes in our own private circumstances· In the time of need, when like Israel "brought low through oppression, through any plague, or trouble," how often has it happened to us that the source to which we looked for sympathy, moral support, or encouragement has failed us! We have found ourselves it may have been in a small and very much more trifling matter, just as cruelly deceived. We have been left to fight our own battle, while the heartless disregard of others seemed to say " What is that to us ? see thou to that," And in lesser matters still we have all experienced the disappointment they thus affectingly expressed.

The " hope deferred that maketh the heart sick " who does not know it in the lesser if not in the greater evils of life ? The visit that you expected that was never paid ; the letter you looked for that was never received ; the explanation you were sure might have been made, that was never forthcoming ; the encouraging word you felt your neighbour knew you needed aye and deserved, but which he was too indifferent to speak ; the help you were sure it was well known you required, but which was never rendered from the quarter, whence you had a right to look for it ; the gift that to you would have been so invaluable, and that would have cost your friend who knew how much you would desire and value it, nothing to bestow, but which was nevertheless persistently withheld— he is a fortunate man indeed who is conscious of no such painful reminiscences that have sorely vexed his soul in days gone by. Well may this same Prophet say " Therefore let no man glory in men."

But to pass from these applications of the words, to a more serious one, and one with which it is more my business here to deal. We cannot read these words without wondering whether in the mouths of some that uttered them, they had not a deeper import : and did not betoken a consciousness that the day of grace was closing, and the greater salvation than a mere worldly deliverance from Assyrian slavery yet un-.

secured. It might well have been so to *them*, for Jerusalem was about to be taken, the temple overthrown, and the candlestick of the Divine presence removed. Jeremiah's ministry had been ineffectual to awaken them to their sin, and to recover them to their God. "The harvest was past." Almost all the God-fearing, taken from the evil to come, like shocks of corn fully ripe, had been gathered into the garner of the Lord, before the day of desolation came. Only the unprofitable and impenitent, like stubble for the burning, now remained in the waste field, which the ploughshare of invasion was soon to break up. "The summer was ended," the sunshine of the Divine favour, while a dreary cold and desolate winter was at hand, when for seventy years the land, which was the glory of all lands, should be forsaken, and the country of Israel, God having withdrawn from it altogether, should be left in sunless gloom.

And though these words have thank God no such intimation of doom to any of us, who yet walk in His light, and are the favoured objects of His continued mercy, and His yet unfailing grace, yet they may and they ought to suggest to us at this season solemn reflections. And if there is within any of us a lingering or doubtful anxiety as to our state before God, and our preparedness for our latter end—if God's Spirit has happily from time to time affected us with a misgiving, which He would have to lead us to repentance, about our religious condition— let us not avoid but rather welcome this time for settling our minds and closing our perhaps too long standing account with Heaven. "The harvest is past the summer is ended." It is so, with us now, *literally*. And in a *figure* too, the words are suggestive. With us it has long been the summer tide of grace and religious opportunity. We have enjoyed a very midsummer of Heaven's golden sunshine. The bleak march winds of persecution have long died out, around the Church of God. And the dew, and the rain of Divine grace have fallen, softly and re-freshingly on the inheritance on which we entered at our Baptism. We have Ministers, and Sacraments, and Prayers, and Sermons, and Psalms, and Hymns, and Spiritual Songs, (and increased life, and earnestness in all), and all that we can need to quicken our faith, and enliven our hope, and fervently kindle our love toward God. We have had Christian education, we are under Christian laws ; and we are surrounded with a Christian influence, that often checks us in evil in spite of ourselves and alluringly draws, almost compels us, to good. We have thank God a social atmosphere around us, which instead of being pernicious and seductive, as in our fathers' times, tends to foster the growth of all things belonging to the Spirit. We are happily free from the moral atmosphere of dissipation which hangs about large towns, and are blessed instead with the comparative peacefulness and purity of village life. Nor do we anticipate as Israel did the immediate passing away of these advantages. The harvest to us, we may be permitted to hope, is not yet entirely past, nor is the summer fully ended. We hope, that long as life itself shall last, we may be permitted to share these benefits and continue to be blessed with these gifts of Heaven.

Still we cannot tell how soon some of these favours of God may be withdrawn. Our lot in life may presently be otherwise ordered than it is. The windows of heaven may not be always so open as now. We may be perhaps soon in places or circumstances where the means of grace we enjoy may be not so abundant, and strange ones may take the place of those Ministers of our God under whose shadow we sit with great delight, partakers of the fruit of God's Word which is sweet to our taste. In the matter of worldly blessings, the calm and even tenour of our present lives may be ruffled we cannot tell how soon by some storm of affliction that shall sweep with a desolating force through our souls. A few months, or weeks, or days to some of us, and we may feel at all events that the harvest tide of enjoyment is over to us for ever, and the bright summertime of our lives is ended.

But must we say with Israel " we are not saved "? Or have we a humble but well grounded hope that we are? The salvation indeed was long ago secured for us all, and has also been covenanted to us each. Have we reason to think from self examination that we are the subjects of it? Are we availing ourselves of it by constant application for the forgiveness, grace and blessing it entitles us to? Or are we neglecting it, living as though we could do very well without it?

> When the harvest is past, and the summer is gone,
>   And sermons and prayers shall be o'er,
> When the beams cease to break of the sweet Sabbath morn,
>   And Jesus invites thee no more.
>
> When the rich gales of mercy no longer shall blow,
>   The gospel no message declare,
> Sinner how canst thou bear the deep wailings of woe?
>   How suffer the night of despair?

Israel felt his weakness and so he looked to Egypt for strength. And when he had long looked, but Egypt came not, he felt his case was hopeless. If you feel your insufficiency to live well through the present, to grasp the future, to conquer sin, and to resist the invading forces that attack your soul, you shall not look as Israel did for deliverance in vain. Egypt did not care to concern itself with Israel's trouble. But your Redeemer with all the feeling of antagonism to *your* enemy that Egypt had for Assyria, has also a longing to come to your deliverance which Egypt lacked. I cannot say whether Egypt grudged the cost of the expedition, or feared its danger, or was otherwise engaged at the time, but I know well that Jesus who spared no cost, but gave His life for your deliverance will spare no pains, as He can shrink from no peril —for he has already overcome them all—and will allow nothing to interfere with the rescue from sin and death for which you appeal to Him " The Lord shall deliver me from every evil work and will preserve me unto His heavenly kingdom " was S. Paul's dying testimony.

Do you say with Israel " we are not saved " or doubt whether you are! He says in reply " Look unto me and be ye saved, all the ends of the earth." What is simpler than a look? The merest infant however helpless and ignorant can look, and will when you call its attention. And the look of faith is just as easy: and as effectual too as it is easy. For this says the Saviour Himself is " the will of Him that sent Me, that every one that seeth the Son, and believe on Him may have everlasting life."

JEREMIAH'S INTERCESSION FOR JERUSALEM DURING THE FAMINE.

O the hope of Israel, the Saviour thereof in time of trouble, why shouldst thou be as a stranger in the land, as a wayfaring man that turneth aside to tarry for a night.
Jeremiah xiv, 8.

The Prophet who comes before us here as so earnest a suppliant for the Almighty's favour, and so anxious an Intercessor for his guilty countrymen, was a true friend of Israel. Not perhaps since the days that their faithful lawgiver had knelt on Sinai with streaming eyes to deprecate on their behalf the anger of Heaven's insulted Majesty in the matter of the golden calf have we such outpourings of impassioned feeling as in the verses of which the text is the first; or an instance of so devoted an advocate to stand in the breach between the unhappy nation and the God they had wronged.

"With strong crying and tears" to Him that alone was able to save in their hour of dire calamity, Jeremiah makes here the most movving supplication. With all the ardour of the noblest patriot, and the heroism of an enlightened religious faith, he threw himself throughout the period his prophecy covers into the cause he here so ably pleads to seek the welfare of Zion. And none but the Psalmist who uttered them could so truly breathe from the heart as he could do the words of self-sacrificing love his whole life expressed," If I forget thee O Jerusalem, let my right hand forget her cunning, yea if I prefer not Jerusalem above my chief joy!"

> If e'er my heart forget to move
> Toward thee Jerusalem in thoughts of love
> If e'er my sorrows cease to flow
> In sad remembrance of thy matchless woe,
> Eternal silence bind my tongue
> By me thy glories be no longer sung
> No more my hands the harp inspire
> Nor wake to rapture the celestial lyre.

Jeremiah was also one of the most tender hearted of men. None save the all compassionate Jesus was ever so ready to weep with them that weep as he. In all the affliction of his countrymen he was afflicted. Over their sorrows he mourned, and over their sins he well nigh broke his heart. For it was not merely with the kindly feelings of a singularly benevolent nature that he grieved over their distresses. He wept over the guilty inhabitants of the land, in the spirit of our Divine Master, mourning as one that had no hope, because they were losing their day of grace and would not hear of what concerned their peace and salvation. He looked on at a moment when they were filling up the measure of their iniquity, and bringing upon themselves a swift destruction. That destruction his testimony had been powerless to avert, nay had rather aggravated. His life among them had been to speak humanly a failure, his prophecy wholly unsuccessful, and his word was returning to him void, having proved rather a savour of death than of life to those hardened men, that had rejected the counsel of God against themselves.

And now the curse of unrepented sin was upon their city. There was dearth in their land, according to the prediction of the Psalmist, the verification of which the prophet most affectingly describes in the verses that precede the text, God had turned the water springs into dry ground and the fruitful land into barrenness for the wickedness of them that dwell in it As an eye-witness of Zion's heartrending sufferings he testifies what he had seen; and with a graphic pen sketches out for us in the first six verses of this chapter a vivid picture of tragedy and woe. In the third verse he tells us he had seen the children of the high born nobles sent forth to the dry cisterns and empty ponds by their thirst-stricken parents. They probably feared to come out themselves, lest they should meet the prophet's reproachful eye, and hear his indignant denunciations of their multiplied sins that had brought such anguish upon them,; "Hast thou not procured this unto thyself, in that thou hast forsaken the Lord thy God." (c ii v. 17 and 19)

In the agonies of burning thirst, with their tongue cleaving to the roof of their mouth, the little sufferers were returning empty handed. Their unrestrained and united cries of disappointment were ringing in the prophet's ears as with feeble and faltering steps they passed him in the streets, their little hands vainly raised to their faces, as he here depicted, as is the manner of children to dry their tears or hide their grief. And many a helpless babe and delicate child nursed lately in the lap of luxury was lying down with others that had fallen in the streets to die. So we see from c. ix v. 21, and 16, and 18 of this chapter, it actually happen ·

The Prophet looked forth again. And far off in the distant fields he saw the faint and exhausted husbandmen. They had set down the ploughshare, in the land that, as Job expresses it, was "crying out against them, and the furrows of which were complaining" of the desolation their sins had brought upon the thirsty ground. For they saw their task was vain. The prediction of Moses was now fulfilled before them, "The heaven that is over thy head be brass, and the earth that is under thee shall be iron." The heavens above them were a glowing furnace, the ground beneath them broken into deep fissures, and parched until it was as unfit for cultivation as a sheet of iron. In the fourth verse he describes the scene. He tells how as they turned bitterly away, and thought of their wives and children that so soon must perish by the cruel death that now stared them in the face, the strong men bowed themselves. They covered their heads after the manner of Eastern mourners; and down the hard labourers' rough faces rolled the scorching tears of despair.

The Prophet looked forth again. And lo, the poor dumb creatures of God were involved in the common misery. Oh, terrible evil that sin is, that visits itself with avenging wrong upon the children of the guilty unto the third and fourth generation and even as we so constantly see it, upon the yet more innocent brute creation! In the fifth verse he describes this next scene. From "the thick bushes" where the Psalmist tells us, she is wont at the voice of the Lord to bring forth her young the hind in the occasion of her need and thirst had fled forth to seek for grass and water. By the instinct of nature, that has made all the beasts of the field to some extent consciously subject to and dependent upon man, she had repaired to the more open country round the city, where man might probably have some store provided for himself. So the wild animal is not unfrequently known to cast itself in its extremity on human aid for succour. And there when she had given birth to her little fawn, she left it if haply man could provide for it better than she could. And with a long and lingering look of maternal fondness she turned away from her helpless offspring; for she knew she had no nourishment in her wasted frame to support and rear its tender life.

And the Prophet looked forth again. And he goes on to tell in the sixth verse, how the wild asses rushed with all the energy of despair to the highest ground their failing strength could take them to. They left the valley springs now all dried up, where the Psalmist tells us they are wont to quench their thirst. And with like wondrous instinct set their faces on the hill tops towards the wind and sniffed the passing breeze. This they did if perhaps it might bear on its wings toward them the scent of distant water, their Maker has taught their nostrils so quickly and keenly to recognise. And though all in silence, their dim eyes and emaciated frames cried with a voice that well He knew to the sympathy of the God of heaven, as "the young ravens do when they wander for lack of meat."

And then Jeremiah thought of the times in the history of Israel, when God had interposed in a similar crisis. He recalled no doubt the story of Hagar and her fainting child; and that of the miraculous supply of water to the three kings. He bethought himself doubtless of Elijah's powerful intercession when "he prayed earnestly and the heavens gave rain, and the earth brought forth her fruit." He perhaps reflected too on that promise recorded by a brother prophet of his a century before " When the poor and needy seek water, and there is none, and their tongue faileth for thirst, I the Lord will hear them, I the God of Israel will not forsake them."

So to Him that "heareth the prayer of the poor, destitute, and despiseth not their desire" Jeremiah addressed the prayer contained in the 7th, 8th and 9th verses of this chapter. "Hath God " he was asking " forgotten to be gracious? Hath He shut up His loving-kindness in displeasure? Will He be no more entreated? And is His mercy come utterly to an end for evermore?" And then comes the enquiry of the text, " Why shouldest Thou be as a stranger in the land, and as a wayfaring man that turneth aside to tarry for a night."

From the circumstances we have now been considering, under

which this cry for help was extorted, let us proceed to observe this appropriate and interesting illustration of the way-faring man, by which Jeremiah represents in the name of his people their feeling of desertion by God. Have we known what it is—no doubt most or all of us have once and again—to entertain for a short period in our house, or even to meet in the society of our neighbourhood, some friend or stranger from a distance or on a journey, who turns aside to make with us a short sojourn? Let him be a well informed or agreeable person, and we know how soon our hearts are interested in such a one. Perhaps he has come to give some instruction in the neighbourhood as a lecturer, deputation or commissioner. He may be a friend on a journey introduced or commended to us by some mutual friend. With him he has brought from his distant abode, and on his travels he has gathered up, much entertaining or valuable information that we are glad to become possessed of. He has seen places that we have only heard of. He has met and conversed with people that we know something of, or have been anxious to hear about. He has been an eye-witness of scenes that are invested to us with ever fond recollections. He has been an observer, or has even taken part in what we have long wished to hear described.

As we sat or walked in the company of such a one, admiring his intelligence, and rejoicing in the perhaps unwonted pleasure of such society and conversation, the hours of his visit have fled rapidly by. Our spirits have risen high within us, and our hearts beaten with animation.

But he can only stop with us a short time, perhaps but one night. The morning of his departure comes, and the stranger goes on his way. He may have been a relative we seldom see, or one who has been heretofore to us a total stranger. But when he leaves our roof or presence there is a temporary blank in our hearts. Like steel to iron his kindly manner or pleasant talk have given an edge to our spirits. A ray of additional enlightenment and kindly humanity had gleamed upon our hearth or path. But with the light of his cheering presence, and genial converse it is gone. We have wished him the parting salutation, and we turn back to our threshold to miss the wayfaring man that turned aside with us lately to tarry for a night.

It is to this emotion or susceptibility of the heart that Jeremiah here appeals, and by this experience he illustrates the case as transferred to themselves and God. For even so turns the lonely heart of the God forsaken to "feel after," and long for the God from whom he has been parted by his sin. He will not very likely confess that craving, as we might not care to do ours for the stranger that had made his abode with our gladdened hearts. But sorely he feels it, and his heart is desolate, and his soul cannot be comforted. "Behold as the eyes of a servant look to the hand of his master," and "the desire of the hireling is to the reward of his labour," so the eyes of Jeremiah and all his few like minded contemporaries, were then waiting for the consolation of Israel, though almost failing for looking so long and vainly, for their now departed God. And yet in the epithets in the text, we see a measure of trustful hope mingled with his sadues. Even in this dark hour he could address God as " the hope of Israel, the Saviour thereof in time of trouble." The faith of the prophet enabled him in the very midst of his desponding prayer, to lay hold as it were upon his God, by these endearing and consolatory epithets. As though he had said with another prophet. " The Lord will be a refuge for the oppressed, a refuge in times of trouble."

Still though thus " strong in hope giving glory to God," there is a cry of bitter want and loneliness here as from the consciousness of the absence of one who had formerly cheered and blessed him with a sweet communion, but who had passed away and left his craving heart unsatisfied. The spirit of that cry reminds us of one who ages before had felt a similar hiding of the Divine countenance, " O that I were as in months past, when the Almighty was yet with me, when the candle of the Lord shined upon me, and I walked in the light of the Lord!"

And to pass from Jeremiah and Job, in the years that are past to God's servants now. To them the Lord's companionship is as blessed a reality, his presence no less dear, as to quote the same figure from the Apocrypha—" the remembrance of a guest that tarrieth but a day." (Wisdom of Solomon v. 14.) To all of us, who have been dedicated as temples for his indwelling, does He come as the wayfaring man, to bless us with His converse, and enlighten us with His knowledge. You can best tell whether you are still keeping at a distance, and treating as a stranger the God and Saviour that awaits your welcome, and is evermore saying to all whom His Gospel calls, " to day I will abide at the home " of your heart. You can tell whether or no you are indifferent to His offered friendship, and saying to Him in your life, " Depart from us for we desire not the knowledge of Thy ways."

Those of you who have received the heavenly visitant, with the confidence, and pleasure you have done, the guest you hold in honour, or admiration, will understand the illustration well. Those whose hearts have learnt to cling to Him will know the feeling of desolation as here described, if for a while He has withdrawn and left you alone. The sinking of the spirit within, when your kindly hearted entertaining or intelligent friend or acquaintance, with whom you took sweet counsel and under the shadow of whose presence it sat with great delight, has passed on his way—is a painful sensation. But though a most apt it is a very faint emblem of the Christian soul's experience, in those sad hours when allowed sin has drawn its dark veil between the Holy God and His for a time unwatchful servant. Beautifully has the Psalmist given utterance to that feeling of desertion in many a moving devotional strain, that I need not now quote particularly. And His gifted and equally inspired Son, has given it expression in the boldest figures of an Eastern fancy in many passages of his mystic song.

O when that blessed inter-communion of thought and love, that subsists between the Saviour and the grateful soul is broken for a moment—when the supplies of grace out of His fulness cease to flow in—when the believer's Beloved withdraws Himself and is gone—all the past joy of fellowship is looked back upon, as gone like a watch in the night, and all the remembrance of former days with the gladness and profit they brought is regretted as the shortest stay, as you look back on the swiftly spent hours or days, of the previous visit when your wayfaring friend rises up to go on his way. But, for ever blessed be His faithfulness! it is not so with our Divine Lord and Friend. He does not pass away like the wayfaring stranger, whom we are to meet no more. To them that look for Him, will He ever appear again. Evermore does He say to the mourning soul He appears to leave, as to the Apostles, "I will see you again and your heart shall rejoice." Linger not on mount Olivet sad disciple! for that same Divine Friend shall so come in like manner as you have seen Him go. "Zion said the Lord hath forsaken me, and my God hath forgotten me!" "For a small moment," is the reply, "but with everlasting kindness will I have mercy on thee saith the Lord thy Redeemer."

So here the illustration of the wayfaring man fails having no further application. Yea thou prophet!—forcible though thy figure be and well as thou hast given expression in it to the thoughts of many hearts thou didst hardly well to think or speak so of thy God and ours. He is no wayfaring man to pass—after tarrying for a little while to awaken the interest and desire of the human soul—carelessly on, and leave it unblessed and uncomforted, more lone and restless than before! The visitor that you have received into your house, or society may possibly be no personal friend. He may be, as I have said, and as the text does, a stranger. There may be no lasting bonds between you and Him. You may have admired and wished you could have known or seen more of him. But *his* business and friendships are elsewhere and not with you: and he passes on. Accidentally and for a while you have met. But it was only as you knew from the first to separate again, after a certain period. And however you might have wished it otherwise, the acquaintance is henceforth to become to you as a thing of the past, and to be as though it had not been. And as you watch him off or hear of his departure, probability forbids your expecting ever to see him again.

But not like the wayfaring man—the mere temporary acquaintance whose business and interests are elsewhere, and who comes to us but to go again, and leave our hearts if they have been attracted to him at all only the more sad— is the God and Saviour and blessed Spirit, that comes to indwell with the believer, and manifest to him their love and their aid. The business of Christ unlike the traveller's, is with all He visits and His interest in them all and each, as though there were none besides to share it. And though in bodily presence, He be necessarily absent a little while. seeing " the heaven must receive Him till the time spoken of by the mouth of His Holy prophets since the world began," He will come again at no distant day; and substitute His personal for His spiritual presence, and fulfill the expectation and satisfy the love of His now waiting Church. And to all of you that traveller now comes.

"Behold says He, I stand at the door and knock!" Our office it is, like Rhoda the doorkeeper in Mary's house, to call your attention to that Visitor. For we cannot open the door of your hearts for Him ourselves. "And if any man," he goes on to say, "hear My Voice and open the door, I will come in to him and sup with him," and abide with

him throughout his life here, and he with Me throughout eternity.
"Even so : come Lord Jesus !"

Long hast thou journeyed with us, Lord
  Ere we Thy face did know ;
Oh ! still Thy fellowship afford.
  While dark the shadows grow.

For passed is many a beauteous field,
  Beside our morning road ;
And many a fount to us is sealed,
  That once so freshly flowed.

The splendour of the noontide lies,
  On other fields than ours :
The dews that lave, you fragrant skies.
  Will not revive our flowers.

It is not now as in the glow,
  Of life's impassioned heat,
When to the heart there seemed to flow
  All that of earth was sweet.

Something has faded, something died,
  Without us and within ;
We more than ever need a guide,
  Blinded and weak with sin.

The weight is heavy that we bear,
  Our strength more feeble grows ;
Weary with pain and toil and care,
  We long for sweet repose,

Stay with us, gracious Saviour, stay
  While friends and hope depart ;
Fainting on Thee we wish to lay
  The burden of our heart

Abide with us, Dear Lord, remain
  Our Life, our Truth, our Way ;
So shall our loss be turned to gain,
  Night dawn to endless day.

PART 2.

JEREMIAH'S INTERCESSION FOR JERUSALEM DURING THE FAMINE.

Why shouldest thou be as a man astonied, as a mighty man that cannot save? yet thou, O Lord, art in the midst of us, and we are called by Thy name: leave us not.
Jeremiah xiv. 9.

It is the character of Poetry and particularly of Eastern Poetry, under which form we have transmitted to us in the original, almost all the writings of the Old Testament Prophets, to deal much in imagery. We cannot read a chapter in the Prophets without noticing how it abounds in illustration, how the inspired writer multiplies and accumulates every variety of figurative expression, around the subject of which he is treating to bring it out as vividly and impress it as indelibily as possible on the mind of the hearer or reader. The heart is besieged on every side, appealed to as it were by its every emotion and worked upon through its every passion.

The gifted writers send forth on broad and sweeping wing their powers of imagination and observation, and gather from every quarter of the world before them, both of nature and of mind, stores of ideas wherewith to point and enforce the deep and weighty truths they have to set forth.

We have seen how Jeremiah did so in his description of the famine in the opening verses of the chapter. With a few rapid touches he concisely, but most vividly brought before us the group of sufferers. Noble and ploughman, infant and suckling, hind and ass, stand forth in life like reality. We seem to see the parched flocks and the thirst stricken cattle. The bleating of the sheep, the lowing of the oxen, and the cries of the perishing inhabitants, ring painfully in our ears. And now, out of the abundance of his heart, out poured in supplication, to Him that was able to save the survivors from this death of torture, his mouth is speaking again.

What hope he was asking himself might he indulge for his miserable countrymen, as regards a re ewal of the grace and love of their offended God? What conjecture could he form about the possibility of any future designs of mercy on His part? Would He return again to pardon, and to help them?—He would outvie the very prophets of Baal, on Mount Carmel, in his efforts to arouse the sympathy and arrest the notice, and awake the apparently slumbering interest of God on behalf of Israel. As they had thought was Baal on a journey, or asleep, so it almost seemed to him. Was God on a journey, he asked himself, like a wayfaring man that for a short time has sojourned and conversed with us and then passes on ignorant, and careless of all that befalls us when he is gone ?   Had He thus passed on and left all thought and concern about those He had so lately known, as our stranger visitant passes on, and amid other scenes, and faces, and business forgets most likely our very names.

And so from this illustration he goes on to another.   If it was not so that God was like such a traveller, what was the reason of his inattention to their case ?   " Wherefore hidest Thou Thy face, and forgetest our affliction and our oppression ? "   Was he as a man astonied, as a mighty man that cannot save," not because he wants the resources but because the force and suddenness of the evil he has to meet deprives him for the time of the power of reflection to use them ?

We shall here consider firstly this fresh illustration ; and secondly the plea in the latter part of the verse by which Jeremiah calls upon God for aid.   We can well understand this figure of a man astonied (or stunned, as the more common expression is, and that in more general use now) stupified and bewildered at the suddenness of some unexpected tidings, of evil for the most part.   It is familiar to us both in instances from Scripture and in common life.   To take the former : Thus it was with the drunken Nabal, when his wife told him how his churlish behaviour to David, and his impious reflections on the affliction with which it had pleased God to visit the persecuted and friendless exile, had well nigh incited the warrior in a moment of excited passion to destroy his whole household.   " And it came to pass," we read, " when his wife had told him these things, his heart died within him, and he became as a stone."

So it was with the aged Eli, the Priest of God, when the messenger came to Shiloh, and told him how the Philistines had triumphed and his sons were dead, and the ark of God was taken.   " And he fell from off the seat backward, and his neck broke and he died."   So it was with Daniel, when the vision of all the destructive empires of the world was revealed to him, and the resistance they should offer to the " Prince of princes."   It was a like shock that made Belshazzar and his lords to tremble when they learnt from the handwriting on the palace wall that their impious career was closed.   So it was with Job's friends when they sat down with him upon the ground, seven days and nights, overcome by the sight of his unexampled misery, " and none spake a word unto him, for they saw that his grief was very great."   And so it was with Ezra when he heard to his horror and amazement that his people had fallen immediately after their return from Babylon into one of the very sins for which God had by that captivity so severely punished them —he says, " I sat astonied until the evening."

All these examples bring powerfully before us the consternation which we have perhaps some of us felt ourselves, or witnessed in others when under the weight of overwhelming fear, or the news of unlooked for disaster the heart becomes chilled as it were for the time to stone.

Now imagine God's infinite horror of sin, when you see how His inspired prophet was taught to illustrate the Divine emotion at the people's conduct by such a figure, not that we can attribute any human passion in the exactness of our own experience of it to the Almighty :

but his feelings are shadowed forth throughout Scripture by ours. They are so represented here. Our love and hatred, our joy and grief, our repentance even, yea, even as here our very dread and horror, and our temporary powerlessness of action under such influence, have their counterpart in Him in the image of whose nature we are made. And though He is not a man as we are, that the pulses of life should almost stand still, and the powers of action be paralysed at the unlooked for announcement of some " wonderful and horrible thing," yet is the Most High God affected by the sins of His presumptuous creatures in such a way no doubt as the emblem before us does to some degree suggest.

Sin—each wrong thought and act of ours—not only each positive offence, but the very negative ungodliness of our nature—sends forth we learn here, though not here alone, a shock through God's moral universe which reaches to the very throne of the Eternal. And while it is given way to and persisted in, it interrupts the communication of Divine grace, breaks off the soul's connection with the Great Lord of Life, in whom it lives, and moves, and has its being, and until repented of and put away does in a manner unnerve that Divine Hand that is mighty to save, and seal up as in a horror of amazement that Divine Heart, that would otherwise outpour itself toward us in continuous love and blessing.

I do not know how the prophet could have set forth the heinousness of sin in the eyes of the Almighty, in stronger and bolder colours than when he depicts it here as bewildering and perplexing with a strange horror the calm clear mind of God, and paralysing for a while the arm of their Great Deliverer. But you know when the first suddenness and force of the blow that has so affected a man is over, he presently recovers himself, and in proportion to the extent of his resources rises to the emergency. He sets himself to consider what is to be done to remove the evil or mitigate the stroke. And accordingly with a strong faith in the invincible power and unfailing love of Israel's God, Jeremiah goes on to appeal to Him so to act. While acknowledging how Israel's provocation might well produce on the Divine mind an effect like that described, he pleads with God that He would as it were bethink or rouse himself. Thus did the Psalmist, " Keep not silence, O Lord, be not far from me. Stir up Thyself and awake to my judgment even unto my cause my God, and my Lord! Thus too did God's own Divine Son, in the prophetical words " Be not Thou far from me O Lord ; O my strength haste Thee to help me."

Like a man astonied God had been so affected by the apostacy and rebellion of His people, that his lips were sealed. Like Laban he had spoken to Israel no word either good or bad. He had ceased to give expression to his feelings as before by the mouth of the prophet. He seemed to him as a man who overpowered by some astounding and dreadful tidings you have brought him, gazes upon you speechlessly. Until he has had time to collect his thoughts he can neither say nor do anything. But now that this moment as it were of confusion might be supposed to be overpast, Jeremiah looks for some revelation of the Divine intention some expression of the Divine feeling. And calling to remembrance the former days of God's long suffering and gracious dealings with Israel, he hopes and prays it might be comforting and favourable. Well He knew that with Him there was " forgiveness and plenteous redemption." So he recalls God's as well as his own thoughts, back to the former days of Israel's happy history when the Lord was yet among them, in the affecting appeal in the latter part of the text. This we have secondly to consider. " Thou O Lord art (or wast) in the midst of us, and we are called by Thy name : leave us not."

And so it was. The Lord of old had chosen Zion for himself, and Israel for His especial habitation. He had chosen this out of all other nations to set His name there. At sundry times and in divers manners He had held with Israel the most intimate communion . " In Judah had God been known and His name was great in Israel." In almost unveiled manifestations of His Godhead He had walked among them and taught in their streets.

Signs and wonders and mighty deeds had He shown towards them that no unbeliever could gainsay and none of all the heathen lands could challenge as tokens of His presence and favour " Did ever people hear the voice of God as you have heard it ? " said Moses. And the same Moses, when on one occasion pleading with God in a strain similar to the prophet's here, urges the same argument. " The inhabitants of this land have heard that Thou, Lord, art among this people ; and that Thou art seen face to face, and that Thy cloud standeth over them ; and that Thou goest before them ." So Isaiah had appealed under the same circumstances a century before, for the restoration of the Divine favour " Return O Lord, for we are Thine. Thou never barest rule over *them* (the heathen) *they* were not called by Thy name." Just in the same way does the prophet call upon God here, as though He would surely help him when reminded of this claim, " Thou Lord *wast* (not so well *art*) in the midst of us : Leave us not," As though he said. We were near once, we were friends once : why not not be near and friendly to us again.

And how forcible do we feel such a plea ! How do we admit and own its power, when addressed to ourselves ! When an acquaintance of early days, or chosen companion of other years comes once more across our path, claims our old interest in the years that are past, and recalls our remembrance to scenes and thoughts that once were dear— how do our hearts wake up within us and respond to the emotions to which they once beat high ! When we meet again our former fellow that shared our labours or our studies—when we revisit the abodes or sojourning places of our youth, and dwell again on the circumstances the places or the persons that developed of old our kindling life, and in which or among whom our heart opened and grew up to its young hopes and joys—when we see once more the long parted friend whom in our former hours of gladness, we used to call to participate our every pleasure, and to whose sympathizing ear in our hours of sadness we were wont to confide our sorrows and as it may have been our wrongs— how at such a moment and when thus appealed to we recognise the power of the past, and straightway surrender our hearts again, we perhaps *all* can tell.

O wondrous provision of grace that God should here teach us to draw as it were upon His feelings of love and interest by this same powerful plea, and to remind Him of all He did and felt for us in days gone by!

But the Prophet does even more than this, He says further, " we are called by Thy name." And here is a handle to turn the heart more powerful still. Inhuman should we think the father that would disown the child, or the man that would desert the woman that had borne his name, and was appealing in vain as a suppliant to the interest and love it might be justly supposed that name would ensure for it. In the bonds of earthly love even the name of such protector or partner, is a strong tower into which the more dependent party runs and is safe. Much more is the name of the Lord, as we are taught in the book of Proverbs, such a tower of defence. Much more surely, if we bear that name, shall we not plead our relationship in vain.

But the agreement " We are called by Thy name! " like a double bladed weapon, has another point of attack. Dear to many a high born noble, or otherwise distinguished family is the honourable name he is proud to bear, and which has been handed down to him from a renowned ancestry as an heirloom of honour to be jealously preserved. But dearer far is His great Name to the most High God. It is the first appeal the Infant lips are taught to breathe " Our Father which art in Heaven." We are taught to use it in our every prayer, and to enforce our every application at the Throne of grace by such a conclusion. The last the almost omnipotent appeal to God, even our own God, is " We are called by Thy Name," and we are the brethren of Thy Dear Son! For our Lord and His Apostle tell us if we ask anything in His Name He heareth us.

Remember the case of Esau, when his Father had hesitated about owning or blessing him. Who has not felt the force of that passionate cry of appeal, which Isaac could no more resist " I am thy son, thy firstborn, Esau? " Put to the test the efficacy of this plea. Go call upon God in the all worthy name of His Beloved Son to whom He has assured us He will deny nothing at all. Put yourself in the place and stead of His Son our Lord, whose name for your encouragement was pronounced over you in Baptismal covenant, as it was in that hour linked with yours for life. His Name and merits and kingdom you were certified these were all, and henceforth available, to you personally. Claim according to your need all that Name guarrantees. And the honour of your Father is pledged in your behalf. The succour sincerely sought shall be given, the blessing, if such it be, *must* be granted " He cannot deny Himself" says S. Paul. No more—to this bears all Scripture witness—can He deny His Son or His name. To it all nature bows and all Heaven surrenders up—I had almost said at our will— its glory and its treasures. Well might David say " They that know Thy Name will put their trust in Thee." Thus he prays himself " Do Thou for me, O God the Lord for Thy names sake." Thus it is written in another Psalm " Help us, O God of our salvation, for the glory of Thy Name: and deliver us, and purge away our sins for Thy Name's sake."

Thus it is in the very prayer of which the petition in the text is a part "Do Thou it for Thy Name's sake." And thus the Church of God in every age with unfailing success has come before Him in the Name of Christ.

> Jesus! name of wondrous love!
> Name all other names above!
> Pleading only this we flee,
> Helpless, O our God to thee.

But through Him we have access with confidence to the Father. And the virtue of that Name is exhaustless and untold.

> For in this hour of glory now
> That precious name is given,
> Above all names to deck His brow,
> And at the name of Jesus bow
> The powers and thrones of Heaven.

THE FRIEND'S WELCOME INTO EVERLASTING HABITATIONS.

I say unto you make to yourselves friends, that may receive you into everlasting habitations. *Luke* xvi. 9.

Our Lord concludes His parable of the unjust steward with four reflections that are, if I may say so with due reverence, highly original. The tale being told He appends to it as it were four morals. The first is to put earthly possessions and temporal advantages to such a use that we may find them turn to our account when stripped of all we enter the life beyond the present. The second is the importance in the eyes of heaven of the lesser, and too often unconsidered duties of life; and the obligation to be attentive to and careful about them which we are apt to overlook. The third is that it is a principle of the Divine Providence in bestowing spiritual gifts, to regulate the granting of them on the scale of our comparative faithfulness in improving and putting to the best account the worldly blessings with which we may naturally be gifted. And the fourth is the impossibility of concentring a supreme affection, and devoting an unrivalled and uncompromising attention to two persons or objects at the same time. They are all great truths and worthy of particular study and full enforcement. But I do not purpose to address myself to the consideration of any of them here. But from the words in which the first of these is set forth, I shall take occasion to urge a lesson which they do not indeed directly signify, but which as might be accurately argued they imply and suggest. I omit the words in the text, "the mammon of unrighteousness," because they restrict to the immediate subject our Lord was speaking of the figurative thought of how we may so manage in this life, as to secure ourselves a welcome in the future. And this commandment like all God's others is "exceeding broad." And the spirit reaches far beyond the letter. With a view to grasp this therefore, I would lead you beyond the occasion, and direct you to consider how in actual fact we may now be providing for ourselves a welcome presently from intelligent beings that have preceded us into the heavenly habitations, "Make to yourselves friends that may receive you into everlasting habitations."

Many are the purposes that different persons have in view, in the seeking of friends. Those who wish only to be amused court the companionship of the witty and the gay, "They have their reward." Such companionship is sparkling, lively and pleasurable. But it is sooner or later felt to be very unsatisfying, and it is for the most part very short lived. Those who have an eye to worldly advantage seek the society of the wealthy. Those who would add to their credit in the eyes of their neighbours strive to attach themselves to the influential and honoured, and boast perhaps of connection with the titled. While those who regard chiefly their own mental or moral improvement think but little of such showy accomplishments or accidental greatness. They are attracted rather by solid merit, and the hidden worth which they have had the penetration to discover, and the sense to admire it may be in some by no means promising exterior, and they have "a *full* reward;" And for such a friendship is likely to be as lasting as it is well grounded. One special and very important purpose to be set before our eyes in the seeking and selection of friends is propoun led here. It is one which is not elsewhere in the Bible directly mentioned, and no where, that I know of, enlarged upon in any other book.

The Lord of life, who holds the keys of death, looks on in the text to that solemn and lonely moment when the creature of His Hand shall be stepping in his last hour from this crowded life to the vaster throng out there! He anticipates what must needs be the shrinking of the soul, the nature of which He, as its Author, knows so well, as it enters the strange assembly the innumerable departed. And He suggests with a wondrous and tender consideration a remedy for what must otherwise be an experience of awful and oppressive loneliness.

> When all is silent, sorrowful, and still,
> And there o'ertakes the heart that sickening chill,
> Felt by the spirit when it stands alone,
> Amid the strangeness of a place unknown.

He bids us, with a view to meet the emergencies of *that* hour, make to ourselves *now* friends who may then be at heaven's threshold to receive us into the abodes of the blessed.

Aye, and we shall surely need some such reassuring presence then. We may have sufficient natural assurance, or we may have succeeded in schooling ourselves into the confidence, to be able to stand with no signs of embarassment before an august company. We may be able to abide with fixed eye and unabashed manner the scrutiny of strange faces, even unkindly and critical. But who may hope to lift his head undismayed and meet for the first time the piercing gaze of the armies of heaven? Who would not wish, as he is ushered by death in a moment into the midst of the holy ones, to catch—as he lifts his eyes on that world and the beings that throng its fields—to catch, I say, at the very first the glance of recognition from some that on earth he knew and loved? Who would not feel a sense of protection and confidence could he reach forth, as it were, his hand, and place his arm within some welcoming grasp, and enter with *human* introduction the High Court of Heaven?

And therefore it was that, knowing what was in man in reference to this coming hour, the Lord in a thoughtful foresight exclaimed, " I say unto you, make to yourselves friends that may receive you into everlasting habitations."

The text, as you will presently see, does not lead me to dwell at all particularly on communion with the living. At the same time I cannot but observe, in passing, what a very suggestive principle we have in it for our guidance in the cultivation of those intimacies to which, as social beings, we are intended, and therefore prone from our earliest years, " Make to yourselves friends that may receive you into everlasting habitations." Friends of such a character, that we may feel instinctively that if they precede us we cannot fail to find them when we have completed our Christian voyage, on the further shore, or that if we are called first to the haven where we would be, no doubt can cloud our confidence that they will surely persevere to follow on. Oh! if we regulated the formation of our earthly attachments on such a principle, and so decided as to the admission into close companionship of our common acquaintances, what disappointment should we not escape in finding our trust misplaced and our associates unworthy. And what strong and sufficient consolation should we secure for ourselves against the changes and chances of this life that so often interrupt and sever the ties of earth.

But it is not only from among the living, but even more particularly of the departed that we may consider ourselves as here bidden to make friends who may receive us by and by, and give us the welcome of Brothers and Sisters, and Fathers in Christ into the home of the blessed. Circumstances may hinder many, and must far the most of us from making such friends from among the eminent of God's living saints. It might be easy for a king on the throne of David to say "I am a companion of all them that fear God." It might be easy for Obadiah, the first in the count of Ahab, to court as he did his fifties of friends from among the prophets of God. And it may be easy for those high in position, and set on the commanding heights of social observation, to number on their list of friends the foremost of the religious champions of the age, to rejoice in the knowledge of those eminent for their piety and distinguished for their spiritual gifts.

But to say to us, make to yourselves friends of such may seem a mockery: for where are they to be found? We are not thrown in such a circle, nor have we the time nor the influence to push ourselves into the charmed company. It is so, doubtless. But yet does the voice of our Lord speak to us all the same, and address us personally as it lays this strange injunction upon us about making such friends, "I say it unto you." And here, mark me, is the secret of this apparent impossibility. From the *living* it may be impossible to seek such. But from the *departed* it is not.

Indeed you may ponder the lives and read the words (which "they being dead, yet speak,") of the heroes of the Bible. And with a wondrous facility you may make these friends of God your own. Brothers once in your conflict, kinsmen still according to the spirit, partners of your spiritual life with its hopes and joys, the sympathy and affection of those blessed ones beyond is far more readily accorded, and far more completely won than of our Brothers and Sisters in Christ who are still in the flesh. The one have their own pursuits and thoughts in life to occupy them. The others have already finished *their* course, and have leisure to look on at *ours*.

Can I doubt that they do look on ?—

> They whose course on earth is o'er,
> Think they of their brethren more ?
> They before the throne who bow,
> Feel they for their brethren now ?
> We by enemies distrest,
> They in Paradise at rest,
>   We the captives—they the freed,
>   We and they are one indeed.
>
> One in all we seek or shun,
> One—because our Lord is one :
>   One in heart and one in love,
>   We below, and they above.

And with what absorbing interest do they not, must they not, so look on. For *our* present struggle was once *theirs*.

> Once they were mourning here below
>   With penitential tears :
> They wrestled hard, as we do now,
>   With sins, and doubts, and fears.

"Who are these that are arrayed in white robes, and whence came they ?" And the answer is—

> These are they whose hearts were riven,
>   Sore with woe and anguish tried,
> Who in prayer full oft have striven
>   With the God they glorified
>   Now their painful conflict o'er,
>   God has bid them weep no more.

The parent or grand parent lives over his days again, and we all, more or less, go back to the days of our childhood, as we watch the mirth of the sportive child. So must they, but with infinitely keener interest, look on at our spiritual life. Assert it who may, with the unbelief of Solomon in his dark days of scepticism, "The dead know not anything, neither have they any more a portion in anything that is done under the sun," we hold by the teaching of the "greater than Solomon," who "hath brought life and immortality to light through the Gospel," that "He hath abolished death," and that "He that believeth on Him shall never die,"—"shall not see death "—but only pass into a higher, and more perfect, and more observant life.

We believe, and our belief rises into assurance as we study the concluding Revelation of the Bible, that we are compassed about in our spiritual course with a great cloud of sympathising and interested witnesses. And we are sure that we are the objects of *their* tenderest solicitude, as we are of the Angels, as Christ tells us, to whom "they are equal."

From the unseen world the arms of an expansive affection, such as exists only in that home of love, are outstretched to sustain and enfold our tried and doubtful spirits. And around the humblest disciple and servant of the Redeemer are waiting those who would welcome him into the everlasting habitations. I say unto you make yourselves friends of such ! Kneel with David as he chants the Psalms in God's house

below. Soar with S. John to the contemplation of the courts above.
Sit at the feet of S. Paul as he expounds to you the Gospel scheme.
Enter into the struggle of Daniel, as he held fast his faith and did not
deny his religion in the face of the lion's den, and the courtiers that
envied and hated him more savage than they. Renounce with Moses
the pleasures of sin and the satisfactions that come of the world alone.
Be brave and fearless with the martyred Baptist. Stand true by your
Master's cross with the noble women of Galilee. Keep and meditate
on the words of Jesus with the blessed mother of our Lord. Be not
ashamed of Him and His words. But unto the end be like the goodly
fellowship of the prophets, the glorious company of the Apostles, and
the noble army of Martyrs. And they are yours in heart and spirit for
ever; and will not fail to recognise you, the moment that death passes
you into their visible presence, and to receive you into everlasting habitations. There—where they

> Have met their other children who have gone
> Before them too—as other years roll on
> And their loved scholars go to them, their hand
> Again shall lead them gently to the Lamb,
> And bring them to the living waters there.

You can imagine what Abraham the father of his faith was to
Lazarus, when the Angels lifted the dying but rejoicing beggar from the
rich man's gate to set him by his side. And the same will these great
pillars of the Church be then to those who have walked in their shadow
and leaned for support on these massive corner stones of God's earthly
temple; " I say unto you make yourselves friends " of such.

Make them your friends by considering their faith and patience;
by imitating the devotedness, the singleness of aim with which they
sought the glory of their Lord; the humility, the forbearance, the self-
forgetfulness with which they bore themselves before their fellow men.
And you shall never miss the certain consequence of being received by
them into everlasting habitations. For at the gate of Heaven you shall
find that they know you even as you are known. They will be there
with a perfect understanding of all you are, and all you have gone
through. Aye, and you shall know them as perfectly as they know you
as fellow travellers on the same road, fellow companions in the same
work. And they shall beckon you forward with the invitation that
was the dearest any earthly friend could utter, as the Psalmist tells us
how glad *he* ever was to hear it, " Let us go into the house of the Lord."

And if it shall be so with those even that Christian believers never
knew in the flesh—strangers that lived in other times and in other
lands—how much more with those who were literally fellow worshippers
and fellow travellers on earth, and fellow heirs of the same salvation! Those that have bowed with you before the same Throne of
grace, listened with you at the same time and place to the same ambas-
sador of Heaven, gathered with you, and the priest that stood to minister
to you in holy things, before the altar of the living God, and eaten and
drank together of the bread and wine of salvation.—Oh let us be only

each one faithful unto death—and how blessed shall then be our reunion in the kingdom of our Father!

Whichever of us be the first to be there let us be prepared to greet the others as they follow one by one into the kingdom of life. And you, me; or I, you, or either and whichever of us it be, let us be the first of all Heaven's company to meet again the fellow worshipper we have been wont to see with us in the sanctuary below, to meet him or her with our reassuring presence, and to "lead the redeemed to the Throne."

THE MINISTRY OF ANGELS.

Take heed that ye despise not one of these little ones; for I say unto you that in heaven their Angels do always behold the face of my Father which is in heaven.
Matthew xviii 10.

"He that despiseth his neighbour," saith the wise man, "sinneth." And alas! it is a common sin. The foolish of the world, and the weak of the world, and the base of the world, the Apostle testifies *are* despised. And we are verily guilty—we all of us have been, we are all continually disposed to be—of this same sin. Did you never stand in the festive throng and see how the shy, the awkward, the unattractive, are neglected, and how the more fascinating and graceful become the centre of admiration? Have you never marked how the conversationally gifted, the beautiful or the accomplished are sought out in society? Have you never gone the way of the unthinking multitude, and as S. James asks, "become partial in yourselves"? Did you never feel the blush of a false shame rising to your cheek as you were found in the company of a poor relative, or humble acquaintance? Were you never conscious of a lowering of your self importance and the working of a miserable vanity, when you have had in the way of duty or kindness to cast in your lot, it might have been only for a brief passing along a thoroughfare, with a mean man, or an ill dressed woman? Did you never feel the rising of impatience at the untimely meeting with such, of which that great expounder of practical life, the Apostle James, accuses the Christians of his day, " If there come unto you a poor man in vile raiment, and ye say Stand thou there or sit here under my footstool"?

"Condescend to men of low estate." I have read the great classic books of philosophy, but I do not know the teacher among them all who gave utterance to a sentiment like this. And I do not know the teacher, save our Lord, that illustrated it in such a practical fashion that he gained in consequence the title of "Friend of publicans and sinners" from those that *did* despise the little, and weak, and base in the eyes of the world.

By the word little ones in the text there is no exclusive, though there appears from the whole passage a first, reference to children. In the text there is first a caution given, and then a doctrine taught.

As regards the caution, we have seen conscience convicts us of its necessity. We have all known what it is at the least to overlook, if not to treat with manifest disdain, the little ones of the world, the poor, the weak, the ignorant, the mean, the small and of no reputation, those of no consequence, as in our arrogance we might deem them. Their Maker only knows of what consequence they are. The Lord has need of them with their poor abilities, their humble capacities, their ignoble surroundings. He shows it by placing them and continuing them there. And what for his own ends in life the Lord has need of let us treat with reverence as His. "Honour all men" says the Apostle. And he learnt his lesson, he might have done so, here. Take we heed therefore that we are guilty no more of the pride of disdain. For what says the Apostle have we that we have not received. Never let us dwell or linger in thought over the imperfections or the failings with which another has been visited. But let everyone see that not in a mere assumption of generosity, but in real lowliness of mind we each esteem other better than ourselves. Avoid we ever carefully the half involuntary smile of contempt, that we have so often given way to, that has indicated our disdainful notice of the confusion of another. Let us not think this or anything too trifling for our care if we would listen with obedient ear to the caution of the text. Take heed that ye despise not one of God's little, insignificant, ungifted creatures.

To come to the doctrine taught in the text, it is unmistakably that of the ministry of Angels. It is a very valuable doctrine, though one undoubtedly too little heeded. The Sadducees, S. Luke tells us denied that there were Angels at all. And there is a kind of Sadducean spirit, I am sorry to say, quite as much in the Church as in the world, which though it does not deny their existence, holds practically that we are little concerned with those glorious beings. Let us then consider this revealed fact of the ministry of the Angels, a fact to which the New Testament gives quite as much prominence as the Old. In doing so let us resolve to know nothing of that unworthy faltering, with which some seek rather to evade than to recognise the teaching of Holy Scripture on the subject. The Spirit speaks with no uncertain sound, nor will we. To His mind the glory of the Incarnate and Risen Lord eclipses not that of His Ministering Angels. And it never shall to ours. A late preacher of our Church (J. M. Bellew) has well said "In our repugnance to the Romish doctrine of the worship of Angels, Protestants have generally surrendered to that Church all regard for an agency which is evidenced continually throughout the Scriptures, which operated on Christ—

On earth by bitter sorrows weighed
He did not scorn His Angel's aid,—

and is spoken of by Himself. I need not remind you how commonly throughout Scripture Angels are made the messengers of God proclaiming His will to man. I need not tell you how they announced the coming of Christ; how they watched over Him when He was a young child, how they came and ministered to Him after the temptation; how they were present with Him at His Transfiguration; and how they had charge over His tomb, and were the first preachers of the Resurrection."

And so the text tells us that our Saviour in His compassion for the innocence and dependence of children, for they are first spoken of, and then of all that are "little," devoid of the good things of this world, the friendless, the unprotected, the poor, the oppressed, the victims of slander and wrong, the sick and the dying, has made for them a special provision.. The want of human patronage, the deficiency in advantages, which the wiser and the stronger have, calls forth the especially mindful regard and protection of their Maker. For indeed a wonderful principle of *compensation* underlies all nature. Whom others forsake the Lord taketh up, as was the Psalmist's experience. And over such He gives His Angels special charge, to keep them in all their ways. And these deputed Angels stand before the face of God. They are peculiarly and immediately in His presence. And He watches and aids *them* as they watch and aid the simple and the helpless. Well may our Saviour say take heed what ye do to these or how ye treat them. For there be mightier than they where you see the weak and defenceless only. And the Lord will avenge their cause, and spoil the soul of those that have spoiled or injured them.

We often hear—alas! the admonition of their presence cannot be too often spoken—of the devil and his angels lying in wait to ensnare and destroy the souls of men. Let us hear with equal clearness the counterpart of the doctrine. Let us have the full benefit of the consolations of Scripture about the Angels of light—Michael and His Angels who fight against the devil, while he does against us—For " are they not all " saith the Spirit.—Are they not, he says, as though knowing full well how in days like ours the truth would be overlooked and lightly dwelt upon.—Are they not he challenges (and who among those that keep back this truth of God, dare meet the challenge with the negative which we think some would willingly do) " Are they not all "—it is a bold statement—ministering spirits sent forth to minister unto the heirs of salvation. " Lord we believe! help thou our unbelief." All the heirs of salvation therefore share their protection. But the little ones of God the timid, the poor, the humble, the ill used, the especially dependent, have Angels that always behold the Father's face, that especially represent Him, and are deputed by Him to watch them as objects of His especial care.

If we have such need to beware that we despise not the *little ones of mankind* those that are little among them, " for that the Lord is the Avenger of all such," how much more reason have we to look to it that we despise not the *little ones of Christ.* The fact that Angels are appointed to confer great services upon Christ's disciples is here revealed ; and we learn from it the honour He sets upon His servants. And first you will observe He calls them little ones. It was a term of endearment which the loving Saviour was accustomed to apply to His disciples " Whoever " says He of them " shall give to drink unto one of these little ones a cup of cold water, only in the name of a disciple, verily I say unto you he shall in no wise lose his reward." He frequently called or referred to them as children. While by the prophet Zechariah in his description of what should happen to these very disciples, when their Master should be betrayed and they compelled to flee, the very expression is used, " I will smite the Shepherd and turn my hand against the little ones, and the sheep shall be scattered." And apart from its use as a term of endearment the description is very appropriate of the professors of Christ's religion, believers in Him. He had just been teaching His disciples that instead of thinking and contriving and ever considering, as you will see they had been doing, how they might be the greatest, and which should be, they must if they would enter the kingdom of heaven cultivate the very opposite temper. They had forgotten (how often do we so) the lesson with which he had begun His ministry, " Blessed are the poor in spirit, for theirs is the kindgom of heaven." And instead of learning of and imitating Him who was meek and lowly in heart, who humbled and made Himself of no reputation, they contended who was greatest. He therefore set a little child in the midst of them by way of example, and declared the blessedness of those who were little in their own sight, like little children. Whoso He says receiveth one such disciple, humble and unambitious like this child, receiveth me. And then He gives a solemn warning against treating lightly his disciples who thus think little of themselves. As though He would say, But let none disparage or slight those who maintain their unassuming deportment that I have bid them show, who refrain from self assertion to which the world is prone. They admit, and are to do, and cannot but do so, their own unworthiness. But they are in My sight of great price. They are little in their own eyes, but great in the kingdom of Heaven. So great that they have Angels who excel in power and might to wait upon them. Those exalted beings that wait my Father's bidding, and " do His pleasure, hearkening to the voice of His word," wait on them too, watch them in their every trial, and minister to their every need.

The Psalmist dwells on this most prominent and inspiriting fact of Revelation "the Angel of the Lord encampeth round about them that fear Him, and delivereth them." S. Paul re-asserted it in his Epistle to that same Hebrew nation, whose history had furnished so many signal instances of Angelic interposition, in the before quoted words, " Are they not all ministering spirits sent forth to minister for them who shall be heirs of salvation." And now the Lord, who though all sufficient in Himself was thus ministered to, stamps it emphatically in this exquisite and touching scene. He sets His hand upon the little child, the symbol of human helplessness and dependance, in the midst of the encircling and attentive throng. He would impress the world most forcibly with a token of assurance how dear to God were His chosen people, how precious in His sight were those base ones of the world, and those in its judgment to be despised, whom it should misuse and neglect as it did their Great Master. And so He broke out into the sublime exclamation of the text, Take heed that ye despise not one of these little ones, these humble ones that believe in me, for God has chosen the mean and foolish things in the world's estimation. And I say unto you that in Heaven they are very differently accounted of. In Heaven when true judgment is given and human characters are weighed in an even balance, they have messengers commissioned to attend upon them from the court of the King of kings. And I tell you furthermore those Angels are accounted worthy for their high office and their important charge of a place nearest to the everlasting Throne. And from time to time as they come to present themselves for fresh instructions or to give an account of the way in which they have exeuted thier high commands they are admitted into the forefront of their fellow Angels in heaven. And while ten thousand times ten thousand stand before Him, as one after another of these ministering spirits wing back their way from earth, they take the precedence of all the rest, A voice is heard, or unheard is felt and obeyed, which for a moment hushes the songs of cherubim and seraphim, that round Him continually do cry. And the ranks of the bright host fall back as they see their brother Angel advancing and gladly recognise the order of Heaven, Give this one place. And, if I may so say, the Divine worship above is interrupted while the Father of heaven enquires and the ministering spirits report concerning His dear children on earth. "Such honour have all his saints!" And perhaps no description however laboured of the estimation in which his humble confiding disciples are held could approach the sublime expressiveness of our Lord's revelation in the text, that ever nearest to the Throne there in their freedom of access are those who are appointed over God's household here, to aid in the work of Redemption and Sanctification in bringing His many sons unto glory.

> 'Tis sweet to think of Him whose Hand
> Caressed the infant race,
> What time with voice Divinely bland,
> He spake these words of grace,
> My children s Angels always stand
> Before my Father's face.

Two remarks are suggested by these words of the text. The first that Jesus evidently anticipated that His humble unworldly ones would be subjected to the world's comtempt. It was in the very nature of things they should. " As long as thou doest well to thyself" the wisest of men has remarked "all men will speak well of thee."

A persistent course of self assertion is sometimes strangely successful. Simon of Samaria gave himself out to be some great one till all in the city were unanimous in declaring " This man is the great power of God." Simon has his followers everywhere. And few of us perhaps have not observed how some persons by putting themselves forward —with no talent to recommend them—have come to ingratiate themselves most successfully with others, and get claims to which they had no title recognised. And on the other hand we all see how the humble and unambitious are liable to be overlooked; how those who ask for nothing are supposed to want nothing; how the meek and retiring are often slighted ; and how people are often valued or undervalued according as they seem to think much or little of themselves. And so our Lord, who knew what was in men, knew how His disciples would come to be treated ; how scornfully the world of the ungodly would be apt to look upon them. Thus in the Apocryphal book of the wisdom of Solomon, we have its confession at the last of its grand and fatal mistake in all along undervaluing the lowly disciple of the Lord.

" And they repenting and groaning for anguish of spirit shall say within themselves. This was He whom we had sometime in derision, and a proverb of reproach. We fools accounted his life madness and

His end to be without honour! How is he numbered among the children of God, and his lot is among the saints."

And so it was in the very same breath, as it were, in which He bade His disciples "walk in lowliness and meekness and humbleness of mind," He sternly warned all others not to take them at their own estimation, but rather at that of Him who would bestow on them the more abundant honour. Thus he turned round abruptly on those who would be only too glad to see His disciples made little of, and humbled to the very dust, and charged them solemnly "Take heed that ye despise not one of these little ones; for I say unto you that in Heaven their Angels do always behold the face of my Father, which is in Heaven."

And how has this our Lord's anticipation of His disciples treatment been verified, but how little has the accompanying warning been heeded! In nothing does the spirit of the world more constantly show itself than in this tendency to treat or speak contemptuously of the humble conscientious Christian. You can hardly take up a newspaper or magazine which that spirit of the world is known to pervade, but you meet with some sneering attempt of this kind; some hit at their views and principles and behaviour; some unworthy or malicious exaggeration of their feelings; some of their doings held up to ridicule; some cold contempt poured upon their profession. Let the children of Ishmael however mock as they will for "as then, he that was born after the flesh persecuted him that was born after the spirit, even so it is now." But take heed that ye despise not the children of the Redeemer—be their inconsistencies and failings what they may. For—while it were better for such a one that a millstone were hanged about his neck, and be drowned in the depth of the sea, than that he should incur the wrath of their Master, and feel the weight of the power of these Angelic defenders—" I say unto you that in Heaven their Angels do always behold the face of the Father."

The second remark is for the encouraging of Christ's little ones. It is a desire natural to us all—and it was the very principle that led to the unseemly strife our Lord was here reproving—to seek and to value the notice and regard of others. But, while he checked the indulgence of it in the way of the world's vain glory, He allowed, yea, even fostered it in His disciples by the promise implied in the text of the attention and notice of God and His Holy Angels. As though he had said, Did they desire to be honoured, would they wish to be attended on, to be ministered to? There were higher than they from whom they were seeking it. Learn to be lowly, contented, not greatly anxious about the advantages of this world. And you shall not be undistinguished. The world may in its folly despise and cast out your names as evil. " But I say unto you that in Heaven their Angels do always behold the face of the Father." By such a prospect as this we would stir you up to consider the high calling and dignity of the Christian. The desire of the approval of those we think greater or better than ourselves is natural to us all. It is implanted by God in order to ead us to excel, to add to our attainments, to become worthier and better. We are not indifferent to the passing recognition in the street, to the salutation in the market place. And well pleasing to us all is the more marked token of our superior's favour. What think you then of the unremitted attentions of the unseen but glorious inhabitants of the world of light?

Poor, unknown, and sharing but little of the interest of the great and the distinguished you may be, a stranger youth or friendless maiden. No familiar face may smile upon you, or voice greet you, as you go to and fro to your unheeded work, unknown or forgotten But I say unto you that with eager interest and affectionate care the Angels of the Lord watch round you. To succour and keep you from falling, to obtain and bring you grace to help in every time of need, they come and go perpetually through the midst of the company that gather around your Father's Throne. Free way is made for them as for His special-messengers, when they come to present your case, and tell your needs. Yea, so honoured are they as your representatives and charged with your interests that to them is vouchsafed a readiness of audience that no earthly sovereign would extend to any subject at all. They have unchallenged entrance into the august presence of the most High King. They have the right of constant converse with Him who is otherwise, and except and upon the concerns of His children, the Great Unapproachable.

They can come and stand unbidden, to quote an illustration from the book of Esther, before His awful Throne with even such a certainty of hearing as is accorded to the Son Himself, our Great Intercessor. And to sum up the meaning of this wondrous passage they can at all times on your account—if I may use so bold an expression in the sense in which an important communication is said to command for itself a hearing—*command* the attention of the very Lord of Heaven.

The use, the practical effect on our lives, which this revealed fact of the presence of Angels among us—interested in our doings and struggles, and watchfully observant of us at all times—should exercise, is too obvious to need enforcing. You know the effect produced upon us all by feeling ourselves in the presence or under the notice of our superiors or friends, or those with whom we would stand well. What restraint it imposes on our demeanour! What guardedness in our words! What carefulness in our actions, lest we should displease or offend!

Seeing then that we are compassed about with so great a cloud of witnesses as the blessed and holy Angels that are appointed to super intend us and minister to us, and report to our Father above, our actions and our needs. Seeing that they are about our path and bed and al our ways, encamping round our souls—as in the Scripture phrase— like an investing army round a city to which all going out and coming in is known—" What manner of persons ought we to be in all holy conver sation and godliness."

O God the Son eternal, Thy dread might
Sent forth Saint Michael and the hosts of heaven,
   And from the realms of light
   Cast down in burning fight
Satan's rebellious hosts to darkness given.

Thine Angels. Lord, we sing with thankful lays,
Dwelling with Thee above yon depths of sky;
   Who 'mid Thy glory's blaze,
   Heaven's ceaseless anthems raise,
And gird Thy Throne in faithful ministry.

We celebrate their love, whose viewless wing
Hath left for us so oft their mansion high,
   The mercies of their King
   To mortal saints to bring,
Or guard the couch of slumbering infancy.

But Thee, the first and last we glorify,
Who when Thy world was sunk in death and sin
   Not with Thine hierarchy,
   The armies of the sky,
But didst with Thine own arm the battle win.   DRUMMOND.

THE CALL AND OBEDIENCE OF S. ANDREW.

Matthew iv. 18-22

In the book of Revelation the Church of Christ is compared to a Woman, and the twelve Apostles to a crown of twelve stars encircling her head. In these twelve Stars there is a like difference in glory, to what we observe in the Stars of the firmament. Some appear of greater and some of lesser magnitude: not perhaps because they are really so, but because of their relative position to us. They are, as it were, nearer to us. Of some of the Apostles we have heard so much, and thought so often, that the very mention of their names seems to call up before us their life-like image. We feel about them as we do with regard to their Lord and ours with whose Name, " Blessed over all," their own is so closely linked in the Gospel history. We feel as though we almost knew them personally, as though if were to meet them again in the flesh we could instantly recognise them.

But to several of the Apostles we seem almost strangers. We see them hardly more distinctly than shadowy forms, that our fancy has never been roused to clothe with an idiosyncrasy of their own. Their memorial has to a great extent perished with them, or survives only in some vague, and as we cannot but feel not very trustworthy traditions. Of many of these " pillars of the Church," wherever the Gospel is preached throughout the whole world, there also what they have said and done in the cause of it is told for a memorial of them, to the praise of the glory of their Master's grace. But of others there is very little known and recorded. Of what persecutions they endured, what miracles they wrought, what particular testimony they bore to the religion for which they lived, and for which they most of them probably died, we have no certain knowledge. Some " being dead yet speak." We may hear their words, may consider their faith, and follow their patience, at least in many instances and sometimes in very full detail. But of one and another of that blessed brotherhood we are forced regretfully to exclaim. " Thy faithfulness is hid from us in destruction : thy wondrous works are unknown in the dark ; and thy righteousness is in the land of forgetfulness."

And it may excite surprise in some minds that these should be alike included in the number of those to whom the Holy Church throughout all the world has devoted a day of separate and especial remembrance. Now we might indeed reply that the simple fact of their being of the number of the twelve, gives each a claim to be accounted worthy of the smae commemoration. For each member of " the glorious company of the Apostles," excepting of course "the son of perdition" is and must be in virtue of his being selected for the companionship of our Lord's incarnate life, one upon whom every subsequent disciple will or ought to feel drawn, to concentre his earnest interest and contemplation.

But the Church as I cannot but think has a further answer than this to give to the enquiry why she has delighted as much to honour the comparatively obscure names of S. Andrew, and Matthew, and Simon, and Bartholomew, as the more renowned and famous characters of Peter and James, and Jude, and John. In this wise provision I believe she would have us know—and very beautifully is the lesson thus suggested—that the Christian life which from the circumstances of Providence is spent rather before the Father *in secret* may be as real, as acceptable as that which in consequence of higher natural endowments, or a wider sphere of influence is rather exhibited before men *openly*. In that state of life to which it has pleased Him to call us who appoints the bounds of our habitation, and determines beforehand the outward complexion of our life, we are to learn and labour, to serve our God and generation truly. All are not disciples like those whom we should deem the chief Apostles. All are not fitted to take rank with them in the forefront of the armies of the Cross. But "let the brother of low degree," the humble Christian who pursues an obscure path in life, following as it were in the shade of the great pillars of the Church around him, contemplate the case of his Brother S. Andrew.

For life is not with all—it is not with the most of us—a round of exciting incidents and stirring adventures : but rather of simple duties and little things. And so it may seem a very unimportant and a very general lesson that the Church has gathered from the consideration of the life of this Holy Apostle, when it merely mentions in the collect his ready obedience to His Master's call, and his immediate and unreserved surrender of himself to follow and to serve ; and calls us in such wise to imitate him. But it is the very teaching which can alone make known to the common average of men, what the Lord who has called them like S. Andrew "to the knowledge of His grace, and to faith in Him " requires of them.

When the Apostles enquiry arises in the awakened hearts of such " Lord what wouldest Thou have me to do," it is not the answer that was given to *him* betokening special functions and extraordinary labours that can be returned to all. We can give no *special* charges, nor point to any *singular* work to which the plain man that would be a disciple of Christ must henceforth address himself.

And yet indeed we quite believe that if he were bidden do some great thing when he comes saying " what must I do to be saved," like the roused hearers of John the Baptist, the convicted murderers of Christ before the Apostles on the day of Pentecost, or the trembling jailor before Paul and Silas at Philippi—he would be much better satisfied. Perhaps a soul is never awakened from the sleep of sin, to serious reflection and religious thoughtfulness, but its earliest craving finds true expression in the spirit of the young Ruler in the Gospel, " What *good* thing shall I do that I may have eternal life." It may be in a measure at first disappointing but, like her Lord, the Church has but one answer to give, to all such as come with the desire and vow of discipleship. " Thou knowest what is written in the law keep the commandments." We find this very noticably in the Sacramental and Confirmation Offices. We have it presented to us very unmistakably in the Collect for this day's festival.

We may even be of opinion that in the Scripture notices of the life of S. Andrew, brief as they are, for as I have hinted he was not " mighty in words or in deeds," there are more striking points that might be made profitable for our instruction in righteousness. We might for example have been called to dwell on his immediate care to bring his brother to Christ, or his joint enquiry with him and the Sons of Zebedee " Tell us when shall these things be," We might remark too on the thought he showed about the solemn future, about which we are ever too indifferent, and the interest he therein evinced on the subject of prophecy and the future of Christ's kingdom. And in this we may well take example by him : for it is the very subject to which our attention is required, and should be given at the Advent season, when this Festival occurs.

We might mention the incident related about him in the Gospel, for the last Sunday after Trinity which is read at this same season, and draw suitable lessons from this appropriate introduction of his name, and significant hint as to his character. But the Church's wisdom will nevertheless be justified of all her children for having given the prominent place that we see here assigned to the readiness of S. Andrew's obedience and his simple following of his Master without questioning or gainsaying.

It is true this readiness was not peculiar to S. Andrew, but evinced in the very same way by three other of the Apostles on the same occasion, as we see from the text And so this temper marks every earnest Christian. Ever as the call of Christ through His Spirit or His Word is heard, it is responded to in the words of the Psalmist, " I made haste and delayed not to keep Thy commandments ; " or of S. Paul when he said in relating his call to the Apostleship, " Whereupon I was not disobedient unto the Heavenly vision."

Why then you may ask if this be so general a feature of Christian character, is it that S. Andrew's obedience and ready discipleship is selected above that of the other three, who seem in the text, the Gospel for the day, equally conspicuous for the exercise of this grace ? And my own answer would be this. In the case of this Apostle we have a record, independent of the text, in the Gospel by S. John, which sets him before us as signally illustrating this self same grace. We have in John, c. i. verses 35-40, an instance of his renunciation for Christ sometime before, which parallels the case before us. S. Andrew left John the Baptist to follow Jesus. Now all Ecclesiastical history, and every-day observation, as well as all Scripture, testify alike directly and indirectly to the strength of the tie that the connection between a disciple and a spiritual pastor or teacher, worthy of veneration, is wont to create. And to John the Baptist the greatest of all human prophets and their father in the faith *his* disciples seem to have been devotedly and jealously attached. It was no slight renunciation then, no easy sacrifice for the blessed Apostle, as far as human predilections were concerned, when at a moment's notice he left John, and that for ever, to follow Jesus. It was no little trial of his faith and sincerity, as one who professed to be looking for the promised Messiah, when as soon as Jesus of Nazareth was pointed out to him by his Master John—as he was walking with him—he left so abruptly his spiritual Guide, for one who to him was as yet personally a stranger. It seems to me then there is more than a coincidence, there is an evident design, in the selection of S. Andrew, to illustrate the grace which so peculiarly characterised him. And well I think may the commemoration of this Apostle stand first as it does, in the Church's calendar in the catalogue of the blessed. For verily we have not found so great or so early an instance of faith and of that particular grace, which he is deservedly chosen to set forth by his example, among the twelve Apostles of the Lamb. Like the law to S. Paul, so was John to S. Andrew, his school master to bring him to Christ. And, "when that which was perfect was come that which was in part," whose aid was temporary, he was willing to give up. The first of all to comply with the Baptist's summons to "behold the Lamb of God." S. Andrew seems to have anticipated by his behaviour then his Lord's after teaching, and to have instinctively grasped the lesson which the prejudices of early training make sometimes so hard, " Call no man your Master on earth for one is your Master, even Christ."

Let us set *ourselves* to learn that lesson. We live in times when we have need to do so, to imitate S. Andrew in his independence of human teaching, though commended to us by early prejudice and strong prepossessions, but to imitate him withal in an implicit and self-renouncing obedience to the unchanging faith and the Great Lord of our religion. Very valuable to us then is his example, and very worthy of imitation his simple Christian character. The gifts of S. Andrew may have been lowly, but his obedience was grand ; his life may have been obscure, but his faith was illustrious. And as we set out on the fresh stage of our Christian life with the recurring Advent season which this Festival heralds, we may all find a pattern in him.

He did not as far as it appears rise above the level of his fellow disciples, nor is he remarkable among them for any superior gifts ; as we do not perhaps rise above the level of the society in which we move, or expect to be distinguished in it. He was simply a straight forward earnest Christian as any one of us may be, who, as the Collect for the day says, " being called by God's Holy Word forthwith give ourselves up obediently to fulfill his holy commandments," and to aim at securing that will of God it reveals concerning us which is our sanctification. He simply strove, as we may hourly strive in our humble life and little duties, to please Christ well in all things. He did so though surrounded by disobedient and Christless neighbours amid whom with his fellow citizens Peter and Philip, he was " faithful alone among the faithless found " Bethsaida, we read, was the city of Andrew. And to this same city, as one before which His miracles had been wrought and His testimony borne in vain, the Lord who had visited it so often and laboured so earnestly protested, " Woe unto thee Bethsaida for if the mighty works which were done in you had been done in Tyre and Sidon, they would have repented long ago."

Be your position and circumstances in life what they may, if like S. Andrew steadfastly dutiful to the calls of Christ and His Word, you will be sure to find yourself encircled as it were with a Bethsaida, that whatever it may own, shows no such allegiance. Walk then so as you have him for an ensample in simplicity and godly sincerity. And " blameless and harmless the Sons of God without rebuke," if like S. Andrew without any marked reputation you shall shine nevertheless as lights in this careless and unbelieving world. And hereafter in that world where the service and faithfulness of the humble Christian can no longer be hid you may shine forth as the sun with this blessed Apostle in the kingdom of your Father.

NEARNESS TO CHRIST.

These are the two anointed ones that stand by the Lord of the whole earth.
Zechariah iv. 14.

This text may well serve as a motto for the subject we consider to-day (May 1), the united testimony. to the faith, of the two Apostles S. Philip and S. James. Why it is that their names have thus become associated in the Church's calendar, we do not know Whether it was that they suffered martyrdom at about the same time, or what other link bound them together in the affections and recollections of disciples of Christianity is by no means clear. But there is certainly one point in which these two anointed ones stand together by the Lord of the whole earth. And that is that they appear among the first in association with their Lord's life. S. Philip—though not actually called to be a disciple of Jesus till the day after S. Andrew (the first called of the Apostles)—followed Jesus with as instant a conviction and obedience. He had not, it would appear, the preparation which Andrew had undergone, who was previously a disciple of John the Baptist, and was by him commended to the guidance of Jesus. His name too stands closely with our Lord's as having maintained that position near Him which he had thus early taken. For he it was to whom application was made by the Greeks, who wished at the Feast to know and converse with Jesus. They judged that, for some reason or other which we cannot exactly specify, Philip would be the most likely medium through whom to obtain the desired introduction. He too stood so in the confidence of His Master that to him—and to see if his faith equalled his singular opportunities of acquiring it—the question about feeding the five thousand was first proposed.

And he it was that, presuming perhaps on his long acquaintance with Jesus, had the boldness to ask in the name of all the Apostles for a like clear revelation of the Father to themselves, to that which had been allowed them of the Son, " Lord show us the Father and it sufficeth us."

S. James, whose life and martyrdom we commemorate with that of S. Philip, is said in the New Testament to have been our Lord's brother. And so by relationship he literally " stood by the Lord of the whole earth." And these two anointed ones we name and think of to day together. The lesson of unity thus suggested comes forcibly after the story of S. Mark we dwell upon only a few days before. On the 25th of April we are reminded of the contention of S. Paul and S. Barnabas, of which S. Mark was the occasion. On the 1st of May we are called to meditate by example, as we were then by warning, on the blessedness of godly concord!

Then we saw the sin of disunion and its painful effects. To-day we learn from these two anointed ones "how good and pleasant a thing it is for brethren to dwell together in unity!" And the text leads us to the secret of that inestimable harmony the very bond of all virtue so comfortable to ourselves, so valuable to the edification of the Church, and all true useful work in it. It is as we stand—and only as we stand—by the Lord of the whole earth that we shall stand together. It is as we look at, as we are taught in the services of the preceding Festival of S. Mark, and "take Him for the Head even Christ, that the whole body of the Church fitly joined together and compacted by that which every joint supplieth maketh increase of the body unto the edifying of itself in love."

I shall say a few words therefore about standing by Christ. These two Apostles stood long and closely by their Lord. They watched His spirit, and they learned His aims. And *so* they became anointed ones fit for doing a great and a lasting work of which we ourselves, and all that we see around us of the present power, and glory, and mightiness of His kingdom upon earth, are in part witnesses and monuments. From them let us learn to stand closely by Him too! If we hope to do any real work upon earth, and to serve our generation well and truly, we must imitate them here.

And this surely is what above all else we long for.

> For what else is the single end,
> Of this life's mortal span,
> Except to glorify the God,
> Who for our sakes was man?

I presume it is your ambition—and it is a high and noble one—to "serve the Lord Christ." You are called, as the Apostles were, in your position in life, however insignificant it may seem, to minister to your Lord. As you think upon the blessedness which was theirs in waiting upon Jesus, in watching and accompanying Him, and in lending their efforts to advance His aims, you envy *their* position who stood in very fact by the Lord of the whole earth.

And yet, though He be not within the vision of sense, *we* stand by Him too. Though our bodily eyes may not gaze as yet on His glorious features, though our bodily ears may not drink the sweetness of His unrivalled words, though our bodily hands may not clasp His own, nor ours lean for support on His "everlasting arms," He is as close to us and as interested in us as ever He we was to and in them.

"Whom having not seen we love; in whom, though now we see Him not yet believing we rejoice!" And *ours* is even a higher blessedness than theirs who "saw and heard and handled Him." For among His last words was the assurance, "Blessed are they who have not seen and yet have believed." We who seem to ourselves so far from Him as we think of the centuries that have gone by since in the visible form of Man He sojourned upon this earth—we who are parted from Him by the veil which this flesh interposes—need truly this encouragement, which He so considerately gave. It is the very assurance we crave for.

> Let me but know that Thou dost truly hear,
> Let me but feel that Thou art truly near,
> Doubt will depart and every dread will flee,
> All will be well if I but stand with Thee.

But where, we ask, is our Lord? We have we know His representatives, His Ministers who speak His word and have learnt something of the spirit and the import of His life. And as we receive them He has Himself said we receive Him. And we know it is so, for we have found it. Their words have brought *Him* near to us. Their life represents His. Would only that it did so more closely! And as we accept their teaching and make it our own, and bring it to bear upon our daily life we feel that we have still Christ as a living power in the world. We place our children in their arms in Baptism. And we know that for all purposes of spiritual blessing it is just the same as though we placed them in the arms of Jesus. We receive from them the bread and wine of very communion with our Lord. And we know that He stands unseen at the Feast all the while, offering and imparting His body for our sustenance, and His blood for our cleansing.

We hear the echo of his Voice underlying the Sermon all through and inspiring all its high thoughts and faithful doctrine. The Benediction that at its close send us on our way to make a fresh start into the world again, to do better and live a more sober, righteous, and godly life, is His own last blessing of peace. He it is after all, and not the Minister who only represents Him by commission, that authorizes the union of man and wife, as He pronounces his sanction at the marriage altar. And His words they are of hope, and consolation, and sympathy that check the mourner's tears, as he weeps and trembles by the loved one's open grave.

We have the Lord Jesus thus, and are brought very near to Him in the Services of His Church. Wholly then and thoroughly yield your faith to this, which is the true and distinctive doctrine, the sum and substance of all Church teaching, that in and through its Ministers and Services, He is with us its members always even to the end. And the more you do so the more thankful and satisfied shall you become, in that which must ever be to you a certain trial, that you walk by faith and not by sight.

But this satisfaction rises higher yet in the light of our Lord's parting assurance, that rather " blessed are they who have not seen and yet have believed," than even Apostles of old who gazed on His features and walked by His side. And we will—we can—no longer envy the privileged ones that stood so long and so near the Lord of the whole earth, seeing that before Him we too are standing. We grudge not S. Philip his three years intimate association with Him, nor covet S. James' natural relationship to the Lord of our faith and hearts, seeing that He is no less ours than theirs.

We are equal to S. Philip who have been called in Baptism to the knowledge of His grace and to faith in Him. And by the side of our one Lord *we* stand on a level with S. James *who* have heard and welcomed with obedient ear and life, His own declaration that " whosoever shall do the will of His Father in Heaven the same is His brother, and sister, and mother."

And we look to stand by our dear and honoured Lord as truly as they within a little while, " Happy," we say with the Queen of Sheba to his " greater than Solomon," " are these men, these Thy servants that stand continually before Thee, and that hear Thy wisdom ! " But we too " have access by faith into this grace wherein they stand." We read in the book of Deuteronomy, " If a Levite come from any of thy gates out of all Israel, where he sojourn, and come with all the desire of his mind, then he shall minister in the name of the Lord his God, as his brethren do which already stand there before the Lord." We are in the position of the Levites, consecrated and set apart to God in Baptism. If we, any of us, with the full desire of our minds, come to seek and crave the blessedness which these brother disciples enjoyed on earth, and now possess in far greater degree in Heaven, of standing before that glorious Lord—we shall be equally welcome to their company, equally accepted in our service here, and blessed as they in our communion with our Lord hereafter. For even now " truly our fellowship is with Jesus Christ." And death and the Resurrection shall only introduce us to a higher and more perfect form of it with Him and all His redeemed before the throne of God.

I conclude in His own words " Watch we only and pray always that we may be accounted worthy to stand before the Son of man."

SCRIPTURE NOTICES OF S. JAMES.

Herod killed James the brother of John with the sword. *Acts* xii 2.

The name and history of S. James is inseparably linked with that of his brother S. John up to the time of our Saviour's death. These two brothers, the sons of Zebedee and Salome, seem always to have been together with Jesus, till the one, John, stood alone beneath the cross, where the other, James and the rest of the Apostles are not found, having forsaken their Lord and fled. After Christ's Resurrection it is to be remarked that S. James is no longer found as before in company with John and Peter. The history of the two latter becomes linked in the earlier chapters of the Acts, while we read no more of James. He, the other of the three most trusted and intimate friends of our Lord, there disappears till the short notice of the text which brings us to his end. It almost seems as though when their Great Lord was taken from their head, James the elder brother felt so strongly that the blessedness of past associations was broken up that he withdrew.   It seems as though he hardly cared to be found in the human now that the Divine companionship could be shared no more.

We learn from the name our Lord gave *him* and his brother, and from the impulsive words and actions recorded of them, to which I shall allude in the closing sentences of this discourse—we learn I say what manner of man he was.   Like his two comrades he was evidently a man of impetuous feeling and temperament. And like Thomas, who was not with them we read when Jesus appeared after His Resurrection, having probably withdrawn in a grief bordering on despair, James is no more prominent.   The iron had entered deeply into his soul, and like the stricken deer that parts itself from the herd, there *might*, there almost *must* have made itself felt in him a deep craving for a degree of solitude and opportunity for self communing.   And the veil that is from that moment thrown over his history seems to bespeak this.   Still of course, for he believed with the rest would he live to proclaim the Gospel message of Jesus and the Resurrection; and tradition says he was even Bishop of Jerusalem.   But S. James once so prominent a figure of the Scripture narrative falls undeniably into the background. Yet to the last—as the historian in the text indicates when he says, " Because Herod saw that his killing James pleased the Jews he proceeded to take Peter "—the unity and commingling of public life between them is hinted at.   They were even then, although we are not told how, so associated, that Herod regarded them as one, and would have destroyed them together.   United in their lives up evidently to the last, in their death they would not, but for the miraculous deliverance of S Peter have been divided.

Ignorant as we thus are of the closing scenes of S. James' life, we are driven back upon the earlier intimations respecting him and his brother together for our estimate of his character. The only separate element in that character peculiar to himself is the feature of soul we may catch a glimpse of, as I have said from the very silence preserved about him towards the end of his life, his apparent voluntary and partial separation of himself from his old, familiar, and to the last trusted Brother Apostles. We are reminded of that notice of Samuel—"So Samuel came no more to see Saul till the day of his death; nevertheless Samuel mourned for Saul." There is a something of gloom overshadowing the great soul of the one as of the other: though in the case of Samuel the grief was for a most unworthy object, Saul; in the other of James it was for the worthiest of persons, Jesus We recall the story of that fond idolater in the Book of Judges, who said in the bitterness of his disappointment,"Ye have taken away my gods and what have I more!" Doubtless the blessed Apostle shrank not from the publicity, nay, eminence, if it was so as history tells us, to which he was called as one of the chief pillars of the Church. But we part with him in the garden of Gethsemane, the night our Lord was betrayed, to read or hear of him no more till he steps forth, the first of the Apostolic band, to be enrolled in that same city among the noble army of martyrs. And so we think of the words of Jeremiah's lamentation, as most applicable to him in the interval, "He sitteth alone and keepeth silence."

We look back then to the earliest notices of S. James. And first we glance at the ready obedience referred to in the Collect for the day with which he heard his Master's call; and left his father, and the servants and the nets to follow Him. We observe how we presently read of his mother also following, and, with some other women of Galilee, ministering to Jesus of her substance. And we wonder if she were encouraged possibly by the prompt faith of her eldest son.

For our next notice of James we follow with him and Peter, and John, as they enter with Jesus the desolated home of the ruler of the synagogue at Capernaum, where lifeless but beautiful there lay the promising daughter of Jairus. Perhaps as they had entered that synagogue every Sabbath day, where our Lord was wont to resort with them they had often observed her a devout worshipper, like Jairus, and an heir of her father's faith. And "now her sun was gone down while it was yet day." The eyes that had been wont to gaze so intently on Jesus as he had then, as His custom was, opened and expounded the Scriptures, were closed in death. The fire of holy animation that had once lighted up that fair form with the unmistakable ardour of youthful piety, had burned itself out into the cold ashes of mortality. The breast that had thrilled with the emotions that His wondrous teaching had kindled in the glowing soul first with anxiety, " What must I do to be saved," then with the hope that maketh not ashamed " and "the love that casts out fear," was still and silent now as it seemed for ever. And James stood by while the gaping, scornful, unbelieving multitude that filled the chamber of death was expelled as alien and out of sympathy with the sacred scene of sorrow and of resurrection. And he saw himself beckoned as one of the privileged three to follow and behold with the father and mother of the maiden the transformation to life. And with chastened awe he drew near the couch of the departed and saw her lifeless hand in that gentle touch of the loving Jesus. And he heard the "Talitha Cumi," "Damsel arise," which awoke the recognition of the soul in the unseen world, just as instantly and perfectly as your familiar voice addressing him does your nearest neighbour. James saw it all. He saw

> When with hushed steps they trod the winding stair
> And from within that awful whisper came,
> "Trouble the Master not for she is dead,"
> How his faint hand fell nerveless at his side,
> And his steps faltered, and his broken voice
> Choked in its utterance. But a gentle hand
> Was laid upon his arm, and in his ear
> The Saviour's voice sank thrillingly and low,
> "She is not dead but sleepeth."

And now he saw how the strange assertion was proved, that the power of death to the Lord of Life was nothing more at all than that of sleep, and as easily broken by a word.

> For at His word lo suddenly a flush
> Shot o'er her forehead! and along her lips
> And through her cheeks the rallied colour ran;
> She clasped his hands, and fixing her dark eyes
> Full on His beaming countenance, arose.   WILLIS.

And from the teachings of this impressive scene we turn to those of the Transfiguration. There James stood again with his brother and Peter, and saw the glory of Jesus and His intimate acquaintance with the beings of the other world, with whom he conversed on the Holy Mount. And from what James then saw and heard of the calmness with which His Master contemplated and conversed about His approaching death at Jerusalem, he would learn much. It could not but be that thus he would gather high encouragement and sustained confidence to contemplate his own which was to follow His Master's so soon. He who saw death stripped of its terror, in the case of Jairus' daughter, and positively looked forward to in the other, the case of our Lord, would be prepared for the decease that he too should accomplish at Jerusalem. And longing as he did, when he prayed so earnestly with his interceding mother for a place as near as possible to his Lord, it could be no unwelcome messenger even though it were the sword of Herod, that waved him once more to the coveted companionship of Him with whom, as we have seen he had, "none upon earth he desired in comparison."

Thrice blessed Apostle! To be seated so soon and first of all the Twelve, in heavenly places at his dear Master's side! Thou Lord hast given him his heart's desire, and hast not withholden the request of his lips! There thou hast never again been grieved with the hardness of impenitent hearts, and stirred to holy indignation as by the cities of

Samaria that refused the Blessed One an entrance! For Angels and principalities and powers vie with one another and with thyself in saying. "Thou art worthy O Lord to receive power and strength, and honour and glory and blessing!" No need for thee to vindicate there the worthiness of thy Master, by thinking to call down fire from heaven as Elias did! For "every voice there," thine own brother has testified —without one dissentient tongue —"heard I saying, Blessing, honour, and glory and power be unto Him that sitteth upon the Throne, and unto the Lamb for ever." No need was there to ask as once thou didst "But when shall these things be and when shall all be fulfilled." For thou wast not kept waiting long; thou didst not need the long patience which some of us do to hold our faith still upon God, and to hold fast our conficence while so many adverse things raise the doubt in our evil heart of unbelief that it is vain, that God hideth Himself, and His word is no effect, and that our Lord delayeth his coming and his promises.

The answer to thee came very soon. And the gleam of the executioner's sword, as Herod flashed it before thine eyes, was lost in the light of the opening heavens. And the sword that smote through the tabernacle of thy mortal body, laid open at the same moment to thy longing and blissful gaze the tabernacle of God beyond, where thou hast been seated ever since in the presence of the blessed and glorious Lord, and where God grant we too in His good time may be seated with Him and with thee!

THE CALL OF S. MATTHEW.

Therefore seeing we have this Ministry, as we have received mercy we faint not; but have renounced the hidden things of dishonesty.   2 *Corinthians* iv. 1.

These are the opening words of the Epistle for S. Matthew's day. None could be more suitable as the expression of the feelings and after-life of that Apostle and Evangelist. The story of his call certainly brings promimently before us two considerations which the text suggests, the mercy of our Lord Jesus Christ shown towards one so degraded, and the prompt abandonment on his part of all, and everything, belonging to the disreputable profession which he had till then been following. These two points we shall observe as we notice *firstly* the change in his name, *secondly* in his outward life, and *thirdly* in his inward character, that accompanied his call to the Apostleship.

I need say little of the fraud and extortion that characterised the profession of tax-collector to the Romans. By S. Matthew's countrymen it was held to be as dishonourable, as it was in their eyes odious. Nor are many words required to magnify the mercy of Him who chose and called with a holy calling one who belonged to a class so infamous. When we observe that both S. Mark and S. Luke, in recording the call of their brother Evangelist give him the name of Levi, we are reluctantly led to a conclusion about him which magnifies that mercy in our eyes the more. If Levi was the name by which he was better known, and which at all events he bore, how great must have been his fall from grace! His very name was suggestive of religious privilege and nearness to God. Levi—was it not his sons, as Moses reminded the apostate Khorah and his company (who like Matthew were, or should and might have been Levites) whom "the Lord separated from the congregation of Israel to bring near to Himself, to do the service of the tabernacle of the Lord, and to stand before the congregation to minister unto them?" No wonder that in his deep sense of humiliation S. Matthew should have dropped the name Levi, and chosen to designate himself by that by which he has been ever since the better known, the name which, as it signifies in the original, is suggestive of that "gift of God which is (and was to him) eternal life through Jesus Christ our Lord." He might and would—for his evident humility has been often remarked upon by Commentators—think himself unworthy to bear again that honoured name. To its memories and glories he had proved himself false, when he chose worldly riches and office under the Roman Emperor instead of the true riches and the high office which had been his under the God of Israel. But not perhaps so much because of the bitter reflections which its mention would awaken in his repentant soul, as because it was a name by which he was "no more worthy to be called," would h resolve to assume, or have it taken up within the lips no more. Let his life—we may so take it as his wish—be associated for the future with the thought of how great things God had done for him—God who remembered him in his low estate because his mercy endureth for ever. And though he were of the great race and lineage of Levi he had no more whereof to boast himself before God, as those who said so foolishly, as though it could profit them anything, " We have Abraham to our Father."

But the Spirit of God has by the independent record of the other two Evangelists shown that he would have us, as we identify him with the name of Levi, observe that name. For it too magnifies not in the meaning, as the word Matthew, but by its associations, the grace of God. For God, it reminds us, will not cast away those whom He has foreknown and chosen unto Himself. Having loved and called them, He loves them unto the end. And Levi whom He had brought into such special covenant with Himself should though a wanderer be restored : " For the Lord thy God," says Moses, " is a merciful God ; He will not forsake thee, neither destroy thee, nor forget the covenant of thy fathers." "Them that thou gavest me," says Jesus, " I have kept and none of them is lost." And the very name of the Evangelist is a living illustration of this, thank God, blessed and abiding truth.

And the promptitude of S. Matthew's obedience is as apparent in the story, as the mercy that called him, or as I think we may say from this observation of the name *recalled* him to the knowledge of His Grace and faith in Him. Very simple is the Evangelist's relation of it as though it was a very simple occurrence. "And he arose and followed Him." And yet we know it was not so small a thing after all, though doubtless in that hour he counted all worldly gain but loss that he might win Christ and be found in Him. He left all says S. Luke. And from an earthly point of view it was much to leave. A gainful profession, sure prospect of preferment, favour with Rome the then mistress of the world, an active life, which always possesses attractions for the capable and business-like and the enterprising ; society among many and varied features and forms of character, beside the companionship of the class with which he had so completely identified himself ; the observation of life in many and interesting phases at the port of Capernaum ; (and such a position of observation is to many minds very attractive as we see by the well-known remark " the proper study of mankind is man.")—all this to be renounced, esteeming the reproach of Christ greater riches.

But it was not here mere external sacrifice only that S. Matthew is set before us as making. The text speaks of renouncing " *the hidden things* of dishonesty." There was far more than a breaking away from external associations. There was the abandonment of inward and long formed habits. And it is in this province that the religion of

Christ exercises its peculiar triumphs. It alters indeed the *outward* complexion of the sinful life. The careless becomes devout, and the churl bountiful. The lover of pleasure becomes a lover of God. The self indulgent becomes the self denying ; the irritable, patient and gentle and self restrained ; and the discontented grateful. Old things indeed pass away and many things become so manifestly new in the word, ways and tempers of the subject of Divine grace that the world looks on surprised and puzzled.

But more, far more than meets the eye is effected in the inward recesses of the soul. *There* are mighty changes which no eye save His that seeth in secret is aware of—changes in the views the soul takes of itself and its Redeemer, and the other world. God's word is changed to it. And the Bible becomes invested with a light and an attraction which it never had before. God's ordinances are changed to it. And they are no more cold and lifeless and formal observances : but they are instinct with warmth and life and reality. Prayer becomes a real transaction with a personal Being, instead of a heartless routine. And praise is not the lifting up the voice in the rhythm of song or metre, but the outburst of a full soul swelling with animation, and sometimes with a rapture and joy unspeakable.

The alteration which the call of Christ made in S. Matthew's inner life took the form of a renunciation of the hidden things of dishonesty. The mean artifices, the low cunning with which he was so familiar were renounced for ever. His words and ways were henceforth straightforward. Sincerity breathed in all his converse, neither was guile found in his mouth. And here was certainly, when we come to think of it, a signal triumph of Divine grace. Some are naturally candid and open like the guileless Nathaniel. But some are close and reserved and given to double dealing. It is impossible to be sure of their designs or feelings, and hard indeed to get at their real mind or sentiments. Counsel, says Solomon, in the heart of man is like deep water. But a man of understanding (he must be wise indeed if he is to succeed in some cases !) will draw it out.

The life of S. Matthew had been an evil school for him. If he had any naturally generous impulses of heart they must have long become overlaid with a crust of miserable selfishness and hardness. The dealings of his class were fraudulent, and the tendencies of their world-worn sophisticated souls were all unfeeling. The undisguised hatred of the Jews they would be apt to meet with contemptuous coldness and bitter resentment. They had them in their power ; and the powerful when unprincipled, like this class, are always disposed to be tyrannical. And this hardness of heart tends naturally to make its subjects worse and worse. For " he that loveth not his brother whom he hath seen how can he love God whom he hath not seen." The unmerciful and the unkind and the inconsiderate, as we see continually exemplified in selfish worldly souls, degenerate very rapidly, and soon reach the point beyond which (of course only humanly speaking) there is no hope of recovery.

And such was S. Matthew, though by the distinguishing grace of

God he was enabled to renounce so entirely the hidden things of dishonesty, and no more as the text goes on to say to walk in craftiness or deceitfully. His life, if we only knew it, would wonderfully illustrate the text which is so suitable a motto for it. The day will come when the revelation of the heavenly world shall supply the blank in his history which imagination is now left to deal with. And we shall then be better able to glorify the grace of God in him.

Meanwhile since we are the subjects of the same call let us see if any such change is passing upon us. We may not be hard, covetous, exacting, oppressive, and crafty, like the publican class to which Levi belonged. But the seeds of these evil dispositions are within us. Lurking within us too are hidden things of dishonesty, crooked ways to be made straight, and secret sins, impulses to and thoughts of evil, which though all the while in the light of God's countenance, as we alas! forget, we should be ashamed to think were known and read of any but ourselves. Hidden things of dishonesty, how striking an expression is the phrase. *Hidden* not possibly observed by any fellow creature, but yet ways that are really unrighteous toward others. Dishononrable motives there are, where all seems fair and smooth and above board, that make the most apparently upright conduct and straightforward behaviour a mockery of integrity, a deception of our neighbour, and a sin against God. Well may each of us say "Search me O God and prove my heart, try me and examine my thoughts, and see if there be any such wicked way in me, and lead me in the way everlasting."

THE EXECUTION OF JOHN THE BAPTIST.

Mark vi. 17-29

The wise man tells us how questionable a matter it is to frequent the house of feasting; and how often "the end of that mirth is heaviness." "I said of mirth (says he) what doeth it." He speaks not of the bright and sunny cheerfulness that overspreads and fills, or ought to do, the joyous life of those who are at peace with God through the death of His Son; and who, being in a state of reconciliation with Him, know the blessedness of those whose transgression is forgiven, and whose sin is covered.

"Let them be merry and joyful," says the Spirit of God. "Let those that put their trust in Thee rejoice: let them ever shout for joy, because Thou defendest them : let them also that love Thy name be joyful in Thee." But he speaks of the reckless God—forgeting mirth of those who are "lovers of pleasure more than lovers of God." "And behold a greater than Solomon, is here," to tell you from the record of His unerring word "what doeth it."

I know not except the awful tragedy of the Crucifixion, and perhaps the tale of the last hours of the sainted Stephen, a more thrilling story than that which here leads us to the end of the greatest of all the Prophets.

Its simplicity is unrivalled. We have in the text no burning words of denunciation of the crime, nor eloquent depicting of the scene. But the account, unvarnished as it is, awakens the fancy, and calls up before us all the attendant circumstances. With harrowed feelings, and righteous indignation roused to a painful intensity, we linger always on the story. Nor can we but speak the thoughts and emotions that God Himself thus stirs within us by His own "quick and powerful Word."

I quote a few words here and some descriptive sentences further on of the opening scene from the graphic pen of the Rev. T. De. Witt Talmage, of Brooklyn, New York.

"It is the anniversary of Herod's birth-day. The palace is lighted. The highways leading thereto are ablaze with the pomp of invited guests. Lords, captains, merchant princes, and the mightiest men of the realm are on the way to mingle in the festivities. There are spiced wines, and costly fruits, and rare meats." The tables are filled with all the luxuries "that can minister to the lust of the flesh, and the lust of the eye, and the pride of life." Though the words had not yet been written there was One, the great hero of whom the text speaks, whose life from his earliest youth had been the expression of that Divine caution,

"Make no provision for the flesh to fulfill the lusts thereof." For related as he was to the King of kings and Lord of lords, he was not "a man clothed in soft raiment gorgeously apparelled, and living delicately in king's courts." But "his raiment was camel's hair, and a leathern girdle: and his meat was locusts and wild honey." But for many months the protests of that bold tongue, and the teaching of that holy life, had been put to silence in the prison fortress.

Into the banqueting house pour the guests in rich attire, anointed and perfumed. The feast of which I tell you now with its wine, and its song, and its dance, and the awful sin which followed, has nothing to do with the sober moderate entertainment in which, under restraint of Christian feelings and principles, we may be free to mingle. I yield to none in keen perception of the seductive power of worldly gaiety. I would speak with no more uncertain sound, and give no feebler warning than any against the perils of worldly company. But I should hesitate to pronounce the sweeping and indiscriminate condemnation which many good and holy persons, take upon themselves to do upon this subject. I should hesitate, I say, when I remember that mirth, music, and dancing, were introduced deliberately by the Lord and Judge of man Himself into that His perhaps most wondrous parable, where He represents the joy in the household of God, the joy of the Father and His Holy Angels, over a returning sinner.

I would distinguish things that differ. And what has the innocent mirth of the select company of Christian people, relatives or friends, in common with the case before us? Here we have a mixed multitude of lawless revellers, a concourse of open sinners, with no fear of God before their eyes. And whenever there is such a gathering, I care not in what class of society it be, nothing but mishief and sin can follow. Let every Christian man and woman, and the young especially, charge themselves solemnly with the Patriarch's holy resolve. "O my soul, come not then into their secret: unto their assembly mine honour be not thou united!" The very inspired book of Sacred Psalmody which ends its gladdening strains by summoning the saints in company to rejoice in their Maker, and their King, with all the accessories of human festivity, the music, and the song, and the dance—opens by insisting on the "separation from sinners, that becometh the saints of the Holy God." " Blessed is the man that hath not walked in the counsel of the ungodly, nor stood in the way of sinners, nor sat in the seat of the scornful." And such were these, the guests in the text, come as though purposely to court the woe with which the words of one of their Prophets had made them perfectly familiar. " Woe to them that rise up that they may follow strong drink; that continue until night till wine inflame them ! And the harp, and the viol, the tabret, and pipe, and wine, are in their feasts; but they regard not the Lord ! "

And presently riot gives place to uproar and blasphemy. The light is dazzling, and the music enchanting. And the graceful and accomplished Salome, the Princess of Galilee, fires the senses of the godless fools and their half intoxicated king. All self control is abandoned, and the monarch has become heedless of his dignity. He aban.

dons shame and moderation altogether. And having no fear of Him whose steward in the kingdom of Galilee he was before his eyes, he wills it away in a tumult of unreason, as though it were his own to dispose of, to the giddy girl before him.

"The magnificence of his realm, says the author above quoted, is as nothing compared with the fascination of the dance. He sits in a transport of admiration before the whirling, bounding, leaping, flashing wonder. And when the dance stops and the tinkling cymbals pause, and the long loud plaudits that shook the palace with their thunders had abated, the entranced monarch swears unto the princely performer, " Whatsoever thou shalt ask of me I will give it thee to the half of my kingdom."

"Now there was in prison at that time, cast there by Herod himself a minister by the name of John the Baptist, who had made much trouble by his honest preaching. He had denounced, not fearing his wrath, the sin of the licentious king, and brought down upon himself the resentment of Herodias enraged at his interference, as she deemed it, with the private actions of her evil life. At her instigation Salome takes advantage of the extravagant promise, and demands on a dinner plate the head of John the Baptist.

" There is a sound of heavy feet, and the clatter of swords outside the palace. Swing back the door. The executioner is returning from his awful errand. The servants hand a platter to Salome. What is that on the platter ? A new tankard of wine to rekindle the mirth of the lords ? No, it is redder than wine—the wine that giveth its colour aright and moveth itself in the sparkling cup on which we are bidden to look with such chastened and bridled gaze—and it is costlier far. It is the ghastly bleeding head of the minister whose faithfulness no others shall ever surpass.—The noble locks of John the Baptist are stained with gore. Those eyes are fast set in the stare of death," that lately flashed with the fire of heaven. The distress of the last agony is in the features. The form of the Princess that swayed so gracefully in the artistic dance bends over the horrid burden without a shudder. She gloats over the blood of the just man and the holy. And even as the maid of your household goes bearing out on a tray the empty glasses of the evening's entertainment, so she carried out with unfaltering touch the dissevered head of him who was great in the sight of the Lord. And all the banqueters shouted with the glee of devils, and thought it a grand joke that in such a brief and easy way they were freed for ever from the plain spoken messenger of Heaven, the troubler of Israel." They would themselves have put him out of the way long ago. But they feared the people for all counted John as a prophet.

O, the forbearance the wondrous long-suffering of God, who can allow space for repentance after even such a crime ! " Surely Thou hast seen it for Thou beholdest ungodliness and wrong ! And yet Thou continuest silent, O Thou Worship of Israel ! "

We leave them, those who contrived the dark deed, and those who as S. Paul says knowing the just judgment of God, that the instigators and accessories to the crime were " worthy of death, had pleasure in them that did it." We leave them till the surely coming day of retribution, when all "they shall have judgement without mercy that have showed no mercy." And even then—when we must stand face to face with the vast throng of our fellow-creatures at the righteous bar, and

> When tyrants to the rocks complain,
> And seek the mountain clefts in vain

—We would to God we may not stand anywhere near that abhorred company. We long, and would earnestly pray if it be the Divine Will, we may not recognise any in the shrinking crowd of the reprobate, who shall be waiting with the conviction of unerring certainty their inevitable doom!

> When sinners filled with guilty fears,
> Behold His wrath prevailing,
> When they must rise to find that sighs,
> And tears are unavailing—

God spare us the sight of these accursed men and women that slew His noble Prophet, and the sight of any like them! The Great God in His compassion to our weakness avert them from the spot where

> Their day of grace now past and gone,
> Trembling they stand before the throne,
> All unprepared to meet Him!

Now that you have watched the scene from the *inside*, come and behold it from the *outside*. Follow me in imagination as I lead you out to contemplate from a distance the startling horrors of this deed of sin. Rise and stand with me aside under the shade of those gloomy trees in the dusky avenue that leads up to the palace of the wicked and murderous Herod. It is night. And as we step together out of the broad avenue into the thick shadows of the intertwining boughs, we can only see our path by the bright glare that streams down from the brilliantly lighted Court. Hush! Let us keep still together in that thick shelter, and see what shall meet our eyes. The sound of music floats down to us on the still night air. And the calm of the peaceful heavens over our head is broken, now again the din of revelry as it breaks fresh and loud on our reluctant ears. Hark! what sounds of tumultuous applause are those that rend the astonished heavens as first the performance of Salome, then the promise, and then the command for its fulfillment, are greeted with the wild cheers of the impious and inhuman crowd!

Now bend forward with me from behind those trees where we imagine ourselves spectators of this tragedy, and look earnestly. Lo the palace doors are opened! And the forms of soldiers and servants, that throng the hall, stand clearly forth to our gaze. From the waiting retinue there steps into the forefront a grim soldier. He is mighty in size and strong in limb, and the undaunted resolution of the battle field speak sin every motion of his massive frame. He is one that "mocketh at fear, and is not affrighted as he goeth on to meet the armed foe." His valour has been proved in many a conflict; and he has borne a charmed life through it all. His comrades yield him the ready palm of superiority. For there is unmistakable might in his strong right hand. And look! the arrogant queen condescends herself to impress the particulars of his awful commission She stands before him in all the haughtiness of majesty, and to make assurance doubly sure, promises, or perchance presses into his hand the wages of iniquity that are to compensate him for his deed of blood Herodias summons the executioner of Herod: and her daughter, a willing agent, stands approvingly and admiringly by her mother's side. And she drinks into the spirit of that nature, the stronger mind that is influencing her young soul, and educating it for a like enormity of sin. O, the wondrous power of human influence! The mighty mystery by which the emotions of one human soul are transferred by companionship to another! The untold responsibility which belongs to us parents, masters, teachers, ministers, superiors, friends, who are moulding the characters of those in contact with ourselves! The example, the emphasis of our words, the very look with which we accompany them, like the iron it is entering deep into the unconscious spirit that is subjected to it, and impressing it for good or for evil, as the clay in the hand of the potter.

Now once more from underneath those trees let me draw you forth to gaze on Herodias, as you see her despatching the executioner from that open door. The fire of passion lights up her expressive eye. And the flush of vindictive triumph is glowing on her queenly brow. And the daughter is like her mother, only she has not as yet—while she has all the propensity for it—quite the same audacity in crime. She fears not God nor regards man. But she has not all her mother's experience of evil. She is reckless, heartless, graceless, but is not yet competent to tread unguided in the same paths of sin. But children of the devil are they both, and enemies of all righteousness. Very beautiful are they truly! and so is the serpent of the East in the grace of its insinuating folds, and the gorgeous decoration of its burnished skin. And so is the savage lurking leopard in its rich colouring and its inimitably graceful form. Very fair truly are those figures before us! But though history paints them as among the fairest women of their age, they are stamped by this story with the deformity of hell.

Should you meet with the plausible evil doer, the fair spoken, or the ingratiating, that would delude you by a specious exterior, a taking manner, a soft tongue, a polite bearing while you cannot but feel confident that all the while they fear not God, and dread not sin, fall not into the admiration of such. Now look again! The executioner makes his rough obeisance, and feels no misgiving about his horrid work. For he is a man of war and blood from his youth. And he too catches the spirit of his mistress and the company. And the gleam of ferocity glares from his malignant eye, as he claps his sword into the scabbard at his side, and descends the steps alone on his unholy errand. Stand back now again with me under the trees of the avenue, and let the executioner pass! For "in the word of a king there is power, and who can stay his hand." The fresh night breeze is on his heated brow and the calm starlight looks down in clear and reproachful gaze, into his evil eyes, as he strides forth at first unfalteringly towards the prison cell. But "the wicked is like the troubled sea." And the holy calm above breathes not on his sin-ruffled breast. And he heeds not, he has never learnt so to look upon it, the reproachful gaze of heaven's holy stars, as they look down as it were in an infinite pity on the men that pursue deeds of darkness beneath their pure light.

The executioner has passed the spot where we are standing together. And we gaze after him to see the end. But mark how his countenance begins to be changed, and his thoughts to trouble him; so that as with Belshazzar the joints of his loins are loosed, and his knees smite one against the other! What means this sudden and unlooked for hesitation? "The expectation of the wicked is wrath." And the hardened ruffian trembles as he begins to contemplate alone, who is that Holy Man indeed, whom all men count as a prophet, who is to be the victim of his sword. Perchance he was himself among the band of Herod's soldiers, whom S. Luke tells us of as trembling before the high Messenger of Heaven, with the multitude at Jordan's stream. Perhaps he was one of them when the almost prophetic caution fell upon their enquiring ears, as John said to the soldiers "Do no violence to any man." Little then did he think that his should be the hand that would be one day uplifted to put the faithful tongue to the silence of its long repose! He might have been the first if so forewarned to protest with Hazael. "Is thy servant a dog that he should do this thing." But stifled convictions had done their work, and resisted truth had sealed his hard heart, until it knew the compunctions for evil, and aspirations after good, of its early days no more. But whether or no he was conscious in that dark hour of any momentary relenting we cannot tell. Suffice it to say he yielded himself in the end, as the servant of sin, the tool of revenge, to the murderers of the blessed Saint.

The prison door is reached. The gaoler recognises the prisoner, reads the errand of the executioner, and admits him to the victim's cell. There, sleeping the sleep of the just, is the long patient and noble witness for Christ.

> Chains and prison, foes derision,
> He endured for Christ his Lord.

And now he is hailed to slaughter by the rough voice (in his ears how welcome!) that bids him rise to the liberty of the emancipated spirits of the blessed dead

> Faith prevailing, hope unfailing,
> Jesus loved with single heart,
> Thus he glorious and victorious,
> Bravely bore the martyr's part.
>
> Lord, give us grace to bear,
> Like Him our cross or shame,
> To do and suffer what Thou wilt,
> For love of thy dear name?

The last moments of the Martyr we have no help from the story to aid us in imagining to ourselves. But our Lord tells us John was no reed shaken with the wind. And so we fancy we see the great Messenger of our Lord raising, for the last time from the floor of the dungeon, that worn body that was henceforth to sleep on and take its long and well earned rest—a rest, till the Resurrection of the just, in the quiet but unknown sepulchre, to which we read his affectionate disciples consigned it.

And now he lifts up for the last time the eyes of faith to the God in whose sight the death of His saints is we are told so precious. He commends his spirit to the Great Master he had served, with such fearless faithfulness, and yet such unequalled humility. He stands alone with the stern executioner, and the onlooking gaoler, and God the judge of all. The record of his last words and looks is hidden with them, till the Great Day of revelation of all the secrets of Time.

Was it with *him* as it is written of his father's namesake—the Son like him of a Priest—" So they slew him at the commandment of the king: and when he died he said (not I suppose in retaliation but in prophecy), the Lord look upon it and require it?" It may well have been: for history gives us a strange sequel to the inspired story, in the narrative of the vengeance of Heaven, that overtook the imperious Queen and her graceless daughter. Or did his "blood speak better things than that of" the other, or of "Abel," and perchance obtain forgiveness at least for the executioner, as Jesus and Stephen did for some of their murderers? This too may well have been: for "the effectual fervent prayer," and surely more certainly still the last dying prayer "of a righteous man availeth much." It may well have been: for the ex. ecutioner and the gaoler were probably heathens in the Roman army; and knew not what they did, like the king and princesses and "lords and high captains, and chief estates of Galilee." And we may indulge perhaps some distant sort of hope that they obtained mercy, "because they did it ignorantly in unbelief;" while the blood-thirsty Herodias and Salome are set forth for an example of the righteous judgment of God. We cannot tell: nor shall we know till "the day shall declare it." But the spirit of the noble Preacher departed to the God who gave it: and John the Baptist was in another moment "where the wicked cease from troubling and where the weary are at rest."

> And though no steeds nor car of lightning bear.
> Thy form triumphant through the realms of air,
> Not less august thy martyred soul shall rise
> Again, Messiah's Herald, to the skies.
> Whence—Oh if stooping from thy starry sphere,
> Thou deignest one future thought of pity here—
> Pleased shalt thou view thy Holy rite confest,
> Thy name revered where glows the human breast,
> Thy Master's reign to age nor clime confined,
> The world His temple and His race mankind.

FAITHFULNESS TO CHRIST.

And Absalom said to Hushai, Is this thy kindness to thy friend? Why wentn
thou not with thy friend ? 2 *Samuel* xvi, 17.

Absalom the rebel son of David, was a very artful man, as a reference to the way in which he "stole the hearts of the men of Israel,"
from allegiance to their king, as recorded in this book, shows particularly.
There are other allusions and incidents mentioned of him which equally
prove him to have been as sharp witted and designing as he was unprin
cipled. In the case to which the text refers he was however completely
and ruinously imposed upon. The wise, those that set up for such,
are often taken in their own craftiness. People are very apt to think
themselves shrewder and more clear sighted than they really are. They
are very quick at supposing they see through a matter of which they
may be all the time in the most profound ignorance. Absalom thought,
I doubt not, his remark a very smart one, and prided himself probably
that he was so keen sighted and ready in exposing the impropriety and
inconsistency of Hushai's conduct. Yet he was all the while the other's
dupe, and fell a victim shortly to his deeper cunning. The taunt with
which Absalom reproached Hushai for his supposed faithfulness to
David may supply us with a profitable line of thought, and is capable of
apt application to ourselves as professedly loyal subjects of the
Redeemer.

Let us take each of the two enquiries. And first "Is this thy
kindness to thy friend?" In all love human and Divine *sincerity* and
fidelity are the indispensable requisites. Sincerity first; "Let love be
without dissimulation" is the requirement of nature as well as of the
Bible. And fidelity likewise ; "for a man that hath friends" said the
brother of the speaker in the text, "must show himself friendly."

Hushai—when the fickle people were deserting their tried old
king for the plausible demagogue, who had won their faithless hearts—
remained as we read in the last chapter firm and true to David. Absalom had hitherto and rightly judged him to be a trustworthy character,
and had never expected to see him join the popular side, and the faction
of which he was the centre. And when he unexpectedly saw him with
his own party, not thinking for the moment of the possibility of his
being a spy, he reproached him with his desertion in these words. I
cannot suppose that Absalom would have uttered them—for he would
have been too glad to welcome any fresh adherents—if it had not been
that he had long hated him for his steadfast decided character. He
could not conceal the malice with which his joy at seeing him as he sup-
dosed falter was mingled. Was this the end he cried mockingly, of all

his hitherto boasted allegiance ?   Was this the [illegible] of which David's friends were made ? Had not he, Absa[illegible] Hushai's professions of attachment to David.   And was this to be the outcome of his attention, his service, and his repeated protestations of loyalty ?

The world is never tired of raising the same sneer against any whom it supposes (often altogether wrongly as Absalom did here) that it detects faltering in their duty to God, divided in their allegiance, and untrue to their professions. But though the world says it in malice and with the devil's triumph—

> Against him I have now prevailed,
> Rejoice the child of God has failed.

Without concerning ourselves about its judgment, let us by all means judge ourselves, and in the way of self examination ask, " Is this our kindness to our friend." Very early in our lives was the solemn vow made with which our Church, and we for ourselves in Confirmation, bound us to God.

> That long as life itself should last,
> Ourselves to Christ we'd yield ;
> Nor from His presence would depart,
> Nor ever quit the field.

If God is not much in your thoughts, nor His Will an object that you are seeking—if you are not concerning yourself about securing His favour or avoiding His displeasure—if you are indifferent to His good opinion ; and all spiritual emotions of love, and hope, and joy in Him are unstirred and cold—we may well ask with Absalom " Is this thy kindness to thy friend ? " Read the vows of God that are upon you, the engagements you have made your own in the Baptismal and Communion Offices ; compare the thoughts that breathe, and words that burn, and the deep earnest emotion depicted and called forth there with the careless, uninterested cold hearts that beat within so many—and you will not say there is no occasion for the preacher to tax you with Absalom's searching enquiry " Is this thy kindness to thy friend." " Do ye thus requite the Lord ! " said Moses to Israel, when reminding them of obligations very like to those which the name of our Redeemer must always call up before our memories. To occasional worshippers only in the place which the Lord has chosen to set his name there, to total abstainers from the bread and the wine He has mingled for our soul's strengthening and refreshing, to prayerless professors of His religion, to disciples that are so in name but never set themselves to learn of Him or imitate Him in anything, to hard unfeeling unloving souls, that gaze without emotion on the Crucified, and think with no promptings of self consecration of His life and His love—To worldly souls that seek their portion only in this life, living without God, just as they would do if they believed there were none, not to say to those whose life is a direct defiance to His laws of peace, and righteousness, and sobriety— we would press most earnestly the consideration " Is this thy kindness to thy friend ? " What will you do that are such, when God rises up for " shall I not visit for these things saith the Lord ? shall not my soul be avenged on such ? " God, no more than man, though he bears long, will suffer patiently the slights, and indignities, and neglect, of those who cannot be distinguished except in name from His enemies. Who of ourselves treats or ought to treat friends and enemies alike? Who is called upon indeed to forbear showing that he is sensible of the difference between the two, and holds the one in honour, while the other he lightly esteems?

But there was a second and equally suggestive enquiry made by Absalom of Hushai. " Why wentest thou not with thy friend?" David had been compelled to flee from Jerusalem, from his home and his kingdom. And how came it that Hushai was not prepared to share his fortune, and stand by him in his adversity? How was it Absalom had not heard of such a devotion to David, as was that of David's great grandmother, when a young widow, to her mother in law. " Entreat me not to leave thee, or to return from following after thee: for whither thou goest I will go,; and where thou lodgest I will lodge. Where thou diest will I die, and there will I be buried." How was it he had heard of him no such vow of devotion, as the very same misfortune of the king had brought out from Ittai the Gittite on the same occasion? For thus had he answered the King. "As the Lord liveth, and as my lord the king liveth, surely in what place my lord the king shall be, whether in death or life, even there also will thy servant be." " A friend (says Solomon) loveth at all times, and a brother is born for adversity." " Affliction is ever—as the test of virtue, so—the touch-stone of sincerity. When the storm arises timorous fowl will hide themselves. But the brave Ocean bird flys rather to welcome it. He loves to breast the swelling wave

> And plants his footsteps in the sea,
> And rides upon the storm.

And the same necessity is in the very nature of things laid upon us, if we would be counted worthy of the confidence of the Friend of sinners. " Whosoever will be His disciple must take up his cross to follow Him.

> Through good report and evil, Lord,
> Still guided by Thy faithful word,
> Our staff, our buckler, and our sword,
>   We follow Thee.
>
> In silence of the lonely night,
> In the full glow of day's clear light,
> Through life's strange wanderings dark and bright,
>   We follow Thee.
>
> Strengthened by Thee we forward go,
> Mid smile or scoff of friend or foe,
> Through pain or ease, through joy or woe,
>   We follow Thee.
>
> Though enemies be round Thy side,
> We stand by Thee, the Crucified,
> Forsaking all on earth beside,
>   We follow Thee.

For whom have we in Heaven alone,
Whom on this earth save Thee to love?
Still in Thy light we onward move,
And follow Thee.

" Master ! I will follow Thee withersoever Thou goest," was the resolution of the enthusiastic scribe. Is it yours? Or I should rather say is it what what you are doing? For I doubt not you have often intended and resolved so to follow. The vows of God are already upon you, that you would walk with Him to your life's end. But some of you are far behind your guide. You parted from Him a long time ago, or it may be recently. You walked with Him a while. But the road presently divided. And He led on the rough and thorny track ; and you preferred the smooth and flowery.

Where are you now? Some are trifling on the world's broad road. There are a multitude of well frequented paths on the highway of life, where Christ is not, but where professing Christians are to be found in large companies. Self-indulgent disciple, that lovest to linger in the sunlight of earthly comfort, " Why wentest thou not with thy friend ?" This was not the path by which Thy Master passed : for " He endured the Cross despising the shame." Thou that " lovest the praise of men, more than the praise of God," to whom the flattery of the world that beseeches you to be of its party is pleasing, and its hollow professions sweet as the breathing incense, " why wentest thou not with thy friend ?" Heardest thou not the voice of thy Master. " If ye were of the world the world would love his own. But because ye are not of the world, but I have chosen you out of the world, therefore (it must needs be that) the world will hate you." Thou that lovest to bask in the smile of the world's vain pomp and glory, whose foolish heart is won by its forced gaiety, and its gaudy glitter, and its empty show, who lookest upon the sparkling cup of pleasure it proffers, and forgetteth the bitter dregs which underlie the draught, and how " at the last it biteth like a serpent, and stingeth like an adder," " why wentest thou not with thy friend ? "

Thy Master hath exposed the cheat that has led myriads to experience a vanity and vexation of spirit, that only those who have drunk deeply of its beguiling cup can know—the cheat that has drawn myriads to the remorse and bitterness of despair, as it drowned them in destruction and perdition-

O world ! with all thy witching smiles,
With all thy fair sunshine,
What mockery of human hopes!
What emptiness is thine!

The expostulation of the text, I observe in conclusion, may happily for us be followed up by an invitation. If you are not found at this moment with your Divine friend, if you have ever wittingly deserted, or some how—you can hardly tell exactly where or in what way—become unconsciously parted from Him, the communion of His love, the light of His favour, and the joy of His fellowship, it is yet open to you to return. Nay the words seem as we dwell upon them, to die off from the lips of Absalom, and to be breathed from those of that Divine Friend and Master of ours, of whom we have been speaking. "Why wentest thou not with thy Friend." It is no more the "taunting proverb" of Absalom, but the gentle remonstrance of the Divine Redeemer, who would fain win back our wandering hearts, "O that my people had hearkened unto me, and that Israel had walked in my ways!"

Hushai could, had he pleased, have given Absalom a reply to the question. But you and I can but lay our hand upon our mouth and remain speechless. Yet not even so. For we can at least put up the prayer, "Turn Thou us O Good Lord, and so shall we be turned." "Draw us and we will run after Thee." "Lead me in Thy truth : for Thou art the God of my salvation, on Thee do I wait all the day. For Thy name's sake lead me and guide me. Lead me O Lord in Thy righteousness make the way straight before my face."

> Jesus calls us, from the evil
>   In a world we cannot flee,
> From each idol that would keep us,
>   Softly, clearly—Follow Me.
>
> Thou dost call us ! May we ever,
>   To Thy call attentive be,
> Give our hearts to Thine obedience !
>   Rise, leave all, and follow Thee.

THE SHAME OF IGNORANCE.

Some have not the knowledge of God: I speak this to your shame!
1 *Corinthians* xv. 34.

What S. John says of some sins which he does not exactly specify,
we may say more particularly of those of Ignorance, "There is s sin
unto death: and there is a sin not nnto death." Ignorance is one of
the most marked and ruinous consequences that the fall of our first
parents entailed upon us. It was with the promise of the very opposite
consequence that the Tempter seduced them, when he said "Ye shall
be as gods knowing good and evil." The knowledge of the latter they
truly gained, but that of the former they miserably lost. And from
that moment the description of Jeremiah became applicable to all their
descendants. "They are wise to do evil, but to do good they have no knowledge." Indeed so wholly destitute are all, until enlightened and instructed by the Word and Spirit of God, of any thought, care, interest,
and even capacty for spiritual truth that they stand in a similar
relation to God and spiritual things, that the very brute creation do
with regard to man, and all those things that are level to *his* understanding. "So foolish was I and ignorant," says the Psalmist referring
to such a state, "that I was even as a beast before thee." And so says
S. Paul "have we the understanding darkened, being alienated from the
life of God, through the ignorance that is in us."

"The natural man understandeth not the things of the Spirit
of God;" the truths, the aims, the objects of Christianity, any more
than "the beasts that perish," can conceive or enter into the aims, the
pursuits, the hopes, the feelings, or affections of human life. Now we
well know that of all knowledge within our reach, as social and intellectual beings, it has ever been an admitted truth, that "the soul be
without it is not good." And in no age of the world has the necessity
been so freely and generally recognised of acquiring and promoting it
to the very utmost as in this. On the same principle as beings capable
of religious improvement, the supply of the natural deficiency of knowledge, should be no less earnestly sought by all: and the more so in
proportion as it must evidently be an object of superior value and
importance.

If the advantage of secular education be manifest and undeniable—
if it elevates a man from the position in which it finds him in society,
and fits him for a superior one—if it opens to him new ranges of
interesting thought and research, as he "separates himself," as Solomon
observes, through the influence of a taste for knowledge "to intermeddle
with all wisdom"—If it is "a defence," as he tells us and "by it there

is profit"—such in kind, though infinitely greater in degree, are the benefits of spiritual knowledge.

Its distinguishing excellence is, as he goes on to observe of it in the same passage, that "it giveth life to them that have it." And to this a greater than Solomon bears His witness. "This is Life eternal to know Thee the only True God and Jesus Christ whom Thou hast ent."

Nor is life only adjoined to this knowledge, but as S. Peter says "all things that pertain to life and godliness." Peace says he is one of its attendant blessings. "Peace is multiplied to you through the knowledge of God and of Jesus our Lord." And S. Paul in like manner says " To be spiritually minded is life and peace." "Through knowledge" it is said moreover "shall the just be delivered." Through acquaintanceship with God and His truth, what snares of evil, and what stumbling blocks of difficulty may we not expect to avoid, and shall we not actually escape, as we pass through this world of offence and sin. "The prudent man,"—forwarned and taught by that God of all knowledge with whom he is in constant communion "forseeth the evil and hideth himself," while "the simple passes on and is punished." And to the same purpose, though in more directly spiritual language, S. Peter teaches us that the "pollutions of the world are escaped through the knowledge of God and of Jesus our Lord."

There is too a satisfaction in the conscious possession of knowledge irrespective of its utility in promoting ourselves and our ends. With what a calm delight does the mind of a successful enquirer, student, or discoverer, rest in the contemplation of the truth it has made its own! Solomon observes how "pleasant to the soul," is freshly acquired information " when wisdom entereth into the heart." When you have mastered some problem that was long a puzzle to your wondering mind when you had secured some clear knowledge on a subject that curiosity had long striven and wished to grasp—with what interest did you ponder over the before hidden mystery, and then go forth with a glad consciousness of power, that was not yours before.

Even so a peace passing understanding suffuses the soul, that rejoices in the knowledge of God. Fresh channels of thought and feeling, fresh objects of hope and pursuit open before the vision of the immortal wondering spirit, and it enters into the experience of the Apostle's rapturous satisfaction. " O the depth of the riches of the knowledge of God!"

And surely from this view of its value and benefits, it follows that to rest satisfied in a state of ignorance on such matters as relate to the nature of God, and the soul, the will of our Creator, and the object or destiny of our creation is utterly inexcusable, and unnatural: that to remain unconcerned about such matters is as unreasonable as it is contrary to all that we approve and do in the case of all other ignorance. God however has not left us to argue about this from reason, but has expressed strongly and unmistakably. His judgment, on this subject All scripture goes to prove that such *wilful* ignorance is in His sight sin of the most culpable nature. Accordingly we find one character introduced by Solomon, owning in expressions of the strongest self-disparagement that he had "not learned this wisdom, nor had the knowledge of the Holy." And on the other hand wo have Balaam rejoicing to a degree of boasting that he was "a man who had heard the words of God, and knew the knowledge of the Most High."

You must now proceed to observe that the text does not speak of ignorance such as that of the heathen, within whose reach the knowledge of salvation has in God's mysterious Providence been never placed. There is an ignorance which from the circumstances of those of whom it may be prædicated is a condition of imperfection rather than sin : an ignorance which is subject of pity, rather than blame ; and which needs forgiveness simply : renunciation of it not being possible. Our Lord frequently in His life hinted an apology which in His death He deliberately offered for such misguided ones. He says " If ye were blind ye should have no sin : " that is, as we learn from His teaching elsewhere, no such aggravated culpability as otherwise would be yours if possessing but not improving the means of " coming to the knowledge of the truth."

Of those to whom little is given, little will be required. The Lord, the righteous Judge will weigh all in an even balance. For " he," He says, " that knew not his Lord's will, but did commit things worthy of stripes, shall be beaten with few." Punished indeed : for even the heathen, S· Paul shows us, might do better, For they have a light of nature, and a law of conscience. And yet with but few stripes. For as many as have sinned without the law, that is the Revelation which is given to the members of His Church, shall be judged without it, not *by* it as the others shall.

And whether such be a case of absolute heathenism of which S. Paul says to the Athenians, " The times of your ignorance God winked at "—or something very like it, as may be the case with many of the neglected of our own countrymen—or whether it be a case of natural infirmity or simplicity, or a want of opportunity, or a visitation of Him who withholds means of grace or knowledge from one as He pleases, which He bestows almost lavishly upon another—there is a certain palliation which the All Wise God has taught us, He knows perfectly how to make. The Saviour of the world knows well when to put up that gracious and all availing prayer of His, " Father forgive them for they know not what they do." The Apostles S. Peter and S. John, admit a certain force in this consideration when, charging the Jews with the murder of Jesus, and urging them to repentance for the crime, the former says " now brethren I wot that through ignorance ye did it, as did your rulers." And so S. Paul " Had they known it they would not have crucified the Lord of glory." And who can tell to what extent we are indebted to that High Priest, to whom we are taught to confess as sins needing forgiveness " our negligences and ignorances," for the remission, through the forbearance of God, of many such that we can never notice or know? It may be we shall look back in the light of eternity, on many a passage in our own spiritual history, and say with the same Apostle's deep humility and adoring gratitude, as we see what has been the at present unimagined efficacy of such intercession on our behalf, "I obtained mercy because I did it ignorantly."

But it is of no ignorance of this sort—no blindness of heathen, no simplicity of the poor and untaught, no ignorance of the unhappily too many who lack the means and opportunity of knowing almost anything—of which S. Paul speaks when he says "some have not the knowledge of God, I speak this to your shame." He does not speak it here, as in the passages I have referred to, to their excuse. The Corinthian professors were not as the heathen, as the Jews, or any in their unenlightened and prejudiced condition. No more are any of us in this Christian land who are within the sound and under the influence of the truths they were, and who pray in our Litany " From all blindness of heart, Good Lord deliver us," " May it please Thee to forgive us all our sins, negligences, and ignorances! " With us it is as with those in the text. For them, as for his other converts, he had not ceased as he tells us to provide, and labour, and desire, that they might be " filled with the knowledge of the Divine Will, in all wisdom and spiritual understanding." It was reasonably expected of them that they should be so filled, and be " increasing in the knowledge of God." To his surprise and regret however the Apostle found that there were those among them, in great numbers, who cared not to possess themselves of that all needful acquirement. And we have to consider the emotion, S. Paul considered such a reflection should arouse in every person, conscious of His ignorance, that of shame. " I speak this to your shame."

Sometimes when writing in condemnation to his correspondents he expresses *surprise*. As to the Galatians " I marvel that ye are so soon removed from grace." Sometimes *anxiety*, " I stand in doubt of you." Sometimes simply *blame*, "I praise you not." Sometimes horror and indignation, as in the fifth chapter of this Epistle. But here he was not so much impressed with the thought how strange it was, or how ungrateful, or how unconsistent, as how utterly shameful! " I speak this to your *shame*."

And why should the inexcusable want of this knowledge, and one's consciousness of not possessing it, be mentioned as a cause on his part for shame! Well we think might he have spoken of such spiritual destitution as a cause for *fear*. For thus it is written " My people are destroyed for lack of knowledge : because thou hast rejected knowledge I will also reject thee." And S. Paul Himself elsewhere appeals on this subject to the same emotion. " The Lord Jesus shall be revealed from heaven in flaming fire, with His mighty Angels, taking vengeance on them that know not God."

Such ignorance is indeed a cause of *lamentation* also. So God complains in the Psalms. "They know not, neither will they understand, they walk on in darkness." In Isaiah, " The ox knoweth his owner, and the ass his master's crib : but Israel doth not know, my people doth not consider." In Jeremiah, " They know not the way of the Lord. They know not Me." In Amos, "They know not to do right saith the Lord." In Micah, " They know not the thoughts of the Lord, neither understand they His counsel." It may well likewise be a subject for *God's threatening*. " I will pour out my fury upon the heathen that know me not, and upon the families that have not called upon My name." And in Zephaniah "Thus saith the Lord, I will cut off those that have not sought the Lord, nor enquired for Him." But the question still occurs. Why is such wilful deficiency in knowledge mentioned as a ground for *shame*?

We shall see perhaps if we think from what source this emotion arises, or what produces it. Without pretending here to any special accuracy of philosophical definition, we may describe shame as a feeling awakened by a consciousness of some defect, particularly if we become aware that defect is making itself observed. And when in the presence or in the imagined presence of one who *is*, or is *supposed to be* a superior in some respect to ourselves the sense of shame is keen. Thus the beggar is ashamed of his rags as he stands amid a well dressed throng, or the " man in vile apparel before those of gay clothing." The mean man is abashed before the lofty, the deformed before the comely, the dull clown before the intelligent. We have felt the emotion as we stood before the person of gainlier gesture, of more self-possessed address, of higher rank or social worth, of more noble endowments than ourselves.

And stronger still is its developement, when it is aroused in the self-consciousness of intellectual, and most of all moral deficiency. Thus is the idle or careless scholar ashamed, when unable to repeat or tell what he feels he might or ought to have known. The trifler in the presence of the wise, the uninformed when he find himself unable to conceal his ignorance of the subject on which he has begun to converse, or answer the enquiry to which he has exposed himself. Thus above all is the evil doer ashamed as his wickedness is uncovered; his unworthy fraud or artifice, his ungenerous conduct, or his concealed villany is detected by his fellow men, and dragged to the light of day. Instances in Holy Scripture abound. It may suffice merely to refer to the case of his servant Gehazi before the prophet Elisha, and the wife of king Jeroboam before the prophet Ahijah.

We think of the difference between ourselves and the One we inwardly feel to be our superior, whether in natural endowment, or mental excellence, and we are ashamed. We are like the children of Israel before the sons of Anak. " We were as grashoppers in comparison in our own sight, and so we were in theirs." The very Angels are thus conscious as they stand before the Great White Throne. And though they excel in knowledge, and know no thought of evil, they veil their faces with their wings in the sense of their infinite distance from the All Wise and Holy God. And so I suppose from the very nature of things that should we be brought face to face in our convicted sinfulness before Him, the impress of whose wisdom we have lost, our first overwhelming emotion in the consciousness of our ignorance and unacquaintance with Him must be that of Shame. It must even precede fear itself, if indeed we can conceive of *shame*, as existing apart from fear. It was so with Adam and Eve. They were afraid indeed to meet God. But it was the sense of shame, that made them fear. Aptly then does S. Paul mention shame in the connection he does here; and say as that which not only ought to be but *will* be a cause of shame. " Some of you have not the knowledge of God." *As that which ought to be.* For if in the consciousness of natural, or intellectual defects we are ashamed, how much more reason have we to be ashamed in the consciousness of spiritual destitution if haply we are standing before His very eyes, worshipping it may even be with the great congregation, kneeling at the mercy seat, without the knowledge of God. And *as that which will be* a cause of shame *as well as ought to be.*

For Ah! It was not merely of the emotion that *might* well have been stirred within the wilfully ignorant Corinthians, that S. Paul thus said, "Some of you have not the knowledge of God, I speak it to your shame." But of the emotion that actually *would.* Terribly significant words! They tell as Daniel's of a coming day when, while "they that be wise" unto salvation shall "awake to everlasting life," they that be not, shall stand forth to "everlasting comtempt."

Even now in the sight of God, and the Angels of light, there can be no such shameful spectacle, as the man that surrounded with the light of truth, and urged and invited to fellowship with God, and acquaintance with His Word and Will, is content to live and die without the knowledge of God, or with a mere form of it only, and with the wondrous capacities of his spiritual nature, undeveloped and unstored.

And where hereafter can the soul that continues wilfully ignorant—never studying God, His nature, and wishes, and the world to come, as it does itself, its own nature, and wishes, and this world—where I ask can this blind soul expect to find its proper destiny when it passes into eternity, but in the "outer darkness?" Indeed there is no other place to which it could pass.

For what reason think you was the unfortunate afflicted with natural blindness forbidden by the Levitical law to go inside the veil, or come nigh the altar, but to shadow forth the Divine abhorrence of that soul, which continues wilfully in its natural darkness, rejecting carelessly the provided aid of an enlightening Spirit and revelation, and for which hereafter shall be found no place at all in the kingdom of Light!

Can God's habitation be a home for ignorance? Can those be there who have neither nature nor capacity to take a part in the pursuit and joys of a Heaven of light and knowledge? It could verily be no more to such, if they were admitted within, than the most splendid exhibition to the man born blind, or the hall of science to the fool. Men think little of spiritual ignorance now. To see them so satisfied in their spiritual destitution you might suppose it was a well established conclusion, that He who came as "the light of the world." was never required in it! that the Spirit outpoured on the day of Pentecost to abide with His Church, to teach and enlighten its Members, was an utterly needless provision! and that the most entire strangers to the feelings, views, ways, words, and works of God would be welcome at last to the mansions of His friends!

But so it shall never be. And just will be the retribution on those who will neither have part nor lot with Him *now,* which has said that they shall not *then.* "Depart from Me I never knew you," will be the sentence which *they* shall hear who now are saying "Depart from us for wo desire not the knowledge of Thy ways." "If any of you," says S. James "lack this wisdom let him ask of God, that giveth to all liberally and it shall be given him." "The God of our Lord Jesus Christ" says S. Paul, "shall give unto you the spirit of wisdom and revelation, in the knowledge of Him. And the eyes of your understanding shall be enlightened to know the hope of your calling, the riches of His saints inheritance, and the exceeding greatness of His power toward us, who believe."

So "grant us, O Lord, in this world the knowledge of Thy truth, that in the world to come we may have life everlasting Amen."

RELIGIOUS EARNESTNESS.

And the Lord said, Whereunto shall I liken the men of this generation? and to what are they like? They are like unto children sitting in the market place, and calling one to another, and saying, We have piped unto you, and ye have not danced; we have mourned to you and ye have not wept. *Luke* vii. 31-32.

The comparative indifference that those around him show to a subject on which he feels strongly, and thinks deeply, must always appear strange to a reflecting person. And more especially must this be the case, when that subject equally concerns those others. The more important he himself feels that subject to be, and the more so he knows it to be to them, the greater does his surprise become, that they are not so affected as he. And if he be at all of a zealous and earnest spirit, the more anxious is he that they should be. Thus it is that—whether the acquisitions of persons of this kind, be in science, art, or literature— they exert themselves to extend among their fellow men, the information of which they have become possessed, to communicate their own views and discoveries, and to enlighten others with those facts or truths, which they have themselve ascertained. And thus it is too that God has provided that the truth He has given to leading spirits in the human race to search out and find, should be set on a candlestick, as it is sure to be, that others may see the light.

We may have felt this ourselves if we have made any progress above our fellows, and if we have pursued enquiry or thought on any subject of knowledge. From the inner chambers of wisdom we look at those who stand outside, and wonder they should manifest so little interest, to know more of that on which we have informed ourselves. The poorest and most ignorant man even, who has studied his trade, and is thoroughly conversant with all branches of his work, no doubt often makes this reflection within himself upon his unskilled neighbour.

And when the case in point comes to be that all momentous, and as it might well be most of all engrossing subject of religion, this feeling about which I am remarking is experienced in its highest degree. When a man has made proof of its truths, and felt its power, his astonishment at the carelessness with which those around him view it, and their disposition to let it be unnoticed, is only equalled by the intensity of the desire he feels to awaken their thought, and arouse their attention, about its revelations and its truths. It is this emotion that has prompted all Christian and missionary enterprise, that has raised up in undying succession all the living witnesses, that have ever striven to commend that truth to every man's conscience, and to stir the world to the recognition of all those by it unseen and unregarded verities that God would bring before it.

From the very nature of things, none could be struck more by this always prevalent indifference to religion, and exert Himself in consequence more strongly to break through it, than the Lord Jesus. He better than all beside knew " the powers of the world to come," and the wondrous value and interest of what He had to reveal. Strange to Him therefore must have seemed, the attitude in which man stood before Him. " He was in the world, and the world knew Him not." He was come to enlighten, and instruct, and open a vast horizon, to men's vision. But lo! they gazed at Him with unmoved eyes and listless souls. He stood and they passed by on the other side. In many passages in the Gospels we have His surprise at all this expressed. In the text we have it uttered in a forcible figure. The greatest Prophet among all that were born of women His own Forerunner, had been among them. And now Himself was come. And when, we read, He saw how many rejected the counsel of God against themselves, He marvelled at them. And then follow directly the words of the text. Whereto could he liken such unreasonable and wicked men? and what comparison could at all describe the posture of the apathetic soul, in the presence of those solemn realities of the spiritual world amid which it stood, and with which it had to do.

An apter illustration than that with which our Lord pointed His remarks on this spiritual indifference, it would be impossible to adduce. In dwelling upon it we shall have firstly to consider the place in which the children were—the market place. Secondly the posture—" sitting." Thirdly the persons with whom they were concerned. " They were calling one to another." Fourthly what they had been doing—playing and crying. We observe firstly the place. There may be many idle corners in a street, but the market place is designed for business. In the 27th c. of Ezekiel we read of the market place of Tyre. There were the merchants, with their vessels of brass, mules, metals, articles of ivory, and other ornaments, weapons of war, jewellery, provisions, and dress. In the 12th c. of S. Mark we read of the market place again, how the scribes and magistrates appeared in it, in their robes of office, and how the people assembled there to consult them. In the 16th c. of the Acts we see it was the same in the heathen cities. And in the 17th c. we see it was there at Athens that S. Paul repaired, when he would converse with the shrewdest, the most intelligent, the most influential, and in a word the greatest number of citizens. If men are found as they may be, standing idle in the market place, they are the exception and not the rule. It is set apart for buying, selling, and business generally, rather than trifling. If you would loiter, or stroll at your ease, the country or the parade is the better place. The market is for the busy rather than the idle or the gay. In such a market place as citizens of this world are we! Transactions of the mightiest nature are passing around us and concern us there. Treasures of heaven are being secured or bartered. Riches unsearchable are to be gained or lost. Interests the most absorbing, that relate to our life everlasting in the world to come, are being decided. Heaven and earth meet here together

God and man confer and treat with one another. And—as in the market place of the cities we have spoken of, where the magistrates met and justice was dispensed—the courts are open round us. The court of Heaven is set: and God is there Himself to adjudicate for us day by day, to dispense justice and mercy, wrath and love; to acquit or condemn to hear petitions, to grant favours, and to transact, to use the figure in the Allegory of "The Holy War," all the business of the city "Mansoul."

And what are *we* in this world, the stage on which affairs of such momentous concern to us all are being enacted, where the affairs of eternity are being settled with us each? Verily we are too like children in the market place, with little more thought or concern about it all than the little child, that sits and plays among its fellows, within the precincts of the busy spot, thinking and feeling only as a child, in perfect ignorance of the conflicting thoughts and passions of the men and women that throng around. In the great mart the destinies of kingdoms may be decided. Success or failure, that shall stamp a lasting character on the life of a nation may tremble in the balance—gains, losses, or events, that may alter the whole complexion of one's life, and turn its current another way, may be experienced. But what knows or cares the unsuspecting child, as it pursues undiverted, by it all, its baby sports, or vexes its little heart, with its infant troubles. And as little recks the worldly soul, while it is engrossed with its short-lived joys, and troubles, its petty cares and anxieties. And yet all the time its destiny to heaven or hell is becoming fixed. In that great mart God Himself spreads out His possessions and Christ sets out His merchandise. "Unto you, O men, I call. Riches and honour are with me; yea durable riches and righteousness. I lead in the way of righteousness, that I may cause those that love me to inherit substance, and I will fill their treasures."

And many a one of us heeds and ponders it no more than the infant in the market place does the trader's cry, and the advantages it might secure by bargaining for his merchandise. We hear the Gospel call to the forsaking sin, to the following after holiness, to the conflict of the spiritual life. We hear it in the word and on the Sabbath. It strikes upon our ear, and startles us it may for a moment, as such a voice might the child in the market. But we turn every one our own way, and recall our thoughts and regards to their old current, as though we had no more part nor lot in this matter than the child in the business of the market place.

Aye we many of us are worse more foolish far than he. There comes with riper years a time when he ceases to think as a child, and speak as a child. He puts away childish things: and rises up in the market place, as eager as those that have gone before him to play the man. Perhaps many of you have not done this. Long years have passed, and you are still as children triflers in the Gospel market place! What business have you transacted with God and Christ? What personal dealings have there been between you? What gains have you acquired out of the Gospel store before you? What debts of sin have you paid off there by your Surety? What benefits of pardon, grace, and strength have you obtained there from Him?

The day to each of us is fast drawing on when, if I may so say, the market shall be closed, the opportunity of enriching the soul, and laying up treasure in heaven be withdrawn. And you must abide thenceforth for ever in your gain or your loss; to rejoice eternally in the one, or mourn everlastingly the other. There is food there offered for the soul now, the bread of Life, there is raiment for it, the righteousness of Christ and the sanctification of His Spirit, in which it may stand faultless and without blame before Him. Ornaments there are in that market well worth securing, to deck yourself withal, " ornaments of grace," to adorn you in the eyes of God and man with " the beauty of holiness." There are houses and lands to be disposed of, mansions eternal in the heavens, and territories as limitless as the Son of man's domains.

And all ready for any applicant: and to be had too, without money and without price! But to you, as to every one shall come a day when you shall be able to buy this costly merchandise no more: when he that is rich, rich in faith, rich in good works, rich in the grace that Christ gives, and His Spirit imparts, and His Church ministers, shall be rich for ever; and he that is not shall remain eternally destitute. Now then while wisdom cries and utters her voice, and proffers her goods in the streets—while the Divine Person represented under that name, is calling to you, as He did to the Church in Laodicea, " Thou knowest it not, but thou art wretched and miserable, and poor, and blind, and naked, I counsel thee to buy of me gold, and raiment."—and while the children of this world stand idle, as regards their souls interests—take you part in its mighty transactions, and lay up for yourself an abiding treasure.

But here we are brought to the second point in the text. The children of this world do not *stand* in this market place. They *sit*. If you see a man standing there, however idly, he may as those labourers in the Gospel, that waited to be hired, be waiting for something. He may be standing till his turn comes, or his opportunity to do something. He may be looking for some one, or stopping in readiness for the business in which he is concerned to commence. Standing is more the posture of expectancy : sitting of rest. And these children were sitting They had settled down there to pursue their childish sports. They had found something to do of their own, or at all events did not mean to take any part in the market business. And this witness of our Lord is true of the multitude around us. The Angels seen by the prophet Zechariah said " We have walked to and fro through the earth:" and behold all the earth sitteth still, and is at rest.

Have not some of yourselves perhaps come to sit as calmly down as regards your spiritual state, as these children, who all unconsciously decided that the market was no concern of theirs? Has there gone forth no voice, though you did not notice it at the time, that has said to you " Soul take thine ease!" and in obedience to it you have settled down in this religious indifference, from which we long to rouse you? You do not for the most part reckon that the man you see sitting idly down is doing any great work. It was this perfect apathy, that affected our Lord as I said so much. This posture betokening it, that he here marks precisely by the word " sitting." He could say with the Psalmist, " My soul is exceedingly filled with the scorning of those that are at ease," with astonishment at the disregard they show. It might be natural for those to sit, who were out of the way in the darkness and the shadow of death. But to sit in the very market place, to continue " wholly at ease and quiet," under the very sound of the Gospel, where the great transactions that concern the soul are brought visibly before men's eyes and the treasures of grace laid open—for them thus to sit instead of being drawn to take part, or possess themselves of the advantages within their reach, were strange indeed!

We observe thirdly the persons with whom these children were alone concerned. They were " calling one to another." With the great characters and prominent figures in the market they had nothing to do or say. There passed it might be the governor of the city! High was his office and responsible his duties. On his wisdom in counsel, his decision in the execution of affairs, depended the welfare of multitudes and these children's too amongst them. But what was he to them? If they gazed at him a moment with childish wonder, in his robes of dignity, and with his train of attendants, they soon turned back their eye with far more interest to their playfellows, and their games. Captains might pass them by, in their pride and their valour, senators in their importance and their talent, lords in their loftiness, or beggars in their rags. The rich and the poor met there together: the mean man and the mighty: the bond and the free.

But little wot the children the thoughts of those many hearts. Little could they fathom the seething tide of human passions, hopes and fears, joys and sorrows, that was surging around them. They had almost no portion as yet in that vast expanse of life. Although in and through the life of those others, their fellow citizens, they lived and moved, and had their own being, they acted as though they were concerned with their playfellows alone, as though they were their all in all.

Our life here, as theirs is wrapt up in a far greater one, the unseen and spiritual, that overspreads us all. We too are encompassed with mighty verities and exalted beings, before which and whom the greatest and most dazzling objects of earthly interest fade colourless away. Around us Michael and His Angels are engaged on the business of man, and the devil with his on the contrary side. That market place of life— in which we sit, so unconcernedly of other and grander presences, calling one to another, and only conscious of our fellows and their concerns, the trivial things of time—is the general assembly ground of aspirations, hope and fears, joys or sorrows, which we must soon share, which are to thrill our souls for evermore.

And what are we who think of and act with our fellow men alone to the almost exclusion from our thoughts and dealings of the God that rules us, and the Saviour that has died and lives for us, and the Spirit that strives with us, the providences that are continually appealing to us, and the evil spirits that tempt us, and the ministering one that wait around ns! What I say are we but these very children in the market place, with a thousand times their trifling, with nothing of their excuse? Harmless indeed was their simplicity, but ruinous if we shall continue to resemble them, shall be our soul destroying folly.

"Be not children in understanding." Be not like children of this world, who are calling one to another, regardless of Him who stands amongst them, the unseen Saviour, on whom they do not call, with whom they hold no communion, with whom they are not concerned, for whom they care nothing. Of the ungodly the same description is given in the Psalm, as by Christ in this passage, "They call not upon the Lord." But our duty towards God, our Church Catechism teaches us from our earliest years to say, is "*to call upon Him*." See that you do so!

Call upon Him as your Master, as you would do to enquire about your work, to receive directions, to tell what you have done, and to see his will, as regards what you think of doing next. Call upon Him as your Friend: as you would call upon a friend, to see what plans or purposes he had for the future, in the knowledge or perhaps arrangement of which you might participate, what trials you might possibly help to lighten, what ends you might take part in promoting, what fresh sorrows or hopes, or joys, you might be admitted to the confidence of sharing.

Fourthly we have to notice from the text, what these children had been doing, and wherein they are here a pattern of the children of this world. They had been playing and also crying. Two things we are always struck with in children: with what little things they will amuse themselves, and with what little troubles they will vex themselves. Volatile in thought, and roving in fancy, a trifle entertains them; and a small thing will divert their attention. Play being wholly natural to their age, they will pursue it in any place, and under any circumstances, even though it be in the market, or any other place designed for graver occupation. And they do so wholly unaware of the incongruity of their behaviour. The proceedings of that busy market place, of whatever kind they be, are a perfect farce and unreality, a dumb show to the little child. They are altogether beyond his mind: and he has even less sympathy with all, and less interest, than the gravest man engaged there has in the child's vain sports.

And what but child's play is the occupation of the mere worldly man, of the votary of pleasure, that passes a life useless and wholly aimless, except for the single thought how "to morrow may be as this day, and much more abundant?" Whereunto shall we liken the grasping man that sets his heart on riches, and gets him ever fresh acquisitions of houses and lands, only to leave all, himself no whit better or happier. or more honoured in the end—but to the child that rises up from its vain pastime? Whereunto the candidate for a mere passing fame, that leaves his popularity and his title to another, as he goes down to the dust, no more to be remembered, where are alike the small, the great, in equal insignificance and in the dishonour of the grave? What but child's play have been all the achievements of the children of this world, laid as they have been or shall be in the dust, by the levelling hand of time? Hear on this point the Spirit's testimony, and God teach you to number your days, that you may apply your hearts unto wisdom. "This I say the time is short: it remaineth that they that rejoice, be as though they rejoiced not ; and they that buy as though they possessed not: for the fashion of this world passeth awy."

But lastly these children had been here crying. We know how prone to such weeping the young child is. As the trivial object will afford it diversion, so the most inadequate cause will affect it with grief. We of riper years wonder as we behold in it how a slight occasion will give rise to such immoderate sorrow and passionate tears. But are the children of this world really wiser, who take the very same over anxious thought, and display a no less undue emotion in things pertaining to this life only? And if so many of ourselves in our puny enterprises and trifling lives, are like children in the market place in their vain and empty games—If so many like them we see as S. Peter expresses the idea before us "sporting themselves with their own deceivings"—how many are like them too in their over eager and passionate solicitude about the things of this passing world! What are the foolish ones, that thus load their heart with a burden of multiplied earthly cares, and bear them about continually: brooding to day on the ills of yesterday, and anticipating those of the morrow—what the distrustful souls, that unwisely vex themselves with the burden of sins that are past, and for which there is such complete absolution, to be graciously, and freely, and at once obtained, that they will be no more remembered against the penitent applicant for mercy in His Redeemer's name—and what are they that continue drinking ever more deeply of that "vanity and vexation of spirit," which is "the sorrow of the world" when "everlasting consolation and good hope through grace," is proffered to them instead in "the comfort of Christ's love and the fellowship of His Spirit"—what are all these who as the prophet says "weary themselves for very vanity," but like unto the silly children sitting in the market place, their own self-tormentors, weeping over their self-made grief if not their imagined and unreal wrongs? We quote the Apostle's words again in this connection also, "It remaineth that they that weep be as though they wept not, for the fashion of this world passeth away."

Sirs ! ye are in the very market place of eternity. Sin, and Death, and Satan. God, and His Son, and His Spirit, all are busy round you. Rise then, quit yourselves like men, in earnest, and in haste ! For the business of that market, as I said, is hastening to a close. Life with its opportunities, Christ with His riches, the Spirit who will help you to secure them to the enriching of your soul for ever, all are before you still, though not for long. "Strive then according to His power, who will work in you mightily, to take your part in the grand transactions around you." Press into the thickest of the throng that are busy about God, and their soul, and heaven. Seek to win Christ and the treasure before you. And you shall. "Your labour shall not be in vain in the Lord." A prize is before you, and success may be won. "For the kingdom of heaven suffereth violence. And the violent (God grant you to be of their number, and not of these loitering children), shall take it by force."

THE AUTUMN OF NATURE AND THE DECLINE OF GRACE.

We all do fade as a leaf; and our iniquities like the wind have taken us away,
Isaiah lxiv. 6.

It is a fact in nature well worthy of notice that the same season of the year, which witnesses the falling of the leaves is characterised also by rough tempestuous weather. Hardly have the leaves shown symptoms of decay, and begun to drop, than for the most part the stormy wind of Autumn goes forth fulfilling the word of Nature's God. It is sent out to hasten their fall, lest they should prove injurious by continuing suspended in a state of decay above and around us; and to scatter wide and far the gathered heaps, the exhalations of which would otherwise prove as noxious as they are offensive. The wisdom and goodness of such provision we may be liable to overlook from our familiarity with the circumstance. But it is one of the beneficent and salutary arrangements of that Divine Providence, ever so "wonderful in counsel, and excellent in working." And it cannot but awaken in the observant mind, the feeling of admiration, to which the greatest of all naturalists gave expression, "He hath made everything beautiful in his time." "God hath set one thing over aginst the other."

And so it comes to pass that, unless in exceptional cases as a wood where the wind has only a limited power, the leaves are no sooner fallen than they are strewn by the wind over the face of the earth. "The wind passes over them and they are gone, and the place thereof knows them no more." It is no doubt from the prophet's observation of this that after his first exclamation in the text "We all do fade as a leaf" he goes on at once to complete the thought and carry out the illustration to the end by adding, "and our iniquities like the wind (the leaf,) have taken us away."

The fading leaf has therefore a two fold end, or there is an account to be given in two particulars: first, in its fall to the ground, when its greenness is withered and its life is gone; and then in its violent removal when, snatched from our eye, it is hurried away by the wind, and carried whither we know not. On each of these points as they illustrate the spiritual life, let us reflect a while with the prophet in the text.

Now it is to be remarked, that when the prophet says here "We all do fade as a leaf," he is not fondly indulging a useless lamentation over the transitory condition of this mortal life. He is not deploring that change which is inevitable, because through sin death has passed upon all men, but a change that had come over his people for which there was no necessity. In other words there is not a reference to the fading away of nature, but to the decay of grace. It was of the freshness of spiritual life, and the beauty of holiness, that he here exclaims "the glory is departed." He was not lavishing his grief in a vain regret over the course of nature, but over the result of sin. It is appointed unto all men once to die, and to all natural prosperity to decline, and the prophet had neither time nor tears to waste over this the ordinance of God. But for the sin of his countrymen of which he here spoke, which had stripped off the glory of the nation, and cast their crown to the ground, for the fading of their spiritual life and the decay of their religious prosperity, there was no such existing necessity.

And it was this that aroused the protesting prophet's mournful exclamation, and infused all the bitterness into the complaint of this sin-conscious cry, "We all do fade as a leaf." It was the passing away of their goodness as the morning cloud, and the early dew : it was the disappearance, yea extinction, in the land of that righteousness, which once exalted them as a nation, that the prophet here regretted. Israel who once was "holiness to the Lord," was now all as an unclean thing. The faithful city, as he tells in his first chapter, was become apostate. "It was full of judgment, righteousness lodged in it." But now he observed in that chapter, and in the verse from which the text is taken, the very contrary.

And thus it is, that of all decay for which man is subject, there is none so sad and lamentable as the fading away of spirituality in a backsliding soul ; that of all examples of mortality there is none so solemnly awful as the spectacle of an immortal being, "dead in trespasses and sins." You have seen fair nature stripped of her graceful Spring, her bright Summer, and gorgeous Autumn-attire, with the like of which Solomon, in all his glory was never arrayed. You have seen her bared of all her beauty, exposed to the violence of the stormy tempest, to be the sport of the wintry wind. You have repeatedly seen the vigour of manhood laid low, and the beauty of youth turned to decay, and the blossom of childhood blighted by disease or death. You have seen the "rich man fade away in his ways," while his wealth "made itself wings and fled away." You have heard how the cities that the great ones of old had built for the might of their glory, and the honour of their majesty, have perished utterly.

So passes everything pleasant to the eyes and dear to the heart, that too fondly cherished its peculiar treasure ! So surely do we all come to prove by sad and repeated experience, that we can none of us hesitate to give a melancholy assent to them the prophet's words." All the glory of man is as the flower of grass : the grass withereth the flower fadeth ! " Sooner or later we are ready to adopt the lines.

> There never was an earthly dream
> Of beauty and delight,
> That mingled not too soon with clouds,
> As sunrays with the night :

That faded not from that full heart
  Where once it loved to stay,
And left that heart more desolate,
  For having felt its sway!

There never was, nor can there be,
  On earth a precious spring
Whose waters to the fevered lip,
  Unfailing we may bring!

All changes on this troubled shore,
  Or passes from the sight,
Earth's transient joys pass evermore,
  And darkness wraps the light!

But to witness the fall from grace, to muse upon some instance of the decline of spiritual life, to behold the withering, like the leaf, of some unhappy one's profession who once " had a name to live," to see some Chorazin, Bethsaida or Capernaum that was exalted to heaven, cast down to hell—to gaze upon some Church that Ephesus-like has left its first love, or some disciple of it that has gone back to walk no more with Christ and His disciples—to see some "turn from the holy commandment delivered unto them," to the paths of the destroyer, and not only the fruits of the Spirit no longer brought forth, but the very leaves of profession scattered by the wintry breath of sin: and to make the reflection of the Psalmist " He hath left off to behave himself wisely and to do good "—this is the spectacle that presented itself to the prophet when he looked forth upon the spiritually dead of the daughter of his people, and cried over them, in the exceeding great and bitter cry, as he saw the end was come, " We all do fade as a leaf, and our iniquities like the wind have taken us away!"

We mourn not, in the certainty of a returning Spring, for the ravage of winter as those that have no hope. Nor do we so sorrow in our sure and certain prospect of the great Resurrection for the ravages wrought by disease and death, on those "who shall be accounted worthy to obtain that world, and the resurrection from the dead." " For this corruptible shall yet put on incorruption, and this mortal immortality." All *natural* loss may be repaired in that hour, but *spiritual* loss, if not made good before, never. " If a righteous man turneth away from his righteousness and committeth iniquity and dieth in them," there remaineth no more hope of restitution to his first state: for his iniquities like the wind the leaf have carried him away. " There is hope of a tree (says Job) though it be cut down, that it will sprout again," yea even for a broken bough, with the leaves upon it, that it might possible be reunited. For it may sometimes be joined to the parent stock, and the leaves revive afresh. But when the wind has borne those separated parts away it is impossible to renew their life.

And even such, as is aptly indicated in the figure of the text, is the nature of all sin. If not only sunders communion with the God of our spirit's life, but it puts the transgressor far from Him, and cuts off his expectation from Him for the future. It drives away from God: ever further and further. Like the Autumn wind—that not only severs the hold of the leaf from its tree, but forces it with all speed from the spot where it had lately lived and grown—so our iniquities the prophet teaches drive us from the God, from whom they have rent us, from the very neighbourhood of hope, and grace, and blessing. So our Lord teaches in the pa able of the prodigal. He not only broke off from his father, but he forthwith went away into a far country. When once God is parted with, He is very soon lost sight of. Jonah, when he had sinned, exclaimed "I am cast out of Thy sight!" Cain, like his father Adam, was very soon driven by his own sin from the presence of the Lord. The prophet here in the very next verse to the text says, "Thou hast hid Thy face from us because of our iniquities." And so the Spirit of God testifies. "They that follow mischief are from Thy law," "The Lord is far from the wicked."

And the effect in the case of the servant of God is the same as in the servant of the wicked one. Sin puts him back, like the hand on Ahaz' sun-dial, many a degree in his Christian path. He may seek and obtain forgiveness for it. But the distance it has in a moment placed between him and God, is not readily recovered. And through many a long day, while he is seeking to recover his steps in the bitterness of repentance, may he have occasion to take up the prophet's lamentation in the text, My iniquities like the wind have taken me away.

And the wind not only forcibly carries away the faded leaf, but none can say where or how far it shall be borne! Thus says David, are "the ungodly like the chaff which the wind driveth away." And, says Job, "They are as the stubble before the wind, and as chaff that the storm carrieth away." Has the wind of iniquity whirled any soul into the course of sin? Has some temptation swept one away in its violent blast? Who call tell how far or where the transgressor may be borne? None can anticipate the vagrant and devious path of the sinner, as S. James says, driven with this wind and tossed. He is arrested, perhaps once and again, by some obstacle that the Spirit of God imposes to stay the madness of his career. He may be checked finally. But if not, he is presently lost to sight, or hope, "like a rolling thing before the whirlwind," like a "wandering star" starting from its orbit, of the destiny of which you can only tell that there is reserved for it a "darkness for ever."

Thus it was with Jeroboam, the first king of the divided nation, to whose name is attached the eternal infamy that he made Israel to sin. He was once a hopeful youth, the stay, it would appear, of his widowed mother, remarkable for his industry, and promoted to office by Solomon, who noticed it. But ambition took possession of his soul, and urged him from one crime to another. He first ungratefully lifted up his hand against the king who had raised him from his low estate, and made him ruler over all the house of Joseph. And ere long the whole house of Jeroboam was destroyed from off the face of the earth. Thus it was with Saul, whom self-will, and then envy, hatred, malice, and all uncharitableness precipitated into a reckless life and a self-murderer's death. Thus it was with Hazael king of Syria. He too was swept into the vortex of crime by the mighty rushing wind of ambition, till, having treacherously put to death his master, Benhadad, by suffocating him as he lay on his sick bed, he fell into a career of savage crime too repulsive even to mention. Thus it was with Herodias. She deserted the home of Philip, her husband, to whom she would not submit herself. And she came at last to stain the soul of herself and her graceless daughter with the blood of the greatest prophet that ever was born of women. And thus it was with Judas. The love of money having separated his soul from Christ, hurried him ever further away, until it "filled him full of all iniquity, and brought him to destruction both of body and soul."

By these and such like solemn instances with which the Holy Scriptures abound we are forewarned of this tendency of evil, and how the wicked, if he become so, is, as Solomon says, "driven away in his wickedness."

When iniquity, like the rising wind, gathers round your soul, when the fierce impulse of passion or immoderate desire lays hold upon your spirit, weak before its blast like the unresisting leaf, bethink yourself of the prophet's reminder here of the incalculable distance to which its violence may hurl you.

Your hopes of heaven, your peace of mind, your fellowship with God and His people, your reputation in the eyes of others (if through grace God has granted you such favour and esteem), the approval of your own conscience, will all be put far from you if *one* iniquity be allowed to sieze upon your unresisting soul, and carry it away captive at the devil's will. "If a man abide not in me he is cast forth as a branch and is withered; and men gather them, and cast them into the fire, and they are burned."

I have said that there appears to be no original reference in the words of the text to the decay of nature. But yet their application to this topic appears to be so natural, and our minds are so instinctively carried on from the words to this idea, that we may dwell on the thought for a moment in conclusion. Let us then ponder in its simplest form the reflection the prophet makes in the text, "We all do fade as a leaf."

The withered leaves that fall around a solemn truth convey,
In wisdom's ear, they speak aloud of frailty and decay:
They say that man's apportioned year shall have its winter too,
Shall rise and shine, and then decline, as all around him do.

They tell him all he has on earth, his brightest dearest things,
His loves and friendships, joys and hopes, have all their falls and springs:
A wave upon a moon-lit sea, a leaf upon the blast,
A summer flower, an April shower, that gleams and hurries past.

Rev. H. F. Lyte.

Perhaps some of us are already becoming conscious of some such change. The eagerness of our youthful hopes, our bright anticipations of the future, our once vivid expectations, are greatly modified. Not only to the Barzillais, the more aged among us, to whom the grasshopper has become a burden and desire has failed, but to the younger and stronger there are ever coming, in the voice of affliction, or pain, or disappointment, or failure of enterprise, the premonitions of this future which is the lot of us all.

> Change is our portion here !
>   Soon fades the summer sky,
> The landscape droops in Autumn sere,
>   And spring flowers bloom to die.
>
> Change is our portion here!
>   Yet midst our changing lot,
> Midst withering flowers, and tempests drear,
>   There is that changes not.

And so, though we too must be borne away by the wind of death which man's sin has set in motion against him, though health and life shall fade by degrees, even the dead, says Christ, all live to God. Though this mortal body be laid aside and perish like the leaf in its hour of decay, in its stead another and more glorious one shall rise. Other leaves in the returning Spring shall take the place of those that have been lost. And thus to the servant of God the prophet's reflection on the autumnal decline has the very reverse of a melancholy aspect. He can add to the words of the lines before quoted—

> It may be so: and well I know, myself and all that's mine,
> Must with each fleeting year advance and ripen to decline.
> I do not shun the solemn truth ; to him it is not drear
> Whose hopes can rise above the skies, and see a Saviour near.
>
> It only makes him feel with joy this earth is not his home;
> It sends him on from present ills to brighter hours to come.
> It bids him take with thankful heart whate'er his God may send,
> Content to go through weal or woe to glory in the end.

The coming autumn of his life brings him only nearer to that everlasting spring that shall follow. If God takes down the earthly tabernacle of the human frame it is only because He purposes, when it is dissolved, to build another and a comelier one, over which sin and corruption shall have no more power. And His servant, as the Apostle says, is only unclothed by the process of natural decay to be clothed upon by immortality, as the beggar might be stripped of his rags by one who designed thereafter to invest him with costly and glorious apparel. While, then, we all do fade as a leaf, for those of us who shall be kept by the power of God through faith unto salvation—for those who seek seriously and cherish constantly that indwelling Spirit who, as the Lord and Giver of Life, causes all things spiritual to live and grow by His quickening grace—there " is reserved an inheritance" and a crown which, as the life of eternity itself, is to " fade not away."

THE MINISTRY OF ANGELS.

Daniel x., 2, 8, 11, 12, 14, 16, 17, 19, 20, 21.

In those days I, Daniel, was mourning three full weeks. (8) I was left alone, and there remained no strength in me. (11) And one (he) said unto me O Daniel, a man greatly beloved, understand the words that I speak unto thee, and stand upright for unto thee am I now sent. (12) Thus said he unto me, Fear not, Daniel : for from the first day that thou didst set thine heart to understand, and to chasten thyself before thy God, thy words were heard and I am come for thy words. (14) Now I am come to make thee understand (16) And behold, one like the similitude of the sons of men touched my lips : then I opened my mouth and spake. (17) Then there came again and touched me one like the appearance of a man (19) And said O man greatly beloved fear not, peace be unto thee, be strong, yea be strong And when he had spoken unto me I was strengthened and said, Thou hast strengthened me; (20, 21) Then said he I will show thee that which is noted in the Scripture of truth.

In these words from one of the lessons for the feast of S. Michael and All Angels we have very fully revealed in the case of Daniel the nature of the offices and services of God's ministering Angels, and the circumstances of God's people which especially call them forth. Daniel, at the time of which the text speaks, you will see by looking through the chapter, was alone, was in a desponding frame of mind, was perplexed and doubtful about the future, and was not at all clear in his own mind on many points of religious interest. He was, moreover, as embarassed in the power of utterance as of thought. He could no longer speak freely to God in prayer, nor to the people to whom he prophesied. He had likewise come to think so humbly and mistrustfully of himself that he had lost all confidence of approach to God, and even the sense of acceptance with Him. Without this last the religious life is a weariness indeed. For there can in no case, as there was not in his, be any peace or joy in believing where doubts are entertained by any one of God's goodwill towards him, and the reality of his being the favoured object of the Divine regard and love.

The Angels, who were sent to enlighten the downcast prophet, addressed themselves to the relief and removal of all these perplexities and doubts. They united first of all in bearing testimony that he was the object of God's deep and earnest love. "O Daniel, a man greatly beloved." For without this knowledge, as a fresh spring of animation to the soul and life, in the matter of Divine as of human trust, the heart of man becomes necessarily and hopelessly discouraged. They each bade him take courage in the words "Fear not." Each addressed himself to the task of opening and enlarging the prophet's understanding. And while one touched his lips, and removed the obstacle that made him falter in prayer and hesitate in speech, the other diffused a peace over his anxious soul, and renewed his broken strength and revived his flagging energies.

The first point to which they directed their attention —like skilful physicians of the soul, which is so open to their watchful and experienced eyes, and of the workings and impulses of which they are, we learn here, so observant—was the awakening of confidence.

We know how without confidence and a certain self-assurance no work can be produced worthy of the author. Without it the speaker, familiar though he may be with the topics of his discourse, and careful as may have been his previous preparation, breaks ignobly down, and the cleverest and most artistic genius fails to his own confusion. The unsympathetic and ignorant observer may even doubt, and will, the capacity of such. He will sooner believe in that of the shallowest trifler who has a flow of speech, or assumption of intelligence, or ease of manner. It was to establish this necessary confidence in the sin-conscious soul that the Angels of God first directed their united efforts when, as " He had brought in His first Begotten into the world," they proclaimed in the valleys of Bethlehem " Peace on earth and goodwill to men." And all through the Gospel we discern a constant aim to break through the needless shyness, if I may so say, with which the humblest sinner is apt to look upon his God, and shrink from His glorious presence. The sense of personal unworthiness must indeed be first awakened, and the foundation of self-humiliation laid deep in the convictions of the soul. But the assurance of the perfect reconciliation that has been wrought by the work of Christ between God and the justified believer God would have to follow directly, and to be impressed deeply. The truth is therefore repeated constantly. " Being justified by faith we have peace with God." " So then ye are no more strangers, but of the household of God." " There is therefore now no condemnation." " Wherefore let us come boldly to the throne of grace." " If any man sin we have an Advocate with the Father; and He is the propitiation for our sins." " Let us draw near with a true heart in full assurance of faith." With such passages as these the New Testament abounds.

And the text teaches that the Angels delight and labour in inspiring this happy confidence in those to whom they minister. They are revealed here as eagerly striving and vieing, as it were, one with another to dispossess Daniel of the mistrust that filled his depressed heart, knowing, as S. John says, that " fear hath torment."

The secret of success they knew, as we, also His messengers, do who would seek in like manner to encourage God's true faithful ones. If they could but awaken in Daniel the sense of his acceptance with God—how dear he was to God, how God was interested in him, and how favourably He regarded him—then Daniel could be courageous and strong and diligent again. And so they said, " O man, greatly beloved."

And what was the condition of Daniel when so addressed ? It was not when he was strong in faith, giving glory to God, and fearing not the wrath of the king, nor the den of lions. It was not when he was eloquent in prophecy, unfolding the mysteries of God in those fearless and glowing words with which this book abounds. It was not when he was mighty in prayer, kneeling in the face of a godless company, and making his supplication to the Lord of Heaven three times a day. But when he was overwhelmed with the sense of his own short-comings and sins—which I suppose no one would see or believe to exist but himself—when the revelation of God seemed sealed to him, and the present a mystery, and the future a blank: when, in his own expressive words, he had "set his face to the ground and become dumb:" when he was humbled to the dust with the sense of defect in all that seemed noble to others, but a failure to himself. " For thus saith the High and the Holy One that inhabiteth eternity, I dwell with him that is of a contrite and humble spirit, to revive the spirit of the humble and to revive the heart of the contrite ones." " And to this man will I look, even to him that is poor and of a contrite spirit, and trembleth at my word."

Those Angels' work is, by God's appointment, continued still. And when the hour of repentance dawns on some humbled soul, when broken and sick at heart, and disappointed at one's own failure or the mighty and crushing power of evil around, some prostrate soul stumbles on the battle field of life, and darkness gathers over the soul where the brow perhaps gives no sign, and a sad hopelessness, and a cold fear, and a nameless dread creeps over the shrinking spirit, those Divinely com-missioned Angels of mercy fold their bright wings around the sacred spot where, in a figure, the disciple, like Daniel here, or like our Saviour in Gethsemane, falls on the cold ground. And unheeded by his unconscious fellows, like Jesus by his slumbering friends in the garden, an attendant Angel is by the frail believer's side. And presently a whisper, unheard by mortal ear, steals over and through the trembling frame, " O man, greatly beloved, fear not; peace be unto thee; be strong, yea, be strong."

And so he rises again: and he may not, like Daniel, have been conscious of the source from whence the fresh vigour came, and that there had "appeared unto him an Angel from heaven strengthening him." He may not, like him, admit it by direct and grateful address. But his life of renewed strength and usefulness gives Daniel testimony to the Angels' ministration. " Thou hast strengthened me." We detract nothing from His glory in admitting the fact, for as we are taught in this very passage it is He that sends them, and from *Him*, though through *them*, cometh our help.

> So cometh still to us from heaven
> A blessed Angel oft,
> A gentle messenger of light,
> With footstep fair and soft.
>
> Oh, on how many an earthly grief
> Or fear a light unknown
> Has with a joyful suddenness
> In heavenly glory shone
>
> To many a tomb of earthly tears
> Comes one of heavenly mien,
> On many a gloomy stone of life
> An Angel sits unseen.
>
> BONAR

And so when, like Daniel's, the heart is slow to perceive and the ears, in a figure, are dull of hearing ; and like his the lips are closed and bound ;and there is no freedom in prayer, nor in speaking of the things touching his King and His power and glory and the mightiness of His kingdom, in religious converse—in which some can speak so fluently and with lips so full of grace and truth—the ministering Angels are equally near. And the brightness that plays suddenly on some doctrine or revelation in which there was little beauty seen or interest felt before is a reflection from some such bright Being sent by God for the encouragement of His servant. A voice unheard has said, as a Being unseen drew near us, "I will show thee that which is noted in the Scripture of truth." And the secret of the new light that flashes from the brightening page or the keener intelligence with which the exposition of the preacher is followed, or the mind's clearer view and more hearty grasp of the doctrines of the Church of Christ, and its fresh appreciation of the power of Sacraments and the presence of the Lord Jesus in the ordinances of Divine worship, might all be read and understood did the ministering Angel, who is, under God, the source and occasion of it, but reveal himself as he did to Daniel. "Now I am come to make thee understand."

And perhaps to the minister in the congregation more especially, whose office it is to minister to the flock—though to others also according as they have need—is this aid granted for the benefit of those whom the minister is sent, like Daniel, to teach. And when, to quote the Apostle's words, the door of utterance is manifestly given to him that he may speak boldly and forcibly as he ought to speak ; and the Church receives edifying—it may be, I think this passage leads us to believe it verily is so, that the flow of words, instinct with life and power, which is so often attributed to human eloquence, has an altogether different origin. It may be that the account which is to be given of it is that of the text, though the inspirited preacher may be unconscious of the source, or hesitate to incur the charge of arrogance or enthusiasm in asserting it. "Behold, one like the similitude of the sons of men touched my lips ; *then* I opened my mouth and spake."

And lastly when, as at the close of some wild stormy day, the setting sun breaks forth through the lately angry but now scattered clouds, and the unveiled blue sky looks down on the green sparkling earth, and there is a great calm on the lately ruffled but now smiling face of nature—so when over some tempest-tossed, afflicted, and care-worn soul there has been seen to pass that strange tranquillity which the world, as it cannot give, can never understand ; and frettfulness dies away in the hush of submission, and the shadow of doubtfulness is chased from the clear brow of trust—the text unlocks the mystery. When the exhausted one rouses himself to "labours more abundant," and the tired one rises up to more self-forgetful services, and the discouraged girds himself for the onward march, as though the world, the flesh, and the devil had never bidden him halt, we that look on and wonder hear no voice indeed, and see no man. But a ministering Angel has nevertheless been there. And in obedience to that mighty voice,

"O man, greatly beloved, fear not; peace be unto thee; be strong; yea, be strong!" courage has been restored, and zeal stimulated; faith confirmed, hope revived, and charity rekindled. And the history of Daniel has been repeated; for the Angelic interposition goes ever on, and the servant who has the greater need is made like unto the Master. And all unconsciously in his life, as in his Lord's, the experience is the same. "Then the devil leaveth Him, and behold, Angels came and ministered unto Him."

THE RAINBOW AND ITS TEACHINGS.

And it shall come to pass that the bow shall be seen in the cloud, and I will look upon it.—*Genesis* ix., 16.

How wondrously beautiful is the bow of God! Cold must be the heart, dull indeed the imagination, and pitifully unimpassioned the soul of any one who can turn to that magnificent arch, the span of the fingers of the Almighty, in its perfect symmetry and glowing colours, without a thrill of pleasure. We know that the Rainbow is but a phantom, an image, a form, and yet to our eyes what a reality! And how apt an illustration thus of the real definite existence of things in the spiritual world around us which, while we move in the body, are to us unseen and intangible. The Rainbow has no substance that could ever be grasped like the sun, or moon, or stars could be, if we could reach far enough. It is the only thing, I believe, we do not see, except it be the electric flash, that has not substance. And yet what more real to the eye! And what, therefore, a better aid to our minds in conceiving how real are the multitude of other creations of God by which we are encompassed which are also without a body. Such are the Angels of Light, and the departed spirits of the blessed while they wait the Resurrection day that shall clothe them once more with material form our hands may handle and our senses take knowledge of.

But the Rainbow stands forth from all other objects of creation with this pre-eminent characteristic which the text mentions. "I will look upon it," says God. It attracts a special observation of its Maker which nothing else—I speak of things that have not life—does. His eye indeed, it is said in the book of Job, seeth every precious thing, and admires it as we do. Mountains and all hills, fruitful trees and all cedars, wild rocks and barren sea, the eye of Him that fashioned all, gazes on with a never resting complacency. But when He bent His bow for the first time after the flood, whether or no it had ever been seen before, He revealed it as a fact that from that day forward He would never cast its arch across the sky without turning upon it, if we may so say, a fuller face, a more fixed attention than on anything else.

Skillfully may the natural philosopher account for the Rainbow by the properties of light. But Revelation leads us one step further back to Him who gave and apportioned those properties. And so, just as Moses' face shone when he came down from the mount from the Face of God, the brightness of the bow is to us the reflection of the very unveiled face of the Majesty in the Heavens. It is with it as with those Angels of His that behold His face, and are bright and glorious in consequence as He is. "In His light we see light," it is said: and we may add we become light. For, says the Apostle, though "beholding but in a glass the glory of the Lord we are changed into the same image." The Arch which He casts on the dark cloud brightens out in the light of the, to us, invisible God, into the radiant hues that by the ever irresistible attraction of Divine beauty presently concentre our own.

Thus said the pious Jew that wrote the book of Ecclesiasticus, some centuries before Christ came : a book which, though not among the inspired writings of the Bible, is, together with the book of the Wisdom of Solomon, the very oldest religious book in the world beside, the most like of all that ever were written to the inspired Scriptures, and the most beautiful to read. "Look upon the Rainbow, and praise Him that made it; very beautiful it is in the brightness thereof. It compasseth the heaven about with a glorious circle, and the hands of the Most High have bended it." A direction this is, and the whole passage itself, worthy of Holy Scripture ; for perhaps to the devout Christian no sight in nature is so fitted as the Rainbow is to kindle that admiration, of which every human heart is conscious, of the bright and the beautiful, into an enthusiasm of worship and of love.

But what, after all, may we learn from these words " The bow shall be seen in the clouds, and I will look upon it ?"

I think there is one emotion in particular of the human heart, to which the Lord of all of us here appeals. He who knows what is in man has thus appealed for the benefit of the devout to that instinct of our nature which can draw strength, comfort, happiness, and an increased sense of nearness and communion from the thought that an absent and loved one is looking upon the same object as ourselves, and at the same moment. It may be one of the heavenly bodies, or some landmark, some lofty object on the landscape within the horizon of two parted friends. And if, by some agreement both are looking, or supposed to be contemplating it, at some fixed moment, the gulf of distance seems in some degree to be spanned, and the spirits of the absent to hold a closer and more perfect communion.

And this is not so only in the romance of sentiment, but in the very sobriety of fact And because it is, God says, " The bow shall be seen, and I will look upon it." He knew that if we would but take in and dwell upon the idea that the Maker of that fair bow is turning His eyes upon it with a special observation, at the same moment that we turn ours, we might come by this instinct of our nature to feel God nearer. And anything that can at any time bring that invisible, and therefore too often forgotten, One nearer serves to us for an invaluable purpose.

And this is one great justification of that so general and (within the limits which Christian simplicity and moderation may seem to impose) *in itself laudable* craving after the aids of art and ornament, music and eloquence in the Sanctuary and its services. Of course the inventions of man to this end partake of his own nature of imperfection, and are often found to tend to excess. But the craving after some material aids—such as it may not be inconsistent with the glory

due to the Creator to employ in His worship, but may be the offering
back to Him in token of the recognition of that glory, some of His best
gifts of nature or of skill—is deeply seated by Infinite Wisdom in our
souls.   And in the one provision, at all events, which the text tells us
God made so early in the history of the world, He has responded to
this craving, and sanctified it.   Surely the cry of nature, " O that I
knew where I might find God, that I might come into His presence,"
is here heard, and at least half answered.   He is of purer eyes indeed
than to reveal Himself with unveiled face as we yet look to see Him in
the world to come to any on this fallen, sinful earth.   But while He
ever says, " Thou canst not see my face," He seems in this promise to
say but if thou wilt thy gaze and mine shall meet half-way.   One
object only shall intervene between the direct gaze of the creature and
the Creator, between the worshipping child on earth and the ever
gracious and mindful Father in Heaven.

> Fair bow ! thy radiant arch we greet,
> A midway station given
> For eyes of God and man to meet,
> In close communion blest and sweet,
> Between the earth and heaven.

But we may read a further lesson in the very form of that wondrous
Arch.   Far as the East is from the West, or the North from the South,
it stretches its mighty span, reaching forth with an equal grasp on
either side from its centre in the heavens.   Apt sign and clear, so that
it might be known and read of all, of Him who has held out from heaven
His everlasting Arms of love, without respect of persons, from East and
West and North and South alike, to gather up once more into the
Heaven above His scattered, and wandering, and fallen children.   Very
and true emblem of Him who, in the hour that He casts it across the
dark cloud that shadows forth His anger, is bending as though with the
outstretched arms of His own bow over His guilty world with a special
care, and thought, and tenderness !   To us, in the heedlessness of habit
to which the bow is no longer a novelty, these thoughts may fail to be
awakened or to occur.   To us they may be overpast with the freshness
of feeling and the vivid imagination of childhood.   But we cannot
ponder on the passage before us without having imagination unsealed,
and the fervour of faith kindling them into life again.   So it was

> When o'er the green undeluged earth,
>   Heaven's covenant did shine ;
> And came the world's grey fathers forth,
>   To watch its sacred sign.
> And when its yellow lustre smiled
>   O'er mountains yet untrod,
> And each mother held aloft her child,
>   To bless the bow of God.

Perhaps indeed before God called the special notice of His creatures
to it as He does in the text, and made it a sign of His presence and
a pledge of His love—the Rainbow may have existed, and Noah have
seen it before the flood.   And then he may have regarded it much in

the same way that we are apt to do with a passing admiration, but with no such abiding associations as ought ever to be attached to it since God appointed it as a sign. There may have been rain, and therefore the Rainbow, before the flood. Geologists tell us marks of rain may be traced on rocks far older than the flood. And yet in the country where Noah lived, whatever it were, there may have been no rain before, just as now in some parts of the world rain is almost unknown. Hugh Miller in his "Testimony of the Rocks" (page 325,) speaks of the "rainless plains," of the country round Caucasus.

But whether at the time of which the text speaks, God set His bow in the storm cloud for the first time in the sight of Noah—or whether, and the passage does not necessarily mean more that this, He only chose a sign already familiar to Noah, to be henceforth the token of His mercy—we need not decide. From the hour of which the text speaks, it was consecrated to be to each beholder, to whom the words should be known, a symbol of God's presence, and a pledge of God's promise. The Englishman's Magazine, page 567, for June 1865, says on this subject. "God had first pledged His word to Noah in the eleventh verse of the chapter. And that would have been enough. But He knew the instability of human faith, and how it needs extraordinary aid to hold its empire against the evidence of the senses. He knew that the experience which Noah had gone through, must have stamped itself on every thought and impulse. So that though faith bade him trust, he could not—when there was nothing in sight to prove that God had forgotten him—but tremble when the dark clouds gathered in the sky, and the rising wind blew strongly, and the sun went down fiery and lurid in the west—so He placed His Rainbow in the sky, for Noah in the hour of his weakness, and for us in that of our depression and faithlessness, when we are tempted to say " My way is hidden from the Lord, and my judgment passed over from my God." Or when again we are disposed in dark moments of unbelief to exclaim or think within ourselves Will the Lord cast off for ever? Is His mercy clean gone for ever? Doth His promise fail for evermore? Hath God forgotten to be gracious? Hath He in anger shut up His tender mercies? He placed it there, that ever and again we, like him, might see as it were freshly created, the pledges of the Almighty's truth, " and seeing might believe and trust."

And what a perfect understanding of our nature and consideration for it is there in this ever fresh renewal of the pledge! How when our fellow creature's promise is delayed, or there seems a likelihood of the word or engagement in which he has caused us to hope not taking effect, do we seek a repetition of his promise, and find ourselves reassured in receiving it again ! " Hope deferred maketh the heart sick." Well has it been said though the words are but those of a song.

> Full many griefs the past has found,
>   To crush the blighted heart,
> And time alone can heal the wound,
>   That rankles from the dart;

But there is yet a deeper grief,
    Than those the past hath stirred,
It is when o'er the sickened breast,
    Is racked by hope deferred.

HENRY LOVELL.

But the promise repeated, or the intention of performance being declared to us to be still kept in mind, will long satisfy our expectation and prevent it from being turned into disappointment.

And each time that the Most High sets His bow in the cloud does He, unasked, assure us again that He has not for one moment let go the government of this world, or retired from it. We may well be tempted sometimes to think so from the hopelessness of the disorder that we see in our own moral nature, and in all around us. And some have even impiously said it, as we read " The Lord hath forsaken the earth, and the Lord seeth not." But no! Forth shines the bow and tells man ever on all through the ages that the Creator and Lord of all is living and ruling still : and that one jot or one tittle, shall in no wise pass from word or promise or threat of His until all be fulfilled. Even so as S. Paul says by two immutable things—the promise for faith to grasp, and the outward and visible sign for sense to lay hold upon—we may have strong consolation who have fled for refuge to the hope set before us in the Gospel.

And last of all to quote from the same article in the above mentioned Magazine, " we cannot look at God's Bridge glowing in the frowning sky, without thinking of that true token of His love and mercy, which has indeed spanned the great gulf that lies] between our fallen manhood and its Maker. The Rainbow must indeed have been a blessed sign to Noah in his age, comforting him with the assurance of the covenanted mercy, when the heavens grew dark with rain, and the evening sky glared with a crimson light. But far more blessed to the Christian is the sign of the Son of Man, the Cross, Rainbow-like, resting on earth, but reaching unto heaven;" interposing—like the bow between the beholder and the threatening cloud—between the penitent sinner that looks to it, and his threatened doom. The Rainbow is God's scroll fixed high in the temple of nature, painted by His own Hand with the inscription, " There is now no condemnation to them that are in Christ Jesus, who walk not after the flesh, but after the Spirit ! "

And thus it is the very antitype of the Cross, which tells, like the other, of darkness and storm overpast, vengeance disarmed, and a once offend d but now reconciled Lord of might, whereunto the consciously guilty, " may flee in all dangers, even in the coming judgment, and so be surely safe. And it is a wonderful thought that He, who is the same yesterday, to day, and for ever—the same when He saved Noah from the flood, as when upon the Cross He saved mankind—has set this token of His Unity even upon the Revelation of latter days. Perhaps it is not only that we may link His purpose into one perfect whole, but also in deep thoughtfulness and tender care for the fears of

His redeemed, that He has associated this symbol with His Revelation of the coming glory," with the scenery of New Heavens and the New Earth of the world to come.

"Perhaps it is that His people may look to Him—in the hour of death, and in the day of judgment," and in the strange moment of entrance after each of them into the kingdom of light—"with more consciousness of security, with a more trusting love," that we read among the pictures of His Majesty in Heaven, "There was a Rainbow round about the throne in sight like unto an emerald."

THE NECESSITY OF GOOD WORKS.

Be careful to maintain good works.—*Titus* iii. 8

This is a direction, as the text informs us, which the great Apostle Paul, prompted by the Spirit, bade Titus continually affirm. He tells him it was his will he should insist upon it most strongly, and urge it to the uttermost. If Titus, the Bishop of Crete, was thus charged to take it as a text, it is a suitable and important one in the mouth of any minister. And I may well take it for mine.

The word be "careful," I may observe in passing, designates in the text turning the mind to or fixing it upon. And the word to "maintain" means rather to excel or take the lead in. The Apostle calls us then to carefulness, or perhaps better and more accurately thoughtfulness.

Here is an object or purpose which they that have believed in God are bidden to study and apply themselves to thoughtfully. It is the prerogative of our rational or thinking soul that we can so address it to any subject we please. We can set our minds to provide for and take measures towards certain ends that come before or are presented to us. And we are here required to prepare and equip ourselves for that one for the attainment of which our very life was given. It is an end which calls for diligent and deliberate preparation. It cannot possibly be secured without such. A real strong effort, or rather series of efforts, is needed. And so S. Paul says, "Be thoughtful" about it. The object of this studious effort, or course of efforts, is the abounding or excelling in those "good works which God has ordained that we should walk in," and "which are by Jesus Christ unto His honour and praise." Works or acts include acts of the soul as well as outward deeds. They need for their performance mental exertion and the exercise of the spiritual power supplied by the Holy Ghost, just as works of the hand or body need for their being put into execution physical powers. To enumerate or describe good works would be the vainest task. The instinct of our religious training tells us all what they are, and suggests them to our minds most readily. Religious observances and moral duties; acts of self-denial and acts of kindness; the exhibition of self-restraint in temper and under provocation, and the exhibition of kindly and generous and benevolent dispositions to those around; assistance rendered to the weaker; condescending thought for the inferior, and respectful demeanour to the superior; lowliness and long-suffering, gentleness and courtesy; "Whatsoever things are true, honest, just, pure, lovely, and of good report;" whatever there is any confessed virtue in, and praise attributable to, this same Apostle says, "Think on," or, as in my text, be thoughtful about securing "These things."

There is an equivalent expression to this of the text, which we often repeat in the Psalms "Are your minds set upon righteousness O ye Congregation." Without thinking or meditating on this righteousness it cannot be attained. The impulses of nature are such that these good works do not come naturally to us. They need to be decided on beforehand. You arrange your worldly plans to a great extent on this principle. You know the value of method or system in matters of this life : and how, with any purpose in view, you take measures to advance it, and govern yourself accordingly. Do the same in things spiritual. Settle in your mind, that under such and such circumstances—trials of your faith, your obedience, your courage, your meekness—you will conduct yourself on such and such principles. And when the hour comes—I will not say of temptation, as is the common way of putting it, but as I prefer saying—of showing yourself loyal and faithful to your religion and Lord, you will not be taken unawares. You will not be drawn in to act according to the course of this world, but in such a way as will prove that you had before resolved to let your righteousness exceed the too low standard of others, and to excel or stand before them, as it is literally in good works. In the Epistles we are very frequently stimulated to a holy ambition, and rivalry to excel in grace. And it is to be deplored that preachers do not follow the example thus set by appealing oftener to the same principle. "Seek that ye may excel." "Covet earnestly best gifts," are the admonitions of the same Apostle. And here he bids us in like manner make it our own care and aim to excel. Natural emulation is declared to be a work of the flesh. But spiritual emulation is an emotion that is commendable, nay that ought to rise in our bosoms above a sentiment to the force of a passion.

Like any sentiment it may be nursed into a passion. And I would have you thus stir it up, and awaken yourself to the influence of so holy an excitement. The way and the means thereto is this, and I beg you to observe the counsel I give in the matter. The direction sounds a little dry and cold. But taking the exact meaning of the words as they are in the original Greek, it becomes you will see a good deal more vivid and interesting. We might translate it freely. "Make it a point of care and thought, to excel others or exceed others in good works." Now you know we are always—we cannot help it—observing the ways and characters of others. And the Apostle tells us here how we may do so and turn our observations of them into a very profitable channel.

You know you almost hourly find yourself reflecting on the conduct or behaviour of some one or other. That conduct may have inconvenienced or in some way affected you, or you may have heard it remarked upon, if it has not immediately concerned you. Now, the next time this occurs—and I promise you you will not have to wait many hours first—consider with yourself, and make an agreement with your own heart before God, and beseeching His assisting grace, that you will make a point, when placed in any circumstances in the most distant degree resembling this offender, that you will act a different and worthier part. Make it a matter of care and thought to avoid that evil yourself, which you see or pronounce to be objectionable in the other. Take a holy pleasure in endeavouring to outstrip the other in that good in which you see or hear him said to be deficient.

Of course you must be on your guard against any self-complacent or self-flattering satisfaction " Not unto us O Lord, not unto us, but unto Thy Name be the praise, for Thy loving mercy and for Thy truths sake ! " " Thou hast wrought all our works in us "—must be your feeling at all times. In the moment of conscious success—and such happy moments shall be yours if you are only in earnest to excel—you will bring your triumph and cast it as a crown before the feet of Him in whose name you have overcome, and say " Of thine own have we given Thee."

For example you shall observe one who has spoken roughly, hastily, unkindly, and ungraciously. And you shall take occasion by his failing to watch to give the soft and conciliatory answer. You shall meet presently with an overbearing neighbour. His insolence or hers shall be undeniable, and he or she shall show you open and unquestionable incivility. Make that transgression your warning : and strive to let your courteous manner and bearing be such as to contrast favourably with the other's want of it. You see certain persons neglectful of the duty of doing good, regardless of urgent claims on their Christian care and teaching. Strive you to fill up that which is so evidently lacking on their part, by being " in labours more abundant," and in zeal more untiring.

Let the rashness of others provoke you to discretion, their ignorance to thought, their intemperance to moderation, their folly to prudence, their heedlessness to guardedness, their dissipation to sobriety, their idleness to double care in the improvement of your own time and talents. Let the unbridled tongue of the tattler or slanderer, afford you occasion to take the contrary part, to check the more firmly the unruly member.

Let the impertinence of the gossip caution you against being ever impelled into the mischief and sin of becoming "a busy body in other men's matters." Let the blame which you rightly attach, or hear deservedly applied to the inquisitive, secure you from the like vain curiosity. Let the giddy trifling of the man or woman that lives only for pleasure, persuade you to " live soberly, righteously, and godly ; " to be self restrained in your use of the lawful things of the world, and resolute in your renunciation of its vain pomp and glory.

Let the notorious way in which you see people deceive themselves lead you to be self distrustful of your own heart and your fallible judgment, and willing to believe it possible when you do not see it, that you are in the wrong.

Let the meanness of the churl disgust you into liberality of thought and judgment, the penuriousness of the niggard awaken a reaction into bountifulness. Let the sight of extravagance arouse in you a horror of waste, the suffering inflicted on those around by the complaining and fretful spirit, stir you to cultivate good humour and cheerfulness. Let the manifest failings of the slow prompt you to alacrity, and the exuberance of the too quick chasten you into a care for due measure and season. Let the irritable and passionate teach you by contrast the blessedness of the meekness and gentleness of Christ

Above all let the too prevalent indifference to anything that is not seen and temporal, lead you in heart and mind to the more earnest contemplation of the things that are unseen and eternal.

Thus as the Apostle says "Let your profiting appear unto all." "Overcome evil with good," and those very points shall promote *your* spiritual well being, which are to *others* an occasion of falling. And your labour be assured shall not be in vain in the Lord. You will gradually come to find that strengthened with all might by His Spirit, you are really adding to your faith as the Apostle bids virtue, that is excellence. And as you outstrip and pass one and another in your spiritual course, you will still be saying all the time you thank God who has given you the victory, and who has enabled you to gain this or that point of advantage. "I count not myself to have apprehended. But this one thing I do forgetting whereto I have already attained and reaching forth to what is yet beyond, I press toward the mark for the prize of my high calling of God in Christ Jesus."

And the mark and the prize shall be presently gained. For He cometh and His reward is with Him. And he who has thus been "careful to maintain good works" shall of the Master's wondrous grace be crowned with glory, honour, and immortality. And at that joyful moment when the approving, "Well done good and faithful servant"— the expectation of which has been the stimulus of all his labour and patience on earth—shall fall upon his listening and enraptured ears, he shall lift his humble and grateful song, in the beautiful words of Bishop Heber's lines.

> 'Tis past! 'tis o'er! in foul defeat,
>   The Demon host are fled!
> Before the Saviour's mercy-seat,
> His life-long work of faith complete,
>   Their conqueror bends his head,
> The spoils thyself hast gained O Lord,
>   I lay before thy throne:
> Thou wert my Rock, my Shield, my Sword,
> My trust was in Thy name and word,
>   'Twas in Thy strength my heart was strong!
> Thy Spirit went with mine along,
>   The glory thine alone!

CHRIST'S REPRESENTATIVES AND THEIR CLAIM ON OUR ATTENTION.

He that heareth you heareth Me, and he that despiseth you despiseth Me.—Luke x. 16

It has always been a favourite reproach of the irreligious world, and of those who take a low view of the Ministerial office, against Christ's Ambassadors, that they are prone to an undue magnifying of that office, and the powers they are entrusted with in order to its efficient discharge. It is a marvel to me how such objectors can evade the clear and strong words our Lord always employs in speaking about His commissioned officers in the Church. Thus saying they reproach Him also. For it is undeniable how largely and heartily He magnified the office. These words were addressed to the seventy whom He sent before Him into every city and place whithersoever He Himself would come. He had before addressed the twelve in a similar way when despatching them on a like errand. " He that receiveth you receiveth me." But it is to be remarked that—though the seventy elders do not appear to have been sent out with quite as full and extraordinary gifts, and as many miraculous powers, as the twelve Apostles—their commission is given in the words of the text with quite as full authority, nay, with the additional emphasis of the latter clause.

And further still we are even more concerned to notice that the same night in which He was betrayed—when looking on to the future government of His Church, and the Ministerial work which was to be handed on through the Apostles to their successors to the end of time —He in nowise modified this strong language. Rather does He assert the fact of such authority, which He willed should be theirs, more forcibly than ever. " Verily, verily, I say unto you, he that receiveth whomsoever I send receiveth Me." Ours be it in the meekness that casts down imaginations and every high thought, bringing it into captivity to the obedience of Christ, to accept without unbelief or unreadiness this revelation of the value of His own appointed Ministry, and to ponder thoughtfully its significance.

I shall take the first clause of the text, and very briefly allude to the latter. " He that heareth you heareth Me." This statement is profitable alike for instruction and encouragement. For instruction truly! For what a wonderful, and, were it not for this revelation, unthought of doctrine is this! That we do really still hear Christ when we hear the Ministers of His word and faith. That He still wields in this world, from the midst of which the heavens have received Him, the power of a living Voice. What an incalculable loss would it have been to the world were it not so! For the voice of the Lord when on earth was a glorious voice, powerful and full of majesty. " His word was with power," " He spake as one that had authority." And all wondered at the gracious words that proceeded out of His mouth—

> For sweet was the voice of the Firstborn of heaven,
> Though poor His apparel and earthly His form,
> When He said to the mourner " Thy sins be forgiven,"
> " Be whole" to the sick, and " Be still" to the storm !

The invitations of the Gospel, the announcements about the future, the injunctions to obedience and faith, with what fresh power would they move our listless, backward, worldly souls, did we but reflect on this solemn assurance of our Master about them as they come to us from the lips of His ordained Messengers. " He that heareth them heareth me." Could we refuse, or at least defer as we do, to yield our faith and to take prompt action upon these words did we but observe, as we are here called to do, from whom those words come and Who gave the speakers their authority ? Hardly should we trifle with the message or directions their words contain did we heed this fact that they speak really what their Master and ours prompts, and what He is waiting to see attended to.

Have you heard repentance or seriousness, humility or perseverance, insisted on from the pulpit ? You have heard, not the words or teaching of man, to which you may allow just what force in your judgment is due. But it is the Master that calleth you, and has laid before you your duty. Have you heard affectionate words of persuasion to be more in earnest, more settled in faith, more joyful in hope, and more rooted in charity ? You may well rouse your soul with the consideration thus suggested.

> It is the voice of Jesus that I hear ;
> His are the Hands outstretched to draw me near.

Have you been plied with exhortations to be more brave and hearty in action, more patient and submissive in suffering, more thorough and painstaking ? They are the words of Him who has endured the cross and has grasped for you the crown. Have you been summoned to be more indifferent to the joys and sorrows, the cares and vexations of this passing world, and more eager about thinking of and looking for the blessedness of the Heavenly one ? It is the call of the Master, who knows, from having lived in them, both this and that, and how the afflictions and interests of the one are not worthy to be dwelt upon in comparison of the glory of the other.

And what encouragement is there too in this fact ? Do we hear absolution for sin repented of pronounced, the favour of God toward us declared, the comforts of the promises laid open to our wondering and delighted gaze ? Ah, if they were but the words of men we should put from us the fair prospect as too good to be true. We might fear to trust them lest we should be deluded. But if he that heareth them the speakers heareth Him that bids them speak, and inspires and guides into all truth their words, what strong consolation is there for those who will but take as truth and follow and be led by what they hear in such a Name!

Well may we lay aside every weight, and discharge ourselves from every burden, and vex ourselves no longer with any care, if the assurance they bring us of release and liberty and the firm ground for confidence, is the word not of an enthusiastic or possibly mistaken human being, but of the Divine One that cannot lie.

> For Thou art true, Incarnate Word,
> Who did'st vouchsafe for man to die!
> Thy smile is sure, Thy plighted word
> No change can falsify.
>
> WORDSWORTH.

Yea, if we take the final and more comprehensive and even more solemn testimony of our Lord which I quoted above, " Verily, verily, I say unto you he that receiveth whomsoever I send receiveth Me," the encouragement becomes yet more decided.

For what would we not, in the moments of our grateful love to our Redeemer, and in the glow of adoration which sometimes comes over the impassioned soul, as it muses on the grace brought to light through the Gospel till the fire kindles—what would we not give could we receive to our homes and welcome before our eyes that glorious Master as did the believing men and women of His day?   What would we not give like Mary to sit at His feet and hear His Word?   Like the women of Galilee to minister to Him of our substance ?   Like Martha and Zaccheus to bid Him welcome to our homes ?   Like the twelve Apostles and seventy Elders to go out on the world's highway to work for Him, and speak for Him, and bid all men turn to Him?   Blessed be the forethought of Him who knows the every feeling of the soul He has created, and has made such ample provision for its every longing, this instinct is not unconsidered nor unprovided for.   And to the devout one that comes enquiring anxiously " Wherewith shall I come before the Lord, and bow myself before the Most High God?"   " What shall I render to the Lord for all the benefits that He hath done unto me ?"— there comes the answer from the solemn stillness of that last dark night in which He was betrayed to die, " Verily, verily I say unto you, he that receiveth whomsoever I send—whether Minister to be honoured, or poor to be relieved, or weary or doubtful to be encouraged, or even child to be taught (see Mark ix., 37)—receiveth me."

The literal joy of receiving Jesus you can never know.   The hour for actual ministration to that Man of Sorrows is happily, as all we who love Him must think, gone by.   Never again can a child of man go forth to call the homeless Jesus to the hospitality of his roof.   He hungers no more, neither thirsts any more, No one again, like the Pharisee after His weary Sabbath, shall call Him, hungry and exhausted, into his house to eat bread.   No woman, like that of Samaria, shall draw water to relieve the burning thirst of long hours spent under an Eastern sun.   No woman shall need to weave for Him the destitute and poor the seamless robe that struck the soldiers who parted His garments among them, for the skill of its handiwork as a prize so worth securing. No one, like the devoted John and the blessed above all other women, shall watch Him hanging on the cross of shame, with their sympathising tears and their longing looks of unuttered love. None, like Peter, shall need again to draw the sword against the ribald multitude that moved to a momentary but righteous indignation the meek and gentle One who resented, just as we should do, with the fire of natural impulse, the wrong and scandal that numbered Him with the malefactors. " Be ye come out as against a thief with swords and staves to take *Me*?" None, like the compassionate soldier, shall need to run and bring the sponge of vinegar to moisten His parched lips and aching brow, and cool the fever in His dying eyes.

" *We* see Jesus for the suffering of death crowned with glory and honour—

> All His woes are over now,
> And the passion that He bore,
> Sin and pain can vex no more.

He is beyond the reach of all this *personally*. And blessed be the God who has thus exalted Him, the joy of our dear Lord is full! " Thousand thousands now minister to Him, and ten thousand times ten thousand stand before Him"—" as the eyes of a servant look to the hand of his master and the eyes of a maiden to the hand of her mistress" —anticipating His every wish.

But all the blessedness of such service may *actually* be yours. For thus He teaches, " He that receiveth a prophet in the name of a prophet shall receive a prophet's reward ; and he that receiveth a righteous man in the name of a righteous man (aiding, assisting, countenancing him, because he is such) shall receive a righteous man's reward. And whosoever shall give a cup of cold water only in the name of a disciple shall in nowise lose *his* reward." "And the day shall declare it" when he shall say to the utter astonishment of His humble servants, " Verily, I say unto you inasmuch as ye have done it unto one of the least of these my brethren ye have done it unto me."

> And hearts are bruised and dead,
> And homes are bare and cold,
> And lambs for whom the Shepherd bled,
> Are straying from the fold.
>
> To comfort and to bless,
> To find a balm for woe,
> To tend the lone and fatherless.
> Is Angel's work below.

You cannot go forth with the seventy in the text to preach the word and turn rebellious careless hearts to their forgotten God and neglected Saviour. But you can smooth the path of the Heralds of the Gospel that do. (Are there any of you that would be willing to incur the guilt of the contrary course ?) You can take up many a stumbling block from their path which your undevoutness and inattention to their words occasions.   And you can gladden the hearts of those that endeavour and long so earnestly to win you to your Lord by giving the more earnest heed to the word that is spoken, more earnest heed each Sunday and in the week that follows, than the last.   You cannot watch with your exceeding sorrowful Saviour in the Garden.   But you can watch to be gentle, and patient, and prayerful, and wakeful as He was there.   You cannot honour directly Him with your gifts and personal service.   But you can most truly do so by reverencing His Ministers, and honouring His true, conscientious, loyal servants, and helping His weak, frail, and downcast ones.

I will not, I should tremble to, dwell at length, on the warning which the second clause of the text, that he that despiseth such despiseth Him contains.

God of His great mercy forbid that any of you should despise the riches of *His* goodness and forbearance, that would lead you thereby to repentance, by slighting *our* message, disregarding *our* teaching, or neglecting the great salvation *we* bring you.   God forbid that any of you should too late have your eyes opened to see the value of what we press upon you, and what you never accepted! God forbid that any now inattentive ears should then hear those awful words, which many in that coming day *must* hear. " Behold ye despisers, and wonder, and perish !"

HEARTLESSNESS.

What is that to us? See thou to that. —*Matthew* xxvii., 4.

Among the mysteries that we cannot fathom in this strange life of ours, not the least is the remarkable manner in which the character of ourselves and others is affected by our association with each other. How it is, and whence, or in what manner operating, is that subtle influence that is radiated from the human spirit upon the inner life of the fellow creature—how it is that the stronger mind disposes and turns the weaker with which it is brought much into contact whithersoever it will—and how it is that two minds of more equal power act and react so strongly upon one another—is a problem the solution of which is known only to the Father of the spirits of us all. But the fact that we are so acted upon, that we are not only directly prompted, but insensibly drawn to good or evil, by our inter-communications and the impressions derived from the converse of one another, is unquestionable. Indeed, so marvellous is the power thus unconsciously exercised by one over another that there are in the lives of many, solemn moments when their eternal destiny becomes to all appearance fixed. And that great crisis seems to be dependent upon or controlled by some action, or disposition, or example, or it may be even word of a fellow creature. What a responsibility then devolves upon us all as keepers of our brother! To think, as it really seems we must think, that we hold in our hands the stake of our neighbour's eternal welfare; that in an hour of which we are little aware, by some perhaps unguarded expression, by some, it may be, mere thoughtless or unadvised conduct, we may cast, as it were, the die that decides his lot for heaven or hell. Oh, it throws an awful and momentous light upon the obligation to take the most earnest heed to our ways, and set the most careful watch upon our words!

We have in the text a painful but most forcible example of the effect to the loss of a soul of the influence which we all more or less are was, exerting upon those with whom we are associated.

The moment that the Chief Priests and Elders spoke thus to Judas Iscariot, and not, as it would appear, till then, that " son of perdition" and in direct consequence of their words, impelled to his doom.

That it was deliberate and self-chosen does not in any way make against the point which I here dwell upon, that it was due in one sense directly to the accomplices of his guilt. So inextricably are our doings intertwined with others that we and they may be equally the causes of our own actions and of theirs. The judgment which shall be passed upon the one either for good or evil may be equally deserved and passed upon the other, to whom the responsibility for the particular deed or course of action is equally attributable.

Judas had now repented, and fully confessed the inexcusable nature of his treachery to his Lord. He went boldly into the presence of our Lord's malignant and powerful foes, and testified earnestly to his Master's innocence. He cast himself, as it were, upon their honour and faith, and seems by his words to have charged them solemnly to release him and themselves from the consequences of their awful and, as he showed, manifest, crime. Alas! It was in vain. "The tender mercies of the wicked are cruel." And Egypt, to quote the figure of the Assyrian captain, is always a broken reed to lean upon. Where there is no fear of God, there is no safeguard of fidelity, and no guarantee for principle or honour. And I counsel you never to trust to the honourable dealing of a fellow creature for whose faithfulness to God and His will you have no security. The prophet Jeremiah earnestly cautions us against such, when he says, first observing that the persons he speaks of did not know the Lord, "Take ye heed every one of his neighbour, and trust ye not in any brother; for every brother will utterly supplant, and every neighbour will walk with slanders, and they will deceive every one his neighbour."

The words of the text give us as vivid a view of the spirit of heartlessness as any that could be imagined. The passage holds the mirror up to nature, as the Spirit of God always does, with inimitable and life-like accuracy. We have the portrait of the hard and unfeeling hearts of the ungodly drawn with that surpassing skill which only He that knows what is in man could exercise. Let us muse awhile on this so true picture of utter heartlessness!

We all know to some extent what heartlessness means We have gone to a fellow creature with feelings aglow, full of some subject on which we felt deeply or were greatly interested. We poured out it may be from the abundance of the heart all that was struggling within it for utterance, and gave free vent to its thoughts and intents. But we found our neighbour careless, or indifferent, or preoccupied. He was cold and unsympathetic. He neither knew nor cared to hear of what we had to tell. And our outpoured or perhaps mute appeal "returned (as the Psalmist says) to our own bosom." It may be well that such disappointment should be ours to teach us the lesson we are always so slow and unwilling to learn—"Cease ye from man, whose breath is in his nostrils, for wherein is he to be accounted of."

To be the victims of heartlessness, as of any other kind of suffering or affliction, may be, and is, a part of that discipline of life whereby we are thrown back, first upon ourselves, and then in the consciousness of our own insufficiency, upon God.

It is thus God would have us to gain moral strength, and to "lift up our eyes unto the hills" from whence cometh our help. But the sin of heartlessness, and its terrible result in crushing out the life and hope, of our neighbour, cannot be too highly exaggerated, or too severely denounced. Suffice it in proof to observe in the text, how it drove Judas to the destruction both of body and soul. Might he not from "his own place," cry with an exceeding great and bitter cry to those graceless men, whose bitter mocking words sent him away to the suicide's doom.

Oh in that hour when thus you saw,
My burdened conscience groan,
Had generous hand or feeling heart,
One glimpse of mercy shown :

Your act had made from streaming eyes
Sweet tears of virtue roll ;
Had fixed my faith, inspired my hope,
And heaven had gained a soul.

We are members one of another. The very law of that charity, which is the new commandment of the Lord Jesus, and the rule of all our life, is " Look not every man on his own things, but every man also on the things of others !" It is not only unnatural, but it is a direct sin against God to separate ourselves from interest in and sympathy with the things that concern the well being and happiness here, the salvation hereafter, of any with whom we are concerned. To pass by as it were on the other side, and leave to his own resources, and therefore to discouragement, and probably error or recklessness, our neighbour who is in difficulty or embarassment :—to mock at his fruitless efforts to extricate himself from what we know we could do much to relieve him, or inwardly ridicule his uncertainty, or confusion—is unhappily a too common sin. But it is identical with the inhumanity of the chief priests and elders, who looked the miserable and despairing Judas in the face and said " What is that to us, see thou to that." In the Old Testament we have one example from life of this same heartlessness. And it is accompanied with a clear declaration of the just judgment of God on the offender. " In the day that thou stoodest on the other side (it was said to Edom) in the day that strangers carried away captive his forces, and foreigners entered into his gates—even thou wast as one of them. For thou shouldest not have looked on thy brother in the day that he became a stranger ; neither shouldest thou have rejoiced in the day of destruction ; nor spoken proudly in the day of distress. Thou shouldest not have entered into the gate of my people in the day of their calamity, yea thou shouldest not have looked on their affliction ; neither shouldest thou have stood in the cross way. As thou hast done it shall be done unto thee."

" What is that to us," said these to Judas when he told of his sin. And was it nothing to them, that had consented to him in it, and urged him forward ? " See thou to that," they added as they left him to bear the consequences alone, as the accomplice of guilt so often does the weaker partner, on whom the consequences fall more directly and heavily. Theirs, above that of all others, as the chief priests and elders, was the duty of charging themselves with the matter of relieving the conscience and enlightening the perplexity of one who so surely needed their spiritual counsel, and cast himself on their aid and pity. Happy for us is it that " we have such an High Priest over the House of God,

who can be touched with the feeling of our infirmities, and will have
compassion on the ignorant, and on them that out of the way." "Come
unto me (says the inviting Voice), all that are weary and heavy laden."

> It is the voice of Jesus that I hear,
> His are the Hands stretched out to draw me near,
> And His the blood that can for all atone,
> And set me faultless there before the throne.
>
> Now on mine ears the gracious tidings fall,
> Repent, confess, and thou art loosed from all,
> And day by day, whereby my soul may live,
> He gives His grace of pardon, and will give.

"What is it" to Him, the burden that depresses our spirits, the sin
that lies upon our conscience! It is His most earnest care, it awakens
his tenderest pity, it moves the heart of Omnipotence to exert Himself
for our help. "See thou to that," He never says. But, "cast your
burden upon the Lord and He shall sustain you." Be careful for, that is
over anxious or concerned about, nothing: but in everything let your
requests and feelings be made known to Him. And the peace of God
shall rule in your hearts.

Alas for Judas that he went for sympathy to the human instead of
to the Divine! Alas for us too if we give as little heed to the sorrowful
prediction of the bitterness which shall be *their* experience, who in the
words of God Himself "trust in man and make flesh their arm, and
whose heart departeth from the Lord."

> When wounded sore the stricken heart,
>   Lies bleeding and unbound,
> One only Hand, a pierced Hand,
>   Can salve the sinner's wound,
>
> When sorrow swells the laden breast,
>   And tears of anguish flow,
> One only Heart, a broken Heart,
>   Can feel the sinner's woe.
>
> When penitential grief has wept,
>   Over some foul dark spot,
> One only stream, a stream of Blood,
>   Can wash away the blot.
>
> 'Tis Jesus' Blood that washes white,
>   His Hand that brings relief,
> His Heart is touched with all our joys,
>   And feels for all our grief.

DR. ALEXANDER.

SELF-SACRIFICE, OR THE CHOICE OF MOSES.

By faith Moses, when he was come to years, refused to be called the son of Pharoah's daughter.—*Hebrews* xi., 24.

To self-sacrifice in the view of a worthy object, in the cause of truth, and righteousness, and honour, the world seldom fails to yield its tribute of admiration. So prevalent and inveterate is the selfishness that clings to fallen humanity, so little disposed are we for the most part to deny ourselves at all, or suffer with equanimity, the loss of anything, that when anyone is seen to take up a cross and deny himself towards the attainment of some palpable and approved object, multitudes will bestow a ready applause, and own the heroi m of the deed. It is only when others cannot understand the prompting motive that they charge him with foolishness or brand him with enthusiasm.

And such is for the most part the self-denial of the Christian. He sacrifices visible tangible good with no corresponding good in exchange. He puts from him things seen and temporal, things which other men seek after as most desirable, things which naturally he is as strongly inclined to seek after as any, in hope of securing things not seen as yet, things which can be ascertained only by the eye of faith, and of which the world therefore knows nothing. And thus like Moses he is subjected to reproach and ridicule from those that seek their portion only in this life, and to whom such strange behaviour is consequently foolishness.

Let us consider the greatness of the sacrifice which Moses made so willingly in hope of a worthier, that is a heavenly kingdom, a treasure more lasting than Egypt's riches, a favour more satisfying to the soul than that of Egypt's king, and a name and a love better than that of Pharoah't daughter. And may we be encouraged by his example in that which, like his, is our great career, to " walk by faith and not by sight ! "

Let us set ourselves to understand the severity of this trial of faith to which this man of God was called, and to meditate on the painfulness of the struggle with flesh and blood which preceded the eventful day when Moses chose before his high position the life of a homeless wanderer in the desert.

" He refused to be called the son of Pharoah's daughter." And who and what to him was Pharoah's daughter? She was his truest earthly friend. When his " father and mother had forsaken" him— been compelled to do so—she had taken him up. From his infancy upwards she had watched him tenderly and loved him fondly. We cannot read the simple story in Exodus of her having rescued him, not fearing the wrath of the king, from his watery grave without an instinctive feeling that the character of the royal Princess was amiable, if not noble. She stands before us at the bank of the Nile in pleasing contrast to her hard-hearted sire, endowed with all the keen sensibilities of womanly affection. She saw the Hebrew babe cast out to perish at the edict of her tyrant father, and behold it was weeping! And the infant's appealing look of helplessness and cry of distress reached her sympathising heart. She was touched with a feeling of its infirmities. And as the high-born maiden lifted the slave child to her arms the voice of Providence whispered to her, " Woman, behold thy son." Whereupon she was not disobedient to the heavenly voice, but from that hour took him unto her own home.

And should Moses now that he was come to years rudely sever the sacred tie, with which each succeeding year had bound him more closely to the generous and devoted friend, that had so loved and cared for him? Should he deny the hitherto recognised relationship, that Divine Providence had formed in the beginning, and refuse to be called henceforward the son of Pharoah's daughter? Yes. For says Christ—and Moses had the faith to grasp the saying long ages before it was spoken— " Whosoever loveth father or mother more than Me is not worthy of Me." Levi, the grandfather of Moses, had done the same. We read in the case of his father and mother: "neither did he acknowledge his brethren nor knew his own children." Pharoah's daughter was an idolatrous heathen. She was, we may suppose, tender-hearted and gentle : but she did not love the God of Israel nor His people. She knew not the God of Moses' forefathers. Nay, she did know something of Him. For Moses must have often told her of the only true God, and of Jesus Christ, Whom He was to send to redeem men from the love of the world, and from sin, to live a holy heavenly life. But she would not serve Him, nor seek to know Him. She loved Moses, but she hated his religion : its strictness that would not allow the pleasures of sin, its self denial that insisted on the mortification of evil and corrupt affections, its devoutness that was continually calling to a worship for which she had no taste, which seemed to her a dull and tedious thing. She was pleased with the vain pomp and glory of the world that surrounded her, and thought of little else. She cared not about " the glory to be revealed," of which Moses spoke. She had no interest in those topics that seemed ever uppermost in Moses' mind, the great realities of the world to come, the diadem of a distant glory, whose far more exceeding brightness dimmed for him the lustre of Egypt's crown, the throne eternal in the heavens, on which his hopes seemed to be centred, and the yet unborn Saviour whom he seemed to think of with such deep reverence, and on whom to set such earnest love.

And Moses felt that he must no longer waste his time among those whom he had vainly sought to win over to his Lord, that he dared not hazard his own soul's welfare, by continuing in scenes of temptation vanity, and open sin. I imagine the consideration of his own ease and comfort, hardly occurred to him : for well he knew that whoever would not take up his cross to follow Christ could not be His disciple.

But consideration for Pharoah's daughter it would seem from the text did for a while weigh withhim. But the time came when that even must no more detain him. Not even for the love of *her*, to whom under God he was indebted for life, and breath, and all things, must he decline the work for which God had raised him up, and Pharoah's daughter had unwittingly preserved him, " to minister unto His people and to give redemption to Israel." And when as S. Stephen says, it came into his heart to visit his brethren, the children of Israel in their affliction, and it had been revealed to him that God would by His hand redeem Israel out of all his troubles, by faith he made the sacrifice of which the text speaks. He believed in the Almighty who had pledged Himself for their deliverance. He believed in the recompense which should be his *then* in the service of Him for whom he was about to make this sacrifice of earthly good ; and thereafter when the Saviour to whose cause and people he was uniting himself, should sit upon the throne of His glory, and he having suffered with Him should reign with Him in glory everlasting. So he refused to be called the son of Pharoah's daughter. He renounced his title as the heir to Egypt's throne. He was content to turn away from the dazzling prospect of temporal honour, and prosperity that might have been his in rich abundance. He determined to forego the accumulated treasures, that were poured freely at his feet.

And he went forth from the home of his childhood and his youth, from the presence of the loved one, that all his life long had guarded and cherished and clung to him as though her own son. He went forth to a life of toil and anxiety, but withal of usefulness, and blessedness, which has hardly been surpassed.

And he had his reward. Around the name of Moses is as bright a halo of " glory, honour and immortality " as around any in the volume of the record of the saints of the Most High. He surrendered his relationship to Pharoah's daughter. But no Old Testament name is linked throughout its history in nearer fellowship than his with that of the Son of God. From the day of which the text speaks, in his voluntary self-abasement, his trials, and reproaches, he became the most striking type of the Man of sorrows.

For He too (Jesus) refused the kingdoms of the world. He too when He was the heir of all, humbled and made Himself of no reputation ; and from a Prince became a servant. He too chose to be the " despised and rejected of men," so that he might be " holy harmless undefiled and separate from sinners." He too refused to come, as we might have supposed would have been most seemly to the Majesty of Heaven, as a man clothed in soft raiment to dwell in king's houses. He too had to refuse, to set on one side a mother, and she the most sainted of all mothers. And bitterer far may we well believe it was to Him, than it could have been to Moses to say to that " blessed above women," " Woman what have I to do with thee ?"

None too was ever more conformed to that Saviour's image than was Moses in the general tenor of his life. He foretold of Christ " A prophet shall the Lord your God raise up unto you like unto me." In signs and wonders and mighty deeds Moses was like unto Him in his character and his office.   Exalted in his life, like the Lord Jesus, he was, like Him, yet more honoured in his death than ever has been any child of man.   For the very Archangel of Heaven, as the High Priest of God, came forth to solemnize the prophet's funeral.   And Michael Himself, at once priest and undertaker, laid the body of Moses in his unknown tomb.

"Those that honour me I will honour."   And he that esteemed the reproach of Christ greater riches than all the treasures of Egypt was chosen to appear with Him in glory at the Transfiguration on the Holy Mount.   Yea, his name stands forth before all others from the very world of spirits as associated with His whose is above every name.   For as the melody of heaven struck down on the inspired Apostle's listening ear, S. John heard the voice or words of Moses before them all, as though he who indeed initiated were then leading, or in some way at least the occasion of, their Hosannas.   "They sang," he says, " the song of Moses, the servant of God, and the song of the Lamb."   Could we but in the matter of life, as it has been said in regard to the moment of death, in the well-known lines—

> Could we but stand where Moses stood,
> And view the prospect o'er!

It could not but be that we should be rising to a higher view of the life we now live in the flesh.   It would open before us in its real grandeur as a probation state for heaven, invested with a dignity and responsibility, with which we had never regarded it before.   And not to " make provision for the flesh," not to gratify the sight of the eye, or indulge the pride of life, not to waste its precious hours in vanity and frivolity or self pleasing, contriving only how each tomorrow in the return it yields of mere earthly good may be as this day, only much more abundant—would you devote your God-given energies of body, soul, and spirit.   But you would redeem it as a candidate for immortality. You would vindicate it from all trifling to the great purpose for which it was given—the carrying on the work of your sanctification, and the advancement within and around you of Christ's kingdom of righteousness, and peace, and joy.

You are reminded for this purpose in the text how it was that Moses was enabled to choose and devote himself to the love and service of his God rather than to that of the world and sin.   It was, says S. Paul, " by faith."   And this says S. John, " is the victory that overcometh the world, even our faith."   This is still the only means of escaping its snares, resisting its allurements, and overcoming its temptations—faith in every word of God and His Holy Scriptures, faith in the great realities of the eternal world, faith in the things unseen, and their preponderant value over what seem the best of earthly blessings. And you shall be kept like him by the power of God through faith unto salvation.

THE DEATH OF AARON AND THE SYMBOLISM OF HIS VESTMENTS.

Numbers xx. 23-28.

Very glorious in his apparel was that exalted dignitary the High Priest of the Jewish Church. Around him was gathered, by the express revelation of God, every symbol of honour and majesty that could inspire and confirm the sentiments of awe and reverence that it was desirable to attach to his Office as typical of that of the Great High Priest to come, whom he represented. It was not of course for h mself, or the intrinsic worth of his ministrations, valuable as they were, as a temporary dispensation—but to reflect the glory of The Anointed One, " full of grace and truth," in Whose his office was to merge. And so it was that Aaron was arrayed with all that the treasures of nature and art could contribute, in elaborate and costly adornment, that no Jew, though a Solomon in all his glory, could or would have dared to outvie. They were " figures for the time then present, which served for the example of heavenly things," as S. Paul teaches us were all the Levitical ordinances.

One whole chapter of inspiration, the 28th of Exodus, is devoted to the ordering and description of his attire.

In the text the Spirit of God has thought fit in the record of Aaron's death, short as it is, to make special mention of the disrobing that preceded it.

Of the closing scenes of life related in Scripture, the imagination seizes upon and ponders with a more painful and wondering interest none sooner than those of the two holy and venerable brothers, that led the people of the Lord from Egypt, but were never permitted to enter, and this one not even to gaze on, the goodly land they had looked for so earnestly and so long. And in the passage before us which briefly tells of the " last end" of Israel's noble Priest we fasten enquiringly upon the only circumstance in it at all detailed, or presenting any surface of actual fact for the imagination to rest upon. And we eagerly ask what this previous unclothing of the body should mean. Why strip off his Divinely ordered vestments, and not let him wear them to the last in token of the respect felt for the Ministrations of which he had grace to make such full proof, and towards the Office he had on the whole so worthily filled ?

Some reply to this very natural and interesting question, some light on the strange treatment to which Aaron was subjected, on his going up to Mount Hor to die—we may derive from the chapter before mentioned, as descriptive of the official dress of which he was here deprived. We doubt not that all the particulars there have a view to spiritual lessons and truths. But what these may be we presume not at all fully to decide. "What man knoweth the things of a *man*, save the spirit of a man which is in him, even so (and much more) the things of *God*, knoweth no man." There are depths and hidden things in the Word of God, and in the full purport and spiritual interpretation of the Mosaic ordinances especially, which after the most careful study we find we cannot pretend to fathom, nor hope to uncover, till we examine the ground again in the superior light that the knowledge of Heaven shall hereafter throw.

In that chapter there are however two articles, out of the many mentioned as pertaining to the sacerdotal garb, in which I discern more obvious significance. They are the *breast-plate* and the *mitre*. I shall firstly show the object of the former, and that the laying it aside might have signified how that Aaron was no longer an Advocate for God's people, but how there was One who unlike him "abideth a Priest for ever." And secondly, the object of the latter—how the *mitre* was a reminder through life to *holiness*, but as such was no longer needed: and how it was a token through life of acceptance, and might therefore be taken off as equally unnecessary.

Conspicuous on the robes that Aaron wore, and very choice in its decoration, was to be the breast-plate of judgment, set with twelve precious stones, bearing the names of the tribes with this intent assigned to, it "Aaron shall bear the names of the children of Israel in the breast-plate of judgment upon his heart, when he goeth into the holy place, for a memorial before the Lord continually." As he went out and came in before the people for whom he was chosen to sacrifice and intercede, he bore ever in his sight and theirs the continual remembrance of all for whose souls he was to watch, and whose cause he was to plead. He stood between God and them; and as near inwardly, as outwardly, to his heart were their names and interests.

But Israel was now no more to have Aaron as a visible friend, helper, or partaker of their joy, or a source of appeal or hope, when "brought low by iniquity, by any plague, or trouble." I say as a *visible* one: because (and indeed this much we may well and I think surely believe) from the unseen world he would probably be one of that "cloud of witnesses," no uninterested spectators, by which the Church Militant is encompassed. But whether he *were* still so or no in any sense, no more should he be *hailed* or *seen* to be "the chariot of Israel and the horsemen thereof," He was to leave them now; and his Office as earthly Intercessor let another take. And let Moses take it from him before their eyes, if haply they might turn their weeping and disappointed gaze from the man that must fail them to the Eternal God, that never could, from the priest that was "not suffered to continue by reason of death," to an everlasting One they were led to believe and know an after age should reveal, whose "priesthood after the order of Melchisedeck," was to have "neither beginning of days nor end of life."

And who can doubt that in that hour he saw Christ's day and was glad: that this last and otherwise sad ceremonial in the deep significance which thus attached to it, brought no pang to " Aaron, the saint of the Lord." The bystanders might mourn for him. Moses that stood to execute upon him the Lord's behest, and cried "Alas, my brother!"— Eleazer that, unless it had been at the bidding of God, would have never submitted to be robed before his very eyes in the official vestments of his dying father—the people that lifted up before him the wail of a sorrow whose bitterness we attempt not, as we must fail, to realise, " Ah, Lord!" or " Ah, his glory!"—all these might "weep and lament." But "a joy unspeakable and full of glory" would illuminate the countenance and stay the spirit of the dying saint.

The sin mentioned in the 24th verse, of which in that hour he was suffering the penalty, had been long ago confessed and forgiven him. The eye, that perhaps in that hour melted again into penitence at the recollection of it, had wept its last tear. God Himself had wiped it away for ever. The bitterness of that death and disappointment that excluded him from the promised Canaan was wholly past. And he would not now have tarried, for all the kingdoms of the world and the glory of them. The Heavenly Canaan was rising before his raptured sight. He had a desire to depart and be there, which was so far better. The one had no longer " any glory by reason of the glory that excelled" in the other, the better country ; for former things were past away.

So the breast-plate was ungirt. And therein engraven before him were the names, and below him in the valley were the tribes, of Israel, for whom he had lived to minister and to suffer. And had he not all his life long borne them before the Lord with a fond and devoted remembrance ? Had he not thrown himself before the very face of an avenging God in the matter of Korah and his company, and stood between the dead and the living with a lofty courage and a fearless faith of which the world has never seen the like, as though he could brave the terrors of the Lord, and say to His wrath—with an almost God-like confidence in the efficacy of that power of intercession with which he was put in trust—Hitherto shalt thou come, but no further?

But though such may be our reflections as we " mark the righteous man and behold the upright" as we are bidden to do in the end of God's saints, they were not his.

As he looked for the last time on the names engraven on the breast-plate, he thought no doubt of Him to whose heart they were nearer still, and of whose intercession his was only a weak and imperfect type. We could imagine him breaking forth into the words of the aged patriarch Jacob to his son—" Behold I die, but God shall be with you." My advocacy of your interests is at an end. My office is fulfilled. My last prayer or sacrifice for you is offered. But the breast-plate is transferred. And God will ever provide a successor to wear it and represent you and your interests before Him, until a High Priest be raised up unto you like unto me, but of a far more excellent and perfect ministry. And "He shall come whose right it is" as the Priest for ever, to bear the name, and plead the cause, and absolve the guilt, and obtain all grace for every applicant.

But there was another ornament, as I said, the mitre, the removal of which was as instructively significant.

Attached to the fore-front of the mitre the Priest wore upon his head was a plate of pure gold engraven with the words "Holiness to the Lord." As Aaron came in and went out among the people, he bore about with him as the mark of consecration the reminder of his standard of aim and theirs. It was just the same as ours under the New Testament rule. "Perfecting holiness in the fear of God" "Ye are not your own. Glorify God in your body and spirit, which are His." *Him* more especially did it become to be holy who was to teach the people righteousness. Often had he put on and off that inscription, worthy indeed of its golden setting, with feelings of shame and humiliation that he so little deserved the motto, and in his heart and life realised the character required. Day by day it had been to him an incitation to press forward the more earnestly, to walk the more worthily, and more and more to aspire to the sober, righteous, and godly life.

And now as he took it off, God comforted his spirit with the assurance that he never should need it again. He was to be Holiness to the Lord for ever without a possibility of falling. And a new seal, as we read in the book of Revelation, was to be set upon his brow, and a new name written on his forehead.

The same prospect of blessedness is held out to the faithful struggling Christian. The Word and the Spirit of God take up to him this urgent cry "Holiness to the Lord." But he is in heaviness often when he hears it, for it calls to remembrance his constant sinfulness, and his own present sense of failure, and makes him doubt whether he can ever be thus holy. Yet of a surety the day to him is drawing on when the admonitory reminder shall be no more needed, the direction shall be no more pressed : for the character shall be attained. The word of exhortation, the supplication for grace to heed it, the conflict with temptation—sermons, prayers, trials, which all aim at promoting this holiness —shall be for ever over, and he shall be without fault before the throne of God.

But there is another point to be observed about the golden signet that Aaron wore upon his forehead. The plate engraven with the letters "Holiness to the Lord" was set on a blue lace ground (Exodus xxviii., v. 37.) This embroidered work signified, it would seem, the elaborate nature of this Holiness to the Lord, the righteousness of the saints, whether that which Christ worked out or which the Spirit works in them with such long and painful toil. It tells of the adornment with which that holiness invests them. The golden plate shows how glorious is holiness. The idea we derive from its embroidered ground is the beauty of holiness. And what shall we say of the rich bright colour, the *blue* of the ground on which those letters were fastened ? It tells surely of the heavens wherein dwells righteousness, where alone that character is attained in its perfection. For here of the earth is only sin. But righteousness is of the Lord from heaven. Green is the symbolic colour of earth, but blue of Heaven. So "Holiness to the Lord" was written not upon a *green* ground, but a *blue* ; significantly showing where and whence it was to be looked for. The robe of nature we see is green. But the other hue is associated to every mind with the blue sky above, the tint which the great Painter has laid on so lavishly on the mighty expanse so far beyond us all. On blue therefore was " Holiness to the Lord" inscribed. The robe too that Aaron wore, we read in verse 31, was " all of blue." And as through the blue heavens we lift the eye of faith to the dwelling place of God, we know that " Holiness to the Lord" is written there on all belonging to the heavenly world. Glorious was Mordecai when he stood in the presence of the king in royal apparel of blue and white, with a great crown of gold. And so, like Aaron when he laid aside the symbol for the reality, shall be the sanctified when he passes to " the habitation of holiness."

But the plate on Aaron's forehead served, we are told, another purpose. We cannot exactly see how it did so. But the 38th verse says it was to be a sign to him that he was to bear the iniquity of those he represented, even as the Great High Priest of an after age " was made sin for us." In some way or other Aaron bore, and was considered as charged with, the sins of Israel. He had to make atonement for all the iniquities they confessed, for which they sought before him pardon, and from which they desired at his hands release.

Beautifully and encouragingly does such a provision remind all penitents now that God has laid upon Christ the iniquity of them all; that not at their hands, but from the High Priest to whom they come as their Mediator and Absolver seeking forgiveness and release, does God expect satisfaction and atonement. Of none of all Israel was it demanded that they should propitiate God themselves. That work devolved upon Aaron, and they let it alone for ever. They came to him, and *he* made peace for them with God. This Christ does for His suppliants. How smooth is the path for the sinner's return to God when he thus learns that Christ is for this purpose set over the house of God to undertake his case, and that " he has an Advocate with the Father, even Jesus Christ the Righteous, and that He is the propitiation for our sins ! "

And so, in this view of what the mitre signified, how grateful to the departing Priest must have been this token of release, as the mitre was unbound from his forehead, as the breast-plate was from his heart! Oh ! his had been an awful and an arduous office! To bear the iniquity of Israel, to have the part he had assigned as to the purging of the worshippers—we feel it must have been a life-long burden of responsibility and a solemn charge the nature of which we cannot adequately even imagine. It was a strange office was that of Israel's High Priest ! We know but little of what it really was. But as we ponder it looms up before us from those olden times invested with mysterious and solemn shadows that thrill our souls with awe. Well we can feel with what a sense of relief notwithstanding all its high and honourable prerogatives, Aaron laid it down for ever. He had only been enabled to bear that mitre as sustained by a special grace and power from God, a grace and power which it seems to me no other child of earth save the Son of Man ever needed to receive as did an High Priest of the Jewish Church.

How could he but be glad to resign it: So they stripped him of his mitre : and to few could the exchange of a life's duty for the rest that remaineth come so sweetly as to him.

The 38th verse says further of the mitre " It shall be always upon his forehead, that they may be accepted before the Lord." Like the Bow in the cloud, was this ornament of blue and gold on the High Priest's forehead, in the eyes of the High and Holy One. Ever as God looked upon it as the appointed token of the covenant between Him and the people, He recalled and respected, that everlasting covenant: and when He was angry His wrath was turned away. He remembered that He had pledged His word to accept and not reject them ; that He was their God, and they His people, sealed in their High Priest's person with His seal. Thus it was that—as Aaron, as the people's head and representative, stood before Him with all their names upon the breastplate on his heart, and all their claims upon his protection and love openly shown before God on that signet " Holiness to the Lord "—" He did not behold iniquity in Jacob, neither did He see perverseness in Israel." So the Prophet Jeremiah says. " Israel was Holiness to the Lord." He neither could nor would impute to them their sins. He neither could nor would withhold the favour and acceptance that plate guaranteed to His people.

And well I observe in conclusion might Aaron consent as he put off the mitre to be stripped of this glorious symbol. In that " holy place, the tabernacle of the most High," into which he was about to enter—he needed whether for himself, or the people, no such token of the Divine acceptance. His consciousness of sins' presence and dominion was never again, as heretofore, to cast a doubt across his mind as to his being the accepted and beloved of God. The time was now come, when he should say with the Psalmist " As for me thou shalt uphold me in integrity, and set me before Thy face for ever." The sign of acceptance was now to be exchanged for the fact. He was to be received into the Great family to whom the Father reveals Himsel, fand whom he loves and blesses evermore with His immediate presence.

Another High Priest should bear the token of acceptance for Israel; but for himself, though he had needed it as much as they till then, he should never need it more. So " the full assurance of faith," would brighten in this last hour into certainty, that his spirit ascending to the God who gave it should be owned with His loving welcome before all the Angels and redeemed children of light, " Behold my servant whom I have chosen mine elect, in whom my soul delighteth. I have redeemed thee : thou art mine ! "

He gave his parting blessing : and the sainted priest of God,
 Unfalteringly the mountain path before all Israel trod,
 Rich his attire of ornament : the Ephod, that he wore,
 Was girt with costly wreathen chains ; on his crowned head he bore

A mitre with a graven plate of finest dazzling gold,
 Inscribed with Holiness, and bound by a lace embroidered fold ;
 The lace, from which the letters shone, and the Ephod, both of blue,
 As though the plate that spoke of Heaven had borrowed thence its hue.

Henceforth a higher priesthood his : so calmly he laid down,
His Breast-plate set with rows of gems, his Ephod, and his Crown,
In token that his Office ceased : then in brighter far array,
God clothed him with His robe of light ; and his spirit passed away.

HUGH ALLAN.

With a life so consecrated and spent in Thy worship and service, grant Lord to us by Thy sanctifying Spirit's help to live ! and in so sure, and certain a hope of acceptance, grant Lord to us in Christ to die ! And let our last end be like his !

FAILURE AND SUCCESS.

Jehoshaphat made ships of Tarshish to go to Ophir for gold; but they went not: for the ships were broken at Ezion-gaber. 1 *Kings* xxii. 48.

Jehoshaphat's design here related appears to have been an imitation of what Solomon had actually accomplished. We read in 2 Chron. viii., 17 and 18, that Solomon built a fleet at Ezion-gaber, and despatched it to Ophir, from which he brought back to enrich his kingdom 450 talents of gold. Jehoshaphat, who appears to have been an enterprising character, attempted the same. But the Divine blessing was withheld in his case for a reason which we learn from the fuller narrative of this incident contained in 2 Chron. xx., 35-37. "Except the Lord build the house (says the Psalmist) their labour is but lost that build it; and except the Lord keep the city the watchmen watch but in vain. It is but lost labour that (in such a case) ye rise up early and late take rest and eat the bread of carefulness." " Ye looked for much, and lo, it came to little; and when ye brought it home I did blow it away," said the Lord by the Prophet Haggai. Success may never be expected where there is reason, because of some unforsaken sin, for the Divine displeasure. And so it was with Jehoshaphat. He had already been warned, in the preceding chapter, that his intimacy with the wicked family of Ahab had alienated from him the favour of God. "Shouldest thou help the ungodly, and love them that hate the Lord? Therefore is wrath upon thee from before the Lord." And now he was to be practically convinced of the reality of that displeasure. For Eliezer (we read) prophesied against Jehoshaphat, saying " Because thou hast joined thyself with Ahaziah the Lord hath broken thy works ; and the ships were broken that they were not able to go."

Ezion-gaber, a sea-port on the eastern arm of the Red Sea, at its northern extremity adjacent to Elath, is mentioned twice as one of the encampments of Israel during the forty years' wandering. It was the place too where Solomon (like Jehoshaphat here) constructed his merchant fleet. But it has passed into obscurity, and its present site is very doubtful. Its name, however, will always be identified with the Scripture record of the unaccomplished purpose of this great King of Judah. And I may take the passage now to lead your meditations to a subject which cannot but be instructive to us all. Compassed about as we are with infirmities and sins, that most easily beset us, sore let and hindered as we always shall be in running the spiritual race set before us—as we daily find we are in the matter of obstacles and difficulties, in our worldly affairs—we may profit by musing on the story of Ezion-gaber and Jehoshaphat, because it is the story of ourselves. It has been well said with a forcible irony against those who indulge visionary hopes of worldly advancement and well doing, who dream of what they *will* do, and talk of what they *may* do, that the best poem is one that has never yet been written, and the best speech one that has never been delivered. And if the wise man has so truly said, that " the soul of the sluggard desireth and hath nothing: but the hand of the diligent maketh rich,"—if there are so many vain dreamers in life, as we know there are, who resemble those of whom the prophet Isaiah tells, " An hungry man, dreameth, and behold he eateth: but he awaketh and his soul is empty: and the thirsty man dreameth, and behold he drinketh: but he awaketh and behold he is faint, and his soul hath appetite,"—the experience is alas even yet more common in regard to the affairs of the soul. Many an Ezion-gaber is there, where on the voyage of life holy resolutions and earnest purposes are broken like Jehoshaphat's ships, and faith made shipwreck of. Well does our Church teach us in her second Collect for Evensong to unite with " holy desires, and good counsels, or resolves," to which those desires after holiness lead, "*just works*" in which they should *result*. And well are we taught in another Collect to pray, with regard to such purposes, that we may have grace to bring the same to good effect.

We have already on the voyage of life, however far or short a distance we may have travelled, come to a stand still at its Ezion-gabers. The child promises to prepare some lesson, to look out some point of knowledge in which it has found itself deficient, and forgets. It declares with all earnestness at the time its sorrow for some childish fault, its determination to guard against the error or failure, for which it has been reproved. But it halts and fails at the very spot from which, like Jehoshaphat's ship, it had promised to make so fair a start. The youth sees, as he is shown it, the necessity of greater diligence in his calling, greater watchfulness against the growing habits of evil that will mar his welfare and success. And the maiden—as she comes to the years when she ceases to think as a child, and speak as a child—is conscious of the same promptings to an earnest useful perhaps God-devoted life. The young man who has entered into business is not unconscious oftentimes of the snare of that idle company, that wastes his hours, and leads him to squander his substance, and incapacitates him for the stern realities of life. The self indulgent thinks seriously with himself to amend his ways, as the intolerable feeling of self-contempt seizes at certain times with resistless grasp upon his soul.

The notorious sinner will listen at times without impatience to the denunciations of Divine judgment on such as he; like Felix will tremble while the preacher " reasons of righteousness, temperance, and judgment to come," and decide at some convenient season, which he flatters himself he will very speedily fix upon, to amend his ways, and let the time past suffice him for following so dangerous a course.

And many a Minister has seen the same as he watched by the sick bed of some irreligious soul, and was made the instrument of rousing him from his false peace, and his unconcern about the things of God.

He has heard the " What must I do to be saved," from lips quivering
with intense anxiety. He has seen the tears of alas! but a short-lived
repentance flow freely, and heard the confession of past sin uttered as
fully as he would wish. And he has seen those impressions pass away
presently as the morning cloud and the early dew when the sun is risen
with a burning heat, and in the scorching atmosphere of the outer world
the frail plant of grace die utterly away. And he has given his regretful
testimony to the truth of the verse.

God called him in the time of dread,
When death was full in view,
He trembled on his feverish bed,
And rose to sin anew.

The illustration I apply to this subject of Jehoshaphat's projected
enterprise fails in its application in one particular. It was through no
neglect, no apathy, no procrastination on the part of the king of Judah,
that his well ordered scheme was never successful, and his enterprise remained uncrowned. In this case God Himself was against him. And
says the prophet Jeremiah " who is he that saith and it cometh to pass,
if the Lord command it not." In matters pertaining to this life it is
often so. That higher Will that claims, as well it may in its perfect
Wisdom, to overrule ours, interposes for its own far greater ends. And
the wise counsel of Ahithophel is brought to nought. And the clever
project is defeated and the likely purpose blasted. Man proposes but
God disposes. But in things relating to the soul there is no such
Divine interference. We are not straitened (says the Apostle) in God,
but in ourselves. We are and shall always be seconded by God's most
earnest Will. For the salvation and the well-being of our soul is far
dearer to God, and an object of far more lively concern, than in the
hour of deepest feeling and most awakened thoughtfulness it ever is to
us. But it is our own fault only, our own most grievous fault, if our
spiritual voyage is broken at any Ezion-gaber, and we suffer a moral
shipwreck on the waves of life.

The complaint of Job is true enough in many a respect " My days
are broken off my purposes are disappointed." For ours here is a
sadly broken life. A condition of imperfection is attached to everything
human. And we seldom reach or can reach our ideal. Cross currents
are met with, and our bark drifts away at the very moment, that land
seems almost touched, from the haven where we would be. The riches
or treasure we had almost secured makes wings and flies away, friend
and acquaintance in the light of whose love we had hoped to journey is
put by death or change far away out of our sight. Into the pool of
Siloam-blessing, into which we had almost stepped, we see another, like
the man in the Gospel, go down before us. And from the good we
craved so eagerly, and which we had made such long and careful preparation to secure, we were sent empty away. The vessel of hope in
which we had looked to cross to the far shore of content, is dashed to
pieces beneath our feet, on the breakers. And we may think ourselves
fortunate if we can escape like Paul and his shipwrecked comrades with
the loss of all its lading to a Milita, which to our chilled souls is peopled

with barbarous beings, where our spirits shiver to follow up the figure of
with the rain and cold of that Mediterranean island.   But it is not so
in spiritual things.   There is no Ezion-gaber like that in the wilderness
of Elath, where storms come down on the unsheltered soul and dash its
confidences to pieces;   or rather, if there be such, there is One at hand
who will say "Peace, be still," to whom the terrified soul can appeal in
its hour of jeopardy—

> Jesus! Refuge of my soul!
>   Let me to Thy bosom fly!
> While the billows near me roar,
>   While the tempest still is high.

Indeed, says the Psalmist, "The floods have lifted up their voice;   the
floods lift up their waves.   But (he adds) the Lord on high is mightier
than the voice of many waters, yea, than the mighty waves of the sea."

> From every stormy wind that blows,
> From every swelling tide of woes,
> There is a calm, a sure retreat,
> The Saviour on His mercy-seat.

And if slowly yet surely, if calmly yet steadily, the fixed purpose of the
believer which, like the will of God, is the sanctification of his soul,
goes ever on.   Across the waves of this troublesome world he pursues
his undiverted way.   And the intended voyage to Ophir for gold is
accomplished in his case.   Yea, an object more to be desired than gold
is his; he is in quest of durable rices better than fine gold.   And he shall
not be disappointed.   Like Abraham, who "set forth to go into the
land of Canaan, and into the land of Canaan he came," he shall never
miss the attainment of his high enterprise.   While he trusts and hopes,
and reposes all his expectation upon God and His grace, final failure is
impossible.   And "Kept by the power of God through faith unto
salvation," he shall be enabled presently to say I have finished my
course, I have kept the faith, and await the crown.   "Therefore, my
brethren, be steadfast, unmovable, always abounding in the work of the
Lord, forasmuch as ye know that your *labour is not in vain in the Lord*."
And that which is, which ought to be, which must be, the grand purpose
of this your earthly life shall not be unfulfilled.

Let it only be undertaken and followed up in earnest.   And
"building ourselves up on our most holy faith" no unsympathetic
beholder like the one in the parable shall ever have cause to mock as he
sees the work of faith broken off, saying " This man began to build,
but was not able to finish,"   " Thanks be to God which giveth us the
victory through our Lord Jesus Christ," the joy of our Lord as the
time of His departure to the Father's house drew near, may in a
measure be yours and mine.   And at the close of life we may be enabled
to say with humble gratitude to the God by whose grace we have been
caused to triumph—and I earnestly pray God we may—"I have
glorified Thee on the earth; I have finished the work which Thou gavest
me to do.   And now I come to Thee!"

THE APOSTOLIC MESSAGE.

I write unto you little children because ye have known the Father. I have written unto you fathers, because ye have known Him that is from the beginning.
1 John ii., 13-14.

Our Lord had intimated in His teaching that He desired as the rulers of His household the Church, faithful and wise stewards, who would know how to give each member his portion of meat in due season. S. John proves in this passage that *he* was so fitted, and could distinguish aright the diverse capacities and circumstances of the believing members of the family of our Lord Jesus Christ. The elders which were among them he exhorts "as one who was also an elder," a partaker of the clearer views, profounder knowledge, and richer experience they had attained, and like them, through the Spirit's training, advancing to the measure of the stature of the fulness of Christ. For those younger in the faith and the babes in Christ, who needed the pure milk of the word rather than the strong meat of doctrine suited for a maturer age, he had also in this Epistle appropriate words of exhortation. He could as perfectly estimate their position and needs; and had suitable topics to present to them, which he could handle as wisely for their edification and growth in grace.

In the text he notes the measure of faith whereunto two classes or ages had already attained; and with a view to incite them to further progress he encouragingly commends the *younger* with a fatherly approbation, the *elder* with the congratulations of a brother and fellow-disciple in the Lord. The latter he addresses as those who had happily acquired the character that S. Paul bade Titus teach was expected of such. They were " sound in the faith." And the yet younger disciples, the infants, so to speak, in the Redeemer's school, he takes as it were by the hand of a gentle guidance, and expresses towards them, as you will presently see, that same affectionate interest which the Apostle Paul did in another passage, when he tells us how he dealt with his young converts " even as a nurse that cherishes her children."

And firstly, as to those who needed it most, he directs his attention and kind concern to those young beginners who were newly setting out on their Christian course. Thus the Good Shepherd Himself does who comes to seek and to save His lost sheep, taking first the lambs in His arms and carrying them in His bosom, as the most helpless dependent. Thus too when He consigned to His Apostles and their successors in the Ministry of His Church, His own pastoral charge and enjoined them to feed His flock, He made the same priority of mention, and bade them first of all to feed His lambs. And so S. John, who had himself recorded this, follows out here the intimation. In the very spirit of his Master he singles out the new born babes of the Christian Church as rightfully and naturally the first claimants of his notice. I speak of course, irrespectively of natural age, of those who are young counting from the date of their *spiritual*, not their *natural*, birth ; young in grace, whether or not so in years. He turns to those whose tender age, and hazardous outstart on the stormy tide of the Christian life and voyage, appealed most strongly to his counsel, his care, and his love.

We learn hence the blessed Saviour's sympathy for His young disciples. The bruised reed He will not break, the smoking flax He will not quench. He anxiously guards and aids those who believe in Him, though with the weakest faith ; and cling to Him confidingly, though with the simplicity of a yet untaught and imperfect love.

And how beautifully and exactly does the Apostle recognise the position and the feelings in the matter of their religious experience, of the younger children of His Lord ! "I write unto you little children, because ye have known the Father." He speaks much in this Epistle of the believer's knowledge of the Father and the Son. But well he knew that the knowledge of God in His Unity, and as man's Father and Friend, must precede the great doctrines and topics of the Christian revelation of the Persons of the Godhead, and the relation in particular of the Father to us in the Son of His love. And so he says "I write unto you because ye have known (not the Son, but) the Father."

Thus had Israel been educated to acknowledge first of all the truth that the Lord their God was one Lord, and to know Him as their one Great Father and Friend. Thus S. Paul at Athens, before he preached Jesus to the citizens, laboured to impress them with the thought that they were the offspring of the One Great God, and that he exercised towards them and in their behalf the protection, the authority, and the love of a Parent. And thus our Lord Himself, when He would lead His disciples further into a Christian faith and knowledge of all truth, built upon this same foundation when He said "Ye believe in God, believe also in Me." And ' as S. John knew how it had been with him in the earlier days of his discipleship, when he and his brother Apostles had so earnestly said with Philip "Lord, show us the Father, and it sufficeth us"—so did he rejoice to think that it was with these young disciples of the faith. They had learnt at the least to say feelingly "Our Father which art in heaven :" and their hearts had turned to the God they had begun to know with the obedience, the reverence, and the trustfulness of a child. He doubted not, therefore, that God would reveal Himself to them, as He had done to him, more and more, and that they would increase in the knowledge of God, and therein of Jesus their Lord. And albeit they did not yet know as they ought to know, and as the fathers in the faith here afterwards addressed Him, the Son, "that was from the beginning with God"—although they had much yet to learn of "Jesus Christ Whom He had sent," and how they were to honour Him even as the Father—he hailed the hold it had been given them to make by faith upon this elementary truth. He knew that He that had begun a good work in them would continue it until the day of His Spirit's revelation to their soul of the Son in the fulness of His glory and the extent of His preciousness.

As the little child that, with the dawn of intelligence beginning to look forth upon the world, for the most part before all other men or objects learns to recognise and love its *father*, so as they looked forth into the spiritual world and life on which they had entered, and to which their eyes were opened, S. John well knew that the object that had fixed their attention and awakened their regard was the Great " Father of Spirits," the Author of their regenerate life. In the consciousness of His Presence they had begun to live and move and have their being. In the consciousness of the benefits they were receiving from Him their hearts were drawn to Him. And in the consciousness of His love and their dependence on Him they were glad.

And of whom should the Apostle speak to them first but of Him to whom their hearts were bound, and to whom they clung in the sense of *their* infinite need and *His* Infinite fulness? Of what would they rather hear him speak than of Him who was now their reconciled Father in Christ? Or to what theme would their filial hearts more gladly respond than to the name of Him to whom they had been introduced by Jesus, the world's Great Teacher and Mediator, and whose relationship of Father was to them a tower of strength and an assurance of love?

And well could S. John so address them. Though he was in experience as well as years old, and they were young—though he had long since been guided into all truth, and they knew but little yet of the Christian faith and the Christian life—he stood here with them on an equality, and shared their every feeling and sentiment towards their Father in Heaven. In His presence S. John could bow before Him as the veriest child with all the self-renunciation and conscious dependence of one of themselves. Full as he was beyond them all of faith, and grace, and knowledge, he knew he needed the aid and sustenance of that Great Father as much as the weakest of themselves. And thus he says " I write unto you because ye have known the Father." Well could he feel as they; for to *him* no less than *them* was their reconciled Father in Christ the object of a most child-like worship and love. What though in the confidence of a long acquaintance he walked with that Father in the close intimacy of a friend? What though in an almost perfect sympathy with all God's views, and thoughts, and feelings, he had come to walk with him as a man of mature years and ripe experience and wisdom might do with his own Parent, as one like-minded and in some respects (if I may say it with sufficient reverence) almost His companion while they, unadmitted as yet to such communion, were in the Father's family only as " little children? " Was he not still before Him altogether such a one as themselves? Other feelings indeed he had towards God. But with all these he still maintained and must needs always do, the lowly reverent submissive attitude of the child ; and share their every feeling of infinite distance and ignorance, and insufficiency.

Did they know Him as, what a father is, condescending towards his children—One whom they had found ready to stoop to their level of helplessness and frailty, and folly, and lift them in His arms of love? Did they know Him as the graciously forgiving One, who had borne with their waywardness, and frowardness, and pitied their foolish ignorance, " like as a father pitieth his own children," and followed them despite all their perverseness with an unchanging love ? Did they know Him as the Father whose labour had been unweariedly expended on their behalf to provide for them eternally, and to instruct them spiritually ? and to supply all their need as a father on earth will do in behalf of his children ? Did they know Him as the Father who had nourished and brought them up, and expended on procuring the things needful for their souls, all that an Infinate wisdom could plan, and Infinite grace secure ? Even just such a Father had S. John himself found Him. And so in a perfect understanding of all they felt for Him, and as a partaker of all their fresh emotions of love and joy in their knowledge of Him, S. John heard with vivid sympathy of their new-born joy in that the First Person of the Triune God whom they had just begun to know, " I write unto you little children because ye have known the Father."

If a writing were to come to you from this departed Apostle, would it think you address you as in the position of these young converts? Were the voice of S. John being dead yet to speak, could he congratulate you in a similar way on your knowledge and love of the Father of Heaven, with whom he dwells ? Without that knowledge you can never be, as he and they have together been so long before the throne of God, in the great and blessed family of Heaven.

We pass to the second division of the text. As the Apostle wrote of the Father, he thought also of His Son Jesus Christ, with whom as truly his own fellowship was. And so he thought too of those " fathers in Israel," who like himself had heard and looked upon " Him who was from the begining." These younger converts had never probably known personally in the days of His Incarnation, "Him the Son of the Father," who was so " full of grace and truth." But *he* had seen with his eyes that Jesus of Nazareth. And though He was long since " passed into the heavens," no doubt the Holy Apostle, like David who foresaw the Lord always before him, had ever before his eyes the vision and the form of his departed Lord. And among those to whom he wrote there were perhaps veteran saints, who had also like himself literally seen the Lord's Christ. Not that I would lay any special stress on this for the *carnal* vision of the Lord Jesus was nothing compared with the *spiritual*. If we think those blessed who saw " the man Christ Jesus," blessed rather He teaches us Himself are they who having not seen Him yet believe. And so says another Apostle of this as a thing that was comparatively of little import, " Though we have known Christ after the flesh yet now henceforth know we Him no more."

And yet I think there is such a passing allusion here, a congratulatory reminding those old fathers of the Church of what they had together been privileged, above all the prophets and kings of an older time, to see and to hear when years ago they had communed with their

Incarnate Lord. "I write unto you, fathers, because *ye* have known Him that is from the beginning." And well might S. John—who, looking at the time he was writing for the hour of his departure, expected to see Him again so soon—recall the happy memory of that outward and visible communion with Jesus of days gone by, that he was so shortly to renew.

If an inward and spiritual acquaintance with that Saviour had been said to be more blessed than a literal one, it was only so as a discipline for a temporary purpose. It could not be more desirable in itself. You never can find such a pleasure in thinking of your absent friend as in seeing him. And so as the time of his departure drew near S. John anticipated that actual vision, with all the eagerness to which absence arouses a strong love. And out of the abundance of a heart "looking for and hasting unto" that coming day when in his flesh he was to see God as he had done before, we may well suppose that his pen would write of a *literal* vision. "I write unto you, fathers, because ye have known Him that is from the beginning." Nor can we afford to lose such a meaning in the passage, as expresses thus forcibly the true and genuine, the living and abiding, love of the Apostle towards the Son of God; and leads us to observe how thoroughly he had learnt from his former association with Him to value and know the blessedness of His Presence.

But whether or know there is implied in these words, an allusion to a previous personal knowledge of Jesus, as I think there is manifestly, well we know they express the Apostle's congratulation on their spiritual acquaintance with Jesus their Lord. No doubt the young converts knew Jesus in a degree. They had cast themselves before Him in the ecstacy with which each converted soul ever exclaims with S. Philip, "We have found the Messias." But they knew Him only as a new found treasure, S. John as a long-tried one. For long years he had studied His character, and sought to conform himself to His Will. "God hath given us an understanding, that we may know Him that is True, even His Son Jesus Christ." These words of S. John seem to betoken a consciousness and a claim of special acquaintance with Christ. And just in the same way S. Paul speaks of a breadth, and length, and depth, and height, in the knowledge of Christ which *he* had, but which those to whom he wrote had not as yet.

And thus it is S. John passes on to address here those old disciples who knew Jesus, as the young converts did not. "I write unto you, fathers, because ye have known Him that is from the beginning." Indeed it was so. They had, as each day the earnest devoted disciple of Jesus gains something in that direction, a richer portion, and greater treasure in their blessed Master's love. They had been growing in grace and the knowledge of Him. As they went daily on receiving grace out of His grace, and strength from His fulness, and pardon from His merits, and the aiding spirit of all goodness as His gift—as they added to their faith in Him virtue, and to virtue *knowledge*, he might well say "I write unto you fathers, because ye have known Him," because they had this knowledge in so pre-eminent a degree above their younger fellow disciples in the Christian faith

And precisely here, as in the case of the more recent converts, does S. John recognise, and address them on the subject, and the person nearest to their hearts, and congratulate each class on what they would feel most especially to be the subject of their glory and their joy. With the fresh convert, rejoicing in the sense of pardon, he speaks like David of the blessedness of the man whose transgression is forgiven and whose sin is covered. "I write unto you, little children, because your sins are forgiven you for His namesake."

And again with the child he speaks most naturally of his father. "I write unto you, little children, because ye have known the Father." And here the fathers, who had long walked in fellowship with Christ, and had come to feel Him the Author and Finisher of their faith, he addresses on that subject of all others so dear to an experienced Christian—Him the beginning and end of their life, Whose preciousness they were ever more deeply feeling, and Whose love they were ever more wonderfully proving—"I write unto you, fathers, because ye have known Him that is from the beginning."

Very observable is the power which is shown in Holy Scripture, inspired as it is by the Spirit who knows what is in man, of gauging the varied depths of human thought, and estimating exactly the position of human feeling. For is not the attitude of the long-tried, and ripe believer exactly delineated here? Is there a topic that appeals so powerfully to an old Christian's interest as does that of the Lord and Saviour? Will he so readily give ear to you when you speak to him of anything, as when it is of the things touching his King. Let the Apostle reply as he says to the Corinthians "I determined not to know anything among you save Jesus Christ," and to the Philippians "I count all things but loss for the excellency of the knowledge of Christ Jesus my Lord." Such as S. Paul's were the views of these elders about the Son of God, and their disposition towards Him.

Well S. John knew it. And well also did he know on what theme they would have him speak. And so S. John said "I write unto you, fathers, because ye have known Him that is from the beginning."

And what think *you* of Christ? And how do you feel with regard to Him compared by the standard of S. John and the fathers before us to whom he wrote? Do you share their affections of deep and self-consecrated devotion towards God's all worthy Son? He is the beginning (says the Apostle Paul,) "that in all things he might have the pre-eminence." "He is the beginning (says this Apostle John,) the Prince of the kings of the earth." "The same was in the beginning with God," His "First-born the beginning of His strength, the excellence of dignity and the excellence of power." Of Him, His glory and His grace, all Heaven bears record: and the Spirit and the Bride, the testimony of His Word, and Church, and Ministers, agree in one. And so I pray with the Apostle Paul, that in the unity of the faith and knowledge of that Son of God, you all may come to a perfect man unto the measure of the stature of the fathers in the text!

THE APOSTOLIC MESSAGE.

PART II.—TO YOUNG MEN.

I have written unto you, young men, because ye are strong, and the Word of God abideth in you, and ye have overcome the wicked one 1. *John* ii. 14.

These words came from the oldest soldier then living in the world, of the Christian faith. Long and manfully had he led the van of the armies of the cross, and he had grown old in his Master's service. The morning that he pressed so eagerly to the sepulchre of his risen Lord, arriving there before any of the other disciples, and outrunning even the quick and impetuous Peter, had been a symbol and an earnest of his after days. S. Paul tells us he was esteemed as a Pillar in the Church : and from what is recorded of him in the earlier chapters of the Acts of the Apostles, we are well prepared to anticipate such testimony. In the course of nature he was soon to leave the work of the Church's vineyard to other labourers and to younger hands. He had nobly borne the toil and heat of the day. And now the Evening of life was come. And he looked for the Master, for whom he had loved to labour, to send him his message of release, and call him home to receive the gracious recompense He had promised him. He was waiting like aged Simeon to see one more promised revelation of Christ. For to him, as to the other, there had been a Divine intimation that till then he should not see death. After that he would be ready to breathe from his heart the words he had heard from heaven in that Revelation. " Blessed are the dead that die in the Lord : yea, saith the Spirit, that they may rest from their labours ; and their works do follow them."

From this brief mention of the writer, we turn to his correspondents. " Young men " they were called. And we have other converts mentioned together with them, and distinguished in the context as little children and fathers. And here we are reminded of the frequency with which this figure of relative age is employed in the Epistles to denote in Christians degrees of spiritual attainments. S. Peter and S. Paul, both refer to the believer's gradual growth in grace, and in the faith and knowledge of the Son of God, to the full stature of spiritual manhood. To such a state these in the text had probably arrived. At the same time there is no reason why we should not regard the expression as pointing also to their natural age. At all events, we will take it as it is, and speak of them as " Young men."

We know nothing of these young Christians, but this Apostle evidently did. As was the case with Gaius, brethren came and testified to him of the truth that was in them, and that they walked in the

truth.   So the brethren at Lystra and Iconium reported well to S. Pau
of the young disciple Timothy.   I wish it were as general, as it would
thus seem to have been in the Apostolic days, for Christian people
to notice, and commend those whom God has endowed with singular
gifts or graces of the Spirit.   It would tend not only to the proper encouragement of such, and their being brought forward to posts of more
eminent usefulness, but to raising the tone of religion, to the imitation
of such by others, and to that spirit of healthy rivalry and emulation
of others in grace, which is perhaps more appealed to in Holy Scripture
than it is by preachers or writers now.

Long perhaps had these "young men" imagined they were labouring
on with self and sin unnoticed by the stewards set over to appoint
Christ's servants their work, to give their portion of meat in due season,
commendations, exhortation, or blame.   And unexpectedly a Note came
to them from the far distant and revered Apostle.   " As cold waters to
a thirsty soul, so is good news from a far country."   And so it was to
them.   It conveyed to them the approbation of S. John and therein of
Jesus also, an assurance like that which made glad the hearts of the
faithful at Ephesus, who received it like these through their Shepherd
and Bishop S. John.   "I know thy works, and thy labour, and thy
patience, and how thou canst not bear them which are evil."   Not only
was their " witness in heaven and their record on high," as Job says.
But in God's kind care that it should be so, they met with a fellow
Christian, and he the great revered Apostle, to cheer them with a word
of seasonable encouragement " Well done thou good and faithful
servant ! "

Well and wisely did this great Apostle bethink himself of his
humbler brethren.   Five talents had he wherewith to glorify his Lord,
and they had but two.   But they were rendering according to their
power of such opportunities of service as God had given them.   And S.
John knew they were equally accepted of their Master, and equally
dear to Him.   If He holds in His right hand the Stars of the Churches,
He enfolds in His loving arms the weakest babe in Christ, the humblest
youth and the lowliest maiden.   And so though their praise was not in
all the Churches as his —though their names were not emblazoned like
his on the scroll of a world-honoured fame—they were whispered in
Heaven by the Intercessor before the throne of God.   And the Apostle's
listening ear, opened by inspiration, had caught those names.   And
with the joy and love of an elder brother he exclaimed " I write unto
you, young men, because ye are strong, and the Word of God abideth
in you, and ye have overcome the wicked one."

Two points have we here to observe.   Firstly, an Apostle's letter
of congratulation.   And secondly, the cause of his so writing.   This
cause is three-fold.   There are three topics of congratulation.   *Firstly*,
" ye are strong." *Secondly*, "the Word of God abideth in you." *Thirdly*,
" ye have overcome the wicked one."

And firstly we observe he wrote to them a congratulatory note.
How naturally do we rejoice in the gladness of a friend!   To rejoice
with them that do rejoice is a Christian precept.   But when our glad

fellow creature is a friend it hardly needs or implies the grace of God to do so. Such a feeling upsprings, and goes forth from our heart towards him, as naturally as our Lord says does even the love of a publican for his fellow. And so far then it is nothing that the Apostle should, with the sincerest feeling, have sent a message of warm interest and kindly sympathy in these young men's advantage and joy. But what does he more than others, or than we ourselves have often done, on hearing of the realization of a friends success, the accomplishment of some desire of his?

He congratulates them on spiritual prosperity. " I have no greater joy (he wrote to Gaius) than to hear that my children walk in truth." Time was when the heart of S. John himself had been filled with worldly hopes and ambitious views. But at the foot of his Master's cross he had laid down all these, and like S. Paul had come to esteem as dross what had once seemed gain the most desirable. And too well did he know, and too often had he seen what a snare to the young, and indeed to any disciple's soul, are riches, preferments, honours, and a multiplicity of this world's cares and entanglements, to make any special mention of these in his words of congratulation, or to venture to desire them even for these young Christians. But there were advantages they had acquired and expectations they had before them, that aroused his most vivid sympathy, and drew forth from him the expressions of his sincerest rejoicing in their behalf.

And firstly in the order of their spiritual attainments, as indeed in the order of nature, they were strong. So he observed " I write unto you young men, because ye are strong." "The glory of young men is their strength," says Solomon : for he knew the gladness which the conscious possession of this gift brings with it—whether it be physical, intellectual or spiritual strength—and S. John knew it too. And he made an apt use of his knowledge here by addressing them on a topic that was sure to appeal to their hearts, and therefore gain their attention.

The prophet Jeremiah warns us how ready is the mighty man to " glory in his might," and the wise man to " glory in his wisdom." Here indeed refers to a vain glorious boasting. And " all such rejoicing is evil "—the Apostle James teaches us. And we are carefully guarded in Holy Scripture against yielding to such a temper—for " the Lord knoweth the thoughts of man, that they are but vain—by such memorable examples as Rabshakeh, Nebuchadnezzar, and Herod.

But with what a natural pleasure, we may yet observe with Solomon, does the young man glory in his strength. How does he delight to tell of the feats he has performed, the distinctions of scholarship he has risen to, the prize he has gained, the contest of whatever kind it be in which he has excelled his fellows ! It was however no corruptible crown of human applause for which these young men had striven. The energies they had put forth, and the strength they had so nobly and honourably exercised, had been directed to the highest and holiest ends. " Strong in the grace that is in Christ Jesus," they had been addressing themselves to the pulling down the strong-holds of sin within and around them. " Strong in faith," they had brought glory to God by their humble

Christian lives. And strong in Christian enterprise, they had been fellow-labourers with Christ in advancing His kingdom. What had been the particular sphere of service to God, in which they had distinguished themselves, it concerns us not to know. Suffice it to learn from the Apostle their labour had not been in vain in the Lord.

Are you strong like these young men, and valiant for your Master? You are not so by nature. With man spiritual strength is never inherent, as natural may be, in a hardy frame and robust constitution. The Angels of God we read " excel in strength," and have done so from the first. With them it may be said, I imagine, to be inherent. But with us since Adam's fall, there is inherent only weakness and frailty. But the delicate and feeble frame has recourse to something out of itself and seeks in exercise, and supplies of external strength—and indeed is able to obtain therefrom in some degree—the remedy of such deficiency. And so in the Lord of all power and might there is an abundant treasury " He giveth power to the faint, and to them that have no might he increaseth strength." All power is committed to him. And to any earnestly seeking disciple will He give power to " subdue kingdoms (whole territories of evil passion and sinful inclination) to work righteousness (even to will and to to do all that is well pleasing to Him), to wax valiant in the fight (of faith), and finally to obtain the promises," He has held out. Need I remind you what are the channels through which this Divine strength flows out to us, the ordinances of Christ's Church, Prayer, and the humble study of His Word ?

Seeing then help is here at hand, and " according as His Divine power hath given unto us all things that pertain unto life and godliness," let us " give all diligence" whereby, as these of whom we are speaking, we may add to our faith virtue, that is excellence and attainments in the spiritual life worthy of the grace so freely vouchsafed for that end.

We pass to the other topics of congratulation, " The Word of God abideth in you, and ye have overcome the wicked one." Now strength is of no avail unless it have an instrument to work with, and an object to work upon. So the Apostles goes on to congratulate them next in a logical consequence, the beauty and aptitude of which is well worth noticing, on their possession of the needful instrument whereby to give exercise to their spiritual strength—the Word of God—; and then to the mention of the object towards which they were directing the whole force of their Christian life and energy, " Ye have overcome the wicked one," or evil generally. They had not only strength, but an instrument *wherewith* and an object *whereupon* to exert it.

And first of the two subjects mentioned, " The Word of God abideth in you." The weapon with which spiritual strength combats, and wherewith it gains all its success, is " the sword of the Spirit, which is the Word of God." S. John's observation on this point accords remarkably with his Master's teaching, as well as with that of his fellow Apostles. He had himself recorded the Saviour's lamentable testimony to the state of the Jews he addressed on the occasion of His healing the impotent man at the pool of Bethesda. " Ye have not His

Word abiding in you." No wonder then that he recognised as a subject for true congratulation the case of these young men who had. And so if we would be strong to do God's will and add to our faith virtue—to our profession of obedience practical worth and excellence—we must be furnished with the same in-dwelling Word. Therefore it is that S. Paul says "Let the Word of Christ dwell in you richly." And observe how Jesus Christ and His Apostles John and Paul all dwell upon the fact that the Word to be of any service must be *indwelling*.

Now if the Word of God be truly indwelling in the soul, the case with that soul will be such as with the inmate of one's own house to oneself. The members of one family have to a greater or less extent common sympathies in feeling, or objects in view or ends in pursuit. They are like-minded. At all events they live more for one another and know one another better than can be with any stranger. You and the inmate of your dwelling are on certain terms of closer intimacy than you are with the rest of the world. You live, and work, and confer together. You aim at similar objects, and promote, or ought to do, each the end that the other is pursuing. And if God's Word is an inmate of your heart the very same will be taking place. It will be helping you as it did these young men to victory over sin, the world, and self. It will be going in and out with you as the friend or man of your own counsel to quote the Psalmist's expression, "When thou goest it shall lead thee, when thou sleepest it shall keep thee, and when thou awakest it shall talk with thee." It will be suggesting this plan or dissuading from the other, disapproving of this or exhorting to that, as is the manner of domestic conference.

And you will be treating it in the same way. You will be paying it the attention and showing it the affection you do to the inmate of your dwelling that you hold dear. You will be feeling it a matter of the warmest interest to carry out its aim, the advancement of Christ's kingdom and your sanctification. You will walk in its company, and enter into its work, and carry out its wishes and directions. Let it so dwell in you. Store up its words of wisdom and its testimony of your heavenly Lord and home. And let them share your hearts, and be admitted into your experience, and shape your life, and come forth in your character. Meditate on those words of it you read and truths you learn, and inwardly digest them. And let it dwell in you richly. Treat it as you would a guest you delighted to honour, an inmate of your abode you laid yourself out to please; yea with infinitely more deference than the most esteemed. Deny yourself for its sake. Lay aside your opinions to adopt its own, your natural pursuits and aims to give yourself wholly to the furtherance of His will and pleasure Whose representative that Word is. For it is worthy. It is the sure guide, we learn from the concluding words of the text, to victory, or the attainment of all the heart can desire, all that is implied in the word salvation.

Here, then, was the object to which these young men in the power of God's Word had directed their strength, and which in the last place the Apostle congratulated them on having so far attained. They had overcome, they had gained a victory. And victory implies spoils, and rewards, and fruits of peace, and abundance for many a coming day. And what victor is crowned with so many such as the Christian's victory over evil within, over his own corrupt nature with all its earthly feelings and tempers? He has his soul recovered from Satan for spoil, and "a good reward" for every earnest, however unworthy, effort he makes to do his Lord's work and copy the example and spirit of his Great Master. And peace above all he has with God, and with a cleansed conscience, for "the work of righteousness is peace, and the effect of righteousness quietness and assurance for ever."

Here, then, was a subject worthy indeed of an Apostle's congratulation. The exact nature of the victory these young men had gained the Spirit of God has thought it unnecessary to tell us. Enough for us to know it was a victory over evil. The Word they cherished as an indwelling guest had pointed out to them what God held evil and would have them fight against. It had armed them for the conflict. And through the might of Jesus Christ out of weakness they had been made strong; and secured a victory that, redounding to the glory of their common Lord, filled with gladness the Apostle's heart. On their behalf his grateful praises were rising to the God who had wrought all their works in them. And they in turn would be invigorated anew by his words of affectionate commendation, and go on their way doubtless rejoicing likewise to win fresh crowns to cast before their Master's feet.

I say we know not the exact nature of these young men's victory. God preserve us only to meet them in Heaven, and with what interest shall we learn it from them there! But we know this much meanwhile that "they overcame by the blood of the Lamb and by the Word of His testimony"—a blood which the Spirit of God will sprinkle on our souls too to the removal of evil within and the sanctification of our services and work for God without—and a Word which we may find no less effectual than they in gaining for us and leading us to the Crown of Life.

To him that overcometh, says Jesus to us by this same Apostle, will I grant to sit with Me in My throne even as I also overcame. May God grant us to sit down there with Him and these young men, and unite our song of triumph with theirs to Him that has loved us and washed us from our sins, and given us the victory over them, making us Kings and Priests, and in the best sense Conquerors!

THE INHERITANCE TRANSFERRED.

God shall enlarge Japheth, and he shall dwell in the tents of Shem. **Genesis** ix, 27.

The prophecy of Noah, in the three verses of which this is one, relates both to the temporal and spiritual history of the descendants of his three sons. Without entering exactly into the question of what were the national limits of the races of which the two here mentioned were the ancestors, it will be sufficient to state generally that from Shem were replenished all the lands of the east in which were the great nations of antiquity, and in his descendants, moreover, were included all the posterity of Abraham, the Jews. As Jacob and Ephraim were chosen by God for His special favour and blessing, to the exclusion of their elder brothers, so also was Shem. Both in political and religious pre-eminence the first in their case was last, and the last first.

The two brothers went out of the ark as far as man could see to a like destiny. They had always lived together, had escaped the same destruction, shared the same experience in life, and witnessed the same events. And as they went out to the same renovated world had not only the same prospects before them, but the same faith to guide them, and it would almost appear a character of equal piety. Yet Shem was in the Divine counsels to be for ages the superior. And though there was no existent likelihood of this, God foretold so it should be. Empire, civilization, and the knowledge of religion, was to be his almost exclusive inheritance, until "the times before appointed," when God had decided to enlarge Japheth. "Japheth was then enlarged, and his descendants spread themselves among the isles of the sea, and thence to newly discovered continents. Theirs was the wide stretch of land whose peoples have contributed so much of the world's history. The second great monarchy, the Medo-Persian, was at least partly of the sons of Japheth; and the Greek and Roman empires were wholly of the enlarged people. The colonies of the world have been chiefly founded and peopled by Japheth and his European sons. "The isles of the Gentiles" were his, such as the British Isles, Australia, New Zealand, Borneo, and many more. India, once partly belonging to Shem, is now wholly occupied by Japheth. The power of Europe now holds Palestine, formerly the possession of Shem, and Jerusalem is trodden down of the Gentiles. America has been discovered and peopled by Japheth. Such is the evidence still accumulating, and even in this our own day sustaining the truth of Noah's prophecy. Japheth is enlarged in population, in progress, in learning, in art and science, in commerce, in arms, in wealth, in conquest, in colonies, in religion, in Bible distribution, in moral worth. In all and each of these particulars the prophecy is made good. And in the tents of Shem doth Japheth dwell, not only by the present occupation of some of the countries of Shem, but chiefly by the spreading of the curtains of that tent in which dwelleth the Lord God of Shem, so as to cover the lands of Europe and their dependencies with the religion of Jesus Christ." (*Editor of Church Standard, August* 18, 1865.)

The nationalities of Europe and America, as they prevailed over the ancient monarchies of the East have verified the prediction. And the northern hordes of Europe and Asia in the earlier centuries, and the southern nations of Europe in later and our own times, have gone forth to enlarge their own heritage, and take possession of and colonize those of Shem. And Japheth in his inheritance of Christianity has come forth from sitting in the darkness of heathenism and an almost unknown history to walk in the light of the Lord, and arise and shine in political and religious exaltation as the great power of the world.

Into Shem's former exclusive inheritance of civilization and religious knowledge Japheth has entered; and will probably be the leader till the end of the world of all human progress, and the possessor of a world-wide influence. Well may we exclaim with the Apostle—as we see how all history, ancient and modern, combines to elucidate this inexhaustible prophecy—" O the depth of the riches both of the wisdom and knowledge of God." Truly says He " I am God, and there is none like Me declaring the end from the beginning, and the things that are not yet done, saying My counsel shall stand, and I will do all My pleasure."

Passing from the prophetic fulfilment of the passage, we ask whether in these words of the text may not be sought a meaning in which we may be more directly concerned. Now " No Scripture is of any private interpretation." We may always press general truths into particular cases ; and fill up with detailed and more individual application the outline presented to us. And prophecy has often a province of *spiritual truth* as well as of *historical fact.* There is certainly such here.

Japheth, in his first unenlightened, and then afterwards highly favoured religious condition, his first straitened and then enlarged territory, is illustrative of many aspects of each one's Christian experience. What God did for him as to his national life, so does He to all to whom He brings " in demonstration of the Spirit and of power" the knowledge of His salvation, in regard to their spiritual life. Not alone does Japheth stand as " satisfied with favour and full with the blessing of the Lord," but rather as the type of the way in which God would deal with us all. That the Gentiles should be fellow-heirs and partakers of the promises of the Gospel ; that past disqualification, sin, ignorance, and darkness, if renounced, was to be no bar in God's rich mercy to the sharing of Christ's salvation—was the great New Testament announcement, and is the same yesterday, to-day, and for ever.

Is there then a Japheth who is conscious of neither part nor lot with God's people, who has the understanding darkened, has been hitherto alienated from the life of God, and has no hope in the world; but who is even now looking with a wistful eye on Shem's goodly inheritance? Is there one who has been labouring on hitherto a hopeless, godless, uncheered life, but is even now beginning to lift up his eyes like Balaam, attracted by the prospect of the Christian's possession, and is mentally exclaiming "How goodly are thy tents, O Jacob, and thy tabernacles, O Israel?" Is there one who has not yet found peace with God through a consciously needed and believingly welcomed Saviour, who has not yet laid down before the Crucified the burden of an accusing conscience, but who is at least indulging the reflection of the Psalmist over a happiness he fain *would* share, "Blessed is the man whose iniquity is forgiven and whose sin is covered?" Is there "one who is walking in darkness and sees no light," but is even now, like the Egyptians in their three days' plague, straining his gaze across the separating gloom to that favoured Goshen where he knows so well that "the children of Israel have light in their tents?" Is there one who longs to know "the secret of the Lord which is with them that fear Him," the secret of their peace and love; to share the Divine communion which they enjoy to whom God manifests Himself as He does not to the world; who sees others walking with God, and wishes to join their company, and is stirring himself up to lay hold on God with the reflection of Solomon, "Happy is the people that are in such a case, yea blessed are the people who have the Lord for their God?" To such as these the application of the text is very encouraging.

Lift up your eyes like Abraham and take in as much as you can of the spiritual territory that stretches out before you, for to you will God give it without reserve. The Saviour's purchased possession, the Spirit's manifold gifts, the gates of heaven's treasures, are all open and free. And unto and upon all them that believe, as the Apostle testifies, shall be all the benefits secured by the Redeemer. Unfit are you for such gifts? Unworthy of such advantages as the friendship of God, the forgivenness of sin, the peace that passes understanding, the hope laid up in heaven, the inheritance incorruptible undefiled that Shem exults in as covenanted and sealed to him? Unqualified we all truly are! So was Japheth to share the blessing of God fearing Shem. I need not tell the state of Japheth, the unconverted heathen world, when the Gospel summoned him to take possession of that "inheritance with the saints in light," of which he was now to become a fellow heir with the faithful in Israel. You know what the Roman converts were to whom S. Paul wrote his Epistle, and with what a catalogue of the features of their former state, his first chapter concludes. You know what the Corinthians were, as recorded in 1. Cor. vi, and how after enumerating the sins of the city, he concludes, "Such were some of you: but ye are washed, justified, and sanctified." You know what the Ephesians were "Ye were once darkness, but now are ye light in the Lord." And again "You hath he quickened who were once dead in trespasses and sins." And the success which it is recorded in the sequel of the Psalm attended the prayer—" Hear me when I call O God of my righteousness, Thou hast enlarged me when I was in distress "—shall be that of all who seek like spiritual deliverance.

From the joy and peace in believing, the comfort of the Holy Ghost, the clear vision of the candle of the Lord, which is the lot of Shem, destitute Japheth is not excluded. " The promise is to all that are far off even to as many as the Lord shall call" within reach of His glad tidings. Only let no one be content to put forth, like Balaam, a momentary aspiration to be remembered with the favour that God bears unto His people, and to be permitted to rejoice in their inheritance. For " the soul of the sluggard desireth and hath nothing." The husbandman (says the Apostle) must first *labour* to be partaker of the fruits." But " follow on to know the Lord." Lay siege with the holy violence of earnest resolution to the kingdom of heaven. And though like Japheth, ignorant, or in the centre of surrounding darkness and sin, though like Japheth, destitute of the " true riches," the " true light," the hope for the future that shall never be confounded—the God of Japheth is ready to be yours, and to " bless you with all spiritual blessings in Christ Jesus."

But Japheth, in his straitened and afterwards enlarged lot, is a figure of another state of spiritual experience. In all his dealings with us we remark how God blesses us progressively, how He delights to add to what He has first given, that we may have more abundantly.

Thus not only is " the *path* " but the *experience* " of the just, like the shining light that shineth more and more unto the perfect day." As there is a developemnt in natural, so also is there in spiritual life. " The Lord shall increase you more and more," says the Psalmist. " God that giveth increase," says S. Paul. And it is a most gracious feature of His Divine character, that He delights to do so. Observe this in the parable of the ten pounds in the 19th of S. Luke. With what pleasure, when there was a pound to be given, did the nobleman who represents Him fix on the one who had already been so largely gifted by His bounty! " Take the pound and give it to him that hath ten. And when the servants hesitated with astonishment, and exclaimed " Lord he hath ten " already. Never mind, says He, he shall have another still. For I say unto you to him that hath shall yet be given, and he shall have more abundantly.

God gives increase in all the gladness of spiritual experience, furtherance of faith and joy, advancement in holiness, ever fresh views of His power, and grace, and truth, constantly additional encouragement and promotion too in His service, and continual growth towards perfection.

Let me from the text appeal personally to any believer, who may need it, and show him the encouragement it affords. Hast thou then, fellow Christian, like the disciples but a little faith ? Dost thou mourn over much proneness to evil ? Dost thou find thyself weak and ready to halt on thy onward path ? Dost thou see yonder Christian, " like the young hart on the mountains of Bether," bounding onward to Zion with enlarged steps ? Dost thou see thy brother with fervent love and mighty zeal shining like a star in the ranks of the redeemed, far up to thy fancy with Christ on the holy mount of transfiguration, transformed from the world and very like in many respects to Christ? And dost thou almost envy him and long to walk like him on the hill of God? Dost thou see Shem thy brother abiding under the very shadow of the Almighty; his faith clear, his mind calm, his hope buoyant, his vision purified and strengthened, so that he seems to walk in the light of an opened heaven? He has no doubts like thine thou dost imagine, and perhaps truly he has not thy misgivings. The love that God has poured into his heart has " cast out fear." And like the Kenite "strong is his dwelling place and he putteth his nest in a rock." And dost thou suppose that no such lot can ever be thine? " Is He the God of the Jews only, and not also of the Gentiles?" asks the Apostle: of Shem and not of Japheth too? " Is the Spirit of the Lord straitened?" the prophet Micah inquires. Has thy Father, as Esau asked so well of Isaac, only one blessing? or is it too hard for Him to raise thee to a like position?

Be of good cheer, fellow Christian, thou mayest yet dwell in the tents of Shem. Wait on the Lord and seek His way, and He shall promote thee to inherit the land. The time may come that " when thou goest thy steps shall not be straitened, and when thou runnest thou shalt not stumble." Hear the Lord's promise to His Church in Philadelphia, " Behold I have set before thee an open door, and no man can shut it; for thou hast a little strength, and hast kept My word, and hast not denied my name." Only see to it that you show all diligence towards the attainment of the other's full assurance of hope, that you " be not slothful but a follower of them who through faith and patience inherit the promises."

Once more we may place these words in another light, and read them as referring to the promise of eternal inheritance to which the multitude of the redeemed who have entered into rest have already attained; while Shem may stand for the Church triumphant seated with its Lord in heavenly places, Japheth is then the correlative of the Church militant " not yet come to the rest and to the inheritance."

Ah! well we know how, as you journey often painfully and discouraged along your heavenward way, this vision will rise before your longing soul, and fill it with a sometimes almost despairing emulation of the happier lot of the sainted dead. The flowing robes of spotless white, the waving palms of the victorious faithful, in which the royal priesthood of heaven stand before the Father's throne and sit at the supper of the Lamb—when the devout mind fixes on these grand revelations of the world to come,

Oh then your spirit faints
To reach the land you love!
The bright inheritance of saints,
Jerusalem above!

When for instance, through the glowing descriptions of S. John the Divine, it has grasped something of what God has prepared for them that love Him, it needs such a promise as this to stay the otherwise impatient expectancy of the kindling sou

> For how can I with such a hope
> Of glory and of home,
> With such a joy before my eyes,
> But wish the time were come :
> Of years the jubilee, of days
> The Sabbath and the sum!

BONAR.

It has been well said—"Compassed about as we all are with infirmity, called upon to do many things for which we are naturally uninclined, and bearing about within ourselves a principle of corruption which continually strives to regain the ascendancy, and which is not to be kept down but by prayer without ceasing, and watchfulness without fainting—indeed it were hard to understand how any believer can often be other than weary and heavy laden, and required to take heed against that impatience over the burthens of life which shall show itself in undue eagerness for the repose of eternity. It is not that he would give up the service of God, but that he may be able to serve God without weariness ; not that he would rest from holy employment, but that he would have employment entail no necessity for rest ; not that he would be released from the struggles of corruption, but that he would have no corruption to struggle with ; not that he would make peace with spiritual enemies, but that he would be encompassed by none but spiritual friends."

And not in such a moment either melancholy or unnatural appears to the citizen of heaven the words of the preacher, "Wherefore I praised the dead that are already dead."   Like S. Paul he is "in a strait betwixt two, having a desire to depart, which is far better." Yet to continue in the flesh, from the consideration that it is the field of discipline, is the more honourable alternative.   Then to check his too fervent eagerness, to strike the balance for the hesitating disciple, comes in the timely assurance of a like inheritance reserved in heaven, and certain to be revealed at the swiftly closing hour of a godly Christian life.

And with the promise of the text, that pledges a dwelling place to those now in glory, the believer can afford like Daniel to stand contentedly in his lot for the few and evil days of the present, like Job to say "All the days of my appointed time will I wait until my change come."

In the tents of Kedar rather than those of Shem is now perhaps your dwelling place.   And you dwell with sinners and vex your soul with their unlawful deeds.   But what are these the nations of the saved, and whence came they but out of the same condition?   They shared your present discipline and passed through your experience.   And you too, who are saying now as they once did, "Woe is me that I dwell with Mesheck"—may yet be "numbered with the saints in glory everlasting."

Time, however, would fail to recount the varied ways in which this general promise is verified in the history of the soul. In deliverance from trouble; in adding constantly to the graces and fruits of the Spirit in which He causes His people to be ever and anew abounding to His honour and praise; in building them up on their most holy faith; and in lengthening the cords and trengthening the stakes of their spiritual life—does God enlarge His Japheth. And as they walk in the foot-prints of those that have passed before them to the heavenly Canaan, as they enter into the joyful experience of all their consolations and their hopes, their victories and their joys—does God make them to dwell even here in the tents of Shem, "to rejoice in the gladness of His nation, and to glory with His inheritance."

But soon the destinies of Shem and Japheth will be unalterably assigned, and the great gulf fixed which shall form an eternal separation between the children of each   Now, while yet you may happily transfer your portion, does Christ offer Himself as your Guide and his Spirit to help you to escape from the lot of Japheth. He will transplace you "by the renewing of your mind" from the ground of Japheth, on which you are by nature, to the possession of His favoured people Shem. He will "turn you from darkness to light, and from the power of Satan unto God; that you may receive forgiveness of sins, and inheritance among them that are sanctified by faith in Him."

THE LOVE OF CHRIST TO HIS CHURCH.

Thou that dwellest in the gardens, the companions hearken to thy voice : cause me
to hear it.   *Canticles* viii. 13.

It is very certain that underlying this inspired writing is a great
mystery, and that it speaks concerning Christ and the Church.   Under
the figure of Solomon—Divinely endowed with kingly gifts and graces—
and his Bride—in her attachment to one so worthy of admiration, and
capable of awakening it as he—we have a shadow of heavenly things.
The Spirit of God has here been pleased to set forth in detailed allegory
the love of the Heavenly Bridegroom, and the soul He espouses to Himself in the Gospel covenant.   The one great character in the book, in
the brightness of his glory and the tenderness of his love, and the other
in her reciprocated devotion, aptly symbolize the Saviour by Whose
grace and to Whose love His elect are one, and the adoring devotedness
of His redeemed.

The whole construction of the book however ; the manners and
customs to which it alludes ; the modes of thought and imagery employed—so peculiarly belong to Eastern life, and pre-suppose such an
intimate acquaintance with it, that by far the greater number of serious
readers even it will ever be perused, if it is perused at all, without much
profit.   And it will perhaps be to a certain extent a sealed book till,
to adopt the figure with which it principally deals, though not it alone
in Holy Scripture, " the marriage of the Lamb is come," and the Church
in the Heavenly state enters on the full enjoyment of Her Lord's love
and communion.

Nevertheless there is in the book of Canticles a repository of instruction, a well spring of devotional thought, and subjects for address
on experimental religion, which it becomes a minister well to make use
of. And many a scribe, properly instructed by education and by diligent
study in the mysteries of the kingdom of heaven has found a store
here from which he has been able to bring forth things both new and
old to the benefit of the serious and prayerfully-disposed, and the
edification of the Church.   In no spirit of presumption, and with no
desire to meddle with things too high for me, but with humble self-
distrusting dependence on the enlightening aid of the Spirit who indited
this Song of Songs—would I too ponder it, and invite you to do the
same.   Only let us sincerely offer the inspired prayer to Him—" Open
Thou mine eyes that I may behold wondrous things out of Thy Law "—
and we may look for instruction from it with confidence.   For thus it
is written " I am the Lord Thy God which teacheth thee to profit."

And again "The manifestation of the Spirit is given to every man to profit withal."

In the text we have firstly, the Speaker's invocation. Secondly, the Speaker's observation of the person addressed, and whose position is described as in the gardens; and what is implied by it—"the companions hearken to thy voice"—Thirdly, we have the Speaker's request "Cause me to hear it."

The Speaker in this verse you must understand and bear in mind is the Bridegroom. There are some considerations that, after even an attentive study of the words as we have them in our English version, might lead us to think they were spoken rather by the Bride. And we might then be very wide of the mark if we went on to interpret the passage for ourselves.

And here indeed we have one striking difficulty which would make the ordinary reader's study of the book sometimes vain. For there is a frequent transition of the two principal speakers in the book. And the English version, from the idiom of the language, is incapable of setting forth to us, as the Hebrew does very distinctly, when such transition takes place, and which is therefore the Speaker the Bridegroom or the Bride. We are therefore left by our translation in doubt, in many passages of the Song, whether we have the feelings of Christ expressed or His people's. But a reference to the original Hebrew decides the point for us. It marks out clearly here who it is that speaks, and who are the companions mentioned.

Both the Bridegroom and the Bride in this book make frequent mention of the gardens of the former. He is represented as going into his gardens to eat his pleasant fruits, to gather myrrh and spices, to partake of the honey comb and fruit of the vine. He repairs there as the bride also at his permission and request, to gather lilies, to see the fruits of the valleys, the flourishing vines, the budding pomegranates, and to be refreshed with the spices that grew there. Solomon had such we know. He says "I planted me vineyards I made me gardens and orchards; and I planted trees in them of all kinds of fruits." And that he was much among these we know also. For says the sacred historian, of his study in the subject, " He spake of trees from the cedar that is in Lebanon, even unto the hyssop that springeth out of the wall." And naturally would his bride be much there also to share his company, to listen to his discourse, and profit by his knowledge on that very subject, as on others. With this brief explanation of the circumstances in which this figure is introduced, I pass to point out the mystical meaning. In doing so I shall not dwell on the correspondence, to the letter, of this to what occurred in our Lord's life. Perhaps it was a new coincidence though not one without a lesson, were I to pause to show it, that that well known Gethsemane to which our Lord "ofttimes resorted with his disciples," and there gave them to see and to know the love wherewith He loved them, was a garden also. But I would rather call your attention to the fact that the garden and the vineyard are the ever chosen emblems of Scripture, of the choice and favoured lot in which the Lord has caused his Church to dwell. As Solomon had his, so are there trees of the Lord's planting wherewith He may be glorified. The figure is consecrated in the New Testament by our Lord's frequent adoption of it in His parables, and by the Spirit in many passages in the Epistles, and especially by His Revelation of the Paradise of God.

There is a secret place of the Most High, where Christ manifests Himself to His people, as He does not to the world, where the Divine Husbandman plants and nourishes and tends His own, where they blossom into grace, and bear fruit unto holiness. Each redeemed soul of Christ knows well that garden, into which it has been transplanted from the world; where it walks and converses with Him, and is filled out of His fulness and ofttimes transported with the sight and the participation of His glory, and His love, and His grace. Jacob was admitted to it on the plain of Beersheba, when the heavens were opened to him, and the Angels of God ascended and descended before him, and he said " This is none other than the house of God. This is the gate of heaven." The Psalmist had been there when he said " O that I might see Thy power and glory, so as I have seen it in the sanctuary." Daniel, and his three friends, in the den of lions, and the fiery furnace, S. Paul in his wrecked ship on the tempestuous Adriatic, when the Angel of the Lord stood by them each—were witnesses to the words of David " Thou shalt hide them in the secret of Thy presence from the pride of man. In the time of trouble He shall hide them in His pavilion." The Apostles on Mount Hermon, S. Stephen kneeling before his murderers' stones, and S. Paul rapt in the third heavens—all saw, like Balaam in his vision, that God makes His " Israel to dwell as in gardens by the river side, among lign, aloes, and cedars, which the Lord hath planted."

Is there not too a resemblance between the garden here, and that of which it is a figure ? Did the bride of Solomon dwell among his gardens, amid all that was pleasant to the eye, and good for food, and eat of his fruits, the honey-comb, wine, and milk, and gather the lilies, and breathe the odorous spices ? And are there not for the chosen ones of Christ promises and consolations in the Gospel, revealed under the same figure of wine and milk ? Are there not prospects for the believer's soul, meditations for his hopes, objects for his affections, and blessings for the satisfying of his desires, sweeter than honey and the honey comb ? Is not the " name " of Jesus " as ointment poured forth ? " and is not his soul refreshed, as with the fragrant spices, by the virtue that exhales from His meritorious sacrifice ? Does he not partake of the benefits of His most precious death and passion to the strengthening and refreshing of his soul ? And may he not expatiate at large through all the walks of Scripture revelation ; through its beds of perfume, its trees bearing all manner of fruits, good for the soul's food and to be desired to make it wise, with leaves too for healing efficacy ? And all the while may he not walk in fellowship with Christ as His Lord and Friend ?

And mark here further in the text how he speaks of it as her dwelling-place not his, as though he thought more of it as hers than his, as though he had laid it out and dedicated it for her ! So does Christ of

Heaven. All Mine is thine says He to His Church. " Father I will that where I am, there they may be also." "All is yours, for ye are Christ's " says the Apostle. He had all Heaven to Himself once, but rested not till He could bring His Church there to share it. He left Heaven as though He could not enjoy it fully till He could chose and redeem a Church as His Bride to be a joint-heir with Him.

Think of this thou elect of God, thou chosen of Christ, whose heart the Holy Spirit has drawn to Him and whose love He has won. Thou dwellest "in the gardens," thou art reminded here. Thou art not in the world's wilderness where thorns and thistles only grow ; but in Christ's garden, in ground out of which He has made to grow all spiritual blessings wherewith to satisfy thy every need. Dost thou need pardon ? Hast thou slighted the dear Redeemer that has bought thee with His own most precious blood, and been unmindful of Him, as the bride in this Song so often and so faithlessly was? Hast thou like her forgotten Him in the hurry of business, or like her parted from His side in the hour of temptation, or like her slumbered unwatchfully when He asked thy presence and thy work ? It was in the garden that Peter and James and John slumbered like thee, and on their repentance were forgiven. He will restore your soul likewise, if you confess your sinfulness, and seek Him again with the earnestness that the Bride does here.

Art thou restless and thy soul vexed with a multitude of cares and fears ? Be careful for nothing. For He that has brought you to His garden will make you to lie down in green pastures, and will lead you beside the still waters : Art thou distressed with one of the rough blasts of adversity ? Weather-beaten with some of the storms of life ? There are trees around thee, beneath whose sheltering branches may be found an hiding place from the wind, and a covert from the tempest. There when the tide of passion rages and swells high among those that are without, and some affliction rushing forth in its might sweeps through others' hearts and leaves them desolate, "My people," He promises, "shall dwell in a peaceable habitation and in quiet resting places." The prophets Isaiah and Jeremiah both employ this figure in assuring God's people how He will guide continually, and satisfy in its every spiritual want, the soul He has brought into the watered garden of His Church. He has brought each member of His Church into that garden, and placed each under the vine and fig tree of Gospel privilege in the midst of abundance and grace, with the free permission " Whosoever will let him take freely."

We pass on to notice in the second place what the Bridegroom observes in the text of her who was so favourably and pleasantly situated. " The companions hearken to thy voice." These companions, we learn by referring to the Hebrew text, were not those virgins the companions of the bride that followed and bore her company on such occasions that David tells of in the 44th Psalm, and our Lord in the parable of the ten virgins. They were "the friends of the bridegroom," such as those whom S. John the Baptist mentioned. In this case they were Solomon's attendants and servants. They, he remarked, could in his absence converse and walk with and listen to her.   And this he intimates, in the words that follow, he would desire himself to do.   This he wished and longed for.   So does Christ from Heaven His dwelling place express His desire for the time appointed at His second coming, to be re-united to His people, and to walk and converse with them again as in the days of His life. What ineffable love of the Heavenly Bridegroom that He should regret the separation from His Church on earth now that He has passed within the veil as it does!   They are parted now; but not more joyfully will His people hail than He the hour appointed when He shall come again and receive them to Himself, and walk with them as in the days of old. The words of the text are an aspiration on the part of the Church's loving and faithful Head.   And no less grateful and satisfying to Him than to us, who wait for His appearing, is the blessed revelation, "Behold the tabernacle of God shall be with men, and He will dwell with them, and they shall be His people.   And he that upon the throne said "Write, for these words are true and faithful."

If two friends are sundered, the one that takes the journey feels the separation as well as the one that is left behind.   And He who took our nature upon Him that He might know the better and love the more the children of men, in whom were ever His delight, as we read in the Book of Proverbs, felt as man and suffered as man.   He feels and suffers still as we should do during a painful separation.   "Still He loves the earth He leaves."   Still He longs, and waits, and works for the hastening of the hour when face to face He shall meet again His redeemed in that visible communion in which—no less than theirs— will be His fulness of joy for evermore.   We are reminded of David, who told in his plaintive song of exile how the very sparrow had found an house, and the swallow a nest, near the altar from which he was debarred access, and could not for many a long day hope to come, as though he almost envied them their near approach to his God.   So here Christ Jesus speaks after the manner of men, as though he could almost, if I may speak it with sufficient reverence—and such is really the thought suggested and conveyed in the text—envy those fellow citizens of His people here, those of the household of God below, their enjoyment of the outward and visible communion of His saints on earth.

"Truly we have fellowship with the Father and with His Son Jesus Christ," and He with us: but not outwardly and visibly as we have with one another.   And it is this direct and present personal association that He here intimates He would were His.   Think of this, thou elect of God, thou chosen of Christ, whose heart the Holy Ghost has drawn to Him, and whose love He has won!   "The companions hearken to thy voice."   You have met these companions of His in the great congregation.   You have prayed for them, and they for you. You have poured out your supplication here before God, and they have mingled theirs with yours.   You have lifted your voice in praise, and they have joined with yours their song.   In your mutual responses in Divine service you have provoked one another to love and to good

works. And as you looked on them, and prayed with them, and pleaded
for them, your faith in God and Christ has been confirmed, your hope
in things to come re-animated, and your love towards God and
them enkindled afresh.

In private as well as in public you have met a fellow Christian,
one of those companions of Christ whom He mentions here. You spoke
one to another of things concerning salvation. You talked of your one
Lord and one faith. You spoke of things touching your King. His
high praises were in your mouth. You told of His glory and honour.
You conversed of His love and His grace. And His companions
hearkened gladly to your voice. And you were drawn nearer in the
bonds of the Gospel, as brothers and joint heirs with Christ.

If the friend of the Bridegroom rejoice thus to hear your voice, as
you to hear his, how much more the Bridegroom Himself! Were it
not that the time appointed in the wisdom of God as expedient for His
manifestation to the Church is not yet come, with what delight would
Christ reveal Himself to you even now; and seek you out with manifold more the eagerness and the pleasure that you do the company of
your fellow Christians or they yours! More grateful to Him is the
sound of your voice than can be that of theirs to you. The heart of
Christ's companion, when he recognised in you a fellow believer was
glad. But He noted it with a far fuller and deeper joy.

And this brings me to conclude with a few words only on the third
division of the text, the request of the Speaker, "The companions
hearken to thy voice; cause me to hear it." You speak often
with your fellow Christians. And He wishes you to do so. The
prophet Malachi says "They that feared the Lord spake often one to
another; and the Lord hearkened and heard it; and a book of remembrance was written before Him." But while you do well thus to speak,
see that you speak often to Him. You meet *them* in the Church's
assemblies and ordinances; neglect not above all to look for *Him* there.
You speak to them of your hopes and join them with pleasure in your
worship; remember that He desires ever to be more prominent than
all: and therefore addresses you each in the text, and charges you to
seek and address yourself to Him. For the Lord our God is a jealous
God. He bids you look through form, and Sacrament, and Minister,
and beyond each fellow-worshipper. "Thou shalt have none other Gods
before Me."

"Let Me hear thy voice," He says again in this same book, "for it
is sweet." And again, "Thy speech is comely, and thy lips drop as the
honeycomb." Ah! sweet to that loving Lord is the breath of prayer!
precious is the outpouring of the heart's abundance, whether it be in
confession, supplication, or thanksgiving! He invites your fullest
confidence. And in these words of matchless favour deigns in His
marvellous condescension to illustrate His own saying, "Ye have not
chosen Me, but I have chosen you." So truly does S. John say "Not
that we loved God, but that He loved us.

I pray Him grant you, to your soul's certain salvation, to respond
with David to this so tender and gracious appeal, "Let me hear thy

voice," " My voice shalt Thou hear, O Lord ; early will I direct my prayer unto Thee and will look up."

FELLOWSHIP WITH GOD.

Walk with thy God.—*Micah* vi. 8.

These words were spoken, it appears, by Balaam to Balak, at that period of Israel's history recorded in the 22nd and following chapters of Numbers. Balak, the King of Moab, was very anxious to conciliate the favour of the God of Israel, with a view to move Him against His people, of whom he was jealous and apprehensive.

In the ignorance of his heathenism, he not only thought that the God of Israel was altogether such a one as himself, to be moved to causeless and unjust anger against His unoffending people, but he thought to compass this, in itself unlikely end, by propitiating Him and His Prophet with costly sacrifices and gifts. In the verses from which the text is taken Balaam plainly undeceives him. He tells him that the God whose prophet he was, was not at all such a one as he supposed: that Balak could never gain His favour, and need not hope to do so by mere acts of outward homage or the offering of the costliest sacrifices; that to do justice and judgment was more acceptable than any gifts; that God required of him honourable and merciful dealing towards His people, instead of the wrong and injury he contemplated; and an habitual walking with, instead of contrary to Him. It is this last point in the direction that I now choose. In the figure in which in the text these requirements are summed up, the religious life God would have us aim at is represented as a walking with and companionship with Himself. And I desire now, on the principles and with the imagery which this simple figure suggests, to set before you the life of faith and holiness whereunto as professing Christians you are called.

The whole of Scripture deals with this figure. Beginning from the garden of Eden, where our first parents were wont to walk with God, we trace it ever onwards. Enoch, we are told, the oldest of the prophets, walked with God for a period of three hundred years. Noah, the first great preacher of righteousness, did the same, setting forth the Divine glory in the eyes of those before the flood by constantly showing his preference for and delight in God's converse and companionship. To Abraham, when he was ninety years old and nine, there came a vision and a voice which said " I am the Almighty God; walk before me and be thou perfect." Of Daniel and Hezekiah the same expression is employed. And of Levi the prophet Malachi says, " He walked with me in peace and equity."

And the direction so to walk is repeated continually. In the New Testament the charge occurs in too many passages to quote particularly. And finally the sacred volume closes with the vision of all the redeemed walking with their Lord in the white robes of sanctification in heavenly places, even as it opened with the like vision of God walking with their first parents in their days of innocence in Eden.

To this companionship we are invited in the text as to something in which is involved all the Divine requirements: a companionship which places by our side all Divine strength and grace to avail ourselves of according to our need; and which is sufficient therefore, if only the privilege could be pressed by us in its perfection, to ensure all virtuous and godly living. " What doth the Lord require of thee but to walk with thy God." I omit the word " humbly" only because it introduces another thought on which I do not wish now to dwell, being anxious to direct your attention at present to the one simple thought of walking with God.

We cannot at the outset but be struck with astonishment both at the condescension and the good-will manifested toward man by this invitation on the part of God. Solomon, in his prayer at the feast of the dedication of his temple, expresses surprise that God should even deign to make His dwelling-place in the very same world which His sinful creatures inhabit! " But will God in very deed dwell with man on the earth?" Blessed be God for His glorious Gospel of reconciliation to our race, He will do even more. He will not only dwell among men as a monarch in stately seclusion, but walk with them as a friend in the freedom of familiar converse.

Now the prophet Amos asks, " Can two walk together except they be agreed?" The very fact of two persons walking together by preference implies a certain degree of partiality. No man, if he can help it, walks with another whom he dislikes. Consequently this very proposal on the part of God bears on the face of it the token of His favour and good-will towards those to whom it is made, whether toward the ignorant, violent, and wicked heathen king to whom it was first addressed, or towards ourselves to whom it is equally made. S. Paul tells us that as early as the days of the patriarchs God preached His Gospel, that is, made known His offers of mercy and His desire of reconciliation with the world. And in such a class of passages as this we may well see that it was so, and that the very fulness of the blessings of the Gospel of Christ, and the revelation of all the gifts and graces God was willing to communicate, is conveyed in such a proposal.

That companionship is truly a necessity of our nature we all must own. That " it is not in man to direct his steps " by himself to his own comfort or satisfaction is a consciousness innate in us all. Accordingly we turn every one our own way to supply that necessity, and think of seeking the object of our need among our fellow creatures, whom we see manifesting it in the same way But the very principle which makes us in so doing select for our companionship, that person or those persons whom we deem to excel in that particular in which we are attracted— might serve to show us that the object of our desire must be most perfectly realized in the worthiest and the best.

In the companionship of One who has the most perfect command of the means of helping, and gladdening, and blessing us we might certainly reckon on deriving the most satisfaction. And who should this be but He from whom cometh every good and perfect gift, to whom we are indebted for every enjoyment we possess, of whom and from whom and to whom are all things, all of plenty, peace, and joy, and comfort that cheers our pathway here—" even God blessed for ever!" And He it is that invites us to communicate and walk with Him all the days of our life: and that more literally than any words can explain. Without reserve and without qualification of meaning, I tell you that the proposal of your Creator, Redeemer, and Sanctifier, is to take His place by your side as a living personal Being, to stand by you evermore closer than any partner in life, and to converse with you more fully and freely than the most intimate friend.

And not at set times, as you may repair to the society of your fellow creature, but uninterruptedly. He will stand by you when you sit in the house, and when you walk by the way, and when you lie down, and when you rise up. When thou goest He shall lead thee, when thou sleepest He shall keep thee, and when thou awakest He shall talk with thee.

Simple indeed is this truth: but when impressed by "the demonstration of the Spirit and of power," its effect thereon is the greatest marvel that human life can show. It was because through the teaching of the Spirit they were persuaded, and availed themselves, of this simple promise of Divine communion that all those worthies of the world, catalogued in the eleventh chapter of Hebrews, achieved their heroic triumphs and gained their undying renown. And the same transforming and elevating power does the belief of this truth work now in the servants of God. When the Christian goes forth in the remembrance and recognition of the fact that he has a God to walk with—he goes forth like Saul from Samuel's presence, like S. Peter and S. John in their Pentecostal boldness, another man. When he walks forth with God upon the battle field of life, and takes God out with him, " remembering that God is his Rock, and the High God his Redeemer," how does he travel in the greatness of a superhuman strength! He is like Job's war-horse, "He mocketh at fear, and is not affrighted: he rejoiceth in his strength, and goeth on to meet the armed men." As, like Gideon, he goes in this his might, he can take up the Psalmist's exulting songs, " The Lord is my rock, and my fortress, and my deliverer; my God my strength in whom I will trust; my buckler, and the horn of my salvation, and my high tower." "The Lord is my light and my salvation; whom shall I fear? The Lord is the strength of my life; of whom shall I be afraid?" In such moments as these—strange as unbelievers may think it—we speak but the words of truth and soberness, he knows what it is to say with the Psalmist, " By the help of my God I shall leap over a wall;" "I will fear no evil for Thou art with me;" with the Prophet "I shall run and not be weary, I shall walk and not faint;" and with the Apostle "I can do all things through Christ that strengtheneth me."

And what a safeguard against those evil communications that corrupt good manners and destroy right principles is this companionship! Strange it is, and humiliating to confess, and yet it is too true that notwithstanding he has deliberately renounced, and does really condemn and hate, the ungodly world and its ways, yet will even the heart of the spiritually-minded betray him. And again and again does he convict himself of not merely falling into but inclining after vanity, and being ready—as the caution of the Scriptures of truth which depict the heart's impulses so accurately teach us—even to "envy sinners."

And what in the view of such a temptation *can be*—yea what I would appeal to the experience of those who are living in communion with God *has been*—so efficient a preservative as the recollection of Him with whom you are walking? When can the godly say so resolutely, and with such abhorrence of their ways and pursuits, "Away from me, ye ungodly," as when he is walking in the light of God's countenance and the joy of His fellowship? At other times when he ceases to walk consciously, and with the set purpose of his heart with God—when he forgets and neglects to seek and maintain His companionship—he is like Samson with his shorn locks among the Philistines. A man of like passions with others, he soon exhibits the same failings and falls into the same sins. But when he goes forth with his Divine companion, there is a hedge about him to secure him from evil. Surely in vain the net will then be spread, and the charmer however wisely charm.

You cannot—if you are walking with another who is taking the lead—turn aside from the way in which he has intimated his intention to go, and you your readiness to follow, as you might do if you were alone. And with God's eye on him, and His voice speaking to him, and His arm holding him, and His finger directing him, the man that is walking with God is not for the time at leisure to listen to other beguiling voices, to follow other by-paths, or to commune with other and alien spirits. He is kept in the strait and narrow path as it were in spite of his own inclination to turn from it. For as the Prophet Jeremiah says, Will the thirsty traveller, as he journeys by Lebanon, leave its snow untasted, or the cold flowing waters from some rock in the field, and neglect to refresh himself; preferring the heat and weariness of the sandy march ? Or as our Lord says, Will the man who is drinking old wine suddenly put from him the better beverage to desire and demand the new ? Thus the disciples of John the Baptist, as soon as they were introduced by him to Christ, and saw His more excellent glory, left even their honoured master to follow Jesus.

Hardly need more be said to commend to you this gracious offer of companionship, the benefit of which must be so transparently manifest, to induce you to respond to this condescending invitation in the words of grateful consent, " Turn Thou us, O good Lord ; and so shall we be turned." "Draw us, and we will run after Thee." O send out Thy Spirit to lead us to Thee, that we may be guided with Thy counsel, and have the fruition of Thy glorious fellowship !

And yet there is one word in the text which seems to make its proposal more binding on us still, to draw us as " with the cords of a man with the bands of love" by an appeal to the power of which we can hardly be insensible. It is the word *thy*—" thy God." For from whom comes this proposal of blessed and most desirable fellowship ? Who is it that so tenderly and lovingly bespeaks our confidence and solicits our converse ? Who is it that thus courts the friendship of sinners like ourselves so immeasurably unworthy of His notice ? Ah! it is no stranger this, that bids us walk with Him, whose terrors we may fear with a troubled mind ; whose intentions towards us we may mistrust ; or whose sympathy with us we may doubt. Though He comes in the majesty of the Lord of all power and might, yet " shall not His excellence make you afraid nor His dread fall upon you." For, says the text to each of you, He is thy God. He is One with whom you are already by Creation, Redemption, and the Christian covenant of Baptism, in the nearest relationship. He is One who has shown Himself devoted to your welfare by the most convincing proofs, by the costliest self-sacrifice, for " He spared not His own Son, but freely gave Him up for us all." He is *thy* God, " the God in whose Hand thy breath is, and whose are all thy ways ;" the God to whom you are indebted for every possession you rejoice in, for every blessing you hope for. It is the God who—neglected it may be, and little recognised as present by your side—has nevertheless followed you all your days : very near at all times, if not yet seen and owned by faith. By Him have you been holden up ever since you were born. He has watched over and walked with you in your going out and coming in. His unsleeping eye has guarded your nightly slumbers. And you laid yourself down and awaked again because He sustained you. It is the Being who has fed you all your life long, and redeemed you from all the evil you have escaped or passed through, and by whose help, as your unwearied and ever present Keeper and Defender, it is that you continue unto this day.

And should we take these blessings given—
The priceless boon of ruddy health—
The sleep unbroken—peace unriven—
The cup of joy—the mine of wealth—
Oh ! should we take them all, and yet
Walk from the cradle to the grave
Enjoying, boasting, and forget
To think upon the One that gave.

ELIZA COOK.

But the word "thy" leads us further still. As we ponder the thought to whom it refers, the glory of that Being into whose presence we are ushered, and which our humanity quails from as too insufferably bright, seems to part with its too dazzling influence. A splendour more subdued overshadows us, and we cease to say " I exceedingly fear and quake." For instead of Him " who dwelleth in the light which no man can approach unto, whom no man hath seen or can see," much less walk with, another vision is before us. And lo! One like unto ourselves, very Son of man, and a voice that seems more familiar to our ears, and in the re-assuring tones of which we no longer tremble, " Fear not, it is I !" I who lived and walked of old in Galillee and Jewry, and whose footsteps you have traced, and whose image you have pondered, till yon must be able to hail me as a Brother, as One who can be touched with a feeling for your infirmities, One who knows your frame, your temptations, and your needs. I, who have taken a human nature, and lived a human life, and sympathized with every human infirmity; and as Man can pity, as God forgive. Would you have testimony to the worth and blessedness of My companionship? Refer to the records of my past Incarnate life: and see how those who shared it rejoiced in it as a privilege so inestimable, and when it was withdrawn, mourned for it as so sore a loss. See how for it they counted it all gain to forego father and mother, and wife and children, and brothers and sisters, and houses and lands, and character and life!

Finally, if you would have an argument from the future as well as from the past, to prove how supremely, how only worthy, is that Divine Redeemer who invites you to a life-long friendship and close communion —take it as it is presented to you from a world of light. *There* where all judgment is rectified, and all things weighed in an even balance— *there* where all objects and persons assume in Heaven's clear light their relative value as they never do now—*there* where infinite discernment rules the every choice, and perfect knowledge guides the every action of those that indwell in its many mansions—*there* where " wisdom is justified of all her children," amid the untold attractions of that vast treasury of bliss, amid the excellencies that that communion of saints shall present, where are Angels and Archangels, and all the company of Heaven—no rival companionship can divert the gaze or distract the devotedness of the redeemed that walk there from their Lord. They follow Him, we read, whithersoever He goeth. Ever is He nearest to them, foremost in their vision, and first in their admiration. Among the many themes for their praise, and beside the "rivers of pleasure that flow at God's right Hand for evermore," they still one to another continually do cry, " My soul doth magnify the Lord, and my spirit hath rejoiced in God my Saviour." And the reason they give for this everlasting preference is still that which the text supplies in reminding us that He with whom we are charged to walk is our own God. For, say they, Thou hast redeemed us to God with Thy blood, and made us as Kings and Priests to sit with Thee in heavenly places.

As you would have that blessed Redeemer say of you hereafter, "Where I am there shall also my servant be," say you of Him now each for himself—and may God the Holy Ghost keep you in His communion—"This God shall be my God for ever and ever. He shall be my Guide unto death!"

GOD'S RECOGNITION OF HIS SERVANT'S LOVE.

If any man love God the same is known of Him.   1 *Cor* viii. 3.

No attentive reader of S. Paul's Epistles can fail to remark the strong persuasion that seems to have taken full possession of his mind, and to which he constantly clung, that he was an object of God's unceasing favour and interest. In his going out and coming in, his perils in the wilderness and in the sea, by his own countrymen and by the heathen, in his vexations and conflicts with false brethren, and his care of all the Churches—one of his chief supports seem to have been his perfect assurance that he was "made manifest unto God." He told the Romans "He that serveth Christ is accepted of God." And he seems to have bound this saying to his very heart. And having "the testimony of a good conscience," that the service of the Lord Christ was the great object of his life, he lived and rejoiced in the consciousness that the God whose he was and whom he served, was always standing by and approving him. "Study to show thyself approved unto God," was his charge unto his son Timothy. And not only did he study to do so; but he took the comfort from that study to which he was entitled, and believed that he was so: The Apostle believed that God and he were one: that there was if I may say, a perfect and lasting understanding established between them, by the atonement for his sins which Christ had made, and he had gratefully welcomed and was sincerely trusting to. He believed that he was walking with God and before Him, and graciously accepted and owned by Him.

"Let him that glorieth glory in this that he knoweth Me," said the Lord by Jeremiah. S. Paul truly did so. Every where he "made his boast in the Lord." And it was with a view to lead us whom his words should reach to the very end of time to rejoice in his gladness and to share his happiness in this knowledge, that he reiterated so continually this truth from the full belief of which he derived such satisfaction himself. "We know God," he said to the Galatians; but he corrected himself at once to mention what was more blessed still, "Yea, rather we are known of God." "The Lord knoweth them that are His," he said to Timothy. And here in the text to the Corinthians and to us, "If any man love God the same is known of Him."

Now we all know what a stimulus to human love and to human action is the recognition of it by him for whom it is felt, or for whom it is done. We are each of us conscious how it awakens the energies and nerves the heart to know that our love for an object of our regard is not unheeded, that our exertions for such a one are not slighted, but that what we feel and do for that person is owned and valued. And just such an incentive was it to the Apostle when through his faith in the Gospel he was made aware of this, one of its most cheering and delightful truths, that His disciple's love to Christ was always known and owned by Him, and that the offering of the heart and the life's service was not in any case despised. S. Paul had not only too experienced the power of this truth himself, but he knew that it is a principle of our nature that we love that one the more, who we know loves us and values our affection and regards our service. And so — in order to kindle the Christian's love and animate the Christian's zeal for the Lord that is looking with such regard upon him from above — the Apostle exclaims, "If any man love God the same is known of Him."

S. John says "Every one that loveth God knoweth God." But here we have the Christian's further experience that he is himself known of Him. When first the knowledge of God in His grace and pardoning love begins to enter the before thoughtless soul, and the changed heart begins to be attracted towards Him as it perceives the preciousness of the Saviour, there is in it of course an immediate awakening of love; but at the same time there is a feeling of strangeness and distance towards God. The new convert is like one who is just beginning to know something of, and in consequence of that knowledge to feel a regard for, another with whom he has had hitherto no personal acquaintance. He esteems the virtues of the character that has come under his notice, or admires the gifts and graces of the person; but as yet he feels towards the person a certain degree of awe and distance; which, however, as he begins to be known of the other gradually gives place to the confidence of intimate friendship. And so is it with the soul of the newly-awakened Christian. As he follows on to know the Lord, and cultivates communion with Him, he begins to find that he not only knows God, but that he is known of Him; that God is favourable towards him; that he reads all the desire of his heart towards Him; and that as he delights himself in the Lord, the Lord too delights in him. And thus, as in human friendship, does increased acquaintance and consciousness of sympathy "cast out fear" and introduce happiness.

S. Paul puts it, you will observe, in the most general way, not as a matter of his experience only, but as a truth of universal application— "If any man"—for he had cases in point to any number that might be demanded to prove it. This indeed is an induction from the whole history of the Church of God from the beginning. All who have consecrated their hearts and service to the Lord, and as He says "set their love upon Him," have united to establish the Apostle's assertion. They have been able to testify, as they followed on to know the Lord, they have felt themselves increasingly to be His accepted and approved; in a word, that "He has made them to know that He has loved them."

Thus Jeremiah appealed, with the satisfaction which this consciousness always imparts to God's people, to this understanding which now existed between him and God. "Thou, O Lord, knowest me. Thou hast seen me and tried mine heart toward Thee." Thus David said—"Thou, Lord God, knowest Thy servant." And again, "This I know that Thou favourest me." Thus Solomon said—"Every man that spreads forth his hands towards Thee—Thou knowest the hearts of all." Thus Nahum the prophet said—"The Lord is good: and He knoweth them that trust in Him." Thus S. Peter—"Lord, Thou knowest all things. Thou knowest that I love Thee." And last of all our Lord Himself bore the same witness. So little was His character and mission known that, as long as He was in the world, He could only say, "No man knoweth the Son save the Father!" He was in the world and the world knew Him not. He walked in its thoroughfares and taught in its streets. And He uttered gracious words such as all confessed that never man beside Him spake. And He manifested actions of kindness, and did deeds of mercy such as made all remark "It was never seen on this fashion." And yet the world knew Him not. Men did not apprehend the love which He had toward them, and which He spent and at last laid down His life in labouring to convince them of. But the Son of God could uplift His eyes to Heaven, and comfort Himself with the recognition of the truth in the text, "But the Father knoweth Me." And still this truth remaineth, for the peace and joy in believing it of all that shall come after to the end. "If any man love God the same is known of Him."

"If any man love the world or the things of the world" his affection may not be returned at all, and in most cases it cannot, and in many it may not even be known of that object. He may set his heart upon the gains, and never realise them; upon the pleasures of this life, and never be satisfied with them; or some distinction, and fail in grasping it; on some fair, excellent, worthy and lawful object, and be unsuccessful in his honest pursuit. His best endeavour may be thwarted, his most anxious aim be missed. But if any man love God, there is no fear of the offering of the heart being slighted, or despised, no hazard of the time and labour, which has been expended in showing its love and winning its aim, being lost, as though the devotion of thought and effort had been thrown away: as there is so often in other aims and and other love, where the object proves unworthy, unreal, or unattainable *There* is no after exclamation of disappointment "Wherefore this waste? For "if any man love God the same *is* known (and will certainly be noticed) of Him."

Very precious in His estimation is the love of us His unworthy creatures. If not a cry can ascend from the helpless young in the wild birds nest—If the young lion in his forest lair cannot utter a hungry roar, but it enters their Maker's pitying ear, and attracts His sympathizing notice—If not a sound expressive of their pain and need can go from His meaner creatures upon earth, "beasts and all cattle, creeping things and flying fowl," without arousing Him to relieve and provide for them —If He has, to quote the Psalmist's beautiful expression, as He has most truly, "a bottle" for every human tear, no matter what the cause that makes it flow, and an ear of kind compassion for every cry that suffering or grief of any kind extorts from the child of man—with what unspeakable interest, yea with what eagerness of affectionate desire, does he mark the uplifted heart, the heaven-raised eye, the first kindling emotion of love to Him from any of His own dear Sons and Daughters! It was for this He sent His Well Beloved Son, to win back their estranged affections to Himself. It is for this He sends His Minister's now, express ambassadors from Him, to beseech men in His Name to believe His love.

And as one after another hearken to their testimony, and yield themselves again to their Father's love and law, from the throne of Heaven His dwelling place, He bends forward as it were to look upon that returning Son or Daughter with all a loving Father's joy and complacency, and exclaims to the Angels that stand around lifting up over him their glad songs of joy "This my child was dead and is alive again! he was lost and is found." His heart was once at enmity with me, and cold and careless, but now he seeks and loves Me.

And as that newly awakened one follows on to know and love the Lord, He watches him with increasing satisfaction and approval. Each desire and labour of love is most fully known by Him who is the object of it. And one sentence of Scripture, the word of commendation to the Church in Thyatira, would interpret the glance of that eye, the meaning of that look that is always so kindly fixed upon him—"I know thy love, and thy service, and thy faith and thy patience, and thy works." "For if any man love God the same is known of Him."

And how encouraging is the freeness of these words "any man!" If any man, no matter who or what he be, will love the Lord his love will not be disdained. It was so in the days of His flesh, when she the penitent sinner, to whom He gave this short but expressive testimony that she loved Him much, stood trembling behind him in the consciousness of her unworthiness; and so far from daring to confess that love, shrunk from the notice of her Lord.

And none but he to whom the words of the text have become subject of his inner experience can conceive the joy with which she found that she was known of Him as she heard this His gracious recognition of that love. And it is so still. For the same Saviour left these words on record for ever, for you and for me, and for every one that would, to take up: "He that loveth Me shall be loved of My Father; and I will love him and will manifest Myself unto him." With Him there is neither respect nor exception of persons. And whosoever will love Him now shall be as cordially welcomed by that Saviour, and He will admit him to as full a confidence, as any of the glorified spirits that minister now before His throne. Let him that heareth come! And he shall share this happy consciousness of the Divine approbation which may be felt but cannot be told.

THE CHURCH'S TESTIMONY TO S. LUKE.

The brother whose praise is in the Gospel throughout all the Churches; and not that only but who was also chosen of the Churches to travel with the gift administered to the glory of the Lord—the messenger of the Churches, and the glory of Christ.
2 *Cor.* viii., 18, 19, 23.

There is no doubt that the person here referred to by S. Paul is S. Luke. Our Church intimates this general opinion to be her own by speaking in the Collect for to-day in quotation from this passage of "Luke the physician, whose praise is in the Gospel." S. Paul calls him in writing to the Colossians "the beloved physician." And it would seem that he had reason so to speak of him from personal experience of his professional advice. For, as it has been well shown by recent writers, the first notice of him as the Apostle's fellow traveller (given by S. Luke himself, when he says "Immediately we endeavoured to go into Macedonia") occurs at Troas where he met with S. Paul just as the latter was recovering from an illness which had detained him in Galatia (see Gal. iv., 13.) In the epithet "beloved" attached to the reference to him as a physician there seems (says Dean Howson) to be conveyed the sense of personal gratitude for benefits received. S. Paul calls him also, in writing to Philemon, his "fellow traveller." And as it is well known we are indebted to S. Luke, as the Author of the Acts of the Apostles, for almost all we know about S. Paul's journeys. It will be remembered too of that blessed Apostle that when he was now ready to be offered, and the time of his departure was at hand, the name of Luke was almost the last to be spoken by his dying lips. Testimony is then given to his fidelity to the last, which must for ever engage and secure our attachment to that noble Evangelist we commemorate to-day. When all others forsook the Church's greatest and most blessed martyr he stood by him to the last. "Only Luke is with me"—we can never hear those affecting words without a fresh impulse of grateful love towards the subject of our meditations for his own heroic steadfastness, and his unshaken faithfulness and kindness to the venerable preacher of Jesus Christ.

This sense of obligation and this admiration, is and has ever been felt throughout all the Churches that have been instructed and edified by those two most full and wonderful books in the New Testament which were written by S. Luke. And such admiration appears from the text to have very early been awakened towards him. The Apostle, who had thus cause from long acquaintance and observation to speak so highly of him himself, here testifies that the opinion of all was identical with his own. It was no partial witness, as of a merely personal friend, that sets forth the praise of the great Evangelist. But it was even then everywhere spoken of. And his praise was *in* the Gospel—perhaps *through* or in consequence of the Gospel that bears his name—throughout all the Churches.

I cannot but observe here that there is none of that affectation of humility and pretence of jealousy for the glory of Christ in S. Paul's writings, which leads so many to undervalue and pass by the burning and shining lights of His Church, and withhold from " the saints of the Most High" the tribute which is justly due to them as examples of grace and God's chosen lights of the world. Our Church falls not into this error. It does not hesitate, and I never do or shall, to commemorate such pillars of the Church, and to call you to glorify the grace of God in them. I am not one of those who can see the smallest ground for apprehension that we are, as a Church, ever likely to fall into the Romish superstition of worshipping Angels, or putting the holy Apostles and Saints into a prominence to be reserved only for the Name that is above every name. And I am not careful therefore to avoid the reproach which the ignorant and the prejudiced cast in their folly upon those that would exalt the Saints to the high pedestal on which God Himself has placed them in His revelation. S. Luke's praise, the Spirit of God tells us here, was in the Gospel throughout all the Churches. And his praise shall be also in my mouth.

Human praise is indeed an object of secondary consideration. We read of those in the Gospel, and their followers are legion to-day, who loved " the praise of men more than the praise of God." But to be insensible to, and undesirous of, the commendation of the good and the worthy is neither natural nor noble. To cultivate a temper of such insensibility is, let others say what they will to the contrary, a grievous error and a fault of great moment. We are bidden to shine as lights in the world. And men do not light a candle but in order that all eyes may turn towards it. And just as the eloquent speaker catches a fresh glow of emotion from the observation of an intelligent audience, just as their manifest appreciation of his arguments and telling illustrations stimulates him to renewed " light, and life, and fire" of diction—so the approval of those whose good opinion is worth receiving is a stimulus and incentive to the thereby encouraged Christian to more devoted effort, more abundant labour, and more hearty service to his Lord. S. Luke, you may be sure, did the work of an Evangelist with none the less singleness of aim, none the less profound humility, for knowing, as he must have known if these words were true, that his " praise was in the Gospel throughout all the Churches." Indeed such esteem is a singular help to those who are so happy as to be assured of it. For it makes them the more vigilant and careful in their lives, seeing that so much is thought of them, and so much therefore expected. Such come to feel that they are really as a city set upon a hill, whose light cannot be hid. And amid the depressing influences of a world of vanity and vexation of spirit—amid the discouraging influences of the felt power of sin within, and evil in such mighty and varied forms without—such special encouragement to those who are called to special positions of trust and usefulness in the Church of Christ is as helpful as it is needful. To plain Christian men and women it is seldom given, because seldom required. But the more eminent who have harder and more extensive work to do, and more in Christ's cause to suffer, need for that purpose extraordinary support. And the Master, who takes delight in honouring His servants that honour Him, gives them not unseldom, as they are able to bear it, and as He sees they will render back to Him the glory, the reward for past and encouragement for future service of unstinted praise. Yea, He gives it not ungrudgingly. And every age produces those who take a high stand before the world as its lights, and in the Church as its pillars, "whose praise (like S. Luke's) is in the Gospel throughout all the Churches." And on the lesser theatre of a life public not before the world at large, but before a more restricted society, in towns, and villages, and several congregations of the one undivided Church of the Redeemer—there are the stars of lesser magnitude that shine in its firmament. And their light is also clear, and their grace eminent, and their faithfulness no less observable, and no less beneficial to their neighbours. Their praise may not be in the Gospel throughout all the Churches, but only whispered secretly, or silently admired with no outward sign or expression of the effect produced on the observer. But even so that effect is real and valuable beyond all knowledge. The kingdom of God cometh not (at all times) with observation. And the trumpet that bids men mark the advance of the conqueror is not always blown. But the day comes, as the Apostle tells those same Corinthians, when "every man shall have his own praise of God." "The good works of some (says this Apostle) are manifest beforehand; and they that are otherwise cannot be hid." But as S. Peter says, the faith of such shall "be found unto praise, and honour, and glory, at the appearing of Jesus Christ."

The text tell us further that the Churches unanimously chose S. Luke to travel with S. Paul, to take their offering to the persecuted and impoverished martyrs, and to administer the same. S. Luke was as eminent therefore in administrative capacity as he was as an Evangelist. It would seem he was another Stephen, "of honest report, full of the Holy Ghost and wisdom" whom it was judged might be fitly appointed "over this business."

The worldly wisdom of a Minister is not infrequently doubted, or even boldly said to be wanting, by a self-conceited world. Let people judge as they will as to the fairness of such a reflection. S. Stephen, and S. Luke and S. Paul and Titus here, were differently accounted of. And they were probably no singular exceptions. The Churches know the Evangelist, and they trusted him. They knew he would serve *them* well because he served his Master well, and whatever his hand found to do, would do it with all his might. Confidence therefore followed esteem, as it always does, or should do, in matters pertaining to this life. Can you thoroughly respect your neighbour, and believe his principles are good, and his aim of life such as becometh the Gospel of Christ ?   Trust that neighbour for righteousness and well-doing in lesser things, where you must needs walk by faith and not by sight. And much anxiety and doubtfulness may be thus avoided.

S. Luke was so trusted. And the Church's confidence was not misplaced. The particulars of that mission of his are among the yet unrevealed histories reserved for our perusal and hearing in the future life. But the Apostle, speaking in the concluding words of the text of S. Luke and his fellow travellers on this business, declares that they are "the glory of Christ." And what high commendation was this in conclusion! An Evangelist of whom it is not only said that his praise is in the Gospel throughout all the Churches, and that he was chosen as the fittest to administer the bounty of the wealthy in other lands, but that he was the glory of Christ—well may we linger to-day on the memory of such a one.

The glory of Christ—the expression indicates one in whose high character and loyal faith the very Lord of righteousness rejoiced. A servant was he of whom his Master, to speak after the manner of men and after the figure of the text itself, was proud. "The Lord taketh pleasure in His people." With the joy and satisfaction with which the captain contemplates his bold and true soldier, the parent his affectionate and dutiful child, the fond one his zealous and devoted friend— did Christ look down on His noble Evangelist. And with the same feeling does He direct our contemplation to him to-day. Behold My servant whom I uphold, Mine elect in whom My soul delighted. I put My Spirit upon him, and he brought forth judgment to the Gentiles." And he did most truly. The beautiful parables, related only by S. Luke, of Simon the Pharisee and the woman that was a sinner, of the prodigal son, of the good Samaritan, of the importunate widow, of the justified Publican, the story of the penitent robber, his especial announcement of "the glad tidings to all people," teach us how fully and persuasively he did the work of an Evangelist to the Gentiles. And well thus did he deserve the title of the glory of Him who came to be a light to lighten the Gentiles, and to be for salvation to the ends of the earth.

Your praise may and will never be, like S. Luke's, in the Gospel throughout all the Churches. But, like S. Luke, you may be the glory of Christ. Serve Him, in however lowly a sphere, with the brave, earnest, persevering, and affectionate spirit of the Evangelist. And you shall one day hear more than the testimony of an Apostle that you are the glory of Christ. You shall hear from the lips of the very Master Himself—as He points you to His right hand to rank with the great and the blessed, the goodly company of the Prophets, the holy fellowship of the Apostles, the noble army of Martyrs and Evangelists—the "Well done, good and faithful servant," that shall honour you before the assembled world and before men and Angels as "the glory of Christ."

THE LAW OF LOVE AS APPLIED TO THE INNER LIFE.

Be kindly-affectioned one to another with brotherly love; in honour preferring one another.—*Romans* xii. 10.

It is difficult to convey into our language the full strength and force of the words thus translated as they exist in the original Greek. The word rendered kindly-affectioned expresses what is elsewhere translated " natural affection," such as exists between near relatives, more particularly in parents towards children. And the use of it here shows that what the Apostle enjoins is that in the household of God, the Church of Christ, there is to be maintained and exhibited the same simple, sincere, artless, and unaffected regard between its different members, which we see, or expect to see, exist in the domestic circle. The Divine family is governed and related and expected to comport itself after the model of a human one.

And you will observe in the first place that the Spirit, speaking by the Apostle in the text, does not concern Himself, as we should be apt to do who judge by the outward appearance, with insisting on kindly acts and generous dealing; but on the inward impulse from which these spring. " Be kindly-affectioned," that is disposed. The Word of God is always a discerner of the thoughts and intents of the heart, and always aims at regulating the sources of action. And so here and in like passages the Spirit of holiness lays a solid foundation for the fabric He would raise. He sounds the very depths of our spiritual nature in the matter of the brotherly love He would evoke in us towards one another when He says " Be kindly-affectioned." He does not pause to occupy Himself, as a human teacher would do, in recommending the cultivation and manifestation of words and deeds of charity. But far down in the moral nature He sows the seed that may bring forth such fruit by urging the cherishing of a disposition—not the performance of an act. And this disposition of good-will, of favourable judgment, of inclination of heart towards our fellow Christians, how little are we naturally habituated to it ! How alien is it to the temper we observe around and detect within ourselves !

To think kindly is far harder than to speak or act kindly. We can force ourselves almost at any time to the one; but long habit and careful attention must accustom us to the other. In kindly words and deeds we may take a pride, for they are known and appreciated ; and therein we have our reward. But the acquisition of the temper of affection is tedious and arduous. And our self-love interferes with our cherishing it, and our self-importance makes us think the object it might go forth to unworthy of it.

Now the precepts of Christianity are remarkable for their being so practical : for their application to us as we are and to our circumstances as they are. And we may see this in the form of the precept before us. We may have little or no scope whatever for showing forth generous actions and unselfish deeds. So far may we be from having an opportunity of doing good on a large scale, that we may be so fettered, as it seems to us by Providence, that we think we can do no good at all. The part of a Good Samaritan it may never be ours in any outward act to be able to play. God, who has ordered our life and sphere, knows that this is so with the greater number to whom this precept shall come. And therefore all He bids us here is " Be kindly-affectioned." So accustom yourself to look upon your neighbour—to look not every one on his own things, but every one also on the things of others—that it may be in your *heart*, even though never in the power of your *hand*, to relieve, and benefit, and bless.

I doubt not for a moment that if you saw your fellow Christian hungry, you would feed him ; athirst, you would give him drink ; a stranger, you would enlighten his ignorance ; in perplexity, you would set yourself to dispel his doubt ; sick, you would visit and minister to him ; in want, you would care for him ; in sorrow, you would sympathize with him. But what do you know of being kindly-affectioned ? " Blessed is he that considereth" such, says the Scripture. What do you know of this entertaining his case in your thoughts, this pondering of his circumstances, this weighing of his affliction, this thought about his probable need or distressed condition ? In this was manifested the love of God towards us. From the far-off realms of bliss He considered the case of His fallen creatures.

He saw, and O amazing love !
He came to our relief.

And this Divine benevolence is to be the pattern of yours. You have frequent occasion to observe the straitened lot, the embarassment, or the trouble that has fallen upon your neighbour. I will not suppose you indulge a secret satisfaction in some cases that he is served according to his deserts, and harbour a malicious feeling of triumph, or a proud one of superiority. For this, if you do, be sure God will call you to a strict and stern account. But do you not for the most part dismiss the unwelcome consideration of the other's grief or need, lest it should disturb your peace; instead of, as you are here bidden, dwelling upon it with a kindly feeling that will presently surpass interest and grow into a warmer and more active sentiment. And the high standard at which we are to aim in cherishing this affection or feeling of the mind is brotherly love.

The affection that subsists between the amiable members of a united, happy family is what God would have to be shed abroad in our hearts towards one another. We have all beheld or reflected at times —" How good and pleasant a thing it is where brethren dwell together in unity." We have seen or known perhaps, or if not we can imagine at least, some household where all the members were one. We have seen their oneness of sentiment, their unity of taste, their care for one another. No suspicion of their intentions clouds the serene faces of brothers and sisters who are thus one. Their relations to each other are perfectly cordial: their communications frank and unreserved. Sincerity breathes in their words, and is stamped in their whole demeanour. There is no standing in doubt of one another's purposes; no standing on guard against something suspected as injuriously meant or designed. There is no duplicity about their actions or words. There may be uncertainty abroad, and clouds and mist in the outer world; but the free and open air of nature envelopes such a home. I may be drawing the picture of an ideal home. But if an abstract idea it is yet a natural one. And if we have not met with the household on earth that exhibited it to any perfection, we shall verify the description should we come, as I pray we may, to our Father's house above. And such demeanour and relationship as theirs, is to be the model for the imitation of the sons and daughters of the Lord Almighty. For this commandment have we from Him that he who loveth God love his brother also.

And says the text last of all, as it lays this charge upon us, "In honour preferring one another." It is comparatively easy to give up to another, to yield the preference. But how hard really to prefer our neighbour to ourself! To think that his judgment may after all be best when ours seems to us so clear—to allow that he may after all be right when he seems so evidently wrong—(I am not of course here speaking of anything that in morals or practice is right or wrong, about which with the Bible's unerring standard of infallible truth, there can happily be no doubt), to believe that the fact may not be as it seems to us, but rather as it appeared to him—to distrust one's own view, and think that the other's may be the more far seeing one—in lowliness of mind to esteem the one with whom we differ, after all better than ourself—Aye these are the triumphs of brotherly kindness and charity.

And the man or woman that has attained to this humility is indeed great in the kingdom of heaven. But it is the standard to which we are here bidden to conform. Not out of mere courtesy, as the educated and refined are taught even by the world to do, but from unfeigned humility, from a bitter consciousness of one's own demerit, and often infirmities,—are we to be ready to stand aside and really feel that the other may be the better and the worthier. We are to be ready even, as the word preferring intimates in the original Greek, to take personal part in putting him before ourselves. We must be willing to take like Haman the office of leading the charger, while the multitude bow to the rider; be content to decrease while the other seems—possibly only seems—to increase. You that have *not* attained to this grace remember that the Spirit of God enjoins it here. Happy are you that *have* attained to it in any measure, for the Spirit of God is truly proved to rest upon you.

And he that humbleth himself shall be exalted. With what measure you mete it shall be measured to you again. And the day shall come when those that honoured Him by the humility He thus commanded He shall honour.   And with a joy which in spite of their instinctive shrinking from such high fame, shall fill their exulting souls, as the expectation of it does now, they shall hear their Lord confess their names before His Father and the Holy Angels, " and give them His gracious benediction commanding them to take possession of His glorious kingdom.   Unto which He vouchsafe to bring us all for His Infinite Mercy!"

THE RECOLLECTION OF THE JUST AND ITS BLESSEDNESS.

ALL SAINTS DAY.

The memory of the just is blessed. *Proverbs* **x. 7.**

The recollection of the past, and the anticipation of the future, are distinguishing gifts and features of our human nature. In the possession of these capacities we chiefly differ from the irrational creatures. With them the experience of the present is—if not the only—far the greater element of life. But we live much more in the *past* and *future*, than in the *present*. The largest share of our thoughts is occupied by the reminiscence of what is to us past on the one hand, by faith and hope about what lies before us on the other.

It is with the former of these that the text, and the subject of the day, leads me to concern myself. Memory, and that not of *events* or *scenes*, which are interesting enough to a certain degree; but of *persons* who have peopled the past, and whose forms still throng the chambers of imagination, and fill the soul with vivid impressions. And the memory of such, the recalling the beings whose forms, and words, and deeds, have left their seal upon our soul, is more powerful and attractive than the memory of places or occurances. For "the proper study of mankind is man."

Aye in that inner life in which—while all around us may be unconscious of it—we are living and moving ever—while eye, and hand, and foot, are busied in the present and the superficial observation of our fellow-creature thinks us perhaps utterly absorbed in it—it is the memory of *beings*, not *places* or *occupations*, that above all else enchains the soul that has wandered back again to the past. We have passed on in the body but we linger behind in the spirit. The eye perhaps may give no sign. The absent look, the uncertain reply, may not, as in many cases, give an intimation that the mind is elsewhere. But which of us is not conscious that the present has oftentimes but little to enthrall the interest and affections of the soul, compared with what is gone before. It may be the recent past, or the past of long ago, the interview or engagement of only an hour since, or the enjoyment or suffering of months or years long elapsed. But the pulse of the soul beats quicker, and the eye flashes with a brighter light, and the soul is thrilled with a far deeper emotion as in its own solitude it recalls those beings with whom its own eager, anxious, and most real and earnest feelings are associated.

And when memory is busy in summoning before us those forms whom absence or distance has separated—whose are the countenances our fancy depicts most readily? Whose are the words and deeds that strike ever and again upon our thoughtful spirits with most powerful influence? Whose are the forms that flit around us most constantly? Whose the smiles that glance into our spirits with the most gladdening light? Perchance you may say the loved. But a moment's thought will make you feel that it is "the memory of the just," that is rather and chiefly "blessed." The memory of the loved indeed is precious, if the loved were really just or good. And it is precious too if they were not really so, but only thought to be. For affection will always invest its objects with "the garments of righteousness," and love them for the goodness which it thinks it sees in them. It is only the evil spirits, that instinctively, and by their very nature, prefer and are drawn towards the evil. But the spirit of man which came to him in the image and likeness of God, though alas now a broken image and a defaced likeness, —even with all its terrible enmity against the good and holy—betrays its admiration of righteousness, and grace, and virtue, by reverencing those in whom they are embodied. And if the goodness be all imaginary, the yet deluded spirit endues with it the subject of its admiration before it falls down to worship it.

And so the memory of the loved we know will cling even when the once blind soul awakes to the bitter consciousness that they are not "just." But "the memory of the *just*," (the righteous or the good), how does it come back to us with an even more repeated and a far more wondrous power! The thought of the just whose examples have told upon our lives, whose saintly teachings, or deeds of kindness, righteousnes, and mercy, have left an impress that the world's revolving wheels can never overcover—how does it steal softly over us in lonely moments and thoughtful musings! How does it shed a light on darkened hours, and pour a balm on painful reflections that the memory of no thing beside can bring. "The memory of the just," of those who have stood by us and helped us to fight the battle of life, those whose high principles have exalted our own, and whose worthy aims have kindled ours; "the just"—those who to us have appeared the good and the noble—whose high character we have looked up to, and by which we have it may be quite insensibly, greatly moulded our own—it is *their* memory, when they are no longer before us, casts a long shadow upon our path which we recognise very soon. They are a power to us still. And we drink into and copy their spirit when we hardly know it; and we are strong to go on our ways, and to work, and to suffer, because "the memory of the just is blessed," because it is filling and inspiring all our soul.

If it seem to you that this is exaggerated sentiment only imagine what your life would be, how utterly lost and miserable, how like unto the very beasts, if the memory of the just could not affect or animate it! Suppose that no recollection of a kindly or generous deed, no impression of a good example, no echo of a holy teaching, no portrait of a good one's face ever lingered a single moment in your soul, or could by any possibility be recollected. Suppose that the spirit of the righteous could never be transfused or the impression of it were instantly obliterated. Suppose that all that now, and ever on through the future, remained in the recollection of your soul were the repulsive visages of the evil : all the hard speeches, the unkindly remarks, the selfish actions, the mean, the cruel, the corrupt deeds, which you have ever witnessed, And you shall admit by contrast, as you imagine how utterly intolerable your life would then have become, that "the memory of the just is blessed."

And so it is blessed because it blesses. For what is it that is the great sweetener of the bitterness, which is so frequent an element in the cup of all our lives, but "the memory of the just?" To what do we revert from the unhappiness of the present, when it is so, but to "the memory of the just" in the past? Of course we turn, or should far more, to the expectation of reunion with them in the future. But this as I said, is not so much within the scope of the text.

And to day, on this most delightful and comprehensive of all the Church's festive Anniversaries of her Sons and Daughters, we may, and are encouraged to summon any and all of them before our review. We hold to day a grand assembly in the soul's reception chamber. And we bid not "the poor, and the maimed, and the halt, and the blind," the outcasts of the world's highways, and hedges, but all the grand, and the pure, and the beautiful characters, whether in the present or the past, that we have known or heard of. And we come in now, like that king in the parable, "to see the guests," that are arrayed in white robes, and whence they came.

In the centre "enthroned and crowned with all renown" is superlatively "the Holy One and the Just," and around Him a multitude whom no man can number of all nations, and kindreds, and peoples, and tongues." As we gaze upon the glorious company, though ranks upon ranks we have never seen before, their bright and happy faces seem almost familiar. There is nothing strange or repelling in their air or appearance or demeanour to us. It is like meeting a circle of Brothers and Sisters not an assembly of strangers : for we "are all one in Christ Jesus!" No one passes us by with the look of indifference that a stranger on earth turns for the most part toward us. And we shrink from none as we do from unfamiliar and unloved faces.

And many a one of those we are called by our Church to meet in spirit to day we do actually know. Pious relatives, and godly neighbours, religious and devout men and women, with whom we were once acquainted, stars of the Churches in the light of whose holy faith we walked long time ago, and from whose burning and shining lives our own weaker faith, and fainter hope, and feebler love, and less vigorous zeal, perchance were kindled, many a one in far distant towns and villages whom we assisted in laying to rest in lovely cemetery or peaceful graveyard, in sure and certain and well grounded hope of a joyful resurrection.

All decked with palms, and strangely bright,
  That living host appears,
And stainless are their robes of white,
  Though steeped in blood and tears.

Fear not to recall those vanished forms, nor think that it will stir the memory of a "bitterness of death" that is overpast, or that you would have to be forgotten in their buried graves. For when the hour and the solemn commemoration of to-day is ended, and their re-awakened forms have melted once more into the dim and hazy past, no aching void, or sense of fresh desolation, need be left in our for a moment forsaken souls. These dead, whom we summon before us to-day shall live : "Together with our dead bodies shall they arise." What we see to-day in fancy we shall behold very soon in fact. And something of the unspeakable consolation and blessedness of the reality shall be ours who set the vision before our soul's imagination now. Lift but the eye of faith ; and these blessed ones are before you, and that at any time, until they are before you for ever. Lo! the unseen world that envelopes us even now is thronged with fair and beauteous forms. I see the gleaming of their pure white wings, and the lustre of their golden crowns. I hear the rustling of their flowing robes of spotless white. I seem to myself to be gazing actually on their clear and unruffled brows, and to catch the glow that lights up their sparkling eyes.

> Their songs of rapture sweet and clear,
> Are falling on my ravished ear ;
> Beside myself I see them stand,
> And seem to grasp their outstretched hand.

God of the spirits of all flesh, help us, who are here to-day to celebrate Thy Saints, to fight their good fight of faith, and gain the crown Thou hast in store for those who like them are faithful unto death! With all our souls we bless Thy holy Name for all these Thy servants departed this life in Thy faith and fear, beseeching Thee to give us grace so to follow their good examples that with them we may be partakers of Thy heavenly kingdom. And with all our hearts—by the blessed memory of these just ones—" We pray Thee help us Thy servants whom Thou hast redeemed with Thy most precious blood ; and make us to be numbered with Thy Saints in glory everlasting."

THE ELDER SON—HIS RETURN FROM THE FIELD AND HIS SURPRISE.

PART I.

Now his elder son was in the field : and as he came and drew nigh to the house he heard music and dancing. And he called one of the servants, and asked what these things meant.—*Luke* xv., 25, 26.

The character of the elder son in this parable is not very easily grasped. With that of the younger we are very familiar. But we hesitate in assigning the exact position which the other is meant to hold when the cases before us are transferred to the characters of our age. We do not readily recognise the portrait, nor the state of mind and the relation to God in which this son or such a one is to be regarded, or indeed where we should meet with such among ourselves. Yet as our Lord enters into it in detail it cannot be unimportant : nor should we be right in judging it merely as a back-ground to the other, and, as it might be thought, more prominent figure in the parable.

Doubtless the parable sets forth the jealousy with which the Jews looked on the reception of the Gentiles into the Divine favour and into the household of God. The instruction here given to the Jewish disciples that they were no longer to consider the Gentiles unclean, but to welcome them, as we see in the book of the Acts of the Apostles they presently did, into their inheritance of a common salvation—is plain enough. But I think we are taught also the far higher blessedness of a lifetime spent in God's service and the enjoyment of His fellowship and love, than can ever be that of one who after years of reckless living becomes the subject of a late conversion. This part of the parable well meets the objection which would naturally arise, and in fact did arise, at the first publication of the Gospel. If sinners are so welcome to the Saviour's pardon and the Father's home, "Is Christ therefore the minister of sin?" Is the tendency of His Gospel to show that it matters little how we live since "the remission of sins that are past" is "through the forbearance of God" so readily to be obtained, and we "may be justified freely by His grace through the redemption that is in Christ Jesus?" "Shall we continue in sin that grace may abound?"

It is to be feared that not only in the early ages of the Church, when Christianity, its effects and tendency to promote holiness, was but little known—was it needful to guard against this fatal misapprehension of the Gospel scheme. To what but this latent notion can we trace the careless and notoriously vicious lives of so many of the lower classes of religious sectaries who "hold the truth." but as the Apostle says "in unrighteousness," who profess and claim to exalt the Saviour,

One whom they believe will save from sin's *future consequences*, but One who has little or no place in their thoughts or teaching as a Saviour from its *present power*? And great need indeed there was to guard against such a perversion of His grace as would make God's charity to cover, as it were in this sense, a multitude of sins; and against the tendency to lose sight of the aggravation in comparison of the elder son's of the younger's misery and loss.

Now I think we may safely say we do not form a correct notion of him if we set him aside from the story as a self-righteous person of whom no heed is to be taken, and in whose example no worthy trait is observable to solicit our imitation. As our Lord introduces him at some length to our notice we cannot be justified in dismissing him, as is too generally done, from the story, as though we had nothing to learn from him. On the contrary, it has always appeared to me that his character is as profitable for reproof, correction, and instruction in righteousness as the other's. I shall endeavour therefore to treat the particulars relating to him as they come before us in the order of the narrative, and extract from them the lessons they seem to suggest and teach.

The text says " Now the elder brother was in the field." Not in the far country wasting his substance in riotous living—not as a companion to the swine of the strange lord his brother had been reduced to serve—not on the homeward journey a beggar and an outcast in misery and shame—not as the other a weight upon his father's heart and a scandal on his childhood's home—was this more happy son. But in the field engaged in useful and honourable toil—the sole joy of his father's heart, and the comfort of his declining years—he was spending his days in peace and the freedom of a comparatively quiet conscience. Of such knowledge of evil as his miserable brother had experienced, who had sown to the flesh, and reaped its ever sure harvest of corruption, he was happily destitute. Not like him had he walked in the counsel of the ungodly, nor stood in the way of sinners, nor sat in the seat of the scornful. And not like him either had he felt the " strange punishment" that God has affixed, as Job says, " to the workers of iniquity" as " that recompense of their error which is meet." He was altogether exempted from his brother's forebodings of aggravated judgment and his depths of humiliation. He never knew the pangs the other suffered when an outraged conscience awoke to vindicate the solemn truth of God as recorded in Eccles. c. xi., 9, that for every youthful excess, for every additional act of hardened impenitence and avowed sin He would exact a terrible retribution. Let not the story of the prodigal give any occasion to think that because grace is so abundant therefore sin is a light thing. For notwithstanding all the merciful provisions of the Gospel for the repentant, not with impunity can one ever deliberately and persistently violate any of the laws of his Creator. " A wound and dishonour shall such a one get, and a reproach that shall not be wiped away." The man that like the prodigal wilfully forsakes the way of life to wander in the destructive paths of reckless sin—even if by Divine grace he arise again to amend his life, and become the subject of that godly sorrow that works repentance unto salvation—may be "saved yet so as by fire" "He shall suffer loss" is the teaching of Scripture, a loss of time, influence, and opportunities of serving his God and generation which can never be repaired, and the extent of which can hardly be over-estimated.

There is mercy indeed free and rich for every returning sinner, a glad and a full welcome for him back to his Father's home, a ready acceptance and an unqualified forgiveness on the part of the compassionate God and Father of us all. Yet who sees not the greater happiness, the preferable lot, of the one who has not run to such excess of riot nor so vilely cast away his birthright? Unprofitable servants indeed are those who have wrought the longest and the best. But the child that, like the one here, has lost the opportunity of manifesting his devotion and obedience to his Heavenly Father, which his brother has improved during years of earnest and filial zeal, cannot in the nature of things have so "abundant an entrance into the kingdom" of glory. He may stand before God in the judgment with equal confidence and acceptance, for the grounds of these depend wholly upon another, the meritorious obedience and sufferings of Christ, "Not by works of righteousness which we have done, but according to His mercy He saves us." But he cannot expect to know the same joy nor to receive an equal crown. "Be not deceived. God is not mocked, for whatsoever a man soweth that shall he also reap." Wherefore look to yourselves that you lose not those things which you might have wrought, but that you receive a full reward.

"As he drew nigh to the house, on his return from the field, he heard music and dancing." It seems to me there is something peculiarly affecting, which we might not at first observe, in this remark. Was this, we are led to ask, an unwonted sound within the precincts of the good man's household? "The voice of joy (says the Psalmist) is in the dwellings of the righteous." But the son seems to be quite taken by surprise at hearing it now. Ah! for many a long sad day had it been there an unknown strain. A chord had been broken in the music of his home, and its former melody was gone. So says the prophet, "Because they have transgressed the laws, changed the ordinance, broken the everlasting covenant, therefore they that dwell therein are desolate. The mirth of tabrets and the harp ceaseth; the noise of them that rejoice endeth. All the merry-hearted do sigh." And so it was in this house. A gloom of grief had long brooded over the good man's roof, and sorrow had sat down as an inmate at his fireside.

Little indeed do the careless, the godless, and the froward realise the sadness their sin occasions. Before them is a delusive light of pleasure, but behind them an ever lengthening and darkening shadow that wraps in a gloom they never think of many a mind, as it will one day their own. The grief of thy parent, the distress of thy Christian friend, the anxiety of thy pastor, the doubts and fears for thy sake that are painfully felt by thy godly neighbour—thou, the unconcerned, the worldly, the trifler, or the inconsistent dost little know. Perhaps to this very hour thou hast made the heart of some "righteous sad whom

God would not have sad," and added a shade to that dark cloud of sorrow with which sin has overspread this otherwise fair and happy world. Thus it was, we read, that over the impenitent and hardened Saul the prophet Samuel, when he had "cried unto the Lord all night," mourned until the day of his own death, departing to his own house, and never visiting him more.

> The last entreaty uttered now,
>   The last remonstrance spoken,
> Grief sat upon that noble brow ;
>   The Prophet's heart was broken.
>
> All vain the last night's bitter cry
>   Of agonized regret :
> All vain the appealing prayer and sigh :
>   The sun of hope was set.
>
> The wilful king he could not save
>   Went on his godless way :
> And onward mourning to his grave,
>   Passed Samuel from that day.
>
> And—while his courtiers still to Saul,
>   Homage of flattery bore—
> He went to weep his monarch's fall,
>   And came back nevermore !

Hugh Allan.

I have alluded to what he heard. I observe next where he heard it, and dwell accordingly on the words " as he drew nigh to the house." Music and dancing are and have ever been well known symbols and expressions of human mirth. By such tokens of festivity the son was perfectly aware there was some special ground and occasion for rejoicing. But he knew nothing of the existence even of such gladness as thrilled the hearts of all within until " he drew nigh to the house." Far off in the field he had no idea of it at all. But as he drew nigh the sounds of an unwonted mirth fell upon his wondering ear. And thus not while he is far off, but as he draws near to his Father in Heaven, does the child of God become conscious of a gladness pervading the household of faith that he had not known before. Evermore there is joy in our Father's house ; for there are themes that call for new songs of praise, and subjects for fresh thankfulness are constantly presenting themselves. Not unwonted is that experience to the Christian that was so strange to this son here. Let us but come near enough to God, and we shall soon be in the midst of a joy we had not known before. The joy of pardon, the joy of conscious fellowship with Christ, the comfort of the Holy Ghost, the joy of a quieted conscience, of a hope that we know can never be put to confusion, and the joy of a satisfying love—these and many more are the notes from Heaven's festive blessedness that vibrate through the soul, as it draws near to God through faith in His Son and obedience to His Spirit.

And daily as you draw nearer to God—in increased watchfulness and humble discipleship, through the means of grace and the Word of God and prayer—will they become to you, as to the son here, more vivid and real, until in the mansions of your Father above, you come into the very scene of rapturous joy, that reigns in the Heavenly household for ever.

Perhaps even now some faint echo of that gladness is borne to your newly awakened and aroused attention, and you are beginning to listen and wonder whether the "joy in believing," of which the Scriptures, and Christians, tell, has indeed any reality. Perhaps God is just beginning to convince you that "great peace have they that love His law;" and you are saying from the far off field, like the Prophet, "From the uttermost part of the earth we have heard songs, even glory to the righteous." If so: keep on and follow up the sound. Draw nearer and yet nearer to the centre whence these echoes come. And you shall know what is "the gladness of His people."

And here the proceeding of the son leads us by a natural transition to what in such circumstances should be our own. "He called the servants and asked what these things meant." At once and wisely he had recourse for the satisfaction of his mind upon the point, to those who had a clearer knowledge of the case than he. Thus when the governor of the feast at Cana, had tasted the water that was made wine, and knew not whence it was—but the servants who drew the water knew—he called the bridegroom, the servants were appealed to, the whole truth came out: and the Saviour's grace and power was known and glorified. So in earlier Jewish times, when those who were strangers to the doctrines and ordinances of their faith should put the question, "What mean ye by this service," God made in anticipation a careful provision, that they should be instructed in His law, and His dealings with His people. So still has He provided that through His "servants," already enlightened and instructed, the knowledge of His ways and grace should be extended. He has appointed them says S. Paul, speaking of the orders of the Ministry "for the edifying of the body of Christ in the knowledge of Him."

Are you with regard to God and His salvation on any point doubtful and perplexed? Are you beginning to bethink yourself of the words and revelations of Scripture what these strange things mean? Are you anxious, as this son, to know the intents of your Heavenly Father's heart, to be informed as to your hopes and prospects? Behold His servants who wait for this very purpose! For this cause they stand continually in His house, and round about, to meet, like these servants in the story, some soul returning from the world's field and coming in the direction of God; and to tell it, like them, of the grace of its Father, and the happiness of its brethren who are already within. They can speak what they know, and testify what they have seen. Ask of them. Come and listen to their testimony. For surely they ought best to know. For "the secret of the Lord is with His servants; and He will show them (and has shown them) glorious things concerning His mercy and His truth." Be not so foolish as to believe the ungodly about matters pertaining to godliness. Take not their opinion in what they have had no experience, nor be guided by those who have neither part, nor lot, nor knowledge in the matter. You ask not the blind stranger for direction on your road. You go not to the ignorant countryman to learn the particulars of the works and transactions of the great city, nor to the unlearned to be instructed in the mysteries of science.

Not so devoid of understanding was this son as to ask his fellows in the field, as ignorant as himself, of the sounds that fell upon his ears, and the doings in his father's house. No vain conjectures, no uncertain explanations would satisfy him. He wished for accurate information. Where to go for it he knew, and there at once he went. So likewise seek of the Ministers of God, who "attend continually upon this very thing." Consult, too, those holy men of old, who spake as they were moved by the Holy Ghost, and who though dead speak still in that Word of God which liveth and abideth for ever. Search those Scriptures in which you have infallible truth. They will tell you of a joy in the presence of God, and the possession of His salvation, and within His household, the existence of which the irreligious must needs deny, because they understand and know it not.

And not to perplex and cause you trouble, as was the effect of the servants' communications in the story, will that blessed revelation tend. Rather "to the quieting of the conscience, and the avoiding of all care and doubtfulness," does the every message of the Gospel speak. With each fresh insight you thus shall gain into the love of the Father, and the sympathy of the Son, and the sustaining power of the Spirit of life, and the privileges of God's people, you shall be more satisfied, and rather able with all saints to comprehend and rejoice in that Divine love that passes knowledge. And thus presently, like the son, when all had been cleared up to him, and every doubt removed, you shall be received and led by a gracious Father to take your part in the never ending festivities of His happy home.

THE ELDER SON — HIS ANGER — AND HIS FATHER'S TREATMENT.

And he was angry, and would not go in; therefore came his father out and entreated him.—*Luke* xv., 28.

The son's mood here appears singularly ungracious and discontented; the father's manner as strikingly kind, condescending, and persuasive. As we first begin to observe the son's mood we are perhaps ready at once to condemn him as a selfish petulant fellow, full of envy, self-righteousness, and all uncharitableness. It is well however, for us all that we stand or fall by a more discerning arbitration than the, for the most part, too hasty judgment of our fellow creatures, that we have, like him, such a Father as can be touched with a feeling for His children's infirmities, and can perfectly understand the particular difficulties and complications that puzzle their path and perplex their minds. Well "the Lord knoweth how to deliver His people out of temptation," and to satisfy them even in such wayward dissatisfied moods as that which we are now to consider; and how to make their own way and His doings plain before their face. He always deals tenderly and is ready to condescend to explain Himself when in the moment of dark and bewildering doubt the evil heart of unbelief is disposed to question His goodness or arraign His wisdom. Even if His child be like the son in the story, or such another as Job or Jonah, he is ever willing to explain His ways more perfectly; and to meet the objections, however foolish and frivolous, that He sees to lie between the earnest soul and the clearer knowledge of Himself. Before His just tribunal there is ever open for any of us a full and free hearing. And if "the Lord hath a controversy with His people," or they one with Him, the Prophet Micah teaches us He will set Himself, and invite them, to carefully plead the cause.

Let us then give the son now as attentive and favourable a consideration as the father evidently did. "He that is first in his own cause seemeth just, but his neighbour cometh and searcheth him." Our sympathies are so naturally elicited in this story towards the repentant prodigal, who is first brought before us, that we have approved him in some degree too much to the disparagement of the other. The humble suppliant here attracts our pity so powerfully that we may have possibly overlooked the hitherto more virtuous but now displeased and unseasonably angry brother. There is such joy in our hearts over the recovery of the lost sinner, that they have been too full to take up the other's case who had not so gone astray. We are so delighted at the sparing of Nineveh, that we have no thought to give, like God, to the difficulty of Jonah in the background, whose words of truth and deeds of obedience have been thereby, to all appearance, made of no effect. No doubt the portrait of the elder son standing outside the happy home, and looking askance at his brother at the blessed moment of his welcome within, appears unamiable. But the candid mind will be anxious to inquire into the matter, and cannot readily suspect that one whom the father acknowledged, and the story shows, to be so dutiful a son, could really be so unnatural a brother as to grudge him his pardon and restoration; and wish him to have perished in the far country of famine, and misery, and sin. He erred indeed, and was re-proved. His selfishness was corrected, and his views were rectified. But in the true-heartedness of his service his father expresses his pleasure and approval. Let us too give the tribute to him which is his due.

We admit there was here shown a temper very alien from that charity which "seeketh not her own." But we may allow something, perhaps not a little, to a virtuous indignation. "Abhor that which is evil" is a Christian principle and one in which the elder son no doubt had been carefully and religiously trained. The course of reckless sin in which his unhappy brother had walked had long, it may be, filled the heart of the elder son with grief and his life with shame. It was true the prodigal was now repentant. But we must remember the elder son had not yet seen and tested the depths of that penitence as the father had. Indeed, as far as we can see from the story, he knew nothing of the other's penitence, but merely the fact of his return. And this he would probably think was for no good purpose. So when John saw many Pharisees and Sadducees come to his Baptism, mistrusting their sincerity, he exclaimed, "O generation of vipers, who hath warned you to flee from the wrath to come?" And if the elder son shrank at first from communication with such a character, even though it were his own brother—allowing, if you ask it, a mingling of less worthy motives—I cannot greatly blame him. To "be angry and sin not" is a possible, but at all times a very difficult thing. But sin is the natural and proper object of that passion of anger which is implanted in our nature. And he did not altogether unwell to be angry at the supposed re-introduction into that home of purity and honour of one who had brought upon it such a lasting shame. Knowing not the genuineness of the change that had passed upon the converted sinner he might well suspect it. He knew that his brother had abandoned his God, the guide of his youth, and his religious profession; and given himself up, to quote the Apostle's strong expression, "to work all uncleanness with greediness." He knew too that in a figure it was as easy for "an Ethiopian to change his skin or a leopard his spots" as for such a one to "cease to do evil and learn to do good."

And I think a certain suspicion on the part of the elder brother was in this case very justifiable. Such conversions as the prodigal's are by no means so common as some seem to think. This was a sincere one; but for a single instance that thus, as S. Peter says, "clean escapes from them that live in error," and by the grace of God arises again to amend his life, and gives his neighbours cause to glorify the grace of God in him, how many more are "again entangled therein and overcome." Our sympathies go of course entirely with the kind father as he points out to him the more excellent way, and the free forgiveness it behoved him, as us evermore, to show, as we would have forgiveness of our offences at God's hand. But at least let us imitate him in the deep sense he may seem to have entertained of the demerit of sin, and the dishonour it does to the Father of Heaven.

It was in such a spirit, and of such open sinners as this son had been, that the Apostle said to the Corinthians "Now I write unto you not to be a companion if any man that is called a brother be a fornicator, or covetous, or an idolater, or a drunkard, or an extortioner, with such an one no not to eat." It is a continually repeated command of our holy religion which bids us "be separate from sinners." And if he showed too little of the humility the Apostle enjoins when he says "Ye which are spiritual restore such an one in the spirit of meekness, considering thyself lest thou also be tempted"—if he thought of himself somewhat more highly than he ought to have thought, and of his brother somewhat less charitably—it is a far more general propensity to think of sin too lightly, and to tolerate its presence too easily.

But another thing we must notice with regard to the son's mood here. I said he might not yet be fully aware of the whole facts of the case with regard to his penitent brother. He had not seen his tears of godly sorrow, nor heard the humble confession that spoke to his father's heart. Nor could he know the keen emotions of sorrow and shame that rent his brother's bleeding heart, the load that bowed his head, and the sting of aggravated guilt that pierced his conscience.

But further than this the information he had received on the subject when "he called the servants and asked what these things meant," was imperfect. The servants knew something, but no more than he could they tell all. It was with them as Jesus said, "The servant knoweth not what his Lord doeth" We are struck with the difference between what *they* said to him, and what the *father* did, in explanation of his brother's reception. After all they only told the bare facts of the case, and even thus their remarks were not at all calculated to leave the impression that we think the father's would. He did well indeed to ask them. But the father had it in his power to throw a far more satisfactory light upon his own proceedings. Who knoweth the things of a man save the spirit of man, which is in him." We often notice how imperfectly others catch the spirit of our feeling or intention. And so it was with the servants. They knew the father had welcomed the younger son gladly and freely. But they spoke of it as though his satisfaction arose from his seeing him again "safe and sound," and not rather from the fact that he was receiving him again humble and dutiful penitent and reformed. But the father had another account to give about the unmerited reception. "This my Son was dead and is alive again; he was lost and is found." He rejoiced over him as one who was "alive from the dead," saved from temporal ruin and eternal destruction. Perhaps if the son had heard this from them at the first, and understood that the rejoicing and honourable reception, was not because the wretched vagabond was " safe and sound," (I always fancy there was a lurking sneer in those words of the servants), but because he was repentant and converted, he might have gone in at once in the first natural impulse of brotherly kindness and charity; and like his father forgotten the prodigal's misery and sin, in the delight with which he must, we think, in the end have hailed his restoration.

And what does this teach us but that if any man lack wisdom he should, as the Apostle bids him, ask of God. Are you in any doubt like this elder son, about God's deal:ngs with yourself or others? Does some difficulty in your hours of thought, and study of religion, weigh upon your mind and perplex you with uneasy and distrustful feelings? Do hard thoughts come into your mind about the justice or even the goodness of God, till you are ready to exclaim with the foolish ones of old with whom God condescended to argue the point so conclusively, " The way of the Lord is not equal ? " You admit that it is inexcusable to harbour such thoughts. But they sometimes force an entrance, and you long for satisfaction. Do what Elihu in the book of Job advises so well in all such circumstances : and say " That which I see not teach Thou me." Go to the Father. Consult Him in prayer. Ask Him to enlighten your mind, and establish your faith that He is doing all things well. Give His Word an attentive hearing while it shows how " righteous are His judgments, and how just and true are all His ways." " The law of the Lord is perfect, converting the soul : the testimony of the Lord is sure making wise the simple : the judgments of the Lord are true and righteous altogether."

And so we pass on to notice how the kind father dealt with his somewhat untoward, but on the whole not very unreasonable child.

Well could he feel his difficulty, and sympathize with all that indignation against sin, that for a moment had shut up his compassion against his brother. And so he dealt with him as tenderly as with the other. " In meekness instructing those that oppose themselves," is the way of God as well as that he has enjoined upon us. And this elder son's opposition was rather as we have seen mistaken than wilful. " Such an High Priest, Who can have compassion on our ignorance," and " help our infirmities " has God in mercy set over His Church. He will deal with His true and faithful disciples, as He did with James and John, when He cannot approve " the manner of spirit they are of ; " and kindly point out the source of their error, and the solution of their difficulty, that they may be grounded and settled. The father knew and felt that it was the very abhorrence of evil in which he had himself so diligently brought up his child, that made him turn away, and manifest a momentary lack of sympathy for the anguish of the penitent. He saw too how the evil spirit was taking occasion to whisper the suggestion that his past integrity was vain and his obedience little approved, if this other was now to be put on an equality. " What profit was there of all his labour wherein he had laboured," and what fruit had he of his many years true service ? Much every way the father could show him : and so he anxiously hastened to meet him with an assurance of his more happily favoured lot, to the quieting of his doubts, and the removal of all objection and disatisfaction.

"Therefore came his father out and entreated him." He would not leave him another moment in this unhappy and ungracious mood. He would not send him a message by the servants. But he would go himself. He would condescend in the most gentle way to show him how needless was his offence, and how unreal was his grievance. "He entreated him." Though he might, from the authority his relationship conferred, have "enjoined him that which was convenient yet for love's sake he would rather beseech him," as S. Paul said to Philemon.

And thus does God oftentimes with man. And how affecting is it to think of His assuming such an attitude! How might it humble and win over the proudest heart to think that the Almighty deigns for man's sake to become his suppliant! A strong lever as we all know is the force of entreaty! Solomon speaks our experience on this point in his sententious proverb "A soft tongue breaketh the bone." When a man will not listen to reason, when he will be moved by neither sense of duty nor power of love, he will oftentimes be open to *this* appeal. And thus you may very probably secure the desired favour, or gain the point you aim at. And as God stoops to use such a form of address Himself, so did He teach His Apostles to move us to obedience by a similar method. S. Paul, thus taught of the Spirit, wrote to the Romans, "I beseech you by the mercies of God that ye present your bodies holy acceptable unto God which is your reasonable service: and be not conformed to this world." So he addressed the Corinthians, "As though God did beseech you by us we pray you in Christ's stead be ye reconciled to God." And again, "We beseech you that ye receive not the grace of God in vain." So the Ephesians, "I beseech you that ye walk worthy of the vocation wherewith ye are called with all lowliness and meekness. So the Apostle Peter addressed the converts. "Dearly beloved, I beseech you as strangers and pilgrims, abstain from fleshly lusts which war against the soul." And so S. John addressed "the elect Lady and her children," when he wished to guard them against heresies and vices of the day, "I beseech thee Lady, look to yourselves that we lose not those things which we have wrought but that we receive a full reward." So to you does God speak by His Word and Ministers. I do not suppose the elder son, who had so long and faithfully served and obeyed his father, would be deaf to his entreaty here. You can hardly refuse the pleading application of the friend you love, and would wish to please. Surely you will not and cannot withstand it in your good Lord and Saviour. Incline ever your ear to His gracious and winning voice. Hear and your soul shall live.

THE ELDER SON—HIS COMPLAINT—AND HIS FATHER'S EXPLANATION.

PART III.

And he answering said to his Father, Lo, these many years do I serve thee, neither transgressed I at any time thy commandment: and yet thou never gavest me a kid that I might make merry with my friends. But as soon as this thy son was come which hath devoured thy living with harlots, thou hast killed for him the fatted calf. And he said unto him, son, thou art ever with me, and all that I have is thine. It was meet that we should make merry, and be glad, for this thy brother was dead and is alive again: and was lost and is found. *Luke* xv. 29-32.

Here stands the young man aloof and will not come near the door of the house. He is glad his father has come out, for he would fain hear his explanation. But he does not go to meet him. With a cloud upon his brow, and a reproachful look of mingled surprise, disappointment and displeasure, he waits to hear the rights of the tale, and to know what the strange things that the servants have brought to his ears can mean. And no sooner does the father approach him than he breaks out into this complaint. Why he wants to know this prodigality of rejoicing this lavishness of affection over a fellow, whom his father had hitherto held up to him as a beacon for his warning? This son of his—had he not despised his father's love, and squandered his goods, and defiled his honoured lineage and name? Might he not for his part appeal to him that it had been his joy to do his will, and that he had striven at least to honour him with the devotion of his best years and love? And surely he did not prefer the other that he had received him with the best of all his house could give, and killed for him the fatted calf! Did he envy his brother? It was "more than all" the love of that father, that it had been the satisfaction of his life to possess and that he prized so dearly, that made him do so! And then perhaps like Esau he lifted up his voice and wept at the thought that his younger brother, who had not sought it worthily and honourably as he, had as he thought supplanted him in the love and blessing of the parent he had lived for and served so faithfully.

Such I think is the spirit of his complaint. But when we come to consider the words themselves we cannot but see that they are hasty, foolish, and ill advised. Anger is a very unreasoning passion. And when it gains as here so thorough a mastery over self-control, the words uttered under its impulse will not fairly and adequately set forth the case. The intemperately angry man is sure to overreach himself, and to put a bar in the way of obtaining the fair hearing or just treatment he wishes for and is perhaps entitled to. In the simple but conclusive words of Solomon "The angry man dealeth foolishly."

In the son's complaint we observe there are three points. Firstly, what he had done. " Lo these many years have I served thee, neither transgressed I at any time thy commandment." Secondly, what he had missed. " He never had been given by his father a kid to make merry with his friends." Thirdly, how his undeserving brother had fared. " As soon as he was come he had killed for him the fatted calf."

And firstly, he desired his father to notice what he had done. He had earnestly set himself to do his bidding and gain his approval. It was an object he had all along prized and steadily pursued. And I take, for my part, but little notice of the self-asserting tone of this remark. If a person imagine himself aggrieved he is very prone, as we all know, to be somewhat vehement in self-vindication. Three of God's most worthy servants mentioned in Scripture are most striking examples of this—Job, Nehemiah, and S. Paul. And most men in such a temper of mind as this son now was " will proclaim (as the Proverb says) every one his own goodness " without your being thereby authorized to set them deliberately down as given to self-glorification. I do not therefore conclude that he was a self-righteous man because under these circumstances he spoke as he did. I bear in mind that he saw at the moment, as he thought, that his sincere and anxious efforts to do his father's will were passing unnoticed. And it is a keenly disappointing thing to find any whose commendation we highly value, and to do service to whom we have laboured patiently and long, unobservant. For I judge from the terms of evident disapproval in which he spoke of his brother's course that he looked upon the contrary part, the life of obedience, as that which he never had a wish to abandon for the pleasures of sin. I see not here any indication of wicked regret that he should have thus laboured in the ways of his father, even if his dutiful piety went for nothing. The Jews in Malachi's time thus profanely spoke of God's service as lost labour. "It is vain to serve God; and what profit is it that we have kept His ordinance and walked mournfully before the Lord of hosts? And now we call the proud happy; yea, they that work wickedness are set up, and they that tempt God are even delivered." The elder son was verging perilously near to this impiety. But he had evidently not deliberately adopted it. In his moment of doubt and unbelief he expressed himself as though he would say, " What was the fruit of his labour he wot not." He seems ready to ask, Is it true—as the preacher in Ecclesiastes had once concluded in the foolishness of his scepticism—"All things come alike to all; there is one event to the righteous and to the wicked, to the clean and to the unclean." I need hardly pause to controvert the saying. One of the first things to be believed about God, next to the fact of His existence, is, the Apostle tells us, that He is a rewarder of them that diligently seek Him." And few truths of the Bible are more clearly revealed or oftener repeated than that " Every man shall receive his own reward according to his own labour," and " He will render to every man according to his works." " Mine elect (God graciously promises) shall enjoy the work of their hands : they shall not labour in vain." As the younger son in sowing to the flesh reaped corruption, so the elder should in no wise lose his reward.   Much every way was the profit of his long true service.

And thus blessed supremely is that child of God who consecrates to Him betimes his service and his life. " Ye shall discern between the righteous and the wicked" He says in His Prophet Malachi.   For I will deal with the one "even as a man spareth his own son that serveth him."   You never indeed could or would to your Father in Heaven make such an appeal as this son here.   But still that gracious and indulgent Lord will be as forward to own you, as you in your heart to desire that acknowledgment, though, i n your consciousness of unworthiness, to disclaim it.   " I know thy love, and thy service, and thy faith, and thy patience."   Christ views His people as " complete in Him," and not as they must ever regard and feel themselves to be—at their best estate altogether vanity.   He is represented in the Song of Solomon as saying, " Thou art all fair ; there is no spot in thee."   And, as the Prophet Balaam said of them of old, we may still say of God's people, notwithstanding their manifold infirmities and failings, " He hath not beheld iniquity in Jacob, neither hath He seen perverseness in Israel."

From the self-justification of the elder son, I pass in the second place to his complaint, " And yet thou never gavest me a kid that I might make merry with my friends."   His father passes the remark by almost without notice.   And we might do so too with a simple observation of the folly as well as the sin into which murmurers and complainers fall ; and the force of that wise admonition " Be not hasty in thy spirit to be angry."   For this grievance could hardly have been a real one.   We cannot bring ourselves in any seriousness to think he had ever before been sensible of the deprivation he now mentions.   But there is one observation to be offered on this part of the son's speech, and a lesson to be drawn from it.   He says to his father " Thou never gavest me a kid."   But we read in the story " He divided unto them his living."   So the kid, we should have said, belonged to the elder son already : and why does he speak then of his father not giving it him ? It is plain from this that when the younger had renounced his father's control and supervision, the elder had very properly continued to submit his own part of the inheritance still to his father's authority.   He wisely saw and felt how well it would be for him to put his affairs wholly and unreservedly into his father's hands, to lean upon his wisdom, and be guided by his experience.

And this is ever the feeling of a dutiful and faithful child of God. He is thoroughly sensible of the significance of Christ's words " Without me ye can do nothing."   Beautifully does our Church counsel us to " submit ourselves wholly to Him, and be ordered by the governance of His Holy Spirit," " Order my steps in Thy word," " Do Thou undertake for me," " Without Thy mind would I do nothing," is the language of the Christian's heart and life.

> Direct, control, suggest this day
> All I desire, or do, or say ;
> That all my powers with all their might,
> In Thy sole glory may unite.

As we read of the believers after Pentecost, "Neither said any of them that ought of the things which he possessed was his own"—so make Him, as Pharoah did Joseph, "Lord of all your goods and ruler of all your substance." Think not to reserve any territory in your heart for yourself to be sovereign in, any prerogative in your life for yourself to dispose. But honour Him with your whole confidence, as One who can order your life with perfect wisdom, and lead you to the attainment of perfect success and happiness. "For as many as are led by the Spirit of God are the sons of God."

This son seems never to have felt before the least occasion for regretting this surrender of himself and property. When he comes to reflect on what he had missed in so doing, he could think of nothing more important than this trifling kid, and that, as we cannot but judge, was a mere pretence. So true is it that all things needful and desirable are the portion of His children. Those that freely give themselves to God freely receive from Him again. "For no good thing will He withhold from them that will live a godly life."

And now I pass on to consider thirdly the elder son's remark about his brother's favourable reception. And here we may excuse in him the hinting at his own prior claim to his father's regard, seeing it was so notably true. But as regards the standing of any of us in the sight of God, "Every mouth must be stopped," and all become (as regards idea of merit) alike guilty before Him. By His grace alone can any of us be justified in His sight. No years of obedience, no plea of outwardly blameless life, no reputation for upright and honourable conduct, such as he here pleaded with his father, can avail us as we seek to be accepted and approved before our Father in Heaven. "For though a man be never so perfect among the children of men, yet if Thy wisdom be not with him, he shall be nothing regarded." (Wisdom of Solomon ix., 6.) As that matchless hymn, in which every denomination of Christians in our land seems to find expression for its feeling of need and dependence on the Blessed One, says—

Nothing in my hand I bring,
Simply to Thy Cross I cling !
Vile, I to the Fountain fly ;
Wash me, Saviour, or I die !

And thus coming is there for any one unconditional pardon and immediate acceptance. The elder son remarks that as soon as he was come he was received and restored. We have reason to thank God for the encouraging truth conveyed in this word "as soon as." When one would be promoted to the office of Deacon in the Church, says S. Paul, "let him first be proved." Let him be designate to the office. And then being "found blameless, and having a good report" of all who know him, let him after a period of strict probation be received. And the elder son seems to have thought such would have been a more fitting proceeding in his brother's case. He would have doubtless said, as the other asked to be, let him become a hired servant, and thus having made full proof of his obedience, and testified the sincerity of his repentance, let him commend himself to his Father as worthy to become a son. And this is the mistaken course that many an anxious soul on first turning to God thinks of taking. But God's way of justifying is not as man's would be. He never intends to take us into His favour or family again (for this is the very error of Baptists in regard to Infant Baptism) for virtue of any obedience we have shown or can show, but only for the sake of Christ's. And so He would have this ground for self-confidence cut away from beneath us, by not allowing us the opportunity of showing it first; by justifying us as we are at the very moment we earnestly turn to Him; and in the matter of Baptism receiving us into His household the Church, and giving us the adoption of sons as early as those who value the blessing may seek it for us. It is not possible, as the ignorant might think, that repentance and reformation could qualify any for his naturally forfeited place among God's children. His past transgression, his sinfulness of nature, needs atonement, and has disentitled him for ever from restoration, even though he could become righteous for the future. Justification and adoption into the family of God *precede* the walking in newness of life. And then, by the constraint of love, and the drawing of the Holy Spirit, is the subject of Divine grace brought to " walk worthily of his vocation," and evince his gratitude by " walking religiously in good works."

But beside the general reception, there was one point in it to which the elder son took particular exception. " Thou hast killed for him the fatted calf." This setting such a dish before a guest, was considered the attributing to the person entertained a very marked and special honour or token of favour. It was thus that Abraham feasted his heavenly visitants, when showing hospitality to three wayfaring strangers he " thereby entertained angels unawares." And it was therefore well chosen by the father to set before the son in whose return in penitence he delighted. And yet this one thing the elder son did not relinquish willingly to his father who had given him so richly all things to enjoy. The calf he had no mind to part with, for he saw no sufficient reason for his being deprived of it.

And is not his temper and attitude of mind strikingly illustrative of that assumed towards God by many of His children when He has seen fit to take from them by an unlooked for visitation some specially valued earthly good? Are they not inwardly disposed to call upon God, as the son did here on his father, to show cause why they should be bereaved of that choice blessing in the possession of which they particularly rejoiced? That friend or relative whom He has put far from them perhaps by death, that acquaintance whom in an undesired removal He has taken from their sight, that position which in the course of providence they have been called upon to leave, that material comfort that had fallen to their lot that was gladdening their hearts— is it not all the grievance of the choice calf repeated in the successive history of God's children?

Be not you then unwilling to part with what God may recall. Grudge not aught you have of which the Lord has need. " Though there be no herd in the stall (says the Prophet) yet will I rejoice in the

Lord." God give you so to live with full trust in His mercy, and filial faith, that when such an hour of trial comes you may be enabled to say "Thy will be done: for Thine is the kingdom and the power!"

And now the father speaks with a fondness and tenderness, and a depth and sincerity of feeling that must have quickly, I think, reassured the mind, satisfied the every doubt, and met the every objection, of this elder son, as his gracious words had already done in the case of his younger. "Son, thou art ever with me, and all that I have is thine." As though he had said "Thou art my first-born, my might, the excellence of dignity and power." Thou art "my joy and crown of rejoicing," and in thee I have always been well pleased. All mine is thine, and I am glorified in thee. Thy labour is neither unnoticed nor unrecompensed. Thou hast my confidence. Thou art ever with me, my friend rather than my child: like-minded, and almost on the equality of the closest friendship. It was meet that we should make merry and be glad; for thy once lost and miserable brother is now humbled and penitent. Thou too will rejoice to hear it, he has bowed himself before the Father in Heaven as well as before me. He is now reconciled to God: and well therefore may we ratify our love towards him. For he whom God blesses is rightly blessed. He comes not, as he went, with a heart set on sin, but a new creature; to "live no longer to fulfil the desires of the flesh and of the mind," but "to do the will of God," and to "bring forth fruits meet for repentance."

And so we leave the elder son. "A soft answer turneth away wrath." And the full and conciliatory explanation chased, I doubt not, very soon the shadow from his ruffled brow and the darkness from his doubting mind. In the clear assurance of his father's love his heart must have been calmed into perfect peace, and he entered probably into a oneness of feeling and sympathy with his father that had never been his before. So soon in the land of light what we do not know now, we shall; so perfectly, when the explanations of eternity shall succeed to the mysteries of time, shall every perplexity be solved and every doubt be stilled. So surely, when the Sun of Righteousness shall shine forth, and nothing that is covered shall fail to be revealed, and nothing that is now hid shall escape from being known, shall God's wisdom be justified of all His children. Yea, there in that land of light each cries to his fellow, provoking him to fresh thanksgiving and renewed love, Holy, Holy, Holy, is the Lord God Almighty!

> Give to our God immortal praise,
> Righteous and true are all His ways.
> Wonders of grace to Him belong,
> Repeat His mercies in your song.

"Tell us, therefore, what thinkest Thou?"—*S. Matthew* xxii., 17.

When "What is truth?" we doubtful cry,
And Babel voices give reply;
Confused what to decide, or how,
We humbly ask, what thinkest Thou?

When, in our ignorance or doubt,
All Nature's light seems blotted out,
To Thee, Infallible, we bow;
"Light of the world," what thinkest Thou?

When oft the world's beguiling voice,
And maxims false would blind our choice;
In Thy consulted will and mind
The safeguard of our faith we find.

When foes malignant on us frown,
And proud ones look but coldly down;
Fresh courage from these words we feel:
What thinkest Thou? is our appeal.

And when condemned with words severe;
Yet in Thy sight if we are clear,
The sentence harsh we lightly deem,
If but approved in Thy esteem.

Shepherd of else but erring sheep,
We trusting own Thy thoughts are deep,
Thy judgment clear; so tell us now
And evermore, what thinkest Thou?

Thy word is sure, Thy wisdom tried,
By "all her children justified;"
We give to Thee the glory due,
The only Guide, all-wise and true.

A perfect understanding Thine,
Thy knowledge infinite, Divine;
Truth's diadem adorns Thy brow,
We therefore ask, what thinkest Thou?

Hugh Allan.

CHRIST ON THE IMITATION OF CHILDHOOD.

Jesus called a little child unto Him, and set him in the midst of them, and said
Verily I say unto you except ye be converted, and become as little children, ye shall
not enter into the kingdom of Heaven.   Whosoever therefore shall humble himself
as this little child, the same is greatest in the kingdom of Heaven.
S. Matthew xviii., 2-4.

The Church's service of Holy Baptism—whether that for Infants
or Adults, though it is the former I have occasion to refer to here—is
absolutely unrivalled except by that the highest and most perfect of all,
the Service for Holy Communion.   Every sentiment breathed in the
Service for Infant Baptism is simple, Scriptural, and sublime.   Every
representation it contains is in the highest degree engaging; every
appeal it makes affecting; every prayer is couched in terms of touching
power; and every emphasis is expressive.   The Gospel it selects for
the occasion is irresistibly tender; and the application of it in the
Exhortation sweetly persuasive.

We are especially charged to observe the good-will of our Heavenly
Father declared by His Son Jesus Christ towards infants, the weakest
and most unprofitable of all His creatures; to consider how by His
outward gesture and deed He declared His good-will towards them;
for He embraced them in His arms, laid His hands upon them, and
blessed them; and above all to remember " how He exhorteth all men
to follow their innocency."

I take this text, therefore, to remind us of, and enforce upon us,
that too much forgotten charge, and to show you how—in what way
and by cultivating what dispositions—we may act upon the counsel.

He called a little child unto Him, says S. Matthew, and set him in
the midst of His disciples.   He set him by Him—at His own side—
says S. Luke.   He took him in His arms, says S. Mark.   And each of
them tell how He bade them imitate the little child if they would be
great, or even have any place at all in the kingdom of Heaven.

Strange teaching! and yet of almost romantic beauty!   What He
could have meant we are attracted to ask with a sort of pleased surprise.
And we instinctively feel that the lesson from so kind and gentle a
Saviour, as Teacher, will be a winning one.

Let us begin by returning in imagination to the days of childhood.
We often do so.   Let me show you how and why by an illustration.

Which of us that has ever taken a long journey on foot, is not
aware of that instinctive feeling that has prompted us to pause, and
look back from time to time towards the point from which we started.
As we reach some eminence that commands a view of the road we have
trodden, and the now distant spot from which we came forth, how
natural the feeling that bids us turn to gaze upon it, and recall the first

moments of our departure, ere we press on afresh to the yet distant goal! As we become weary with the way, and our steps perhaps begin to falter in our doubtfulness of the yet untried road, with the toil of that which has been overpast, and it may be uncertainty about the scenes and persons, all strange to us, to which we are journeying—we know what it is thus to cast ever and again the lingering look behind.

In the journey of life such retrospect is equally instinctive. " The great Apostle in the midst of his labours and his grand career, thought upon the days when he spoke as a child, understood as a child, and thought as a child. Which of us has not done the same ? As we climb the steep ascent whereon the path is tracked which conducts us onward, how often do we look back and down into the plain as it were, on the scenery of early associations." (J. M. Bellew, in a sermon on the sanctity of childhood, which suggested this one, and from which some sentences here are quoted.) The impressions of childhood, effaced almost perhaps in the graver experiences of the days that followed, come vividly out in the foreground of memory at such a moment of thoughtful musing. We remember how we used to watch the smoke of the house that was in view from our nursery window curling over the adjacent roofs. We remember the very forms of the windows opposite that met our eye as we pursued our childish tasks. We remember the very figures of the passers by who have long since gone the way of all flesh, but whom we can never forget. Their looks, and occupations, and very bearing and attitudes, we recall with an undimmed power of recollection. We stand in a moment in fancy before the garden gate that bounded so strictly the roving steps of our childhood : and beyond which we were wont to gaze, with wondering awe and infinite longings, on the busy, but to us so distant, world of life. We see before us the adjoining lane where we watched the carts and cottagers go up and down; the adjacent fields where we played so merrily with brothers and sisters, some of whom perchance we are to see no more till the Great Father and Judge of all call us to meet before IIis throne. Before us are the sunny banks on which we sported, the meadows where we wove the daisy chain, and fashioned that marvel of our young delight the cowslip ball. And once more we climb to the window sill, or go forth with our nurse or mother to the hill or bridge from which we looked for the well known form, or listened for the familiar foot-fall, of " our father, returning homeward at the close of day."

Thus far our musings on our youthful days may be only a matter of sentiment. And yet it is a sentiment which can hardly be idle or vain, since it touches a chord that vibrates in the hearts of us all. When we come to feel that " among all the influences that operate upon us there is none so touching as that of childhood, we think there must be a value in the sentiment. But that sentiment expands into nobler proportions in the light of the text." And when we come to see that it is that which our Lord selected to appeal to on subjects of the mightiest moment—we cast away all suspicion of romance in dwelling upon it ourselves. In His treatment of it it is no bare sentiment, but a lesson as practical as beautiful.

And when or wherever was the lesson before us—I will not say so engagingly and strikingly drawn—but where indeed was it ever drawn at all? "It was reserved (says the before quoted preacher) for Him whose heavenly glory was, that He was a Son obedient to His Father who is in Heaven, whose earthly claim upon our love was that He was a Son, the Virgin's Child, of like nature with ourselves—it was reserved for Him who, whether we contemplate Him as Divine or human, is for ever associated in our minds as a Son, the Son of God or the Son of Man—to vindicate the honours and the deep significance of childhood; to make it the emblem of His holy religion upon earth, and its spirit the only warrant of greatness in Heaven."

Where, before the age of this wondrous Teacher, was the imitation of the comparative innocence and simplicity of childhood enforced by any human teacher upon the disciples of His faith?

And what is the import of the Master in doing so, and what are the characteristics of childhood that command this Divine regard and commend it to our notice? I shall mention three—Innocence, Humility (and included in this Docility), and Trustfulness.

And first Innocence. (Of course I mean comparative.) The young child "thinketh no evil." It is evil in its nature, and it yields to evil, and does evil. But it does not at first premeditate or design evil. It is entangled in the snare of the devil in a moment, and at first involuntarily. Until its conscience becomes enlightened it is with no knowledge that it is evil. Like Abimelech, in "the integrity of its heart and the innocence of its hands," it involves itself in that against which it has to be warned by the older and wiser who are aware of the consequences. It does that, and goes where, it ought not. But it means no harm, and suspects no evil, and is ignorant of devising it. And until it has learnt that "fear of man that bringeth a snare," it is candid, and outspoken, and truthful. It is almost a stranger to that ruinous dissimulation whereby we learn to consider "even good itself an evil, and indiscretion, if it appear impolitic in the eyes of the world," injurious to the self-interest of the hour, out of harmony with the sentiment of the company.

What does it know—and how happy is it in its ignorance—of that miserable worldly wisdom that corrupts the principles, and vitiates the aims, and silences the tongue, and masks the profession of the Christian faith and duty? What does it know of the "corruption that is in the world through lust" that we daily witness and deplore?

And childhood is distinguished for its humility, the great requisite and ever insisted upon element of Christian temper, arising from a sense of helplessness. The absence of pretension, the recognition of the ignorance and powerlessness of our fallen state, is the indispensable, but sure condition of pardon and salvation for us all. Whereas says our Saviour, "now ye say we see, therefore your sin remaineth." And so He warns the church of the Laodiceans, and every church and member of it that shares this self-righteous and therefore fatal confidence,

' Thou sayest I am rich and increased with goods, and have need of nothing, and knowest not that thou art wretched and miserable, and poor, and blind, and naked: I counsel thee to buy of Me."

The child, conscious of ignorance, knows that it must depend upon another for information, guidance, and direction : conscious of inability to provide for its own wants, it never ceases to look for sustenance and provision elsewhere beyond itself. If we could and would but learn to be like it in things spiritual, then were our salvation sure. For what the parent is to its mortal frame, that is or will the Father above be to the immortal spirits of us all. Indeed—thanks be to God for this glorious Gospel—whosoever shall humble himself as the little child shall be great in the kingdom of Heaven, and that with a greatness we cannot limit. He cannot look nor ask for too much. For the kingdom of Heaven is constituted after the pattern of the relation that parent and child stand in here. Provision is made for all man's spiritual helplessness and need, even to the uttermost. The acknowledgment of the one draws down the other : and the Father of Heaven comes forth with open arms and boundless store, to fill the wants of His dependent child. And the awakening the sense of dependence is the beginning and end of all Christian teaching. It is all that is meant by faith, or at least the feeling of which Faith is the outcome. If you can but be brought to possess and exercise it, simply and thoroughly as the little child, you are already and therefore great in the kingdom of Heaven. " In Thee, O Lord! I have put my trust: I shall never be put to confusion ;" never in the consciousness of sin, never under the accusations of the adversary, never in the hourly conflict of frailty with temptation, never in the hour of death, never in the day of judgment—the hour and the day when this the entire helplessness of man in the hand of the Great Parent of his being shall be felt and known as it never was by any of us before.

And in thus observing the *humility* of childhood, we are led to notice its *docility*. The little child is very yielding. With its hand in yours it is quite content to go where you whom it trusts may take it, and turn where you may lead. I know well how soon the spirit of wilfulness will develop itself. The doctrine of the Bible is " They go astray as soon as they are born." But still it is not at first disposed to assert a claim of choosing or judging for itself about its ways and occupations. It gives way readily to your powers of selection and decision, which it instinctively recognises as superior to its own. Could the Saviour have taken an apter, a more almost perfect symbol of the attitude of spirit which becomes and marks the child of God. " I am Thine : O save me !" " Lord I will follow Thee whithersoever Thou goest !" " Thou art my defence and my refuge." " Lo I come to do Thy Will O God !" " It is not in man that walketh to direct his steps." " Thou shalt be the Guide of my life." " Be it unto me according to Thy Word."

And so we pass to the trustfulness of childhood. For in this our ignorant imperfect life we too, like the little child, walk by faith. We know not, nor can we understand the aims and purposes of that August

Being in whose governance we are as passive as the child in its parent's power. Only let us learn that child's submission. "It puts forth obedience and receives back protection." And if we are but content to be ordered as He shall see good, and know no Will but His—we are safe, and of as great account in the kingdom of Heaven, as the docile trusting child in the eyes of its wise and tender guardian. Do we think sometimes that it must be very hard to enter into the kingdom of God? This one thing which of us is there that cannot do—cast ourselves on the Infinite resources of the compassionate Father, and His Son, our Lord Jesus Christ, in the recognition of the truth we have thus already begun to feel " Without Me ye can do nothing?" And "the Eternal God shall be the refuge "of His trusting child," and underneath him the everlasting arms. What man if his child ask food will do otherwise than supply him? So likewise, with the same loving and liberal readiness, will your Heavenly Father give to them that need and ask Him.

Do but picture to yourself in conclusion the look and attitude of that confiding child, whom Jesus took and set in the midst of His disciples—set by His own side, and took in His own arms—and translate it into the life of your own spirit. And you shall have learned the lesson and ensured the blessing of the text.

Fancy him set in the midst of that strange throng! turning upon them his wondering eyes, and clinging to Jesus- with the instinctive intelligence which taught the winds and sea to obey ; and the unbroken colt, whereon yet never man sat, to submit itself to His blessed and gentle Will! There is the loving Jesus, whom the little child had never probably seen, known, or heard of before. And He lifts him, with the Good Shepherd's tender touch, and sets him by His side. And the lamb knows His voice, and trusts His care, and shrinks not from the strange position. And if perchance his guileless eyes look up appealingly in a momentary apprehension to his unknown Protector—the light of love that beamed so softly and yet so grandly from that gentle Eye re-assures his hesitating soul.

> See the kind Shepherd Jesus stands
> With all engaging charms !
> Lays on the child His gracious Hands,
> And folds him in His Arms.

The little child could not know or imagine the meaning and extent of those wondrous words that followed which no expounder or interpreter of Scripture has ever fathomed. " Even so :t is not the will of your Father which is in Heaven that one of these little ones should perish," and " I say unto you that in Heaven their Angels do always behold the face of My Father." But they soothed, we may be sure, his throbbing heart ; and they charmed away his infant fears, as the mighty throng pressed round to gaze upon the little child enfolded in the caress of its Maker's arms.

So let that same Good Shepherd with His gentle constraint of love lay hold upon you, the wayward, the wilful, the worldly, the wandering.

And all the strangeness of experience that you think you must go through will vanish. He may be as unknown to you in reality, though you have heard so much of Him by the hearing of the ear, as He was up to that day to the little child. But the heart of man, of each of us, happily answers very soon to its Maker's when the Spirit of God reveals Him to the soul. It takes us, it may be, long years to know and trust a stranger. And which of us is quite sure of our nearest friend? We only half trust the sympathy of any, and only half believe in their good-will towards us. It shall not be so in our experience of our Redeemer. Who ever that came near shrank or could shrink from His loving presence? Who ever found himself in a strange or uneasy state as he drew near that attractive Being who is gradually drawing "all men unto Him," and who so retains the spirit when it is once drawn within the circle of His influence as to enable it to say " I am persuaded that nothing shall be able to separate me from the love of God which is in Christ Jesus our Lord."

Thrice happy and great and honourable those among us who in the consciousness of their own insufficiency, but in full reliance on the wisdom, and might, and love of their Father and Protector above, cling confidingly, and lovingly, and undoubtingly to Him as the children of their Redeemer!

CHRIST THE INTERPRETER; OR, THE REPORTERS OF THE GALILEAN MURDER.

There were present at that season some that told Him of the Galileans, whose blood Pilate had mingleh with tdeir sacrifices.—Luke xiii. 1.

The multitudes that pressed upon our Lord to listen to His discourses, and be the eye-witnesses of His actions, included, as we know, persons of every variety of character and every possible state of mind. The wisdom of the one none could dispute. For, even His adversaries themselves being judges, never man spake like that man. And the power of the other was equally undeniable. For in this the universal testimony alike of favour and prejudice was agreed that " it was never seen before on this fashion." And thus alike believers and unbelievers, those who simply wondered at Him, those who wished for further satisfaction about Him, those who were drawn by the most earnest and humble desire for instructiou, those who affected to despise, and those who more openly opposed and would have crushed Him— came eagerly into His presence, and sought most anxiously for opportunities of conversing and becoming acquainted with Him.

The consideration of the text will afford us an instance of the widely different spirit iu which the same subjects were proposed and inquired into by the various classes of our Lord's followers. It was then as now some "worshipped Him, and some doubted ;" some mocked, and others said " We will hear Thee again of this matter."

A startling and " horrible thing had been committed in the land ;" and the awful tragedy had raised the minds of the people to a state of painful excitemeut. Every mouth, as it is always in such cases, was full of the story. And free expression was given to the popular feeling of indignation at the outrage, abhorrence of the cruel act, and terror of the lawless Governor of Judæa.

And as the Great Prophet among them had always appeared to invite inquiry of every kind, to be ready to express His opinion to the avoiding of all scruple and doubtfulness, and to give a clear intimation of the Divine counsel on all matters of faith or practice—there were many that hastened to bring this one before Him. We find from Scripture it was a part of the Prophetic office to promote a judicial satisfaction among the people, as well as righteousness and true holiness. We read " They were wont to ask counsel of the seer" (the old name for the prophet), and so they ended the matter. "The Prophet's judgment was in Israel what the Apostle says " the oath in controversy" is generally, " an end of all strife." And so it was a point to which Jesus devoted a singular attention to hear the communications, to solve the difficulties, and to unravel the perplexities of all who came confessing His superior wisdom, and ready to bow to His superior authority.

And so to Jesus of Nazareth were propounded all the vexed questions of the day: The problems of ecclesiastical casuistry, decisions of a legal nature, arbitrament between political parties, the settlement even of domestic differences, were referred to Him, as to One Whose wisdom was unequalled in Judæa, and Whose justice was absolutely unimpeachable.

So too, the story of the Galilean worshippers who in the midst of their solemn service were suddenly surprised by Pilate's soldiers and cut to pieces with the slain victims of sacrifice before the Altar of God —was told in the ears of the Lord of that Altar who was Himself a Galilean. The particulars of the tragedy are not revealed, nor are they at all important to my present purpose, which is only to inquire into the spirit of the narrators, and the spirit of the hearing they received from Christ.

The spirit in which we come ourselves before the Lord is always of great moment. And if through that of others we may gain an insight into our own, and be guided to observe the direction our thoughts and feelings within ought to take, or are improperly taking, the subject will be to us as profitable as it must be instructive! May the Spirit of God, as we consider the text, make it so to us now.

And firstly there were those who related the tragedy to our Lord in a spirit of dismay and altogether bewildered feeling. "The thing that is done upon earth He doeth it Himself." This is one of the first principles of revelation. Every mind that admits an overruling Providence feels the force of this that " the Lord reigneth, be the earth never so unquiet;" and that without His notice and permission is not anything done that is done, whether good or evil. And yet the events that actually occur in this disordered world, whose very foundations seem out of course, are so strange and startling—so abhorrent oftentimes to the whole mind of God—that astonishment is only the natural attitude of the beholder. Judgment is in every sense, as the Scripture saith, God's strange work ; and not the least so those judgments that befall the world as it goes on in its natural and daily course. They are most truly—and felt by us all to be—past finding out. And most of all are those so which relate to God's Church and people. That God, as Elihu says, should strike wicked men in the open sight of others, because they turn back from Him and will not consider His ways, may occasion us no surprise. But that He should permit His worshippers to suffer in a similar way was a puzzle through all the ages of the world—as it was to those who came to tell their Lord how it had befallen the worshippers of His Father—until it was seen that His well-beloved Son in whom He was always pleased had to undergo a similar discipline. And then, that became a part of the Church's privilege of faith, and has ever since been unquestioned which before was dimly and more hesitatingly recognized. So David exclaims somewhat doubtfully "Surely Thou hast seen it; for Thou beholdest ungodliness and wrong." So the Prophet Habakkuk, "Thou art of purer eyes than to behold iniquity ; wherefore hidest Thou Thy tongue when the wicked devoureth the man that is more righteous than he." To still this doubtful questioning of the soul Solomon says, "If thou seest the oppression of the poor, and violent perverting of judgment and justice in a province, marvel not at the matter ; for He that is higher than the highest regardeth it, and there be higher than they." Indeed the truth was admitted by one here and there in far earlier times. For in the days of Job Eliphaz the Temanite set himself to enforce it on his doubting friend. "Behold, happy is the man whom God correcteth ; therefore despise not thou the chastening of the Almighty." And Moses said to Israel "Thou shalt also consider in thine heart, that, as a man chasteneth his son, so the Lord thy God chasteneth thee."

And though this be ascertained now beyond a doubt, there are moments when to the thoughtful and really believing soul the old perplexity will recur. The old difficulty of Job, " The earth is given into the hand of the wicked. If not, where and who is He the Judge of the world ?" still makes itself felt. And the inquiry of the suffering wife of Isaac, " If it so be why am I thus ?" is still repeated. If it be so, if God is loving and "a rewarder of them that diligently seek Him," why is it thus with me, and why so with the world ? Why do I seek my Father and His kingdom sorrowing, while my heart is staggered, and my faith so sorely tried with the sight of the world misgoverned or the Church betrayed ?

" The faithful are minished from among the children of men," while "the wicked are increasing ever more and more." Pilate triumphing, and the unavenged and hapless Galilean failing and crushed, instead of outwardly accepted and blessed, in his deed of sacrifice and worship, do you not see the old marvel still ? Ever is it repeated all through the Church's history, all through the Christian's experience. "And yet Thou continuest silent, O Thou Worship of Israel !"

We naturally think it strange that Jesus should have taken so little notice of the story then: that not only was His arm not outstretched to smite the proud persecutor and avenge His Galilean brethren *at the time*, but that *even then* when the impiety of the unrighteous and cruel Pilate was fully declared to Him, and the blood of the murdered worshippers cried to Him in the voice of those that reported their murder, —no direct condemnation was uttered nor immediate response made to the appeal. Manifestly our Lord meant in that hour to plainly teach, as He did afterwards by the vision at the opening of the fifth seal in the book of Revelation, that for a short season still the Church and each disciple of Christ must be content to rest in faith, committing a cause that He holds no less dear than they, in full assurance of His wisdom and eventual succour, into the hands of " Him that judges righteously."

How long, O Lord, how long? they cry,
Beneath Thine Altar, day and night,

> Who with deep yearning hearts await
> The fulness of celestial light.
>
> How long, O Lord ? creation cries :
> The tribes of men take up the strain ;
> When shall the poor oppressed go free,
> The captive cast away his chain ?

Well may we wait His time.   For, says the Prophet Isaiah, and S. Matthew repeats the saying, " He shall not fail nor be discouraged till He have set judgment in the earth."

> And when His wisdom can mistake,
> His might decay, or love forsake—
> Then may His children cease to sing
> The Lord Omnipotent is King.

But among the multitude who pressed upon the Saviour's attention the direful tale of the Galilean slaughter were some, we doubt not, in the second place whose apprehensions had been roused on behalf of Himself.   With hearts full of tender concern they lost not a moment in repairing to Him they had learnt to revere and love, to give Him timely warning of His danger in Jerusalem; little thinking how unfailing were His own resources, and that Pilate, as He afterwards told that tyrant to his face, could have no power at all against Him except it were allowed from above—they took upon themselves to put Him on His guard.   Their views of His person and nature must have been most unworthy.   He was wiser, says S. John, than to commit Himself to them : for He knew all men, and needed not that any should testify of man.   No man could take His life from Him against His will, seeing as God He was beyond the reach of the will and power of man. But for all their ignorance and littleness of faith their love to their Lord was true.   And therefore—although the idea they entertained was derogatory to His character, and even dishonouring to His work and Himself—He intimated His disapproval of the spirit that incited them to the narrative of the Galilean tale, only in the gentlest way, by a suggestive silence.   " He will not be always chiding."   He had answered the very same error on one occasion in the severest language when S. Peter took and began to rebuke Him for His intention of going to Jerusalem to certain death.   But there was not quite the same presumption here.

Still it was very foolish and altogether wrong to think it devolved on them to guard Him.   So S. Peter did when he drew his sword in his Master's defence, to smite the High Priest's company, in the garden of Gethsemane, and was again rebuked.   Yet there was a solicitude about the safety of Jesus that we cannot but admire, a humble appeal, as it were to Him that He would preserve to them the life they held so dear. The feeling that prompted them was like that with which His disciples said when He was going to Bethany to raise Lazarus, " Master, the Jews of late sought to stone Thee : and goest Thou thither again ?"

How loving is our Master! And how tenderly does He deal with His weak disciple! Like the Good Shepherd that takes the feeble in His arm, and gently leads those with young—like the father, that when He might reprove some fault of an erring child, forbears if he knows only that he is striving to do his best, and earnestly desiring to know and follow the more excellent way, "lest (as the Apostle cautions parents) their child should be discouraged" — so does the long-suffering Jesus. He "comforts the feeble-minded, supports the weak, and is patient toward all." Be your ignorance that of a babe, your simplicity that of a child, your apprehensions and views of His power and Himself as elementary as these by-standers', yet if you come to Him with their attachment and confidence as all your salvation and all your desire, you shall never be despised. He will take you, as it were by the hand, and lead you on to a riper knowledge and a clearer faith. For "to him that hath shall more be given."

With a similar object to induce our Lord to flee from the neighbourhood where such lawless crime might seem rife, and such a general insecurity prevailing, but prompted by a far different motive, there was a third party who united in carrying this tale to the ears of Jesus. And our Lord, who could discern things that differ, and knew they told Him only because they wanted Him *gone*, as the others had done simply because they wanted Him *safe*, treated them in a very different manner. They came to Him like the Gergesenes, and though ashamed to confess their wish for His departure so openly as they, He saw the language of their hearts was also "Depart from us, for we desire not the knowledge of Thy ways."

These were the irreligious men who in every age—how many do we know and see, and how do the hearts of some of ourselves perhaps inwardly respond to this feeling of impatience—can scarcely or at all tolerate the restraints of religion and the Bible. Like the bullock, the Prophet tells us of, unaccustomed to the yoke, "they kick against the pricks", the driver's goad. Conscience is an unwelcome inmate, whose voice they would gladly stifle ; the Sabbath, and the worship of God it calls them to, is a weariness to them. They say of it, as the Prophet Amos tells us, When will it be gone, the prayers over, the sermon finished, that we may get to our buying and selling again, our business or our pleasure. And the Minister or the man of God, whoever he may be, is to them a Michaiah. Like Ahab, somehow or other they hate him. Evermore he that is not of the light hates the light. The words, the bearing, the very presence, of the godly he shrinks from. He is like the bird of darkness, like the burrowing mole, or the worm of the clod in the atmosphere of day. Bring the religious atmosphere to bear upon him and he is manifestly uncomfortable, and would fain evade it. The word of the just is a reproof to such, his silence a reproach. And they say of him as Amaziah, the man of Bethel, did of Amos to the King, "The land is not able to bear all his words."

With wonderful power and knowledge alike of Scripture and human nature does John Bunyan describe in the trial and condemnation of Faithful the feelings of such towards the Christian:—"Said Mr.

Malice, I hate the very look of him.   Aye, said Mr. Love-lust, I could never endure him.   Nor I, said Mr. Liveloose, for he would be always condemning my way.   My heart riseth against him, said Mr. Enmity. Let us dispatch him out of the way, said Mr. Hatelight."

If we go back to a far older source, from which I am inclined to suppose this description taken, the oldest religious book in the world after the inspired Old Testament, we read in the Apocrypha how the ungodly said "The righteous is not for our turn, and he is clean contrary to our doings: he upbraideth us with our offending the law, and objecteth to our infamy.   He professeth to have the knowledge of God: and he calleth himself the child of the Lord.   He was made to reprove our thoughts.   He is grievous unto us even to behold: for his life is not like other men's, his ways are of another fashion.   We are esteemed of him as counterfeits: he abstaineth from our ways as from filthiness."   (Wisdom ii., 12-16.)

So came these men to Christ.   But not perhaps daring, from the estimation in which he was held, to be so outspoken, they hinted in their tale, which they eagerly brought as most apt for their end, how expedient it was for him to go away.   For was not He too a Galilean? And as a notable one, and a religious one too, often in the temple, might He not fall a victim to Pilate's enmity or revenge?   For Pilate was at known enmity with Herod the Tetrarch of Galilee.   This might even have had something to do with his late assassination of Herod's subjects.

Our Lord, however, deigned them no reply.   Most artfully was "their wickedness covered with deceit, but in the end (according to the true Proverb) it was showed before the whole congregation."   And when at the end of this same chapter, on the very same occasion, some of the Pharisees felt themselves constrained—if they would hope for any chance of success in this way—to use greater plainness of speech, and said "Get Thee out, for Herod will kill Thee"—our Lord, who does sometimes withstand to the face those that are so foolhardy as to fight against Him, bade them open defiance.   He would neither go out of Galilee to escape Herod, nor keep away from Judæa to avoid Pilate. "He said unto them, Go ye and tell that fox, Behold, I do cures to-day and to-morrow;" as though to say I shall continue my work in spite of thy malice and guile until it shall be "perfected," and at the appointed time I lay down my life.   For "I have power to lay it down, and power to take it again."

How dreadful it must be to be exposed in the act of rejecting God's Son, and the driving out His Spirit, and the putting from us His salvation—we may here take warning.   "He that rolleth a stone it will return upon him."   And if that stone be the chief and precious corner stone that God has in mercy laid to be the foundation and object of our faith, and any of us, like the builders the Prophet and Apostle tell us of, should reject it in their spirit, "We will not have this Man to reign over us," upon whomsoever that Stone shall fall it will grind him to powder.

As Moses charged Israel with reference to this gracious, glorious, and at the same time awful Being, "Beware of Him, obey His voice, provoke Him not," as these His wilful rejecters. There is none other Name given under heaven whereby you can be saved than His. "There remaineth no more sacrifice for sin" if you secure not the benefit of this. "Be wise now therefore lest He be angry, and ye perish from the right way if His wrath be kindled," as here.

We have had a repulsive picture in the portrait of these last relaters of the Galileans' end, though one that has suggested deeply practical lessons. And yet I think there was even a fourth class among those that brought these tidings to Jesus, of more wicked and hardened spirit still. I fear, looking at this in the light of kindred passages in our Lord's life, the inference is too plainly supportable that there were some who turned the story to a still baser purpose, and made it the vehicle and expression of a yet more bitter enmity and avowed hatred to the Nazarene of Galilee.

There was, we know, a feeling of prejudice and contempt for Galilee, in Judæa. And we find from the Evangelists that the reproaches of those that reproached these fell on Him. The Prophet Isaiah hints at the existence of such a feeling even in his day. And it found expression in such sayings as "Can any good thing come out of Nazareth?" "Out of Galilee ariseth no Prophet."

And it would seem as though some felt a malicious triumph in telling of the Galileans' tragic end, as though they would mock their enemy with the slaughter of His Galilean countrymen, "There, there so would we have it" with Thee too, Thou Galilean! And so we will, some day. Even then were many conspiring to take away His life, and marking Him out as a "sheep appointed for the slaughter." They spoke even then perhaps in the sure and certain hope of the accomplishment of their dark design, in diabolical anticipation of the time when, by the sufferance of this same wretched Pilate, the innocent blood of a Galilean worshipper should yet again be mingled with the sacrifices of the people at the high festival of the Jewish Church. And indeed if such was the purport of their words they came true at last. Alas, too true! The words, whether or no indicative of their design, have at all events a Caiaphas-like significance.

But what lesson from the mocking and threatening tone of these blood-thirsty and avowed enemies of our Lord shall I gather for ourselves? Notwithstanding the Apostle's notice of those who by a reckless course of bold impenitence or persistent backsliding, "crucify in a sense the Son of God afresh, and put Him to an open shame," we feel instinctively, and I think not incorrectly, that these men stand in history almost alone. And wondering at the blindness of their bigotry and the darkness of their malignity, we start always with fresh horror as we read of those that "crucified the Lord of glory." Through all ages their crime will command, as it has done, the world's universal detestation. And I certainly wish and mean to press no comparison here. I do not even suggest it. For I fully grant you will never, thank God you never can, commit the unpardonable sin of some of these. They had the most powerful drawing and witness of the Spirit in the attractive and visible exhibition of the exceeding great love of our Master and only Saviour. And they shut their eyes, and closed their ears, and hardened their hearts against the acknowledgment of the truth and their own salvation until they filled the measure of an iniquity which the world shall never see repeated, and are set, if I may so say, on a pedestal of solitary, almost unapproachable, crime, as having sinned against the Holy Ghost. I add one word only here. "Because of unbelief *they* fell: and *thou* standest by faith. Be not high-minded, but fear." Take heed lest your hearts become gradually and insensibly "hardened through the deceitfulness of sin."

One other class there was among our Lord's informants: and their error He set Himself at once to refute. This was those who were in heart referring the late judgment to some supposed crying sin for which, though it had escaped the observation and punishment of men, "the vengeance of God had suffered them not to live." From the days of Eliphaz there had been lingering a belief in the religious mind that sudden and swift destruction was a proof of God's particular wrath against the sufferer. I need not say how many and just were the grounds for this conclusion, which nevertheless was pressed much too far. "Who ever perished (said he), being innocent? or when were the righteous cut off?" And so these, coming before the Lord with the self-complacent spirit of the Pharisee, God be thanked we are not as other men are, not with humble gratitude for that adorable grace which alone makes any of us to differ—were met and at once checked by the startling assurance, "Except ye repent ye shall all likewise perish."

May God write this warning upon our minds too—especially on any of us who may be inclined to be self-satisfied and self-reliant—and give us "repentance unto life." And as the blood of these Galilean worshippers in their cruel death was mingled with the temple sacrifices, so may the blood of that other and far greater Galilean, the crucified Jesus, be mingled with the else unavailing sacrifice of our faith and obedience, prayer and praise, repentance and devotion. And so shall our poor, weak, and unworthy services, and the living sacrifice of our life's work be rendered—what otherwise they cannot be, but what thus they shall verily become—"a sacrifice acceptable to God through Jesus Christ our Lord."

"Master, we know that Thou art true."—*St. Matthew* xxii., 16.

They gather round in envious strife,
The foes that watched His blameless life ;
With their feigned doubts, one thing they knew,
Master, that Thou art surely true.

Grand witness to Thy glory, Lord,
Which all Thy tempters thus record ;
Diverse their parties, one their view,
Master, we know that Thou art true.

E'en thus while party watchwords range
Opposing hosts, in conflict strange,
Unvarying as then, so now,
Master, we own how true art Thou.

Whate'er of new time's teaching bring,
To this confession will we cling,
And steadfastly affirm all through
Master, we know that Thou art true.

E'en thus as oftentimes we find
The trusted human guide but blind,
The firmest fail, faith's leaders few ;
Master, we know that Thou art true.

E'en thus as on the wisest friend
We learn how little to depend,
We turn with comfort ever new,
Master, to Thee, for Thou art true.

E'en thus as earthly prospects fade,
And disappointment's gloomy shade
Obscures hope's evanescent hue,
Master, we know that Thou art true.

E'en thus as doubting and perplexed,
We sometimes falter, pained and vexed,
Life's tangled path has one clear clue,
Master, we know that Thou art true.

HUGH ALLAN.

THE SAVIOUR'S LAMENT OVER JERUSALEM.

Matthew xxiii., 37, and *Luke* xix , 41-44.

The time of the end is always in human things a time of increased preparation and redoubled earnestness. No matter how thoroughly we may have been working up to it, the consciousness of its approach stirs to the more diligence and heedfulness. In all worldly business and all human engagements as the crisis draws on there are signs of unwonted effort and heightened interest. Our Lord was perfect Man. And so we observe the same symptoms in Him as the great event of His human life and of the world's life drew on. As His hour neared, "a deeper seriousness (says the late Rev. Denis Kelly in a sermon on the same subject) appears to characterize His teaching. His parables have a more pointed significance. His warnings and threatenings are louder. His expostulations are more tender. His words and acts betray an inward conflict of feeling which is most affecting. His heart seems moved with a positively unutterable compassion towards the deluded people. And His indignation rises proportionately against the blind guides at whose door the greater guilt of the national rejection lay, those who had been their deceivers and destroyers." And yet even when His indignation is at the highest a gust of uncontrollable sorrow breaks forth from Him. And now that they had reduced themselves to that hopeless condition that the Son of God Himself, as it would appear, could do no more than bewail their incorrigible obstinacy, He gives expression to His regret in that burst of anguish conveyed in the text.

> 'Tis evening over Salem's towers,
>   A golden lustre gleams,
> And lovingly and lingeringly
>   The sun prolongs his beams.
> He looks as on some work undone,
>   For which the time is past,
> So tender is his glance and mild
>   It seems to be his last.
>
> But a brighter Sun is looking on ;
>   More earnest is His eye.
> For thunder clouds will veil Him soon,
>   And darken all the sky.
> On Zion's hill He bends as loth
>   His presence to remove,
> And on her walls there lingers yet
>   The sunshine of His love.

'Tis Jesus ! with an anguished heart
  A parting glance He throws,
For mercy's day she has sinned away
  For a night of dreadful woes.
O would that thou hadst known, He said,
  While down rolled many a tear,
My word of peace in this thy day ;
  But now thine end is near !

Alas ! for thee, Jerusalem,
  How cold thy heart to Me !
How often in these arms of love
  Would I have gathered thee !
My sheltering wing had been thy shield,
  My love thy happy lot.
I would it had been thus with thee ;
  I would, but thou wouldst not.

"There can be no question that our Lord in His human nature had an especial regard for the land singled out for His kinsmen according to the flesh by the Providence of God, and selected as the land of His own birth. There can be no question that the strongest and most fervent expressions of attachment to the land and her people which are contained in the sacred oracles found a ready response in our Lord's bosom. "The Lord loveth the gates of Zion more than all the dwellings of Jacob. Very excellent things are spoken of thee, thou city of God. Beautiful for situation, the joy of the whole earth, is Mount Zion." It was the place where the Virgin Mother watched over His slumbering infancy. It was the home of His innocent childhood and stainless youth. And who can picture the peacefulness of that bright and holy home in Nazareth which was adorned for years by the very presence of Divinity. In that town were those with whom He took His walks of holy meditation. Who may have been the persons that shared occasionally that blessed companionship, and walked with the youthful Saviour through the glens and vales of Nazareth, heard Him sweetly and engagingly dwell on the teachings of nature around, and gently lead the heart of the wrapt listeners up to nature's God ? Who gathered from His young lips the interpretation of the ways and work of His Father, the Creator and Upholder of all around ? What old men or women of Nazareth were wont, as they passed Him in their village streets, to look wonderingly on that strangely beautiful but calm and collected face ? and, as they halted onwards to their not distant tomb, see the light of the life beyond dawn on them through those clear and speaking eyes ? Which of its busy cottagers were wont to ponder the salutation of blessing that would fall from His kindly lips as He passed them by, and carry on from His presence thoughts of a higher and a nobler life, amid the engrossing occupations of their own ? Who were the young man and maiden, that would pause in the impetuosity of that period of our years when the pulse of life is throbbing quick and high, to learn from His winning lips the lesson they will hardly ever be persuaded to learn from ours—the importance and blessedness of moderating their over eager affections and chastening their over sanguine expectations ? Who were the little

children that would leave their childish sports to gather around the
knees of that gentle and holy One who could guide heavenward their
young thoughts, and desires, and hopes as no other could—who could
tell them, with words such as never other man spake to fascinate the
roving attention of childhood, the sacred stories of their land or their
people?   Why was no record kept of such interviews and scenes which
amid all the books, of the making of which, as the wise man says, there
is no end, we feel would in this Christian age command the study, and
enthrall the interest of myriads?   Aye, it was kept, only the record is
above.   And even the Bible *here*, over which uncounted generations
have lingered with admiration no eloquence could tell, is but a mere
page to the volume *there* kept in store for our future perusal.   Who
would not pray and strive to be of that blessed number who shall hear
from myriad lips, touched with the inspiration of heaven, the recital of
that wondrous grace, and love, and life of which we have the barest
outline now!

But we return to the thought of our Saviour's interest in the land
of His birth.   "There must (says the author before quoted, some
few more paragraphs of whose discourse on this subject I shall add)
have been spots in that land associated in His mind—a mind of such
sensibility—with touching recollections which softened, if aught there
were to soften, His pilgrimage of woe.   There were those hallowed
spots where He held sweet communion with His heavenly Father. There
were those calm retreats where He retired so oft and lingered all night
long in prayer.   In that land also were many whom in His human
nature He loved with the tenderest regard.   Though it was an evil
generation, yet there were many of His Father's dutiful children there.
Amias, Zacharius, Elizabath, Nathaniel, the Marys, Lazarus and his
sisters, and many who followed Him from Galilee, not exceptional cases
of piety, but rather samples of a numerous class.   And dear to Him
was all that was sacred in the land.   No less than any of us could He
say—

> And dear to me the winge 1 hour
> Spent in Thy hallowed courts, O Lord ;
> To feel devotion's soothing power,
> And catch the manna of Thy word.

Dear to Him were the Sabbaths and synagogues, and above all that
glorious Temple, the special residence of Him from whom He came, and
to whom He so longed to return that He said—and to my mind it is
one of the most touching utterances of His own personal life—" If ye
loved Me ye would rejoice, because I go to the Father."   None that
ever trod its courts breathed forth more fervently than He, the Psalmist's
ejaculation, "How amiable are Thy dwellings, Thou Lord of hosts."
And there is more still to make us feel His human attachment for that
than the glory of all lands.   His beautiful addresses, His allusions, His
imagery, His parables, His expressions of admiration of the works of
nature, of the garniture of the fields, of the lilies of the valley—all con-
strain us to think that He must have gazed with a fond and partial eye
on all that was fair, and sublime, and picturesque in that land.   Dear

to Him, we are thus assured, were its verdant fields, and cloudless skies, and balmy airs, and peaceful vales, and snow-clad mountains, and golden sunsets, the land which God Himself called a delightsome land. It was the land of miracles and of Angel visitants for which He had laboured, and watched, and prayed without ceasing, and was providing for even still. For it His chief miracles had been wrought and His discourses uttered. At Jacob's Well at Sychar He showed how dear this labour was to Him. And the joy that He felt in Simon's house over the mourning penitent proclaimed it." He loved the people "for their fathers' sakes." And there is a peculiarity and intensity of feeling in such love (of the offspring for the sake of the parent) as possibly we may know, which was singularly shown in Him.

And now when compelled to abandon them as incorrigible, with a burst of anguish, which we in the guardedness and reserve peculiar to our nation should never have expected, He pronounces His last farewell in the text. Those tears of the Saviour are dried. The bitterness of His grief for Zion is overpast. Shall they be caused to flow afresh for any hardened unimpressed soul of ours? For His heart is still the same :

> That hour has fled, those tears are shed,
>   The agony is past;
> The Lord has wept, the Lord has bled,
>   But has not loved His last.
> His eye of love is downward bent,
>   Still ranging to and fro,
> Where'er there roams this wilderness
>   The child of sin and woe.

From the commanding height of the upper world He looks upon us now, us who stand in the stead of Zion, who have all the love that she shared lavished upon us, who have the very prophets that ministered to her addressing ourselves, and the very words of her Saviour handed down and sounded in our ears to-day. The special favour that His Providence bears our land is in the eyes of the world unquestionable, and our succession to Israel's lost inheritance undeniable. We have almost all they had, yea, in reality more. For us He has laboured, and watched, and interceded above from our earliest infancy. To us He has spoken by those Ambassadors of His who come, as you know, with His very words and utter all His mind. As our day of grace goes further on I see the shadows of thought and concern gathering fuller and darker on His anxious brow. As we near the end (which of us shall say we may not be very near it?) He gazes on us each yet more earnestly and lovingly. As we leave His house time after time; as we turn from His presence here to go each our own way ever and again; as the habits of life are settling upon our souls; as the entanglements of the world possibly are thickening; as the chains of besetting sins, it may be, are rivetting closer; as the impenetrability that ever comes of much hearing but little practising of the word preached is steeling our hearts and making them ever more cold and passionless; as the eye becomes listless which once used to give far more earnest heed, and the demeanour restless that under the preaching of the Gospel was once so noticeable for its fixed attention and solemnity, I seem to hear a voice from the upper world, and to read a look the meaning of which is touchingly significant in the words of the text. That voice and look is for *you*, you who come as His people come, and who sit before Him as His people sit, but whose hearts are not with Him all the while. Wouldest thou but learn, it says, even thou at least in this thy day the things that belong unto thy peace! You will observe, the sentence is unfinished. Our Lord does not say what in the case of such attention would be the consequence, but the blank speaks volumes, as we may say, for the blessedness it would bring to you and the satisfaction it would occasion Him. You know how you sometimes break off unable to complete a sentence, or express yourself as you would, when emotion within rises very high. So in this sentence the tender and loving Saviour is able to speak of the peace obedience would bring to *you*, " the things that belong unto thy peace," but not of the joy the witnessing or the conferring that peace (for it is His to give as well as witness) would bring to *Him*.

By which motive—the peace to you or the joy to Him—should I urge the yielding the obedience we ask to your Lord, and the accepting the salvation that from Him we bring? Shall I press you by the blessedness of the former? "The Lord shall give His people the blessing of peace," it is said. And I might seek to persuade you by this priceless offer. The peace of a quieted conscience, the peace of a contented and trusting submission to the will of a Father in His Providential government of you and His direction of all your ways, the peace of a confident anticipation of the future, and the peace of a Christian death-bed—the falling asleep in the safe keeping of Christ, as the child falls calmly asleep without a thought of fear in its mother's lap—this is what the Gospel and what we as its Heralds and the Ambassadors of the Lord of Peace are charged to offer you. " Great peace have those that love Thy law, and nothing shall offend them." Or shall I impel you to the obedience of faith and the service of my Master by telling you, as He here fails to tell, of the joy with which He would welcome you to such? Can I reveal the infinite longings of that gracious One to see you turning to Him, drawing nearer and closer to your Redeemer, and Guide, and everlasting Friend? "Thou (He says) even Thou." He addresses you each—young men and maidens, old men and children. And He calls you afresh by name to gather one by one and come to put your trust in the shadow of His love. That joy I confess *I* know not how to attempt to describe, when *He* left it as beyond the power of words to tell. But the joy that a parent feels when a much loved but perverse child becomes dutiful and affectionate—the joy that a Sovereign feels when a rebel people turn back with a loyalty that shall know no change—the joy that any one of us may feel when we greet the return of an alienated but repentant friend—the joy with which we can imagine one long thought to be dead, is received alive again—the joy when one long lost is found—the joy with which the ministering Angels of gentleness and tenderness hail the sinner that repenteth, and the rejoicing Shepherd takes to His arms the long sought lamb — these are the

Scripture illustrations and symbols of the joy of Jesus over His redeemed, the rapture of which none but His compassionate and full heart can know.

May that joy which springs from His infinite love and desire for our salvation be His over some erring ones among ourselves. And

> By Thy tears of bitter woe
> For Jerusalem below,
> Let us not such love forego!

CHRIST'S TESTIMONY TO THE DEVOTION OF HIS APOSTLES.

Ye are they which have continued with Me in My temptations! *Luke* xxii 28

These words of Jesus were spoken under very especial circumstances, and with a very unusual emphasis. The deep emotion with which they were spoken by their Lord would be met, though it could not be equalled, by that with which they were listened to by His Disciples. On *His own* part they breathed a spirit of more than tenderness, an absolute fondness, and if I may so say, pride in their fidelity, which is not that I am aware of matched by any of His recorded words to them. And on *theirs* they would, and must, have been received with a grateful satisfaction at His recognition of their devotion, and a glow of adoring love with which they could hardly have heard any words from Him before. Everything, as I said, combined to give these words, both as spoken and heard, the utmost intensity of force and feeling. It was the hour immediately preceding that of the most bitter bereavement that any of the sons or daughters of men have ever experienced when their Master and Lord was taken from the midst of them to die.

At the moment He thus spoke He was uttering to them His last words of consolation and affection, as He lingered on till the midnight hour, over the table in Jerusalem, where He had celebrated with them His last supper. And He was concluding that interview of full and free converse with them which was to be the last till He should meet them again and sit down with them, and us, as I hope, and all the blessed of age, and clime together—the great multitude whom no man can number—in the kingdon and house of His *Father* and ours. His outward and visible association with those true loyal ones " the glorious company of the Apostles" who had followed and served Him, and were still to do so more nobly, with a devotion which the Holy Church throughout all the world has never ceased to admire and striven to imitate—was on the point of closing. The blessedness of it to *them* and the joy in it to *Him*, was almost overpast. With that expiring hour a change was to pass upon their lives ; and He and they were to stand towards one another in an altered relationship which awoke all the feelings of that heart of Divine and Infinite sensibility. And so it is that His farewell words, as recorded in several following chapters in S. John are imbued with a power, beauty, and depth of feeling, which 'even readers who are not spiritually minded reverently pause as they come to, and wonder at.

And now ere He rises from the table, and goes forth in the darkness of that last night in which He was betrayed, He breaks off in the midst of all those concluding admonitions, prayers, and consolatory addresses.

He gazed upon the assembled eleven, whom He had chosen as the companions of His Incarnate Life, and loved unto the end, and borne with so graciously in all their ignorance and prejudice, and their strife with one another as you see in the context. And His soul overflows with that Love of His which is ever "stronger than death," and triumphant over all unworthiness. And pausing, as one does in a moment of excessive feeling and high wrought emotion, to collect and gather up the crowding thoughts and mingled, perhaps conflicting sentiments—with a glance upon them the speaking power of which we can well imagine, such for example as that which He presently cast upon the faithless Peter, He gives this fond testimony to the sincerity of their allegiance, and the value He had been pleased to set upon their after all so unperfect loyalty. "Ye are they which have continued with Me in My temptation."

And like unto the profound emotion with which *He* gave this honourable and high testimony, though as I said not with an equal intensity, was the joy with which *they* heard it. Great indeed that joy must have been to them. Very like to that with which we shall hereafter hear—if God keep us but faithful unto death, and we for our part are true to ourselves, and our profession. and therefore to our Lord — the "Well done good and faithful servant," with which we shall be greeted and hailed to the fellowship for ever of All the Saints. I can imagine the kindling light that flashed, as they listened to the wondrous words, from their tearful eyes. I can fancy their down-cast faces raised in that blissful moment the fond approving smile with which their Master regarded them as He thus spoke. I can see as I said the glow of adoring love with which they welcomed them, for words would fail as all inadequate. But their eager upturned faces would acknowledge them with the rapture that Thomas did "My Lord and My God!"

And why you may ask do I say so positively that the emotion, which I grant was profoundly deep, with which the disciples heard, was comparatively superficial to the depth of that love of Christ which prompted them? I might indeed answer because in that Infinite Being there is, as the Apostle says of the love of Christ, a breadth, and a length, and a depth, and a height, which passes knowledge. So it is most truly!

> And fainter than the pale star's ray,
> Beneath the noontide blaze of day—
> And lighter than the viewless sand
> Beneath the waves that sweep the strand.
> Is all of love that man can know,
> All that in Angels' breasts can glow,
> Compared O Lord of hosts, with Thine,
> Eternal fathomless, Divine!

But there is a further answer than this to be given, and one well worth consideration. The sensibility of the Divine Saviour's soul was and is always unvarying and perfect, whereas in every human soul it is becoming constantly impaired. We know how truly it is so that, as philosophers teach us, the mind from the constant impressions it receives, becomes less impressible: how to any passion or affection of the mind, whether of fear, or shame, or grief, or hope, or gratitude, or love, we are apt to become more indifferent as we become more familar with it.

Take for instance the emotion of mercy. "The tender mercy of God" is to be the pattern of our own. And in its exercise, and even in the cherishing of the sentiment is said by the Prophet Micah to be one of those three points in which is summed up all religion " What doth the Lord require of thee, but to love mercy." " Blessed are the merciful, for they shall obtain mercy." And yet we know how the world with its rough ways and chilling atmosphere tends to harden us as we go on in life—how alas people can become regardless of sorrow in their fellow creatures, that once moved them to compassion, and sin that stirred them to indignation. We see alas in others, and perhaps recognise in ourselves, how, for example, familiarity with the suffering of the brute creation tends to produce a callousness about it which we should ourselves call shocking if we reflected upon it— how natural compassion is often restrained till it ceases to be felt at all—how we become tolerant of injuries and wrongs committed against our brother, that would once have roused us to indignant protest—how we learn to speak without the former bated breath of the evil of oppression and cruelty, and to witness it without the flush of shame. Well are we taught to pray, " From all hardness of heart, Good Lord, deliver us." And so it is with every other affection or temper of the soul. What causes us dread or fear, at one time we gradually cease to be apprehensive of. Hope loses insensibly its powerful charm : and the object of our love often ceases to be attractive in our eyes.

So even the Apostles, who prized their Saviour's approbation and fellowship so dearly, would hear the words although with pleasure, with a far less degree of intensity of feeling to that with which He spoke them. But " with Him is no variableness nor shadow of turning." He knows no change of mood like ours. Impressions on His soul are never effaced, and never become less vivid. Thus it is that having loved His own He loves them to the end. Thus it is that despite all the wanderings of our own hearts, and all the provocations we may have offered His Holy Spirit during the past week or year, He loves us to-day each one as much as He did last Sunday, or when twelve months ago we concluded, with the Festival of All Saints, the lessons set us in the Church's Calendar.

Thus it is that after training one generation after another in the faith and holiness of His Gospel, and in obedience to His Spirit, He is ready to devote equal attention to us to-day, and to draw us to Himself and to Heaven, with as untiring pains. Which of us could do so. What Parent, what Father, what Minister, what craftsman of whatsoever craft he be, who has set himself to instruct and discipline others— do we not see as life wears on glad to retire, and leave the work of training and education to fresher and more vigorous minds ? But " hast thou not heard (says the Prophet) that the Creator fainteth not neither is weary " ? All the longsuffering and the Divine Patience He has ever exercised in days gone by, He exercises with you; and He will with your sons and daughters ; and their children after them, till time shall be no more. All that He has been in the years that are past (and we have heard with our ears, O God, and our fathers have told us what Thou hast done in their time of old!) to His creatures, will He be to you. The protection He extended to them, the forgiveness with which He blessed them, the goodness and mercy with which He followed them all their days, the gentleness with which He met their perverseness, the pity with which He restored them when they fell, the renewal of mercies with which He overcame their ingratitude, and at last melted them into love—it is all for *you*, and for you *now*. For "Jesus Christ is the same yesterday, to-day, and for ever."

Yea, Thou art God, the One, the Same,
O'er all things high and bright ;
And round us when we speak Thy name
There spreads a heaven of light.

"Ye are they which have continued with me in my temptations." Does not the kind Saviour always credit His servants in His infinite love, I need not hesitate to say fondness, with more than they deserve ? For did they so continue ? Alas! no. For even on that very occasion He had predicted a melancholy faithlessness. "The hour cometh, and now is, when ye shall be scattered every man to his own, and shall leave Me alone." And so it came to pass, for in the self-same night they all forsook Him and fled. They stood by Him when many were offended at His words. They kept true and unfaltering when many turned back and walked no more with Him. When rulers and Pharisees agreed together that if any man confessed Christ, they should be put out of the synagogue, *i.e.*, formally excommunicated from the Jewish Church and all its privileges—when the name of "the Holy and the Just" was cast out as evil—when He endured the contradiction and reviling of many against Himself as a blasphemer, a Sabbath-breaker, a friend of publicans and sinners, a mover of sedition, a Samaritan, and one who was in league with the devil—they clung to Him the closer, and honoured Him with the practical avowal of a more unbounded admiration and a yet more unshaken loyalty. Even then, and far more afterwards, they declared with their lives, as the Apostle with his words, "Who shall separate us from the love of Christ ? Shall tribulation, or distress, or persecution, or nakedness, or peril, or the sword ?" "Lord, I will go with Thee to prison and to death," said Peter. "Likewise also said they all." And eventually they did. And we wonder not then—though the flesh were weak, and they drew back for a short moment in one hour of trial—that their Lord should have acknowledged their fidelity, as His Church has delighted to do ever since, in her monthly commemoration of one or other of the twelve Apostles of the Lamb. In the light of His love we understand the words of the text, which show that these are they that He delighted to honour, "Ye are they which have continued with Me in My temptations."

You cannot have this grateful acknowledgment from the lips of the Blessed One of your personal attendance and steadfast faithfulness to Him in the hour of His reproach, desertion, and rejection. But where His Church is, and His people, there is He. Cast in your lot with His Church, and make the cause of His people, of any disciple that stands in His stead, yours. Take you but your humble part unswervingly against the impugner of the Church's faith, and the scorner of its ordinances, and the adversary of any of His Great Father's laws of justice, and mercy, and charity. Make common cause with the weak, and the oppressed, and the suffering, and the injured, and the unjustly abused, and the despitefully treated. Fight on manfully under His banner when the spiritual conflict seems to you a losing one, and your success in well doing absolutely hopeless; when for all you have done and are doing the power of sin within you seems as strong as ever; and the goal as distant, and the prize as far beyond you, as it seemed when you first entered the lists with the world, the flesh, and the devil. And verily, as my Master's words are true, you shall be beckoned before an admiring world in the great coming Day to join the ranks of His Apostolic champions. And with the same affectionate pride in His Heart shall the words be uttered again; and with the same rapturous and unspeakable joy listened to on yours— "Ye are they which have continued with Me in My temptations."

Ye are they which have continued with Me in My temptations. And I appoint unto you a kingdom,—*Luke* xxii., 28, 29.

His eye with fond affection and with pride
Gazed on the trusting followers at His side;
And with these thrilling words, in gentle tone,
He praised their truth, and blessed them as His own.

Long have I watched you with delight, rejoice
In listening gladly to your Shepherd's voice;
Seen your devotion to your Lord and Friend,
And found you now unshaken to the end.

Reproach, desertion, slander, I have borne;
Been bowed with sorrow, and with labour worn;
By contradiction and abuse been tried;
But *you* were ever loyal to your Guide.

When in temptation coward spirits failed,
Heedless of danger *you* by faith prevailed:
And in allegiance to your Lord and vow
Faithful you have continued until now.

When waverers doubted, *you* were firm and bold:
You faltered not when faithless hearts grew cold;
Nor shrank from sharing My contempt and shame,
But still confessed and witnessed to My name.

When all refused to listen, *you* were they
With love unchilled chose ever to obey.
Many offended turned away. But *you*
When all forsook Me were unchanged and true.

And yours shall surely be the rich reward
Reserved for His true servants by their Lord.
Counted as worthy, you shall sit upon My throne,
And all the Church your tried fidelity shall own.

HUGH ALLAN.

CHRIST'S BURIAL AND DESCENT INTO HADES.

He descended into the lower parts of the earth.—Ephesians iv. 9.

It is a well known condition incident to our frail humanity that when the mind has long been over-wrought by the eagerness of expectation, the strain of stirring events, or more surely still the suspense of suffering—there presently comes a re-action. And if the excitement arise from a combination of all these causes the re-action is proportionately severe. The spirit of man, though it will sustain the mental conflict long, will not, cannot, as the Prophet says, always strive. It fails exhausted before a too protracted trial. Illness often in such a case succeeds in the physical frame: and in the moral the energies of the living soul cease to operate with their wonted force; the very power of thought is paralysed; and the heart's impulse to further enquiry or exertion is overborne.

And so it is that while the details of the crucifixion are in all the four Evangelists very full, the allusion to all that took place after Christ's death, in regard to His burial and His soul's repose in Paradise, is but slight. I would not seek to attribute too unguardedly the exactness of our own experience in the matter to the blessed Evangelists. "They spake as they were moved by the Holy Ghost," and consequently communicated more or less of information on this part, as on all the other subjects of their narrative, not as they were disposed themselves, but as they were led by the Spirit to do. But at the same time I cannot doubt that we have in this law of our nature an explanation—at least to some extent—of the fact I have referred to : a fact which may, which almost must, have struck us in dwelling on the closing scenes of our Lord's life. The tongue of the sacred historians seems to falter as they draw near the bitter end. And the re-action of an overpowering grief seems to check the current of their words, even as we know it did for a time at that solemn crisis the powers of their remembrance and reasoning. It was with them, as we read of the mourners beneath the cross, "All the people that came together to that sight, beholding the things that were done, smote their breasts and returned." But besides being then incapacitated by grief to look further they were antecedently disinclined to do so.

When their trust that this was He which should have redeemed Israel gave way, and hope died within them with their expiring Lord—when all save the faithful Galilean women, with Joseph and Nicodemus, deserted the crucified body—it was clear enough that they cherished no curiosity about, and felt no interest in, the mysterious abode to which the soul of their Lord had passed. And it may lessen still more our wonder at this if we bear in mind with what feelings the Old Testament Saints were accustomed to view the state beyond the grave. We believe and are sure, since our Lord revealed it as the Paradise of His presence, that " the souls of the faithful after they are delivered from the burden of the flesh are in joy and felicity." But they had no such happy assurance. The hopeless cry of David and Hezekiah—" In death there is no remembrance, in the grave no giving of thanks"—reflected only too accurately the dark and dreary view which up till then had been for the most part entertained of that unseen state. The most enlightened even seem to have deemed with the Prophet Isaiah (xxiv., 17) " Fear and the pit" (that is, Hades, the unseen state) to be so coincident as to be almost synonymous. Death was deprecated by them as the worst of evils ; and the cry of the Psalmist was ever on the lips of the truest believers, " Let not the pit shut her mouth upon me."

And so when the disciples had contemplated to the last in their Lord's decease the terrors of death, no marvel that they shrank from the dreaded threshold of the pains of Hades. And when too the gloom of that grave and gate of death was dissipated a few hours afterwards by the gladness of the Resurrection morning it is no less natural that the disciples, as we see to have been the case with them, should have had in their fresh flush of joy no leisure or inclination to revert to the subject of the intermediate state. But well it becomes us who view the whole transaction of Calvary with no confused and dark uncertainty as they—in the light of accomplished revelation, and not in the distraction of an almost wild despair—to linger around the tomb and to penetrate, as far as it is given us to do, the Paradise into which the Father of Heaven translated the commended spirit of His Son. To us it is given to calmly contemplate, in a sure and certain hope, that scene in the presence of which they mourned without any hope at all.

The very title by which the Church has designated this day—*Good Friday*—reminds us of the brighter aspect under which *we* may regard its dark transactions. To us it is not, as it was to them, to quote the words of the Prophet Zephaniah, " a day of wrath, a day of trouble and distress, a day of wasteness and desolation, a day of clouds and thick darkness, a day of the trumpet and alarm against the fenced cities and high towers of blinded men that had sinned against the Lord"—the men of Zion who had crucified the Lord of glory.

To us, to quote what we read in the book of Esther of " the days wherein the Jews rested from their enemies," " it is turned from sorrow to joy, and from mourning to a good day." And so we call it Good Friday. I trust indeed that we gaze on the cross to-day affected none the less deeply because it must be from our sustaining hope and enlightened acquiescence in our Lord's death less passionately than they. But still the fact remains that that cross is to *us* the centre of our believing joy which was to *them* the very climax of despair. We can even thank God in the midst of our recoil of shame that He *was* wounded, seeing that it was for our transgressions that He was bruised ; seeing how by His stripes we are healed ; that He died and was buried, and went down into hell; seeing in His death we live, and from His burial and descent we derive new revelations for our faith, and fresh accession to our joy!   And so *we* can take courage where *they* could not to follow Him in imagination as His body is deposited in Joseph's tomb, and His human soul consigned to the Hades of departed spirits.

Isaiah had prophesied that the rejected Messias was to be " with the rich in His death."   And meet indeed it was that He who came so bountifully to enrich the world should thus be honoured.   It was meet that as at His birth gold, frankincense, and myrrh were offered to Him that was " born King of the Jews," so now the costliest oblations customary for royal burial should be again presented to Him who claimed, and was even allowed to the last, as the superscription on the cross witnessed, the same august title.

And so in God's Providence two of the wealthy of the city, an honourable counsellor and a Master in Israel, and all the women from Galilee who had hitherto ministered to Him of their substance, united with one consent to pay the last tribute of honour that love could prompt, or wealth provide, to their crucified Master.   From the presence of Pilate—leave having been gained for his pious purpose—Joseph hastens to the place of merchandise.   Of him we may say reversely what was said of Tyre—" The prince was a merchant, the honourable of the land became a trafficker."   He bought fine linen, says the text—a Sindon it is in the original (as the late Melville explains)—a very precious and rare robe, no mere shroud for the dead, but an attire worn, it is said, by some among the devout Jews who could afford to purchase it, as a symbol of special sanctity.   And if so, there was, it seems, a peculiar and observable fitness in its selection for investing the body of " the separate from sinners," the Holy One of God.   Nicodemus also, S. John informs us, brings an offering of myrrh and aloes, about an hundred pound weight.   And the women at the same time contribute those the last offices of devotion which their hands may fitliest render to the person of the dead.

And so the mutilated and dishonoured form, which in a few hours more was changed according to the working of His own Divine power into that all-glorious body, into the likeness of which the bodies of all that die in the Lord shall be hereafter fashioned, is dressed for the burial.   And the face, marred more than any man's, and the brow distorted with the pangs of the late anguish and the scars of the thorny crown—the face that might have well drawn a world to worship in the light of its unearthly loveliness, and the brow that might have attracted the coldest to sun themselves in its beaming beauty—is veiled for ever from that hard world's gaze : *for ever* until He come again at the end of all things and every eye see Him in the majesty and lustre of His resurrection-body.   And what an act of unrivalled faith was the homage rendered in that hour by those few sainted disciples who hid not their faces from Him when all the other disciples and the very Apostles did !   Their devotion was shown to the body of the Nazarene in the moment of its very deepest humiliation, when the self-abasement of Him who " humbled Himself even to the death of the cross" had reached a point from which all others recoiled with horror, as unable to tolerate the indignity and the shame.

And as it has been beautifully said by one who has commented upon this scene, " Henceforth we shall forget it of Joseph who now went so boldly unto Pilate that, as S. John tells us in his account, he had hitherto concealed his discipleship for fear of the Jews. We shall forget it of him that he had acted as if he were a stranger to the Lord, seeing that when Christ was in such a special sense a stranger on the earth he opened his own new sepulchre to take Him in. And we shall forget it of Nicodemus that it was for a like reason he had come to Jesus by night, seeing that upon this last evening he came forth so openly with his costly offerings to embalm Christ for the burial. Of the Galilean women indeed we have nothing to forget."

But we shall remember them all the more gratefully and reverently for this their exceptionally pious care. As we watch the women from Galilee following after (as S. Luke tells us they did) as Joseph and Nicodemus carried the body to the tomb ; as we see them beholding the sepulchre and (expressive addition that gives so accurately the very touch of a woman's nature of tender, loving, even extreme solicitude) " how the body was laid ;" as we see them (as S. Matthew shows us) two of them at least far through the falling shadows into the cold still night, sitting, after all was over, against the sepulchre ;—we shall say assuredly no earthly love ever passed the love of these blessed women. For three years of eventful journeyings up and down the land they had attended Him through good and evil report. Though the reproaches of them that reproached Him would fall bitterly on them, regardless alike of fear or slander, they confessed Him openly to the last. And now they were not ashamed of His bonds or His cross. And beyond the scene of His crucifixion, through the hour of its desertion, they lingered by His lifeless body, till, aided by them, devout men carried It to Its burial, and left them alone through those hours of horror to watch heart-broken by the dreaded tomb.

And thus the great Lord was buried. And as His worn body was peacefully interred at last in the rocky recess of the rich man's garden, His spirit passed, as He foretold to the dying thief, to the repose of Paradise, the Garden of the soul. For, says our third Article, " as Christ died for us and was buried, so also is it to be believed that He went down into hell." And by the word " hell" we mean not the place of torment, at least not necessarily, but simply the unseen assembly ground where human spirits await their re-union with the bodies they have ceased to animate, and their joint remission with those bodies to their future destiny upon the judgment day.

And yet hardly more sure the stone, the watch, the seal that guarded from any further intrusion of friend or foe the sepulchre that contained the body of our Lord, than that which shuts to from our eyes or imagination the door of this mysterious abode to which His soul was then consigned. It is a secret thing, that mansion of Hades, which belongs to the Lord our God. There, our Church teaches us in her Visitation Service, " the souls of them that sleep in the Lord Jesus enjoy perpetual rest and felicity," though not the perfect consummation of bliss reserved for body and soul together after the Resurrection day. But into the nature of those habitations it is altogether vain for us too curiously to inquire. Yet one fact connected with them we are able to ascertain ; and we ought therefore to turn to a practical use.

S. Peter in his address to the multitude on the Day of Pentecost speaks of his Lord's soul being in hell or Hades. And though he had nothing to reveal and little to suggest on that subject *then*, the Spirit, who was to teach the Apostles all things, seems at some subsequent time to have made to him a further revelation concerning it, for he has more to communicate afterwards. In his First Epistle (iii., 19, and iv. 6) he speaks of our Lord's spirit as preaching to the spirits in that prison or house of detention, speaks of it too in immediate connection with the subject of Christ's death. And he seems certainly thus to intimate some work in which Christ's spirit was engaged during the interval that his body was in Joseph's grave. Our attention is therefore specially called to the subject by our Church in the Epistle for Easter Eve. Here we have, if we accept the Apostle's statement in its natural and simple sense, a plain historical assertion in the 19th verse—just as we have two other plain historical assertions in the verse before and the verse after—an assertion that after His death Christ preached His Gospel to certain spirits in Hades. This is alluded to as a simple undoubted fact by the same Apostle in that other passage in his Epistle to which I have referred (iv., 6). It is introduced as a simple fact about the reception of which S. Peter at least seems to have felt no difficulty. Others have done so in the self-sufficiency of a captious reasoning, and, with a less simple faith than his, have thought it needed explaining away.

And we need not, we do not, wonder that this allusion to that truth stands almost alone in Scripture when our Lord expressly tells us that He alone has the keys of death and Hades, that He reserves to Himself the prerogative of unfolding their secrets after this life is ended, that it is not His will we should know much about them before. But we take up this fact, that S. Peter has been permitted to give us, undoubtingly. We think it not even strange that he to whom the keys of the kingdom of heaven were specially given, should have been inspired as no other sacred writer has been to disclose this much. And we accordingly accept it—although it may seem an otherwise unsupported fact in Scripture—as yet a fact that when our Lord died and was buried He went in the spirit into Hades ; and, in the converse of His own spirit with those others sojourning there till the morning of their resurrection, unfolded the consolations of His glorious Gospel. And who were the subjects of His instruction in the Gospel scheme : the spirits of the faithful only, or some of the disobedient also ? What saith the Scripture before us ? It unquestionably leads us to suppose the latter, those that in their life time had been disobedient. That the obedient were it seems very natural to conclude, and it has been very generally believed in the Church. It may well have been that those who before His coming saw His day, believed on Him the foretold and forcordained Messiah who was to be the Saviour of the world, and departed this life, although under the older dispensation as Christians in His faith and fear—were permitted to hear published by its Author the Gospel of salvation in the hope of which they had lived and died. But this is not the statement of this passage. Its obvious sense is that after His death He went and preached in Hades, and that His auditors there were certain spirits who when in the body had been disobedient. To say, as some do, that He went and preached means that He sent His Holy Spirit some centuries before to preach in the time and person of Noah, is an unwarranted interpretation which seems to me presumptuously to set aside the plain words of Scripture. But if we receive the idea most naturally suggested here—and I doubt whether, seeing it is so directly suggested, it would not be unbelief to deny it— we shall very largely extend our conception of our Lord's work in Hades, and of the magnitude of the triumph that S. Paul tells us was there gained over the powers of darkness. And thus we would infer that others too who knew comparatively little or nothing at all of the salvation that was to be, such as the men of the antediluvian world to whom S. Peter in that passage refers, others who died without the knowledge of God and His Son, shared in the Preacher's sympathy, and were graciously allowed to lay hold on the hope set before them in the Gospel which they then for the first time heard.

And to what deduction does this intimation of His work in Paradise lead us?

Jesus Christ is the *same* yesterday, to-day, and for ever. And if so, to the dead that henceforth die in the Lord, that being absent from the body are present with Him, awaiting the accomplishment of the number of His elect and the coming of His kingdom, His office and work must be still the same. He still, therefore, in the first place consoles the spirits of the blessed dead with the expectation of the consummation of bliss reserved for them at His glorious appearing at the end of the world.

And in the second place, if the further supposition be correct—and correct it is if the passage before us is to be taken and understood, as I have said, in its obvious meaning—there is then more than a reasonableness, a positive analogy to the case before us, in the admission that if others of the departed than Christians welcomed the tidings of redemption then and there in Hades, it may be open to the *same class* in our Lord's unlimited compassion to do so still.

If we understand this Scripture aright that our Lord in Hades preached to the heathens of the antediluvian world, those that perish in heathenism now—heathenism in the widest acceptation of the term, heathenism in our own as well as pagan lands—a multitude, whom no man can number, who die unsaved simply because untaught, are not, we may with some probability hope, debarred of the same benefit still. We leave them as in the hands of a merciful Creator to His uncovenanted mercies. For such mercies we are perfectly assured there must be, and that the thoughts of "the Saviour of *all* men" toward them are "thoughts of peace, and not of evil."

And though we believe in no Purgatory, we would fain cherish a hope that many such shall obtain mercy, and be brought to a knowledge of Christ and to faith in Him after death, seeing no opportunity was theirs of arriving at this saving knowledge *before*. And perhaps such mercy and participation in Christ's salvation as we doubt not will be granted to " those who perish without law" (God has given us for our satisfaction His express and positive promise "for they shall not be judged by the law") then may come through this very channel, through some such revelation made to them *exceptionally* in the intermediate state to which they, as we *all*, must pass.

But observe, I say to them, the heathen and untaught, *exceptionally* and *exclusively*: to those only who by reason of tender years or an inevitable ignorance, which another Apostle leads us to believe God may overlook, (Acts xvii., 30) may claim the benefit of the Redeemer's dying prayer (Luke xxiii., 34.) For to *us* who have been baptized and brought up as Christians, and to whom the Gospel revelation is granted in our lifetime, no truth of the Bible can be more explicit than this, that there can be, there shall be, no such after revelation. Indeed we do not, thank God, need it. For *we* at least, though we may rightly expect to be made wiser on an infinite variety of points in that abode of the departed, expect not to be made *wiser unto Salvation*. Well we know that however it may be with others on whom the Gospel Day star has never in their life-time shone, to all of *us* the day of salvation is now. For us who have received the knowledge of the truth that we might live to God, and who if we sin and die in sin will have sinned wilfully and not ignorantly, there certainly remaineth no more sacrifice, and no more hope, and no further proclamation of Gospel mercy after this life is ended.

But if to you Christ is not dead, nor His Gospel preached, nor this day's commemoration of Calvary all in vain—If with grateful penitent hearts, and a true and lively faith you have gazed to day on the atoning death of your crucified Lord—if you go forth from your late meditations on His sufferings and His death, minded like Him to suffer as a soldier of the cross and to die daily unto sin :—then sweet, pleasant and unspeakable is the comfort you may draw from His descent into Hades, and from the *everlasting* nature of His office and work in that abode.

I say He lives and works there evermore, and that His presence there with the spirits of the departed is continued. And yet I know we are distinctly told the spirit of the man Christ Jesus was only detained there for the few short hours that His body lay in Joseph's tomb. But indeed there is no contradiction here. We profess the truth as formulated in our fourth article, " Christ did truly rise again from death, and took again His body, with flesh, bones, and all things appertaining to the perfection of man's nature ;" the " all things" of course including equally His human soul that " was not left in Hades" with His body that was not " suffered to see corruption." " And therewith He ascended into heaven, and there sitteth until He return to judge all men at the last day."

But we likewise believe that in virtue of His Divinity, which renders our Lord Omnipresent in His universe, He revisits the abode where, like His own at this time, the spirits of all flesh rest in the interval of putting off the body's tabernacle, and returning at the general Resurrection to re-inhabit it. The confidence of the Psalmist is the belief of the faithful through all ages of the Church. "If I climb up into Heaven Thou art there: if I go down into Hades Thou art there also."

Yea, and there in Hades we too, if we die in the Lord, shall find like him, the Blessed One. If Christ has been our Guide and Lord through life, and we have died in His faith and communion, trusting ever in His cross for pardon, yielding ourselves ever to His Spirit for sanctification, there on the very threshold we shall meet our all-glorious Redeemer waiting to receive our departing spisit into Paradise as we commend it to Him in the words of the martyr S. Stephen. And in that presence of His we shall find our "fulness of joy" until the time come at the end of the world for the entrance of all the risen saints together on that kingdom of light, the inheritance reserved for them at the Resurrection day.

CHRIST'S ASCENSION.

Acts i. 2.-12.

The forty days that intervened between our Lord's Resurrection and Ascension was a period which to us seems very obscure and mysterious. That He shewed Himself alive during it to His disciples by many infallible proofs, and that He spoke of the kingdom of God—we are distinctly told. But we none of us can take much interest even in worldly matters in what is unreal to us and in things of which we have had no experience. Talk to a person on a subject beyond him, on a matter with which he is in no way conversant, and he listens without evincing any feeling beyond perhaps the appearance or assumption of it which politeness requires. And so when we think upon our Lord's sojourn among us, it is only natural that we should dwell upon those portions with which we have the closest and most complete sympathy. Jesus sitting upon the hill-side and teaching the multitudes with a simplicity, and wisdom, and authority which no teacher had ever exhibited before—Jesus healing all manner of sickness and disease among the people—Jesus receiving all that came to Him, hearing their stories of sorrow and of sin, and counselling them in His Divine and wondrous wisdom—Jesus weeping at the grave of Lazarus, and going with the father and mother of the maiden to the couch where lay the body of their departed daughter—Jesus entering the group of mourners at Nain, and tenderly addressing the widow, and restoring the dead young man to his mother's grateful arms—Jesus blessing the little children and telling to the gathering crowds his tales of attractive and touching power—Jesus weary, and hungry, and suffering, and dying—we can grasp the central figure in these exhibitions of His perfect humanity.

But when we come to the forty days that intervened between the Resurrection and Ascension, we are sensible of a mighty change. He no longer lives with His disciples as one of them, suffering with them, subject to all that affected them, ministering to their wants, and ministered to by them. Those days are gone by or only recalled for an hour or two by the scenes recorded of His occasional appearances. And He seems to us to dwell apart: and if the same yet with an indescribable difference. The same indeed for He said "Handle Me and see that it is I Myself." And yet different, for now He comes and goes as a spirit. He eats and drinks with them. And yet He vanishes when they seem to see Him most clearly. · And so there is a temptation to regard His existence at that time as wholly beyond the sphere of our thoughts, and thus practically to neglect it.

And yet these forty days were very important: important for the testimony they afforded to the reality of this Resurrection they were more important still for the teaching they contained. It was in those days that the Lord instructed His Apostles more completely concerning the nature of His kingdom. He opened their minds to understand things which they could not understand before. He made their hearts ready for that great outpouring of the Holy Ghost which came upon them on the day of Pentecost. They had no ministry of their own to interfere with their progress in Divine knowledge. Preaching, healing the working of miracles were all apparently suspended. They had to "wait for the power from on high." It was a time of holy rest and calm perhaps the only such time they had known since they became Apostles, or ever knew afterwards. "And it was a time which was well spent" in preparing for that storm of affliction, and that pressure of labour which were to follow and which were never again to cease till they were succeeded by the rest of Heaven.

Alas! it is clear they did not so improve that period when He spake of the things pertaining to the kingdom of God, by the very last question they put to their Master immediately before He was "received up into glory." "Wilt Thou at this time restore the kingdom to Israel"? Here was the old notion of the restoration of Israel's glory, not the new Gospel notion of a Holy Catholic Church to be established throughout the world. They had profited little from the instructions of that Heavenly Guide. And so the Lord was taken from His disciples —not while in more lively faith, and vigorous hope, and ardent love, they were professing their allegiance and renewing their vows of devotion and obedience to Him to their life's end—not while they were showing by their whole conversation their fitness after such careful training to be left to a certain extent alone—but while they were uttering words which seemed to prove conclusively that hitherto they had not been able to understand their Master's teaching, and that a vail was still upon their hearts.

And when do we ever improve as we might the opportunities that are ours. In earthly matters do we not continually think of what wo we had intended to say when the visit is over, or the letter is closed? In spiritual matters are we not like Zion knowing not the day of our visitation till the sunlight is over, till the offer is withdrawn, till the probation is at an end. I am not speaking of any final rejection of grace, but of the way we miss the blessing or treasure within our reach. You will kneel in your pew, and the prayer will be half over before you collect yourself to see its significance. The Hymn will be sung, not once but many a time perhaps before you discern its beauty. And many a Sermon shall fall upon heedless ears ere they observe a lesson profitable for doctrine, reproof, or correction in righteousness which many that have preceded it have equally well furnished.

The first part of our Lord's answer to their vain and foolish enquiry I pass over, the rebuke being too plain to need enforcing. "It is not for you to know the times or the seasons which the Father hath put in His own power." But the second part of the answer "Ye shall receive power,"—the power that is of the Holy Ghost coming upon you—is very noticeable. Our Lord saw the desire that underlay this interest they showed about the kingdom being given to Israel. He saw that there was in "their hearts an ambition for power." That ambition is not always vain-glorious, or deserving of the censure with which it for the most part meets. In their suspicion and jealousy of their fellow creatures, people are slow to give any one credit for desiring power on such a ground. But there is such a thing as what we may call honourable ambition, prompted by a man's consciousness that he possesses capacities for exercising power well and usefully.

And these disciples long association with the Lord of all power and might, their observations of the restraint which He imposed on Himself in the exercise of His hidden powers, and which He had taught them to do, had qualified them to be rulers in His spiritual kingdom, as He had meant them to be. And *power* He would have them to know that they should have, for " the Spirit of might," should rest upon them. God, says the Apostle Paul, " has given us the spirit of power," and again, " according to the power that worketh in us."

Do you know—are you invested with—this enviable power?—the power to get the better of evil within you, and to resist it steadfastly in the world, the power to deny self, to crucify the flesh, to overcome the world? That you should possess and wield it, if you will, is the promise which God for His part made you in your Baptism. No matter how deficient you may be in it now because you have not claimed the promised gift, out of weakness you may yet be strong.

No sooner did the cloud receive their ascended Lord out of His Apostles' sight than they looked steadfastly after Him, and began to long for and feel the value of their Redeemer as they had never done before.

It is always so. It is the ever remarked frailty of human nature that we do not know the worth of our friends till we lose them, the dearness of our relatives till we are bereft of them, the blessedness of health till we come to lie on a sick bed, the delight of exercise till some restraint confines us to our homes, the joyous sense of liberty till some engagement deprives us of our freedom.

The disciples must needs be roused too from the reverie in which they had enjoyed rest in the society of their Lord. And this was a hard thing for them. It needed the rebuke and remonstrance of Angels to turn their thoughts and recall their interest to the sphere of duty. Our own experience affords the key to reveal to us *their* feelings then. When some favourite pursuit of ours is suddenly interfered with, when some congenial study is interrupted, when we must needs arise and quit some pleasant companionship, when the season of relaxation is at an end, and duty asserts her stern claims once more— who knows not the rude shock that vibrates through the soul? " Like as a dream when one awaketh" the image of the happy past is vanishing. And all the future is for awhile a blank.

" Why stand ye gazing up into Heaven?" The Angels needed not to ask, for they knew the preciousness of the vision that was now gone by, and could surely sympathize with the lingering look after departed blessedness. But the words reminded the disciples that there was hard work yet to be done, and that human effort was required for doing it, and that *they* were to be the honoured instruments of its accomplishment. And so we may reflect from this that we are not to be seeking too anxiously the luxuries of the spiritual life, the indulgences that are yet in store for the faithful and the true.

> There are mansions exempted from sin and from woe,
>   But they stand in a region by mortals untrod.
> There are rivers of joy, but they roll not below.
> There is rest, but reserved in the presence of God.

We have as His disciples a great work to do for our Master. Like these Apostles we are to be His witnesses, and the representatives of His self-denying, peaceful, blameless, spiritual life. Infinite results depend upon our doing the work of God with a cool head, a steady hand, a zealous heart, and an unbroken perseverance. Let that work be done vigorously and well, though it be in the solitude of homes where no eye save His who seeth in secret smiles on our earnest effort to please God well in all things: though the door of the solace we crave is shut upon us, and no heavenly revelation animates us to our unheeded enterprise. Alone must they return to Jerusalem, without the companionship which was to be theirs no more for a little while. But still they were to know they had " a faithful Witness in heaven" who would watch their labours for Him, and crown each enterprise with good success, and presently send for them to the blessed mansions which He would have them regard as *their future* as much as *His present* home. And they believed it thoroughly. And perfect faith dispels all sadness, as perfect love casts out fear. And so we read "they returned to Jerusalem with great joy, and were continually in the temple praising and blessing God." There was no more selfishness in those Apostles' love to their Lord. They rejoiced in His triumph.

> Thou art gone up on high!
>   Thou who didst first come down
> Through earth's most bitter misery
>   To pass unto Thy crown.
>
> Thou art gone up on high,
>   To mansions in the skies!
> And round Thy throne unceasingly
>   The songs of praise arise!

And the confidence of the Apostle, " He ever liveth to make intercession for us" was theirs.

It is pleasant and encouraging to know, as you turn your thoughts to some distant town, or village, or household—in some time of need or distress, when many have turned against you, and your name is cast out as evil—there is one at least who will plead your cause, one who will rise up for you against the adversary, one who will stand up to take your part in the strife of evil tongues; and when appearances are against you will vindicate your honour, and assert your innocence, and contend for your fair fame.

Your heart glows with affection towards the faithful one who is not ashamed of you and your cause, nor afraid to contend for you in the gate of the enemy. Such a one is the Lord Jesus, the kind Friend and Advocate whose help is offered to us all. Truly we need His Mediation, with enemies around us, and sins to rise up to our confusion! But even so surely we have it. And, says the Apostle, "Who is he that condemneth, seeing He ever liveth to make intercession for us?" "For if God be for us who can be against us?" The belief in His uninterrupted advocacy was the secret of their confidence and joy. And it was an adequate justification of it. The grand tidings of the Ascension is that the same advocacy is offered to you. He is willing to throw the shield of His loving protection over you, and to answer for you when the adversary clamours for your condemnation; and, in the conviction of your sinfulness, your own mouth is closed. Make that advocacy your own by taking up the Psalmist's prayer, and saying to the ascended Jesus, "Thou shalt answer for me, O Lord my God."

THE CLOUD AND ITS TEACHINGS.

A MEDITATION FOR ASCENSION-TIDE.

A cloud received Him out of their sight.—Acts i., 9.

A cloud suggests four ideas.   Firstly, the idea of multitude, for it is composed of numberless units.   Secondly, the idea of a barrier or obstacle to the sight, slight in itself, yet impenetrable.   Thirdly, the idea of a veil, which prevents the clear perception or right estimate of an object which may be near yet unintelligible.   Fourthly, the idea of something which is in its nature very transient or temporary.

The cloud in the text may have been one literally.   But it was undoubtedly a multitude also of the heavenly host   A multitude are often so called.   The Apostle Paul speaks of the inhabitants of the unseen world, to whom our ways and lives are open, under this figure when he would remind us how we are ever under observation; and encourage us to do our best, as you know we generally do, or aim to do, when we feel ourselves under observation.   He says, speaking of the blessed dead, " Seeing we are compassed about with so great a cloud of witnesses, let us run with patience (or perseverance) the race set before us."   And he reminds Timothy that the Angels are observing him in the striking and solemn words " I charge thee before God and the elect Angels that thou observe these things!"

And I must remark, in passing, how useful and inspiriting a revelation we should find this fact to be did we give it the heed we are called to do in this and other passages.   It often happens, as we well know, that we have to go through some duty which no reward will follow but the consciousness of having gone bravely through it.   We learn here, however, that the solitary resolve or action, the self-denial, or hard but never noticed task whatever it was, was observed with eager and affectionate sympathy that we should never have thought of; that some, I am sorry to say, will not think of, nor believe even in the light of a passage which seems so clear as this.   They, the unseen witnesses—through the same inspiring motive of allegiance to God and duty—overcame in days gone by as we have now to do.

> The justified spirits that meet at the throne
>   Have passed through our conflict and care;
> All our joys and our sorrows are still to them known,
>   And keenly our struggle they share.

HUGH ALLAN.

They watch us, the book of the Revelation clearly tells us, and for my part I thoroughly believe sustain us too, with their perfect knowledge of our present position and their infinite sympathy. Let who will doubt, I believe from the teaching of the Bible in the *certain* consciousness of the mighty spirit throng of our inner life, and in the *possibility* of their aiding and sustaining us therein. And I hold this doctrine to be a great secret of power to those who have faith to receive it. I quote this passage here, however, in connection with the text simply to show what was the probable nature of that cloud that received our Lord out of sight. It was "a cloud of witnesses," "an innumerable company of Angels." For we are distinctly told that our ascending Lord was so welcomed and accompanied back to the heavens above. Speaking of that event, it is said " The chariots of God are twenty thousand, even thousands of angels, and the Lord is among them.

> As slowly toward the expecting sky
> That sky's Creator rose,
> The Angel watchers ranged on high
> Bade Heaven's bright gates unclose.

And the illustration of the cloud is herein a very suitable one. For as a cloud is composed of a collection of individual drops, each perfectly distinct, yet all combining into one great whole, so is the heavenly host.

The cloud conveys to our mind secondly the idea of a barrier. That barrier is very slight indeed in itself, and yet is of a nature that the eye cannot penetrate. It is just such a barrier which separates the Lord of man from the recognition of His believing disciples, and the departed who died in penitence and faith from us to whom they were dear. A cloud as it were : something very slight in itself, and like the thin cloud having the peculiar property of veiling utterly from our sight and knowledge what is only just beyond. It is only a cloud which interposes between us and our ascended Lord, between us and the faithful dead.

> So—as we leave the world in which we are,
> And look to that in which we hope to be—
> It after all is not so very far !
> Nor yet so vast the dark mysterious sea
> That flows between the future home and this—
> This land of sorrow, that the land of bliss.

But thirdly we use the word a cloud too of something which is not quite intelligible, which we cannot explain. We say a man is under a cloud when there is something that we cannot quite make out about his relations to his fellow-men, the circumstances in which he is involved, the light in which he is viewed. And in something of the same way does S. Luke tell us that " a cloud received Him out of sight," when he would relate that mysterious change that passed upon our risen Lord, that somehow altered relationship in which He would henceforth stand to His fellow-men.

The eye could no more see, nor the ear hear, nor the hand be outstretched to lay hold upon Him as before. He is still amongst us, one of us, in all our proceedings interested : yet—gaze upon Him as by faith we may, and study His clear character and intentions as we will—He is to us all the while as under or beneath a cloud. We lack the insight that can make us as yet altogether, as we may say, *understand* Him. He stands by us in His Infinite Majesty; and "full of grace and truth." But like Eliphaz, with regard to the spirit that appeared to him in vision, we cannot "discern the form," and can only exclaim with the Prophet Isaiah, "Verily Thou art a God that hidest Thyself."

But painful and embarassing as is such an experience, and trying as it is to faith, it is no strange thing to any of us : but in a degree and measure that which we are accustomed to in our relation to one another as well as to Himself. "What man knoweth the things of a man save the spirit of man which is in him?" It is the manifest intention and arrangement of "the Father of spirits" that in this world we should all be more or less strangers to one another. This may seem a paradox when we consider how He has ordained and constituted us for social life ; but it is nevertheless true. There is evidently lacking at the present a capacity for grasping or understanding the being of one another. The man who has respectively the natural senses of sight, and hearing, and speech, knows more of his fellow-creatures than he who is without any one of these But a further faculty of reading the heart and judging with any accuracy the real character is evidently wanting. We admit it when we say that we cannot quite make out or understand such a one. Nor shall we until that missing faculty is no longer withheld ; and, in the world to come, as the Apostle says, "We know as we are known."

"A cloud received Him out of their sight." Of how much in our lives here is this the history ! The companions of our childhood and the friends of our youth ; the acquaintance whose help or presence we felt so indispensable ; the friend that was as our own soul, yea that we loved better than life, on the arm of whose counsel, guardianship, or kindly and ever present sympathy, we had long leaned—is by the changes and chances of this mortal life put far from us. And a cloud receives them out of our sight. A misunderstanding has arisen we can hardly tell how, and a cold shadow of doubt comes across our minds, or an impatience of the other's apparent foolishness or perverseness. And the cloud gathers thicker and darker and receives him, *as we knew and trusted him*, out of our sight.

And it is just the same with all that gives life, and comfort, and animation to the soul. The throne of grace at which we were wont to bow, the mercy-seat where we gathered with the great congregation, the Scriptures under the shadow of whose teaching we sat with great delight, the altar of God where we loved to kneel in a blessed calm (sometimes a fervent transport) of adoration—there rises up between these and us the cold imperceptible mist of unbelief. We gradually retire, as we should from some creeping mist, instead of pressing forward, as we ought to do, the more steadily, and grasping the more firmly the object of our hope, and comfort, and love. And so a cloud receives it out of our sight.

And yet, be it observed, the cloud has no power to change that which it has received out of our sight. Our own vision is affected, but not necessarily what is intercepted. We often imagine or complain of a change in what we had valued and clung to when in reality there is none. It is only that a cloud, caused by our own want of intelligence or clear insight, has gathered over. And so it is with our unseen Lord. He is, as the Angels said in the passage from which the text is taken, "that same Jesus" still, notwithstanding the intervening cloud. The fact that we lack the faculty of discerning Him behind the cloud does not remove Him the further, or alter the relationship to us in which He stands who is "without variableness or shadow of turning." The very words of the text lead us to this comforting thought "A cloud received Him"—Him as He was before—And, "out of *their* sight." And if out of *their* sight shall we think it strange or hard, that He is out of ours? "The disciple is not above his Master," He was thus withdrawn from the very Apostles, who had shared on earth His companionship and especial love. They still held on their believing way: "returned to Jerusalem with joy;" were kept by His power through faith; and grew in grace, and knowledge, and fidelity as though it were expedient for them that He should go away.

And with what gladness then may we too contemplate His Ascension: knowing that it is really to us a source of power in our own spiritual life, that we are no losers by the absence of the visible Lord of our faith and hearts!

No need our longing hands detain,
Christ on His upward way,
The change to *us* as *Him* is gain,
Nor would we have Him stay.

And last of all I would have you consider that the cloud is in its nature transient. It fleeth as it were a shadow. It passes away and is gone. In wintry days it may wrap us even weeks together in sunless gloom. But the scattering power of the Sun is stronger than the adhesive power of the cloud, and so its end is to pass utterly away. The Sun must sooner or later break forth and disperse its shadows. And so according to the prophecy of Isaiah shall the Sun of Righteousness. "He will destroy the face of the covering cast over all people, and the vail that is spread over all nations." And then, as the Apostle teaches, "shall the Lord be *revealed*." Not perhaps actually draw any nearer to His Church and each member of it than He is now. For says He "Lo! I am with you always even unto the end of the world." But He will manifest Himself to His people, and them to one another.

For that day in which He is revealed is also called the day of "the manifestation of the Sons of God." Then in His Light shall we see light—not only seeing Him as He is, but each other also in His perfection—The final barrier to that Communion of saints, which is so delightful in theory, so unreal and impossible of attainment now, shall be taken out of the way.   For indeed all must be one in Christ Jesus.

The earnest pursuit of a like end, the hearty attachment to the same objects draws us wonderfully together now; and makes us contemplate the common object of our desire or admiration with like emotions and sentiments.   And how much more shall this unity of soul be attained, when " with one heart and one mind even as we are called in one hope of our calling," we worship and serve together our one Lord, and follow and celebrate together the same Jesus.   When a man expresses heartily an opinion that you thoroughly share, when he utters a sentiment that you deeply feel, when he casts himself into a work that you long to see successful, when he strives for an end that you have long tried to advance—your heart is drawn towards him, and you feel that you are one.   So shall it be with the redeemed that gather around the throne of God.

Soon may all the clouds of unbelief be scattered before our eyes: and the light of joy, and fellowship with our Redeemer and with His blessed break upon our now bewildered but then enraptured souls.

Where they need no star to guide,
Where no clouds His glory hide !

CHRIST AND THE WOMAN OF SAMARIA.

John iv., 5-42.

Our blessed Lord was sitting faint and weary in the noontide hour hard by Sychar or Shechem, one of the towns of that region of Samaria to which His ministrations of grace and life had not yet been extended. Exhaustion left the " Lord of all power and might," who thus humbled Himself that He might know and feel for us in our daily infirmities, unequal to the short distance that remained to complete the journey into Shechem. And His faithful followers passed on to provide and bring Him the needed food in the strength of which He was to complete His mission of mercy and salvation to the town. He in whom is the Well of Life sat meanwhile thirsty by the fountain side, in that wonderful self-control He always imposed upon Himself. Let us pause as we see Him sit thus on the well, to bethink ourselves how He has left us an example to imitate that power of restraint He always exhibited over, not appetite only but will, and impulse, and affection of every kind. Let us observe too in Him that Divine patience and meek submission to the Will of the Father above who appoints us our hourly trials of fortitude, and perseverance, and self-denial, and pray God enable us to take it increasingly as the model of our own. He was content—let us strive more at all times to be so—to wait the Providential hour of relief and the disposal of Him who orders all things "after the Counsel of His own good-will." His eye was dim with thirst : but the gentle light of love was as marked in its glance as ever. It was fixed with all the expectant eagerness of nature on the source from whence the so urgently needed relief was to arise. Yet :t was not for a moment unobservant of all around. And I can suppose how as it wandered over the country His mind would revert to the memories of the past.

For the most part when we find ourselves waiting for a little while, or unoccupied in any place, we direct our thoughts and reflections to the persons around us whom we know to be living there. But if the place be a strange one, where we know nothing of the people, where every face before us is alike a blank, and as sojourners only, we feel no interest or care about the persons that are dwelling around or moving before us—our mind turns to the history of the spot, and what we have read or heard of it before. And if the spot be a lonely one in the scenes and objects of which there is little or nothing that is suggestive in the *present*, our thoughts, by the law of association, recur to anything that has made it memorable in the *past*. Where there is no province for *comparison* there may be for *contrast*. And as we look upon strange faces or scenes we are presently carried back to something of which we are—we cannot tell exactly how—reminded.

And so the place and country recalled to Him, persons and events that had given of old, and have preserved to Shechem till to day, its undying renown. For though He had never trodden its hills and valleys before in the flesh He was perfectly familar with its history.

Underneath the oak which was by Shechem, Jacob, on his return from exile from his native land buried the idolatrous ornaments of the household he had brought with him from the heathen Syria. " Put away (said he) the strange gods that are among you." "There he erected an altar and called it by the name of the God of Israel." In its neighbourhood his flocks were pastured by his sons who, like the inhabitants of Shechem at the time of which the text speaks, had forsaken the ways of their godly father. Indeed the apostacy of Shechem had been singularly marked. It had been a city of the Levites, where resided a great company of the teachers of the faith from which the Samaritans had declined. It had too been a city of refuge. And what need had all its citizens then to fly for refuge—with far more eagerness than ever the pursued manslayer from the avenger of blood, to the shelter it afforded—to the hope set before them in the Gospel. Within its walls was now to be proclaimed a Gospel not of *temporal* deliverance such as had so often gladdened the hopeless stranger, that under the circumstances referred to had escaped there for his life, but of *eternal*. Shechem was the place too where before his death Joshua had assembled all the tribes of Israel, and pledged them to keep eternal covenant with the God who had " stablished, strengthened, settled" them in the land of promise. " Now therefore fear the Lord and serve Him in sincerity and truth." But with what a contrast would the present religious condition of the place affect our Saviour's mind! For He shows His sense of the extent of their backsliding in His words before us. "Ye worship ye know not what, but salvation is of the Jews.

Hard by were interred the remains of Joseph, who, by faith in and love for God's promised inheritance, gave commandment, says the Apostle, concerning his bones. On his death-bed in Egypt he desired they should be carried up when the time of departure for Israel arrived, to the land he and his fathers had loved, because it was to them the type of the better, that is the heavenly country, to which they looked ever onward. Shechem was the scene too of the adventures of Abimelech, the perverse child of a godly father, the famous Gideon. And it was enlarged and then chosen as his home by " Jeroboam who made Israel to sin."

And now the pious memories which immortalized it lingered but in the traditions of the people. For they had forsaken the faith in the fathers of which they still prided themselves. And of those forefathers now mentioned, they had followed rather Jeroboam, and Abimelech, and the sons of Jacob, than Jacob, and Joseph, and Joshua, and the Levites, who had sojourned there.

These reflections, mingled no doubt with prayers for that blessing on his projected visit to the town which so signally followed, were interrupted by the arrival of the woman of Samaria. She was to be the first to hear the glad tidings of pardon and a gift of God, even the water of eternal life, which so far exceeded in value, that gift of old for which the townsmen still gratefully celebrated the name of their father Jacob.

Heedless she came : as we go out and in, little thinking how what we may hear and see, and the persons we converse with are leaving for good or evil their impress on our lives : how we are about to meet encounters or occurrences that may presently alter the current of our thoughts, the order of our purposes, it may be finally the complexion of our lives. Her errand was a very simple and ordinary one. But she does not seem to have been altogether an ordinary character. There are indications of powers of observation, and an acquaintance with human nature about her remarks, and even a respectfulness in her manner, notwithstanding the assumed pertness and flippancy which meets us on the surface, that has engaged and compelled the interest of every reader in the story of the woman of Samaria. She knew both the history of the place and the points of controversy between her own people and the Jews. She knew so well the force of bigotry as to express her surprise that the stranger, who was manifestly a Jew, should ask drink of her, "for the Jews have no dealings with the Samaritans ;" and thus show Himself so entirely superior to the prejudices of His age and people. Many would have refused the request the stranger proffered, as she thus intimated to Him. Yet she did not, though the favour He craved was such an unwonted one. Nor did she, after the first naturally guarded answer, "I have no husband," seek to conceal from Him, whom she owned as a Prophet, the secrets of her life. She first yielded the respect He deserved, and then treated with full confidence the Messenger of her God. She admitted all. And when she had owned her need of His ministrations she sought them to the uttermost. "Sir, give me this water that I thirst not." The language is figurative, as had been His. But there is no mistaking in it the cry to its God and Healer, and the Great Interpreter of life, of a sin-conscious and unquiet soul.

The interview being ended by the return of the disciples from their errand of ministration to the wants of Jesus, the woman left her water-pot at their service while the intended meal was taken : and with a laudable zeal hastened to communicate with her fellow-townsmen the news of the presence of the great Messiah. And though—to convince those blinded prejudiced men that He was truly a Prophet who could read the heart and decipher the life—she must needs tell how He had read her own, she shrank not, in order to bring glory to Christ, from the painful avowal. She knew best, from acquaintance with their sentiments and feelings, what was needed to convince those men of Shechem. The invitation to "Come and see" alone was not enough. They had other things to see, and think of, and concern themselves with than a stranger Jew of the people they despised. So with a plain spoken but noble boldness, a sacrifice of feeling, but one acceptable and well-pleasing to God, she was not ashamed to add—though she, better than we do, knew how much that addition conveyed—"a man that told me all that ever I did." "A Prophet? Yea, more than a Prophet," they thought to themselves this must surely be. So they went out : and those that did so found it even as the woman had said.

Nor do we wonder that those who " believed because of His own word" should have said to the woman, " Now we believe, not because of thy saying : for we have heard Him ourselves, and know that this is indeed the Christ, the Saviour of the world." But we are likewise told " Many of that city believed on Him for the saying of the woman which testified He told me all that ever I did." And on this verse I always linger with a wondering interest. It could hardly have been those simple words of hers alone that produced this strange conviction and conversion of their hearts to the Lord. If this were the substance of her testimony we feel we must fill it up with an earnestness of tone, a vivacity of feeling, a genuineness of emotion, and a persuasiveness of manner which raises highly our opinion, and enlists our interest, and arouses our admiration towards this great herald of the Redeemer in Shechem. A humble woman, and yet so mighty a missionary, so impressive a preacher! Herself a convert, and yet in a moment almost a converter of multitudes of disobedient to the wisdom of the just!

O the power of Divine Grace! How it quickens the life, and transforms the soul, and ennobles the character! What a blessed impulse it communicates to naturally lively energies, and what a warmth it infuses into feeling souls! On what principle are we to explain such an effect as that produced by her words except that " the voice of the Lord is a glorious voice, powerful, and full of majesty?" " Many believed for the saying of the woman which testified He told me all that ever I did." Well may we explain with the Apostle, as we read of such a result from such a cause, " It has pleased God by the foolishness of preaching to save them that believe!" and " I am not ashamed of the Gospel of Christ, for it is the power of God unto salvation."

Of the after life of this woman of Samaria, and her perhaps yet more abundant and successful labours for her people and her Lord, we shall know nothing until we meet her—as I pray God we may—in the kingdom of the blessed. From the story we learn clearly that she heard meekly, believed implicitly, reverenced trustfully, and ministered readily to the Saviour of the world. And then that she hurried eagerly and laboured sincerely to do the work of an Evangelist when there was no one else to do it in Shechem. And she has for ages been reaping her rich reward.

Before the throne of the Saviour she heard, and reverenced, and proclaimed, she has long ago sat down, with the fellow townsmen she was the means of enlightening and winning to her Lord. And He has told her and them far more than ever He did before. And she is learning still, and worshipping as she converses face to face with the Lord of all. She knows now, better then ever, Him in whom she so confidingly believed. And she is drinking of the water of life where at His right hand it is flowing in rivers for evermore. No shame of former sin rises up, as of old, to confuse her unruffled brow ; and no shade of doubt gathers in her untroubled eye ; for she is " without fault before the throne of God." "And the Lamb who is in the midst of the throne leads her to the living fountains of waters," where they that drink never thirst again.

The well by which the woman of Samaria met the Lord and Giver of Life, in her earthly days, as He sat exhausted in the noontide hour, flows now no more. A few years back only it was closed by the envious Arabs. But the joy, and peace, and consolation He there declared Himself charged and willing to bestow, has been gushing in a dry and thirsty world, and springing up within, and overflowing the needy, longing, restless spirits that have sought it of Him ever since. And the spring is open for you now.

> They have stopped the sacred well which the patriarchs dug of old,
> Where they watered the patient flocks at noon from the depths so pure and cold
> Where the Saviour asked to drink, and found at noon repose;
> But the living stream He opened then no human hands can close.
>
> They have scattered the ancient stones where at noon He sat to rest.
> None ever shall rest by that well again and think how His accents blessed.
> But the Rest for the burdened heart, the Shade in the weary land,
> The riven Rock with its living streams for ever unmoved shall stand.

"Ho, every one that thirsteth, come ye to the waters!" "Come taste and see that the Lord is gracious, and that blessed (as this happy woman of Samaria) is the man that trusteth in Him!"

THE BEAUTY OF HOLINESS.

Adorn the doctrine of God our Saviour in all things. *Titus* ii. 10.

The love of ornament, and the desire to surround oneself with things ornamental, is a deep instinct of our nature. From the wildest savage up to the most refined subject of civilization we trace the workings and behold the power of this universal taste. Indeed there can be no question that man inherits it from the Creator. He has decked His workmanship, through the whole range of His manifold works, with surpassing grace. The heavens above. the earth, the sea, and all that is therein, bear witness to the bounty with which He has provided what is fair and pleasant to the eye, and meets the human craving for adornment.

" Beauty (it has been well said) is one of the chief ends and aims of the Creator. For the ground beneath our feet is decked with flowers, and the sky above our head is painted with a thousand colours to cheer man as he goes to his work in the morning, and to fill his heart with thankfulness as he returns at evening." Indeed I think there is an especial significance which the thoughtful mind will note in the beauty of the morning and evening sky. The clouds of summer and sunset seem as though charged with a particular lesson from God to man, as he thus goes forth to the work of the day, or returns from it. Each seems to certify him of a world of light and beauty above. The reflection of it in the morning sky seems a glimpse given as though purposely to nerve him for the conflict of the day, and cheer him with the prospect of the coming Resurrection morning, that he may walk in the light of the Lord's countenance, and in the expectation of His glory to be there revealed, all the day long. And the golden beauties of the evening sky repeat the provision, as though they would irradiate his mind with the hope of the glories of which they are the emblem, console him after the trials and labours of the day with the sure and certain hope of Heaven's happier life, and seal his slumber with the vision in antitype of that " Sun of Righteousness" that " shall no more go down !"

God tells us Himself how He gave his " goodly wings unto the peacocks, and his feathers unto the ostrich." In the 39th chapter of Job, in which He does so, He draws attention to the strength and glory of many of His creatures. And in His very language there seems to breathe an admiration of the same kind as that which we feel in the contemplation of such bright and beautiful objects. And we learn thus that from His own delight in adorning His creatures He gave " the leopard his spots," to the dove her " silver wings and her feathers of yellow gold," and to beast, and fowl, and creeping thing, to the flowers of the field, yea, to creatures of His that are impalpable as the clouds and bow of heaven, their graceful forms, and burnished plumage, and radiant colours.

And man has the same natural pleasure in surrounding himself with ornamental work. God Himself recognises the taste when He asks " Can a maid forget her ornaments or a bride her attire ?" And we verify it in our houses and in the streets of every city which exhibit to us as we pass along in countless variety ornaments graven by art or man's device. Every craftsman, of whatsoever craft he be, presents such specimens to our eye, here in the merchandise of gold, and silver, and precious stones ; there in divers colours of needlework, silk, and fine linen, and embroidery ; and here again in all manner of vessels of precious wood, and brass and iron, and marble, and fresh articles that the inventive genius, His Creator has endowed Him with, is ever originating.

It is the same love of ornament that inspires the painter's or the sculptor's fancy, that guides the ready writer's pen, that moulds the sentences that fall from the lips of the eloquent orator, that breathes in the utterances of the poet, that attunes the composition of the musician that plays well upon an instrument. None of these are satisfied with merely performing the task they have to do. Each and all aim at beauty in the execution of what they undertake ; and strive, as each ought to do, to render it as of the ability which God giveth, and to set it forth according to the Divine example as complete as may be with all the grace and ornament with which it is given to them to endow it.

And when the question come to the highest work in which a man can be engaged, to that which is of all others worthiest of adornment— when the man is concerned not with corruptible things which beautify them as you may endure but for a while, but with that which he hopes to be to him his joy and crown for ever, an inalienable property, even his Christian profession and religion—what forethought should he not take, what energies should he not concentrate, what pains should he not devote, and withal with what an ardent eagerness should he not strive according to the bidding of the text to adorn the doctrine of God our Saviour in all things !

And this is the work of adornment referred to here, the setting forth the holy religion you profess, and in the way of obedience to which you hope to be saved, with all the christian graces with which its Author when on earth exhibited it to an everlasting admiration. And when I tell you that this, to which every one that bears the name of Christ and the seal of His baptism is summoned, is a work that will bring the greatest glory to Him that has called you to the knowledge of that one only pure and true religion—when I tell you that the adornment of that doctrine is the most acceptable and pleasing sight on which the eye of God can rest through all this world, which He has for His pleasure so richly decked—when I tell you that of all the beauty that encircles us on every side there is none so grand and bright in the eyes of God and man as " the beauty of holiness"—when I tell you this work will not only redound to the praise and glory of His

Grace, but will fill the hearts of your fellow men with the greatest amount of gladness which you can be instrumental in conveying to them and your own with a joy, and peace, and comfort that no other work to which you can lay your hand shall bring—well may you rise up with all and manifold more the eagerness with which you ever addressed yourself to the work you loved and could do the best, and go forth to it in the strength which will be freely and abundantly given to you of God, and in the might of the Psalmist's prayer, " Prosper Thou this work of our hands upon us, yea prosper Thou our handiwork."

And this work of adornment is one in which the most uninstructed in other arts of ornamentation can engage. You may be no cunning workman like Bezaleel or Aholiab to devise works of skill or memorials of human art such as you see around you on every hand. You may neither be able to handle the brush of the painter, nor the instrument of the musician. You may have neither " the tongue of the learned" nor "the pen of the ready writer." You may have never had the leisure to give the attendance to reading, nor the opportunity of storing your mind with the treasures of literature, or the instructions of science. Poor you may be in this world's riches, ignorant in this world's knowledge, and devoid altogether of this world's genius. But you can avail yourself of the example of Him who taught and set forth in His holy life the doctrines of His Gospel of salvation, and of the aid of His own provided Spirit, whose province it is to teach and enable His disciples to show forth " the doctrine which is according to godliness." And therewith your " profiting shall appear unto all," as you " labour according to His power working in you mightily" to accomplish that which is in His sight of so great price, the adorning the doctrine of God your Saviour.

Perhaps, however, it may occur to you that to " work out your salvation" is by itself a sufficient task : that it should be for others who may have more leisure, more influence, more talent, to recommend that religion on whose principles they act, and by whose rules they live, by the attractions of manner, or the singular devotion to its cultivation implied in this direction to adorn it. And so you may wrongly imagine some hindrances, peculiar to your own case, may render it a very unlikely or almost impossible thing that you should be ever able to rise to this distinction of not only *maintaining*, but positively *adorning*, the doctrine of Christ. The cares of your family, your daily struggle with poverty, the want of those gifts of attraction or influence over your fellow-men with which others are liberally endowed, the peculiar temptations that surround you, the unusually strong passions or besetting sins with which you have to contend, the presence in your household of members of it of very trying or untoward tempers, some special unkindness or opposition which you are called to meet from unreasonable or wicked neighbours, or some natural infirmity or affliction of which you are the subject—all these, or a variety of others, of which your heart only knows the bitterness, may seem to you impediments that make it hopeless for you to think of ever adorning, however you trust to *cling to and live by* the doctrine of God your Saviour.

Earnestly would I caution you against entertaining any such thought as this. The idea is as destructive to the interests of godliness as it is incorrect in fact. The adorning the doctrine of Christ our Saviour is not incompatible with any worldly circumstance, however undesirable; with any situation, however trying or obscure; or with any relationship to the cares and troubles we meet with in the ordinary course of Providence, however engrossing or vexatious. And perhaps it is for this very reason that the precept of the text, though applicable to us all, is given, as you may see, to servants, or, as they really were then, *slaves.* And I suppose none will deny that of all possible positions in which any man could be placed there could be none so unfavourable, so apparently irreconcilable with the life and duty of a Christian, as the lot of a miserable slave in those heathen countries and in that lawless age. Would you observe more particularly the vile character of those to whom these Christian converts were slaves, see Titus i., 12-16, and iii., 3. And if the Apostle, writing by the Holy Ghost, deliberately commanded these wretched bond-slaves, whose whole lives, actions, and very persons, were subject to the will of their infamous masters, to adorn the doctrine of the Saviour to whose religion and laws they had been converted in all things—judge ye how inexcusable it must be pronounced for any of us, who are within the pale of civil liberty and under the guardianship of Christian laws, if we fail in effecting that which even they were expected to attain! Judge ye how vain are those pretexts under which a man, woman, or child, poor, ignorant, or ungifted as you will, should plead an exemption from this universal obligation to adorn the doctrine of God our Saviour in all things!

And what you now ask is it thus to adorn Christ's doctrine, and how can it be done? The verse before the text briefly teaches this art of adornment, as it bids us to please well in all things those with whom we have to do. And in another of his writings we have the limit which this Apostle sets to this pleasing. "Let every one of us please his neighbour for his good to edification." As has been said, the very nature and aim of material adornment is to please the eye and gratify the sense of natural beauty. In one word, to adorn is to please. And it is the province of this adornment to which we are exhorted to please and attract those before whom it is exhibited by the graces of Christian temper and the consistencies of Christian character shown forth by the disciple of Christ. In word, in conversation, in spirit, in manner, it is his to present afresh, as his Lord's representative, the attractions of His blameless life. And following in his Master's steps to be so "harmless and without rebuke in the midst of a crooked and perverse generation" that his fellow-men beholding, albeit as in a glass darkly, the lustre of his Lord's righteousness, may be drawn to admire, and thence perhaps to imitate.

You well know that it is the way of men of the world—though this their way is their foolishness—to credit Christianity with the faults of its professors, to take exception to its Divine teaching because of the weakness, harshness, or the want of amiability of some who are its champions. I pray you therefore to strive constantly to remove from such every stumbling block of infirmity of temper, narrowness of judgment, pride of your own opinion, inconsideration of others, and, in a word, to walk towards those that are without in denial of self, kindness, humbleness of mind, and all long-suffering. And thus, to quote the words of this very passage, "He that is of the contrary part may be ashamed, having no evil thing to say of you." Endeavour, as a living Epistle of Christ, to commend —by all that may be winning in manner or deportment to the regard and acceptance of all who can observe your life and disposition—the holy teaching of your Master. Let your words and ways in your dealings with others be as it were an advertisement of the excellencies of the religion you profess.

But in enforcing this, as all the general directions of Scripture, a word of more particular explanation and special application seems to be called for. It is easy for any one to exhort in general terms. But it is the province of the expounder of the Bible and of human life to point out the bearing of his subject on cases and persons. And first it would seem that on the Minister of the Gospel, whose office it is to speak and teach of the doctrines of Christ's holy faith, it must be peculiarly incumbent, and that it must add a weight to his teaching when his hearers are disposed to be guided by it, to adorn that doctrine in all things. Through a Minister the charge in the text was given to the Cretans. And, says this same Apostle, "Thou that teachest others teachest thou not thyself. ?" Let the Minister then heed it carefully. Let him learn and carefully practise to adorn that doctrine in his very manner of setting it forth. I mean not of course the mere embellishing his theme with "enticing words of man's wisdom." For the same Apostle earnestly disclaims as unworthy of its momentous verities, the mere art of the orator who would treat the Gospel of the grace of God as only a grand subject for the display of natural powers of eloquence. As soon, he tells us in his own emphatic style, might he be " a sounding brass or a tinkling cymbal," for all the good *he* may expect to do by his arguments or words, who makes this his aim. But I do mean to say, as the Spirit of God has said, that the preacher will " seek to find out acceptable words," even those words which in the lips of the wise are " as nails fastened by the masters of assemblies." I do mean that he should not think to serve God, in the preaching of His word, of that which doth cost him nothing. But rather " as of the ability which God giveth" to the painstaking, should he present to his hearers the truth with which he is charged, in such harmonious colours, with such correctness of argument, such force of illustration, and such power of appeal, as the Spirit of God, in whose might, strength, inspiration, and guidance he ministers, will not be wanting to supply. The reckless, presumptuous, self-reliant preacher, who is not careful to guard his discourse from rambling common-places and vain repetitions, but habitually " darkens counsel by words without knowledge," and utterances wholly unpremeditated—dishonours his Master, and does His

Gospel a grievous and far-reaching wrong. Highly culpable is he who is not particular to gather out from his teaching inaccuracies, though he may deem them slight ; modes of expression that offend against the refined taste and sense of propriety that becomes a Christian, as well as an educated man of the world: who brings forth from the treasure house of Scripture knowledge of which he has the keys nothing new, which he is charged to do as well as the old ! I do say that such a one (and many such unhappily there be !) does not—however sound be his faith, and however earnest his devotion to truth—carry out as he might and ought the injunction of the text to " adorn the doctrine of God our Saviour."

And on *you* whose duty it is rightly to *receive* as it is *his* worthily to *proclaim*, the teaching of the blessed Redeemer—is a like care imperative. " In all things shewing thyself a pattern of good works," it is said in this passage to Titus. And while we accept it as the rule for the Minister, we charge it also upon *you*.

There is a word of exhortation here for all classes, conditions, and ages. And firstly for classes inferior and superior. Are you *a servant* or one under authority ? You will adorn the doctrine you profess by " shewing all good fidelity," as you are charged in the very verse of the text : by making your employer's interest your aim, and his will your study. Are you a Master ? You will best adorn your religion in the eyes of your servants by forbearing all harsh words or treatment, and making them feel that you consider their welfare, even as you expect them to provide for yours.

Secondly there is a word here for all sorts and conditions. Are you a neighbour ? You will most attractively adorn your profession by kind actions and little self-sacrifices and readiness to oblige and befriend. Are you successful in life ? Have you a sufficiency or abundance of this world's goods ? You will adorn the doctrine by remembering the poor, and giving to him that needeth, and scuding forth the light and the truth of that doctrine into heathen lands, and dark places of your own that sit in the shadow of death. Are you, or have you been the victim of some wrong or injustice ? On the side of your oppressor was power. And you had none to rise up in the judgment for you to avenge you of your adversary. You were slandered and you had none to make your righteousness clear as the light, or your just dealing as the noonday. Commit yourself to the hand of Him that judgeth righteously, And adorn the doctrine of your Saviour by imitating His spirit of meekness, and forgiveness, and self-forgetfulness. Are you the subject of some disappointment ? And your heart aches with its burden till you are ready to cry like Naomi. " Call me Marah for the Almighty hath afflicted me." Yield not weakly to the sorrow of the world that worketh death. Think as the pious servant of God of old time, " what shall we receive good at the hand of God, and shall we not receive evil ?" And adorn the doctrine of that Saviour, who teaches that in the world you shall, you must have tribulation, by lifting up your heart only the more earnestly to the treasure, and the friends, and the inheritance above, on which the hopes that are fixed are never put to confusion.

Thirdly, there is a word here to those of every age. Have you arrived at years of discretion when you have to make the great election of your life, and choose and resolve and act for yourselves? You will brightly adorn your Redeemer's doctrine by setting an example, in industry, temperance, or moderation in all things, and sobriety of speech and demeanour, to those of your own age and rank, as they observe you remembering your Creator in the days of your youth, not forsaking the assembling yourself together in the congregation of the saints and at the feast of your Lord, honouring God's Holy Name and Word and Day, calling upon Him in prayer, and walking watchfully in His fear. Are you a young man? You will adorn the doctrine by your known steadiness, sober-mindedness and purity, and by taking heed to your ways according to God's Word. Are you a maiden? You will do so by exhibiting that ornament of a submissive and quiet spirit (the very opposite of that alas now so prevalent one, " the loud and froward," the unrestrained and fast), which God has declared He esteems in such of great price : and which He would have you more diligently see to, than broidered hair, more assiduously clothe yourself with, than costly array. Are you a man in the forefront of the battle of life, going in and coming out in the eyes of your neighbours? You will adorn the faith and doctrine of your Lord by bold integrity, high principle, and Christian consistency. Are you a matron? You will adorn it by exerting in behalf of God and godliness, the influence which it is given to all your sex, and especially to those in *your* position, to wield.

Are you an old man or woman that has well nigh filled your days : and the hands tremble, and the knees wax feeble, and the eye is dim, and the ear is dull of hearing, and the head is heavy, and the limbs are chill, and the well-springs of life are gradually sealing up, and the very grasshopper is becoming a burden, and desire is failing, and your little remaining strength is only labour and sorrow? You think, it may be, your working time for God is past. But indeed you can richly and nobly adorn the doctrine of your Saviour by " bringing forth more fruit in old age." " A crown of glory is the hoary head if it be found in the way of righteousness." Take up the cross of those infirmities during the few days of your pilgrimage that yet remain, with patience and hope, and the meekness of uncomplaining submission. For in the land where your youth shall be renewed like the eagle's it shall be hereafter your joy and crown of rejoicing to have borne it for the Master's sake. And as you halt feebly to the tomb in the cheerfulness for which your possession of the peace that passes all understanding can alone account— your faltering tongue still speaking of the things touching your King, and your dim eye still fixed upon the glory that is to be revealed—the light of your Christian faith shall not be hid. And one or another of those who are to you near and dear may be led to *notice*, or, perchance long after your course is finished and your rest entered on, to *recall*, the grace that marked the life of your latter [days, and to " glorify your Father which is in Heaven."

" Finally, Brethren, whatsoever things are true, whatsoever things are honest, whatsoever things are just, whatsoever things are pure, whatsoever things are lovely, and whatsoever things are of good report, if there be any virtue and if there be any praise think on these things." Produce in your life, and in your transactions with your fellow-men, practise these things. And so shall you with the help of the Blessed Spirit, Who sets you to this work in the charge of the text, and Who has promised you His aid in fulfilling it, be adorning the doctrine of God our Saviour.

FINIS.

H. Jackson, Printer, Market Place, Olney.

www.ingramcontent.com/pod-product-compliance
Lightning Source LLC
Chambersburg PA
CBHW031152120726
47905CB00006B/1923